Stark Raving Sober

a memoir

Donna Bailey-Thompson

Donna Bailey-Thompson
November 2006

To Maria —
Thank you for
your help —
Donna

PUBLISH AMERICA

PublishAmerica
Baltimore

First printing

ISBN: 1-4241-3001-8
PUBLISHED BY PUBLISHAMERICA, LLLP
www.publishamerica.com
Baltimore

Printed in the United States of America

The genesis for the book *Stark Raving Sober* was first published on January 16, 1983, as the cover story of *Northeast Magazine*, part of the Sunday edition of *The Hartford Courant*. At that time, the author used the nom de plume Rebecca Bass.

For my children
Elizabeth and David
and our family
with love.

Acknowledgments

I am beholden to Al-Anon members and my Spofford sisters who through sharing their experience, strength and hope, helped me to reclaim myself. I am particularly grateful to my Al-Anon sponsor, Idora, for her understanding patience, encouragement and wisdom.

The feedback I received from friends near and far was invaluable.

Writing is a lonely process. A cheering section is a great morale boost, and especially when it includes constructive suggestions. During the editing process, a number of computer glitches were resolved—and disastrous panic attacks averted—thanks to the unselfish help from technically savvy friends.

My longtime dear friend Marie Greco transformed a self-conscious photo session into a relaxed visit and worked magic with her digital camera.

Buttressing my spirits throughout the writing, re-writing, editing, and tweaking was my valued friend and colleague, Thayer Bennett.

From the moment I tackled this manuscript, I benefited from the loving support of my daughter, Liz. When I spoke about quitting because revisiting some memories were particularly painful, she convinced me to keep writing.

I discovered that writing a book also takes a village.

Author's Notes

Stark Raving Sober is a true story. I have written it from my perspective which means I have looked at my life experiences through one prism—my own. With the exception of using real names to identify Sandra Cohen-Holmes, my children and myself, all characters have been renamed.

Because I wrote the journal entries with no idea one day I would quote them in a book, their spontaneity is retained "as is," and editing occurs only for the sake of clarity

My opinions are mine. I speak for myself and no one else. I found answers that work for me. I agree with addiction and mental health professionals that those affected by alcoholism can benefit from learning all they can about this insidious, cunning and subtle disease; and when symptoms suggest the presence of an additional problem, such as bipolar disorder, knowledge can lead to the management of its symptoms.

If I had not rid myself of hateful resentments and changed my attitudes, I could not have written this book. The writing demanded that I dredge up the past. I remembered the feelings, at times strongly enough to laugh aloud or to weep. Some were difficult to write. One especially tore me apart with such shame, embarrassment and anger with myself that I came close to abandoning the book. I am relieved to let the old feelings return to the past where they belong.

In 1983 in a letter from Lary Bloom, then editor of *Northeast Magazine*, he wrote: "I have this theory about life, unproven, of course, that sometimes in the great cosmos there appears to be a reason for pain—and that something good can come from it."

Yes.

Contents

Alcoholism isn't just drinking.

It's a family disease. It causes the wife and kids to become as addicted to the alcoholic as the alcoholic is to the booze.

While the alcoholic lies passed out, anesthetized, the family goes through the years of his drinking—stark, raving sober. Their world is like no sane family's world. They believe lies, expect miracles, have him locked up, bail him out, wish he were dead, and pray that he gets home safely.

From the introduction to "Getting Them Sober,"
Volume One by Toby Rice Drews.
Recovery, P.O. Box 19910, Baltimore MD 21211
Reprinted with permission from Toby Rice Drews

Foreword by Dr. Roger A. Rhoades

Fasten your emotional seatbelts—you're in for a ride. I have long been a fan of Donna's writing, seeing her grow as a wordsmith and a person by putting parts of her own life under the microscope. Now she has stepped up to the task of taking us on her personal journey in book form. We don't have to read between the lines or string together snippets of information. In this book we are able to have the full experience. *Stark Raving Sober* brings all the elements together in one place and allows us to gain insight into a person who is struggling to get life right, only to have it jump back and bite her on the butt.

As a talk show counselor for more than ten years, I have often been frustrated by people who come on television and radio shows to explain their lives in sound bytes. They recount only the bullet points of their problems and then expect the viewer or listener to understand where they are coming from and perhaps even take their side. Donna is not part of this group. She writes from a place of both pain and victory. Concerned with presenting reality as she knew it, Donna does not attempt to show herself as superior and never paints herself in a deceptively favorable light.

Stark Raving Sober is a book about love and its steep cost. It is about insanity and how it can infect someone's life before they even realize it. It is about addiction and how it grows into a monster that ruins everything and everyone it touches. It is about humor and how without it, only despair is left. It is about infidelity and how others use it as a tool of manipulation. Finally, it is a book about redemption and how no matter how bad things are in a person's life, and they get really bad for Donna, she is able to find her sanity again and reclaim her life.

In *Stark Raving Sober*, Donna writes with exceptional transparency about a brand of love that is very popular and dysfunctional. In this brand of love, you will see that initially she is looking for someone who through marriage will make it possible for her to become part of an existing, complete family. When someone is looking for another person or in Donna's case, something else to complete them, an unhealthy person will seem very appealing. An unhealthy person will come on so strong that it will sweep a gullible person like the young Donna off her feet and create an illusion of romantic love as represented in movies and television. Whenever someone expects an individual to make their life complete, then they are more likely to select an impaired person. An unhealthy person who looks for someone to heal them will feel like they are getting deep care from the one who answers that need. Once either partner finally realizes that it was an unrealistic expectation that drew them into the relationship in the first place, they have invested too much of themselves and feel trapped.

When working with people as a counselor, I am shocked by the effects addiction has on not only the person drinking, but also on all those people who live with the alcoholic. I cannot tell you how many times I have seen spouses of alcoholics get away from the alcoholic, only to end up remarrying that same problem drinker or finding another alcoholic. As for the children, often they grow up to marry alcoholics themselves. The level of denial is huge and in *Stark Raving Sober* you, the reader, will see how this invisible evil comes about without the people involved even being aware that it is happening. If you have always wondered how someone with seemingly good common sense could find another version of the same person they chose to divorce, then reading Donna's journal entries will help unscramble that mystery.

People who have some of the same issues that Donna reveals in her book will see how she harnessed journaling, one of the greatest therapeutic tools in use today. Journaling one's daily events and thoughts provides an excellent way for a person to gain insight into their own life. It is easy while living with an alcoholic to lose perspective and many times even doubt one's own sanity because the alcoholic is either passively or aggressively convincing. Donna's journal entries, included in the book just as she wrote them at the time, reveal how this excellent therapeutic tool helps her make it through some of the most horrific moments in her life and gain a more accurate perception of the events surrounding her.

Another important therapeutic tool confirmed in this book is the use of a proper support system. The reader will see how Donna makes the mistake early on of seeking support from people who are not capable of giving her the solid reinforcement she needs to break from relationships with addicted individuals. When she became willing to swallow her pride to seek help from people with the professional depth to help her, then her forward path to healing could begin.

It is not unusual for anyone who is caught up with an addict to believe that they alone can come up with an answer all by themselves. As you will see, a few knowledgeable people made an effort to inform Donna of the destructive path she was about to take. Donna does an excellent job in explaining how her distorted thinking kept her on an emotional roller coaster and unable to heed the warnings of those who had already experienced the craziness she was about to encounter. As a therapist, I see this type of thinking every day. People who live with an alcoholic have to live in a deep level of denial otherwise they could not stand the pain of everyday life. These people go to a therapist like myself and think that if the therapist can say the right words or perform some special treatment, then the "person with the drinking problem" will start living a "normal" life.

Another side of therapy is also addressed in this book. When anyone has lived with an alcoholic for an extended amount of time, then they, too, acquire many of the same traits as the person who has been "using." With the help of professionals, Donna discovered that about herself.

Many people find it hard to continue living with an alcoholic who has stopped drinking, especially if that person seeks true recovery. A typical pattern I have seen manifested many times is that the attraction of the relationship was based on the addictive qualities of the user and once the user is in recovery, the partner has to look at their own issues. It is at this shift in the balance of the relationship that many partners will encourage the alcoholic to start drinking again or will create some kind of crisis which will bring on a relapse.

Not many people are willing to sit down and write about the "dark side" of their life. When someone has to write about the ugly things they have allowed others to do to them and the people they love, the first thought is to throw away the paper and forget about it. Donna decided to confront her own personal shame and embarrassment and face her demons head on; consequently, you will be treated to vivid tales of chaos and confusion.

For those readers who have been exposed to the same issues that Donna writes about, hopefully this book will be a wake up call because your life may depend on it. If you are a friend of someone who is presently living in a destructive relationship, then this book can be a great therapeutic tool to help those who might be in the same kind of denial Donna was early in her life. If you have heard about women in destructive relationships and always wondered how they got themselves into such a mess, then you are going to get a front row seat to a good woman, wanting love, finding sickness, and then finally she stopped digging herself in deeper and instead climbed out of the hole.

I am excited that Donna has been willing to open up her heart and her life for the sake of personal healing. In *Stark Raving Sober*, she places the reader in the mind of a life spiraling out of control. Through each chapter when you, the reader, think things could not get any worse, you will be shocked by the despicable way one human being treats another human being. Hopefully, Donna's story will shed much needed light on how a person who has been beaten down can rise again to a new and better life.

As a therapist, I have seen how hard it is for a person to make a fearless search of their life and take responsibility for their choices. So many people want to get better, but are unwilling to do the painful work. Donna is showing all of us all how to move beyond the pain and into a life fully lived. I hope that everyone who reads this book will be as inspired as I was when I read it. I am so glad that I have had the privilege of knowing Donna and seeing her face her own shame in an effort to help others who are still living in their own personal hell.

Dr. Roger A. Rhoades, a licensed professional counselor for more than 20 years, is a popular relationship therapist who has gained a national following through his appearances on television talk shows. He is also a frequent contributor to notable magazines on such subjects as dating, breakup recovery, and infidelity. He has a Master's Degree in Religious Education with an emphasis on Marriage and Family from New Orleans Baptist Seminary, and a Doctorate Degree in Ministry with an emphasis in Pastoral Counseling from the Graduate Theological Foundation. His most recent book, Living in the Moment, is available online through his cyber office at www.greatstuff.com

Prologue

I sat for hours in a dark living room, quietly, and I thought logically, plotting how I would murder my husband. My children and mother were asleep upstairs. Across the entry hallway of the old farmhouse, Steve was passed out on our bed. He drank heavily that day and the day before; it was inevitable he would wet the bed again. With each bout of drinking came another volley of diabolical meanness, outbursts of violent verbal attacks, punches and slaps, and threats of bodily harm to me, the kids, even my elderly mother. He told me he would break her arms and throw her down the hill. He added, "And I hope she breaks both hips." Yet Steve was the one who invited her to make her home with us.

Steve collected guns. Some were kept in custom-built cabinets; rifles and shotguns stood in corners throughout the house. All were loaded, including the .38 detective special he gave me one Christmas that I kept in our bedroom, in a bureau drawer. I thought if I used the Luger he kept in his top dresser drawer that it would look less like premeditated murder. I visualized the oozy, bloody mess, and I hoped he would be aware, between shots, that I was killing him. Next I would upset lamps and tear at the curtains to make it appear there had been a struggle; that I killed in self-defense. I walked into the bedroom several times, checked the accessibility of the Luger, stood by the bed and stared at the snoring beast. I loathed him for his cruelty to me and my family, to our animals. I wondered if the intensity of my hatred could cause his heart to stop.

Because he had earned a town-wide reputation for having an explosive temper and had alienated many, I thought I might get away with justifiable homicide. But if the jury was not convinced I had acted in self-defense, I would be separated from my children. That they would be relieved to have him removed from our lives I had no doubt, but who would raise them and how would they cope with the knowledge their mother had killed another human being? Reason intervened. I dared not kill him.

The long hours awake in the sleeping household, planning a murder and considering the consequences seemed rational. For me to relish the idea of shooting bullets into my husband's chest was incongruous with my basic temperament—then and now. I abhor violence. As a youngster, Mother had to take me out to the lobby during *Snow White and the Seven Dwarfs* and *The Wizard of Oz*. Even as an adult I wince at the brutal shenanigans in cartoons. As teenagers my children cautioned me against seeing certain movies because they knew I would be upset. I was roped into seeing *Taxi Driver* and for days its savagery clung to me like a shroud. I avoid exposing myself to violent situations, even on a printed page. If faced with possible bodily harm, I rely on my wits because I lack physical strength and self-defense knowledge. Ergo, I am a physical coward.

On the New England night in 1971 that I contemplated murder, thinking of adding my own violence to the violence Steve had already brought into our lives, I was on the brink of emotional bankruptcy. At that time, not widely known nor understood were the behavior patterns that constitute what eventually became known as "domestic violence." The symptoms are universal and timeless. In 1971, shelters for battered wives and children were still a few years away.

With the help of hindsight and discussions with a number of physicians, I believe Steve suffered with a mental illness, possibly bipolar disorder. Depending upon which cycle was in control, ingesting alcohol either exacerbated his already agitated mood or deepened a depressed mood. But when his mood was pleasantly upbeat, he passed for a normal social drinker. His mother and brothers told me that even as a child, he displayed a mercurial temperament and needed to be handled carefully. After I divorced Steve, I married Harry and learned to recognize the symptoms manifested by a bonafide alcoholic who was rampantly promiscuous.

This is a true story about emotional chaos and reclaiming my self. Through reading about my experiences that are similar to their own, and by combining new insights with awareness gained from other sources, I hope readers who need empowerment to break out of the debilitating smog of helplessness will find it soon. And to those who are dumbfounded as to why anyone remains in an abusive relationship, I hope these pages will provide perspective and appreciation of why a seemingly simple decision is fraught with complicated emotions.

Part One

Mayhem

Chapter 1

Mother had been widowed five months by the time I was born, three days after she watched eggs frying on a Kansas City sidewalk and six weeks before what would have been her first wedding anniversary. Mother received no death benefits because my father had neglected to change his beneficiary; the insurance money went to my adult half-brothers, children from my father's first marriage, which they used to cover final expenses and to help keep the family business going. Mother's income from the company ceased when I was ten months old. One year into The Great Depression, I slept, burped and cooed in a hammock hung in the back seat of a green DeSoto touring car, my father's wedding gift to Mother, while the three principal influences during my childhood sat in the front seat during our trek to New England—Mother, her mother, and her youngest brother whom I knew was my uncle but I called him Daddy. We were headed east to the area where they had lived and now would become home for me, too. Once back in Massachusetts, we stayed with relatives before moving into our own apartment. Mother found a challenging position in nearby Worcester as YWCA Business Manager and Director of Maintenance, a dual position she held for the next 32 years. Almost everyone on the staff, from janitors, maids and cooks to the executive directors contributed to my upbringing.

Until I was almost five, we lived in South Lancaster, a sleepy college town. Chameleons purchased during circus visits lived on the kitchen curtains and ate sugar from our fingertips. Daddy didn't have much luck finding work but he was jubilant in the middle of the night he awakened us with the news, "I've got London on the radio!"—a crystal set. While Mother commuted to work 20 miles away, Grammie cared for me and indoctrinated me in her strict fundamentalist religion which seemed to be against almost anything that was fun. When I was sure she could not see me, I danced in the living room in front of a picture of my father. I believed he could see me.

I was told I was born with a beautiful disposition; that I always woke up smiling. I was told I was a happy child and I can agree with that, but no one knew I feared that my mother might die and leave me an orphan. That would have meant Grammie would raise me, and although I loved her with all my heart, I did not like how serious and pious she was most of the time, reading and quoting the Bible, always talking about Judgment Day when Jesus would come again and know if I were good or bad. I reasoned it was important to be good so God would not punish me by taking away my mother. When it was time for me to begin kindergarten, Mother moved us all to Worcester.

For the next nine years, I attended the neighborhood grammar school. I enjoyed school; I liked my classmates; and the neighborhood kids were great playmates. When I was six, I told Mother she was wicked because she went to the movies; another time I told her she was wicked because she ate meat. Both were pleasures Grammie's religion forbade. When I was seven, I stopped participating in dancing class because Grammie had told me dancing was wicked. Mother intervened. She told Grammie I could continue going to Sabbath School and church with her on Saturdays but once Mother and I found a church we liked, we would go together on Sundays to the new church.

Grammie threatened to leave unless Mother relented. Mother stood firm. Grammie moved back to the little college town but not before telling Mother, "God will punish you for this. Something terrible will happen to Donna." A few days after Grammie left, I came down with chicken pox, and Mother was scared. This was the first of many childhood illnesses that were monitored by worried looks and anxious questions, thermometer readings, gargles, alcohol rubs, and prolonged gradations of recuperation. Before I could resume a normal lifestyle, my temperature had to be at 98.6 or below for at least 24 hours. A reading of 98.8 was not acceptable. I was also carefully overdressed by Mother during cold weather in long lisle stockings held up by a garter belt harness that hung from my shoulders. I had a poor appetite and for a while, the doctor prescribed that I walk before breakfast. Between meals I was allowed to snack on fresh fruit or raw vegetables. Soda pop was verboten except I could sip ginger ale when I was sick. Sugar was not added to my cereal. We never bought white bread. I may not have eaten heartily but I ate healthfully. Practicing my piano lesson daily was expected, from age four until I was almost 18. I had many friends but not having a father made me feel different.

Following Grammie's departure came a succession of live-in housekeepers—all of them kind, some more strict than others and some openly affectionate—who carried out Mother's instructions to the letter. I may have been more closely supervised than my friends whose mothers were at home. With Grammie's prediction never out of Mother's mind, I was overly protected. I thought of myself as delicate. On the few occasions I experimented climbing fallen trees with my energetic and daring peers, I exalted in the joy of pushing my body and spirit into somewhat precarious situations and then felt guilty because what if I had gotten hurt? Mother took pride in seeing I was well dressed in classically simple clothing that more often than not was purchased in Filene's bargain basement. Piano, dancing, and voice lessons ate into her limited budget. I was acutely aware of the need to economize and of her sacrifices.

I longed for Mother to remarry because I wanted the security of having two parents and having my mother at home. Daddy was a pretend father, and I knew that. I loved to go into the bathroom after he shaved to smell the mixture of aftershave lotion and the smoke from his cigarette, which he always tossed into the toilet bowl where the paper disintegrated freeing tiny squiggles of tobacco to float in the water. My happiest times were when Mother's brothers and their families gathered to celebrate holidays, including Mother's Day. My uncles' wives never spent Mother's Day with their own mothers. Instead the daughters-in-law acquiesced to their husbands' lifelong devotion to their mother: Grammie lived to be a spry and mentally acute 101. This diminutive woman who barely cleared five feet, who bore seven children, she of the snapping brown eyes and strong will was tendered obeisance by all who knew her. Mother showed courage when she declared she would take me to a new church on Sundays.

The best family gatherings occurred when unexpected snowstorms prevented everyone from returning to their homes. Front seats removed from cars became makeshift beds. Uncles, aunts, and my beloved boy cousins filled the house. The organized confusion, the joking and good-natured bickering, the profusion of so many *relatives* all under one roof filled me with happiness. For however long it took for roads to be plowed, I was not an only child of a widow but an integral part of a large family. I was in hog heaven.

With many of the same schoolmates I had known since kindergarten, I enrolled in the college preparatory Classical High School. I began dating, an extracurricular activity I considered of equal importance to studies. I didn't have swarms of boys buzzing about me but I did not lack for dates. I was more interested in quality than quantity. I had my share of hurt feelings. Mother reminded me that every disappointment was "character building," a phrase I came to hate so much I vowed I would never inflict it upon any children I might have. As usual, however, Mother was right.

I flirted with romantic love and then with one boy, Dane, our dating progressed from reciprocal attraction to falling in love. When after months of dating he asked me to go steady with him, my happiness was complete. I loved him, loved knowing I did not have to guess if he really liked me, loved feeling I belonged with him, the sense of emotional safety. Those were the days when going steady meant commitment and sometimes it was a forerunner to becoming engaged-to-be-engaged. A few times we teased about marrying one day; we even chose the name for our first child, a son, of course. The future included graduation from high school, then college. Even with interim separations, I could not envision a future that did not include him. He had the attributes I wanted in a mate—intelligence, dry humor, socially well-developed, wide interests, kind, courteous, and a strong moral code of right and wrong. He seemed to be his own person until the dreadful day he succumbed to peer pressure: his buddies who were temporarily without girlfriends convinced him that going steady was both too limiting and too expensive. My heart was broken. But I accepted invitations from other boys and dated frenetically. I'd show him! I went through the motions of having a wonderful time but when alone, I cried. I mourned. A few months later Dane phoned and we resumed dating but I dared not invest myself in him again. Neither then nor now, decades later, do I underestimate the power and depth of so-called puppy love. In conversations he and I were fortunate to have 30 years later—yes, he matured into a fine man—he asked, "Whatever happened to us?" After my daughter met Dane, she said, "He's the one you should have married."

When I was introduced to Brad, I wondered, "Will I know when I meet the man I'm going to marry?" A year went by before I saw him again in October of my senior year. Although I would have denied it, I was rebounding from my first love and was primed to be swept off my feet by a handsome young man who, although only a year older than I, had graduated from prep school (valedictorian) at 15, attended college for one year, enlisted in the army to qualify for the G.I. Bill, became the youngest member of OSS (clerk typist), and was stationed in Trieste where he became engaged to an Italian girl who worked at the British Embassy. She predicted their romance would end when he returned home. After Brad was discharged from the Army, he monopolized my time. He introduced me to his parents and kid sister and their black cocker spaniel. Through the stars in my eyes, I saw an idealized family, a complete family unit. Our romance flourished. Brad's father told him, "You know, with the G.I. Bill, and with us and Donna's mother helping out financially, you and Donna could get married." The idea had not occurred to either of us, nor to my mother. We had college degrees to earn. Brad's parents presented what I eventually referred to derisively as The Master Plan: while Brad accumulated degrees, including a doctorate in mathematics, I was to acquire a business education so I could augment the G.I. Bill with my earnings. Mother was crestfallen. I waited for her to veto the marriage because I lacked the gumption to challenge Brad's parents but even she was overwhelmed by their public relations campaign. While compiling the invitation lists, Brad's family were not pleased when they learned my list included not only the YW's professional staff but the maintenance people, residence maids, and cafeteria cooks, all of whom had a hand in raising me from babyhood. Brad was upset because I was including boys I'd known since we sang in the children's choir, some I had dated. He manifested such unreasonable jealousy that I wanted to cancel the wedding. But I was assaulted by the admonition, "What would other people think?" The pressure to fast forward the marriage obliterated common sense. His parents urged us to have a secret civil service a few weeks prior to the wedding so we could have a longer honeymoon than the time allotted between the church service and the beginning of classes. Brad pressured me. But I refused because if I were no longer a virgin, it would be dishonest of me to wear a white wedding dress. While I waited with Daddy at the back of the church for our cue to walk down the aisle——I in my white dotted Swiss gown——I wanted to bolt. But, what would other people think? And so on a hot August day, three weeks before my 18th birthday, I married Brad. I had cancelled my dorm registration at Rhode Island School of Design and with it my personal goals. I loved Brad but married him for the wrong reasons: I wanted independence and to become an integral member of a ready-made family. For years I mentally adopted my girlfriends' fathers. When I was in public with Brad, his younger sister and parents, I hoped strangers mistook me for being a daughter, not a daughter-in-law. Years of fantasizing about the joys of a complete family were to be paid off by the real thing. I saw Brad's mother and father as ideal surrogate parents. Disillusionment occurred two years into the marriage when I had a miscarriage and Brad and his parents responded in a hurtful way that was neither kind nor supportive. Their words and behavior demonstrated they wanted the miscarriage so that I would not be prevented from fulfilling The Master Plan—earning money to help support Brad while he completed his education.

Brad was a scholar with genius mentality. His humor was sophisticated, subtle, at times delightfully childlike. He knew he was a disappointment to his parents because he excelled in the classroom, not on the playing field, although he was varsity tennis in prep school and college and on the chess team. Eventually he cautioned me not to introduce subjects into conversation with his parents but to let them choose the topics with which they were comfortable. I developed violent headaches whenever I knew we would see them. Between aborted graduate studies at Harvard and Brown, Brad joined a major life insurance company as an actuarial student. He studied year round, year after year. I was an executive secretary. We rarely socialized except to play bridge and to see almost every movie that came to town. His personality quirks, which at first I found amusing, became irritating. He was absent minded to the point of discourteousness and created dangerous situations when behind the wheel. He had inherited his father's preoccupation with his health; hypochondriac episodes became common-place. Librium was prescribed for tachycardia. Five years into our marriage, he said, "I'm glad you haven't conceived because I do not want to reproduce myself." That should have sent me screaming for help but I thought I needed to love him more. After all, hadn't his parents said to my mother during the bridal dinner the night before our wedding, "We hope Donna can do for Brad what we've been unable to do." They expected me to change an intellectual recluse into a sociable extrovert. But his anti-social behavior deepened. During our tenth year of marriage, a young relative of mine, age 14 going on 30 and deeply disturbed, lived with us for six months. Brad, twice her age, told me he was in love with her. I squelched the infatuation, but the incident compromised my trust in Brad.

We conned ourselves and an adoption agency into believing ours was a healthy marriage. I wanted children and stupidly thought a child would create a family. We were married almost 11 years when six-week-old Elizabeth was placed in my arms. Within hours my bond with my daughter was solidified. A year and a half later, three-month-old David was handed to me, and another bond was formed. However, the already deteriorating marriage went on the skids. I consulted our family doctor who suggested counseling. We saw a psychiatrist with whom Brad connected but I found unapproachable. Instead, I counseled with a psychologist who helped me regain my feelings of self-worth even while Brad continued to tell me no one liked me, that family and friends only pretended to like me. During the last two years of the marriage, Brad chose to sleep in another bedroom. I was ready for divorce but the psychiatric consensus was for me to delay initiating proceedings until Brad could cope. That year was permeated with sadness; my heart went out to Brad as it never had before. But I believed that to remain together would have been mutually destructive. So I bided my time until early one afternoon he walked into my office (I was general manager of a summer theater) to tell me, "The die is cast. I have filed for divorce." By early evening I had counter-filed. Our marriage ended after 15 years.

In 1963, a divorced mother of two little children was not commonplace. I was scared but convinced I had made the correct decision. The beautiful home in the suburbs was sold, and on a dead-end city street in Springfield, I rented a three-bedroom house with a large fenced-in backyard across the street from an elementary school and its playground. My job with the theater led to an offer from a local radio station. Every weekday morning I left Liz and David at a fine nursery school, continued on to work, and picked them up at the end of the day. When they entered public school, I was fortunate to latch on to a wonderfully kind and competent housekeeper who came in by the day. I loved my job—a daily on-air program about the performing arts, interviewing the near great and formerly great, covering area professional and community theaters, occasionally New York theater, Ice Capades, movies, books, and even doing a play-by-play of the Shrine Circus. For evening assignments, I had a stable of reliable babysitters.

And I enjoyed my kids who were bright, witty, inventive, loving, and very active. I felt guilty about depriving them of a father figure, which I felt compounded the emotional loss they had suffered due to their respective birth parents' decisions to release them for adoption. I had grown up without a father; I didn't want them to. Everyone I dated I appraised as potential husband-father material. Some might have acquitted themselves well as fathers but not as husbands, or vice versa. I was embarrassed and a new date probably alarmed when my kids asked him, "Are you going to be our new father?"

Chapter 2

Nine months after my divorce, on a blind date arranged by a mutual friend, I met the man I would marry two and a half years later. Steve was a USAF Lt. Colonel, a jet fighter pilot, with almost 25 years of service. He was 6'2", powerfully built, vain about his appearance, especially his legs, and exuded animal excitement. Less than a mile from the house on our first date, Steve told me to reach over into the back seat and mix us both what he called a "jar of candy"—vodka, 7-Up, fresh lime. He was the only man I ever dated who had a portable bar in whatever vehicle he drove. Suddenly the admonition "don't drink and drive" seemed to apply to other people so I construed the bar in the back seat to be an extension of his glamour. I was captivated by his charm, magnetism, his combat experience, and worldly sophistication. His assignments overseas had included Europe, the British Isles, the South Pacific, Japan, and Taiwan. I admired the ease with which he met and mingled with people. Here, I told myself, was a well-developed social being. The only fly in the ointment I could see was our mutual friend had been mistaken about Steve's divorce, but he cleared that up at once. He told me the divorce was in the works, but on the advice of his attorney, he had not moved out. He said he and his wife, Maggie, occupied separate bedrooms and had for some time. He had two children in their early teens. The fact he was already a father enhanced him in my eyes.

On that first evening he also told me that his wife often behaved like a crazy woman, that once she had attacked him: X-rays, he said, showed she had broken two of his ribs. He said she threw a fork at him another time and often she yelled and screamed, indoors and out, making the neighborhood privy to their problems, and this he found reprehensible. He said she would just fly off the handle for no reason. But, he added, Maggie was a good woman and a good mother. It did not occur to me to wonder what provoked her rage because he blocked the question by saying she flew off the handle for no reason.

During the initial hours of that first evening, I was on assignment. For the first time, after clearing it with the headliner, I invited Steve to sit in while I taped an hour interview with Tallulah Bankhead in her dressing room. Afterwards we watched her dominate a run-of-the-mill play, transforming it into a personal tour de force. I sat in a darkened theater fascinated by the scenery-chewing technique of a living legend and enthralled by the charisma of the man at my side. Much later I learned about Miss Bankhead's personal battle with alcohol but it was years before I realized Steve had a compulsive drinking problem.

Two weeks later over pre-dinner cocktails, Steve said, "Will you marry me when my divorce is final?"

I replied, "If I feel the same way about you then as I do now, yes, I will."

The following week we drove to Uniontown, Pennsylvania, where he introduced me to his mother and the members of his large family who still lived in the area. Steve told me his mother interfered with his first real love by advising the girl not to marry him. "I've never forgiven her for that," he said. I had yet to learn that forgiveness was not one of his better qualities. He implied his mother thought no girl was good enough for him; I was already nervous about meeting her because I was self-conscious about being a divorcee. Mom, as I came to call her, greeted me warmly and from the first, I felt at ease with her. A few months later when she visited me and my children, she advised me not to marry Steve.

"You're too nice a girl, and I don't want to see you hurt." I had no reason to doubt Mom did not care for me nor did her behavior ever arouse concern that she wanted to control Steve. But then there was the story Steve told me about his first love, the girl who pinned on his wings, and the broken engagement he blamed on his mother.

Mom spoke of visiting Steve while he and Maggie were married and how "Those poor children used to go off to school in the morning in tears." Based upon what Steve told me about Maggie's erratic behavior, I assumed Maggie upset the children. Mom mentioned that Steve had always been headstrong;

that to get him to do his chores, she used psychological persuasions "Steve, when you split and stack wood, you always do it so much neater and nicer than the other boys." She added to me, "I found I could get him to do what I wanted if I didn't order him." I was not hearing anything I had not discovered for myself. Steve also warned me that Mom, now in her seventies, tended to become confused now and again and sometimes said things that were not true. During the years I knew her, she was honest and mentally sharp.

A few weeks into our courtship, on the day of his annual physical, Steve said he might be a little late for dinner. He was several hours late and arrived reeling drunk. After the physical which included several shots, he and some others at the base had a few jars—Steve's appropriate word for a drink because he preferred a drink big enough to fill a jar. He sprawled out on the couch and then staggered to his feet and announced he was leaving. "Where are my keys?" he demanded. I said he was in no condition to drive. He became angry. "Give me my keys!" he thundered. I was concerned he would awaken Liz and David. My shushing only made him angrier. He walked right by the keys on the desk where he had put them. I scooped them up and hid them behind a book. He turned back to me, his eyes on fire. There was no hint of love in his face. I felt as if I were being burned with hatred. He lurched about the living room and kitchen, then back through the front door and down the front steps. He leaned against his car, demanding I give him the keys. I knew he kept an emergency set gripped by a magnet under the hood and I expected he would use them. Instead he called me names, swore at me, "We're through!" cursed God, and said, "I'll walk home." He lived 20 miles away. I pleaded with him to come back into the house. He pushed me away. I followed him to the edge of the yard and stopped: two little children, hopefully still asleep, were my primary responsibility. I watched him reel from side to side, sometimes falling, until he disappeared around the corner. He was in uniform. My knowledge of military rules came from movies about the Second World War. I feared if the police picked him up there would be hell to pay. I had to talk to someone. I called the only person who knew about our relationship—his attorney. He told me not to worry. "Steve's a big boy. That's one of his problems; he's never grown up. If he gets into trouble, I'll get a call." I felt like an idiot. It took me hours to fall asleep.

The next morning on the chance Steve might return while still drunk, I drove his car to work. Throughout the day I tried to reach him by phone. He was not at his office and he did not answer at his house. I was beside myself with anxiety. I described what happened to one of the radio station salesmen who listened sympathetically and tried to assure me that Steve had a little too much to drink, that I shouldn't pay any attention to what he had said, that Steve obviously adored me, and once he felt better, everything would be fine again. That was advice straight from the horse's mouth: the salesman was a heavy drinker. By mid-afternoon, Steve's car was gone from the parking lot. My first thought was that it had been stolen but then I wondered if he had remembered about the keys under the hood. I continued calling his home and finally he answered. His voice was thick.

"Are you all right?" I asked.

"I'm sick."

"Do you have the car?"

"Yeah, no thanks to you," and he hung up.

The salesman said, "See, what did I tell you? He'll be okay."

I heard nothing from Steve until the following evening. He telephoned, his voice low, measured, and said, "I love you." His next words made me laugh. "I'm starved. Would you fix this old goat some breakfast?"

I felt happy again. Steve was fine and he still loved me. I prepared a huge breakfast. He arrived with an armful of packages which I mistakenly thought might be peace offerings for me. No, he had bought new clothes for himself. He was a clothes horse. He interrupted his attentiveness to scold me for letting him just go off the other night and sleep in ditches. "I could have died," he admonished, which I doubted because the summer nights were balmy. I wondered what he thought he could have died from. I felt guilty.

"I tried to stop you," I said.

"You didn't try hard enough."

"I couldn't leave the children."

"You care more about them than you do me."

"Steve, I couldn't go off and leave them alone."

"Never mind. It's history now." He explained away his drunkenness as a reaction to the immunization shots. Of course the shots he had a reaction to were those containing ethyl alcohol but because I knew nothing about drunkenness, I swallowed his excuse and felt more guilt. My God, he could have died from a reaction to the shots. I would have to try harder to be perfect for him.

I learned how to mix jars of candy to his satisfaction. His favorite before dinner drink was a vodka gibson, mine a bourbon sour, but I changed to a vodka gimlet and sometimes shared a pitcher of martinis with Steve. My limit was one, occasionally two, but I preferred eating to more drinking and fortunately still do. But with Steve as my teacher, I was introduced to the ritual of the cocktail hour. He expanded other horizons for me too. He was an excellent, inventive cook, and I learned more about cooking from him than anyone. He enlarged my vocabulary with colorful words and expressions I could not use in public. He chided me about having "led such a sheltered life." He took pride in my work and bragged about me to others and sometimes in front of me which both embarrassed and pleased me. He had great curiosity, a tremendous zest for life and drained the last drop from any experience. He introduced me to hunting—deer, pheasant, partridge—and to deep sea fishing. He encouraged me to learn how to fly. Later I soloed in a Cessna 150. He treated me to commercial air travel and the wide open spaces of the American West and Southwest. He made acquaintances out of strangers and often exaggerated the association by saying they were personal friends. He introduced me to the excitement of automobile racing at Watkins Glen, New York, and Sebring, Florida. In New Mexico he introduced me to an Apache Indian family where I rode one of their ponies in a swirling snow squall; through them I interviewed the son of Geronimo. Between us, we introduced each other to people from many walks of life and socialized comfortably with all of them.

Best of all, he was good to my children—at first. We played hide 'n seek in the house where he helped the kids hide from each other—swinging little Liz up onto the top of the refrigerator, helping little David curl up in the cupboard, stuffing one into a broom closet and the other into the bottom of the linen closet—outlandish, ridiculous hiding places that sent us all into fits of laughter. He was firm but loving—at first—guiding, correcting, chastising, praising. Here at last was a real engaging father figure for them. Finally my fantasy of a complete family was coming true. I was delirious with happiness— at first.

Months passed while his pre-divorce negotiations dragged on. Maggie and their children moved back to her home in Georgia. There was another drunken incident while we visited his family in Pennsylvania but stayed at a hunting lodge in the nearby mountains that belonged to a love of a man, Kenneth, whom Steve adopted after his father died when Steve was a teenager. "Dad died just when I needed him the most." The man died of stomach cancer, but Steve implied his father elected to die because he knew Steve needed him. I learned not to argue. At the lodge, Steve showed colored slides of his trips to the western states. He had captured the panoramic grandeur of the mountains and in close up shots the delicate beauty of wee desert flowers. Frame after frame was breathtakingly beautiful. He added to the entertainment by giving a travelogue and natural history information. He enjoyed having an audience. He was also rather tipsy but he remained in good humor. Suddenly we smelled something burning. He had left a slide in front of the projector bulb too long. We alerted him, but he did not react. He seemed confused. The image on the screen turned from orange to brown to black. He caught on to what was happening and clicked to the next slide. That slide, too, he left in too long and it burned. More than a dozen slides were destroyed, but he seemed not to care. He laughed. When the show and burn act ended, we drove the guests into town and then headed back into the mountains. Steve was happily drunk and his driving was terrible. I asked him to let me drive so he could relax, and to my surprise and relief, he agreed. He put his head on my shoulder and began singing raunchy ditties, some of them outrageously funny parodies of epic poems. Several times he kissed me and said, "I love you," and somehow I kept the car on the road. The night was crisp and clear. Soft music played on the radio. I was with a man I loved, who loved me, and he, was happily, rather than unhappily, drunk. I thought it was all wonderfully romantic. I was reminded of a movie scenario, one of those lovely, sophisticated comedies Hollywood turned out during its golden years. I giggled and said, "You Gable. Me Lombard." He enjoyed being likened to Gable and especially to John Wayne. Often when he was really full of himself, he walked like the Duke, hip joints swiveling. He cultivated his macho image and—at first—I was thrilled with his taut spring prowess. With my first husband I thought that if we were somehow caught in a barroom brawl— highly unlikely because we never went to bars—Brad would have hidden under the table and let me slug it out. With Steve, I felt I had found my protector. I would hide under the table until he finished mopping up the bad guys. I had found a lover for me, almost a husband—and a father figure for my children.

But the price was high. I had to use diplomacy. Even after I chose words with great care, Steve accused me of "blurting" or "talking without thinking." Often he shot me down saying, "Typical female talk." I wondered how he could love me and also have such open hatred for females in general. He seldom used the word "woman" except in a derogatory sense. More often than not, he called me, "Girl", but that was usually spoken with tenderness. When angry, he snapped, "Sister!" He told me, "A female's mission in life is to make man happy." He never said "male." Further, "As long as you keep me happy, you'll be happy." I wanted so desperately to be happy, to have a happy home life for my children, and because I believed such happiness was contingent upon Steve being happy, I knocked myself out trying to please him. I hoped that if I never made the same mistake twice, I would win his blanket approval and unconditional acceptance. I was flabbergasted by the number of things I did or said which he judged to be mistakes. "I'm disappointed in you," he said, and I withered.

And poor Liz and David! Being just kids, they made normal mistakes I could roll with but which infuriated Steve. He was a strict disciplinarian. He not only expected perfection, he demanded it. Yet there were times when he let them be just what they were—normal kids. Then he referred to them affectionately as "ankle biters" or "house apes." He had already raised his own two children into their teens, and so I understood his reluctance to repeat the process with mine. But there was one thing I made clear to my children and to him: the kids and I were a package deal.

Chapter 3

After Maggie and the children left the area and Maggie and Steve's house was put on the market, Steve spent more time at my place. One day it dawned on me that Steve and I were living together. There was never any discussion; it just evolved. This gave me the opportunity to really get into playing house, pretending we were, indeed, a family, hoping the property settlement would be resolved soon paving the way for divorce proceedings to begin and that one day we would be legally a family. Steve told me, "In the eyes of God, we are married." That somewhat assuaged my concerns about what the neighbors might think.

For our first Christmas, I continued the custom of giving the children their own Christmas trees to keep in their bedrooms where they could decorate and un-decorate as their imaginations suggested. This spared the lower branches of the living room tree from spontaneous creative disasters. Steve lavished me with gifts; by actual count, seventeen. What I especially remember is a street-length white wool sheath that caught his eye while driving by a store window.

While I behaved as a wife/mother, Steve's conduct varied between husband/father and footloose bachelor. During that spring I was ill with, of all things at age 34, Scarlet Fever. Steve had a bonafide commitment out of town but he could have returned. Instead he took a long weekend and phoned me once. I felt sorry for myself. I was sick in bed with a high fever and it was Mother's Day. When he finally returned on Monday, he said he had swung by to spend a day with a brother. But on the dresser he tossed a matchbook that inside had the name and telephone number of a girl. A few months later there was a party at her apartment where I watched her like a hawk. On a Friday afternoon during our second summer together, he informed me he was going to Long Island and, no, I was not invited. He spoke of a house party where Johnny Long's orchestra would entertain. I envisioned unattached, beautiful women. I panicked. I can see myself now pleading with Steve after he got into his car. I cried hysterically. I even held onto the door handle as he backed out to the street. Among other names, he called me "stupid." I felt stupid—and rejected. Early that winter I was recuperating from an accidental cut to the bone on the middle finger of my right hand. In response to this problem Steve took off, he said, in response to a call from an old friend who needed to talk. I was livid because I couldn't use my right hand that throbbed incessantly and because the old friend was an attractive divorcee and because he did not return until the following afternoon. What was his excuse? He told me he swung by the home of a couple we both knew and spent the night on their couch. A few weeks later at a dance, I thanked the wife for letting Steve sleep on her couch. "Steve's never slept at our house," she said. When I confronted him, he took the offensive. He said what he did was none of my business and to stop embarrassing him in front of his friends.

And then he had an affair with Margo, half his age. I did not know this when I wished them a safe trip from Massachusetts to Utah and Colorado where Steve wanted to scope out areas to live after retiring. He had asked me to accompany him, but he knew I had used most of my vacation time. Later I realized they had already made their plans but at the time I told myself the pangs of jealousy I felt were silly and without foundation. I hugged and kissed them goodbye. Steve said, "I wish you were coming with me." Months later when Steve was temporarily stationed in Nevada and was hammering out a divorce agreement so we could marry, he and Margo spent a weekend together in Mexico. When I joined Steve in Las Vegas for a month, thinking we might be married there, I learned about their affair while putting clean socks in his drawer that also held letters I had written to him. While reading my letters, I discovered Margo's letters to Steve sandwiched in with mine. Prior to the Colorado trip, they had already enjoyed a rendezvous or two at the shore. During Margo's dalliance with Steve, she advised me by mail to reconsider him as a prospective husband because he was 10 years older than I and would be an old man while I was still relatively young. At the same time, she was writing Steve that my indecision about remaining with him was driving her nuts. It was convenient for me to blame Margo for seducing Steve, but hindsight tells me they were equally at fault. I never did tell him what I knew. But when Margo twisted the truth about the character of one of her friends, I blasted her in a letter, effectively ending our association.

Chapter 4

According to an entry in my journal written during one of our many crises, two years into our relationship and ten days before we became officially engaged, "Steve spoke of how we argue, bawl and make love." The entries demonstrate I was unable to integrate my intellectual awareness of a no-win situation with emotional realization. I walked into the marriage with my eyes wide open. The problem was cataracts—a fog of ignorance about mental illness and alcoholism as well. I did not have the fortitude to break with him. I tried. I broke off the relationship in January, again in February, almost in March and April, talked through a break in May, and in June I cried hard before calling his favorite brother who was kind enough to tell me: "Steve has never known what he wanted; he's two people. For a long time I didn't even speak to him. My wife and I love him very much but we could never live with him." Minutes later, I acted. I packed Steve's clothes in a box, placed it on the front porch, and taped an envelope for him to the door. I wrote in my journal:

Maybe I'm doing right; maybe wrong, but I can't go on like this and keep my health. His brother said maybe Steve needs a real shock to change him—if that would do it. I doubt it. I'm afraid of Steve's temper and I couldn't stand a parting scene with him. I'd break down. I still love the kind Steve but I hate the mean Steve.

Years later I learned that one of the most common expressions used by people who live with bipolar disorder and/or active alcoholics is that there are two distinctively different personalities, like a Dr. Jekyll and Mr. Hyde. I dubbed Steve, "Steve White" and "Steve Black." Any assumption I made about his drinking was fuzzy. I knew I was losing my self-esteem. Only three years earlier, I had felt resolute about divorcing Brad, scared but nevertheless confident about my decision. Why was I turning into a wishy-washy *female*? How could I feel like a strong woman one minute and a directionless ninny the next?

To avoid seeing Steve, the kids and I visited Mary Jane and Barny, a loving couple whose home in the country was always open to us. They had rolled with the on-again, off-again bombardment of my vacillating emotions. They took me out to dinner and when we returned we found a quarter of a bottle of vodka in a paper bag on the back steps and a note from Steve that said, "Have a good time." The next day he phoned. "Let's give it one more try." We did, but before the month was out, a journal entry reads:

I'm crocked on three Jim Bean sours. I feel as if I'm seeing things so clearly, as if I should phone Steve, "Tout finis. Get lost, buster," because really, how can I be content with him? Can't. Wish I could be whisked away to a new environment. Last week was perfect. If I could break with him and have him leave me alone so I could follow through. I have such enjoyment with other people that I know Steve isn't suitable for me. But, how can I escape? I love him, but love is not enough. Am really at war with myself.

By August I sought direction from Barny and Mary Jane.

Barny said I have to make the decision, that if I can stand the crap Steve dishes out, that if I feel the children and I will be financially secure, then okay, but that it's my decision. I can answer "yes" to Steve offering me financial security. I cried. Mary Jane comforted me and it seemed strange because she prayed aloud: "Dear God, bless this woman. Help her to make the right decision." Prayer unsettled me. She said I am the healthy one and should never doubt it.

The following day I made what I thought was the final break with Steve.

My heart is breaking.

Two days later, he called. "I loved you from the first. I love you now. I'll always love you." By the following week Nick, someone I had known professionally for years, gave me a heady, romantic rush. I relished the refreshing difference, how the dates were quiet, relaxing, "unfearful." I even wrote:

My feelings for Steve have gone.

Ongoing phone calls from Steve buttressed my determination not to see him again. I had heard all the apologies and promises I could stand.

I like being treated nicely too much to ever experience again what I did with Steve. Too much agony for too little ecstasy.

But the calls kept coming from Steve, some businesslike, but some so emotional that I captioned one:

A dilly. He asked for another chance. I said I'd been hurt too much, that I need time to think, to recuperate, to mend. I told him I'm not saying I don't ever want to see him again but that I don't know. He asked, "How will I know when you know?" I said, "I'll call you." His voice cracked several times. I got so upset, tears, pain in stomach, and damn blocking of ears. I felt sick, all the hurt and pain all over again, especially hearing him talk about marriage. How could I ever trust him again? I couldn't.

But I did. After an especially enjoyable evening at the theater followed by a reception, while I sat in bed at two in the morning writing about the day, Steve telephoned. We talked for four hours. His persuasiveness was compelling. Neither of us had slept; we were hungry. He asked if he could come over for breakfast and continue our talk. I agreed. The kids were still sleeping. We embraced, went into the bedroom and made love. He asked me to marry him. I responded, "What about...?" and I rattled off a grievance. As soon as he answered it to my satisfaction, he again asked me, "Will you marry me?" I had another issue I wanted clarified. He gave me the assurances I wanted to hear and at once proposed to me again. There were at least a dozen questions and a dozen clarifications and a dozen proposals. When I had exhausted all my questions, I believed we were home free. I said, "Yes, I'll marry you."

We were in the kitchen making breakfast by the time the kids woke up. I told them we were going to marry. Liz, who was six, disappeared for a couple minutes and returned to give us a wedding present—four dimes she fished out of her piggy bank. David grinned. We knelt down and put our arms around the children. We were all half crying, half laughing. Steve looked at the dimes and said, "Each dime is one of us, our family." Later that day he glued them to heavy paper and placed them in a glass frame. That afternoon he took me to a jeweler where I passed up a diamond solitaire in favor of pearls flanked by diamonds set in platinum. The wedding ring was a platinum band of diamonds.

During the four month engagement, more red flags waved under my nose that I chose to overlook. Maggie phoned very late one night and talked for two hours. "Steven really loves you. He never really loved me." She alternated between saying kind things about Steve and criticizing him. She spoke of how many times he had been fired, and I thought the woman must be daft: how could Steve have been fired in the military? She said that several times they left a base in disgrace to go to another where before long, Steve antagonized superior officers and they had to move again. Not until after she left him did she begin to hear about his flirtations with other women but she added I would not have to worry because, "Steve loves you." She was very angry when she said, "He has lost his children. They want nothing more to do with him." She told me how much she had loved him but that she obviously had not loved him enough. She said, "He's a terrible liar." I gave little credence to her words because I believed I was listening to a jealous woman. Besides, Steve had told me she was unstable. I did not realize that Maggie's confused emotional state was due primarily to her 15-year marriage with Steve. I did not know that already I was caught up in a similar merry-go-round. Eventually, Maggie's words, all factual, came to haunt me.

Steve was away on frequent trips, and we ran up astronomical phone bills. I wrote off his mood swings to pressures he was under and perhaps they contributed. At four in the afternoon, he told me he would call me later that night. If he did, he was often blue, maudlin, sometimes crying.

Steve told me he's going hunting this weekend and that I'm to stay put in the house, not go anywhere or see anybody. I called him back. "Things can get mighty tough, and I don't think you're capable of handling it. Stay out of my life until Christmas 1969, 79, 89." I asked, "What are you saying? Do you want me out of your life now? If so, I can be out of it tomorrow." He said, "Just as I thought. You're frivolous. You couldn't care less. You're just exactly as I figured. Just thanks very much. I'll blow my brains out."

The next morning Steve phoned before seven. He had no recollection of my call to him last night but said that must explain why he was so tied up in knots. My freedom to move about was resolved. I could go to movies alone or with female friends, and with them and their husbands. He said he's so jealous he doesn't want anyone else to even look at me, that he's madly in love with me. I told him I can't be smothered, and he agreed. And yet within a week, I wrote about my own feelings of jealousy:

I doubt his sincerity and inside I was in shreds. He tried to reassure me of his love and devotion to me but I was more pacified than assured. I won't be able to believe anything completely until—if and when—we are married.

All common sense had long since disappeared. I, who had divorced after 15 years of marriage was back to buying into the romantic notion that vows and a piece of paper created a passport to living happily ever after.

We entertained. We threw impromptu parties to celebrate obscure historic anniversaries and for changing the clocks from standard to daylight, and back again. Steve surprised me with birthday parties. On Thanksgiving following a long lull between crises, I wrote:

For the blessing, Steve said, "We thank You for this wonderful day. We thank You for this wonderful food. We thank You for this wonderful family." We did our share of happy bawling while preparing dinner. This was the happiest, most thankful Thanksgiving I've ever had because the four people whom I love the most—Steve, Liz, David, Mother—were there.

Chapter 5

Late afternoon two days before Christmas, we were married in the chapel at Westover Air Force Base in Chicopee, Massachusetts, in a solemn and moving ceremony. Mother presented me in marriage. Mary Jane was matron of honor; Barny was best man. Liz and David were our honor attendants. Steve wore his dress uniform and all his miniature medals. I wore a street-length champagne lace cocktail suit, daisies in my hair, and carried a single daisy. Several times my eyes filled with tears as did Mary Jane's. Steve and Barny wept openly. After we returned to the rambling old colonial house we had moved into months earlier, friends and acquaintances arrived for an impromptu reception. Close to 60 people milled about; there were congratulatory phone calls and a witty, loving telegram from Daddy.

I was exhausted. A few weeks earlier, Maggie contested the Nevada divorce; Steve flew to Nellis AFB near Las Vegas, to challenge her claims. Two days before we were married, he prevailed and flying a fighter jet, streaked back to Massachusetts in record time. While he was in the air, Mother, the kids and I shopped for our wedding finery. The next day, Steve and I met with a judge in his chambers to request that he waive the three-day waiting period. On the morning of our wedding day, I saw a doctor who prescribed tranquilizers. Not until the last guests left in the wee hours did I swallow the first one. Steve held me in his arms while I wept and my body jerked in one spasm after another. On Christmas Eve snow fell steadily all day. We admired the tree Steve found and decorated. I was a zombie. The bedtime spasms continued. Christmas itself was beautiful; I enjoyed the day through a haze of fatigue. Again that night my limbs twitched and jerked. Steve said, "I'm going to take you where it's warm. We're going on a honeymoon. I have leave coming to me." Mother agreed to stay with the children, and off we went to Florida where I was pampered and cuddled and loved by my new husband. The body spasms stopped, and I stopped taking the tranquilizers.

Two months later Steve was transferred to North Carolina, and we moved into a brick three-bedroom ranch, one of four designs in the sprawling base housing complex. I was apprehensive about military protocol, fearful I might make a social gaffe that would embarrass Steve. He told me I had nothing to worry about. He was right: good manners are good manners regardless of the setting. Initially I was reluctant to join the Officers Wives Club because I did not enjoy organizations; Steve said I could do as I liked. But every wife who called on me had such complimentary words about the OWC that I did join and soon had many new friends. Within a few months, I became editor of their monthly magazine. My life was hectic and fulfilling. Liz and David had no trouble adjusting to their new school. Most days Steve came home for lunch and shared work stories with me, often regaling me with hilarious accounts of military mickey mouse. Repeatedly he remarked, "I'm so happy! I love my wife, my kids, and my job. I'm not mad at anybody and nobody's mad at me. It's so wonderful to be able to tell the truth!" I planted flowers and wondered why I had been so foolish as to doubt I could be content with Steve. The turmoil of the previous year must have been nothing more than a bad dream. One evening at the Officers Club, Steve introduced me to the Base Commander, a man he had known and served with a few times before. The Colonel held my hands in his and said, "You have my deepest sympathy." Surely, I thought, he's joking. After hesitating a moment, I laughed. No one was going to spoil my happiness. Steve was drinking more and often had a couple drinks at home "to relax and get in the mood" before we went to social functions where liquor was served. I rationalized that the military was a heavy drinking crowd.

On a glorious spring day just before Steve was to leave on a three-day cross-country flight, he picked a fight with me in the kitchen, something stupid to do with onions. He continued his harangue in the driveway. He insisted I drive him to Base Operations. By the time we said goodbye, I did not care if he crashed. My head spun from his verbal abuse. After only five months of marriage, had he stopped loving me? I thought of the fights he instigated before we married whenever he went TDY (temporary duty). Was he trying to justify his right to play bachelor during his 24 hours on the West Coast?

I arrived home to find Clara Marshall in the kitchen talking with Mother who was visiting us. Steve's ranting had alarmed Mother enough for her to call Clara. Clara's husband, Monty, had served under Steve before, and we had become instant friends. In the military, time does not permit the luxury of developing friendships slowly. Clara suggested I talk with her priest, one of the base chaplains, but I dared not; Steve had told me that anything a wife might do that was at all untoward found its way into his file, too. Sometime during the night, Steve phoned from California, his voice in his boots. I could tell he had been drinking. He told me he was sorry, that he loved me. He cried. I cried.

Late the following afternoon, I reported for my regular flying lesson. With my instructor beside me in the Cessna 150, we taxied onto the base runway, and flew to a strip about 20 miles away where he had me perform a series of touch-and-go landings. On the third or fourth approach to the runway, he told me to land, taxi to the end, stop, and let him get out. That could mean only one thing: he believed I was ready to solo. He told me not to forget to come back for him.

The exhilaration of one's first solo flight cannot be exaggerated. For the first time, I heard wind in the cockpit because the instructor was not there filling the space. I was so exhilarated that I likened myself to Lindbergh on his history-making solo flight across the Atlantic, a partially-eaten sandwich on the cowl, the lights of Paris just visible and Orly, his destination, was dead ahead. I felt a sense of freedom and accomplishment—me, the coward of all time, flying an airplane all by myself. I teased the instructor waiting on the ground by making a touch-and-go landing in front of him. I waved to his surprised face and lifted off into the darkening sky. The runway lights were on, twinkling little yellowish-red gems. I circled and brought the plane down for a kissing-smooth landing.

Steve returned that evening and was jubilant when he learned I had soloed. We stayed up half the night drinking a rhinegarten wine, the closest we had on hand to champagne. The next afternoon Steve arrived home at the usual time and on his heels were a dozen officers. During a staff meeting, he had handed a note to the officer seated next to him: "Donna soloed yesterday. No brass band to meet her. How about coming by for a jar—pilot to pilot? Pass it on." There I was with less than 14 hours flying time which included one solo in a rinkydink 150, surrounded by fighter pilots with thousands and thousands of hours of flying time, and they wanted to hear every last detail of my solo flight. They shared memories of their own. Everybody drank up a storm. One jar became two, three, until well beyond the dinner hour they serenaded me with the Fighter Pilot's Song before they weaved their way out the door to their cars.

The 24 hours following my solo are significant because it was the longest period Steve and I shared a quadruple closeness—emotional, intellectual, physical, and spiritual. I was doing my best to be part of his world—flying, hunting, attending auto races. However, during the five years of our marriage, my interests were given short shrift: we attended only two plays, half a dozen movies and no concerts. Steve dominated my life, my thinking. I was on the alert for changes in his moods so I could adapt mine to suit his. In almost the full sense of the term, I was his woman—except for one section of my brain that strived to be both a mother and me. The continuous stress took its toll. I became short-tempered with the kids and too often spoke sharply to them. I did not want them to do anything to send Steve into a fit of rage. But my boiling point was seldom far below the surface. The kids found the stick of gum I'd saved from the day I soloed and chewed it. I had planned to frame it. I was furious. I put the wrapper back together and framed it anyway with this legend: "First stick of gum not chewed by DSM during flight. Discovered on top instrument panel following first solo 21 May 1967." I keep it on my desk. At times I look at it and think, "Well, since I could do that, then I can (fill in the blanks)."

Steve's moods became erratic. If the kids and I could avoid saying or doing anything that might aggravate him, he was good to us. And when Steve was good, he was very, very good. No one could have asked for anyone who was more kind, considerate, fun, and loving. More often than not, drinking put him in foul, abrasive humor. I was glad we entertained often because, by the time the drinks hit him, the kids were in bed and so escaped antagonizing him. His nephew lived with us for a few months and one day he said to Steve, "You're killing your wife." I thought, "Is it that bad?"

On a summer day we joined many military families at an outing held at the Base Pavilion. Others arrived in cars; we made an entrance in our new 30-foot motor home (Steve had the bumper extended to support a trail bike). Steve was one of the few officers present and he was in his glory as a man with authority hobnobbing with his men. In all fairness to Steve, he looked out for enlisted personnel under his command; he never forgot he was an enlisted man who came up through the ranks. The outing featured a never-ending supply of beer and mixed drinks. Many fathers joined the kids in pickup ball games, there was easy camaraderie, a mix of ages, and I enjoyed big family feelings. I especially enjoyed observing David and Liz having such a good time playing with the other kids. When it grew dark, Steve ordered Liz and David to bed down in the motor home. The other kids, many younger than they, continued playing. Expecting Liz and David to lie down and go to sleep was not only unfair but unrealistic. They knew it; I knew it. But the three of us knew that to protest would invite trouble. Hindsight suggests that Steve did not want any interference with his drinking. A sergeant invited many of us to continue partying at his house. After seven hours of concentrated togetherness and many showing signs of drunkenness, I preferred to go home with the kids and let Steve go on by himself. He overruled the idea. When the kids sat up to look out the window, he yelled at them to keep their heads down. What was he trying to do? Demonstrate how well he ruled his own family? He parked the motor home across the street from the sergeant's quarters, spoke sternly to the kids not to look out the windows, to go to sleep, and then told me to come along. We had been inside the house for only a couple minutes when a youngster told Steve he had seen Liz and David looking out the windows. Steve thanked the boy, turned on his heel and marched towards the motor home. I started to follow him. "You stay here!" he commanded. I caught up with the tattletale and chewed him out, and told him he had no idea what kind of trouble he would cause. I was wild with anger and fear. Steve returned to hear me scolding the boy. He pulled me aside and in a quiet voice the partying people wouldn't hear, he told me I had no business talking to the kid and further, he was not going to stand for having his whole family embarrass him. When I started to walk away, he ordered me to return. My fear of him had yet to paralyze me and I kept on going. I found my kids, then 8 and 9, lying on their beds. They told me Dad had hit them. I reminded them of Dad's order not to look out the window. They were sniffling.

"Mommy, David's bleeding."

I turned David into the light from the street lamp. Blood was smeared across his face. I could not see any cut and assumed he was struck hard enough to make his nose bleed. That monster had struck the child and made him bleed because he had looked out a window! (Years later, David told me Steve had held him with one hand at the front of his throat and with his other hand punched him with his fist). David whimpered. "I'm all right, Mom." I quickly checked to make sure his legs and arms were okay. Both kids urged me to leave, to return to the party. "It'll go hard on you if he finds you here!" I knew

51

that as soon as Steve missed me, he would be angry with all three of us and most likely come to the motor home to inflict more punishment.

I said, "Come on! We're getting out of here before he comes back." They didn't move. "Hurry!"

"But what about Dad?" Poor scared kids. They did not know whom to obey, an enraged father or a mother in panic.

"Come on!" I insisted. We dashed into the backyard of the nearest house. I had only a vague idea of where we were; all the houses looked so much alike and one street was almost interchangeable with any other. We hid in shrubbery whenever we saw headlights or thought we heard Steve running after us. We ran and zigzagged our way through back yards. Before crossing streets, we made sure no motor home was in sight. When we reached our neighborhood, we made a wide circle to avoid our house and went to the Marshalls'. They were not at home. We hid in their bushes and waited. The kids were convinced Steve would find us. I was as scared as they were. Finally, the Marshalls and all their children returned. We told them what happened. They were shocked to see David's swollen face. I washed off the blood. Monty swore. Clara telephoned their priest who offered to let the kids spend the night at his house where they would be safe. For me to stay there also would have been improper, so I stayed at the Marshalls'. Every so often, I sneaked through the back yards between their place and ours to check if Steve had returned. Eventually he did. I crept around to our bedroom window and listened. He was snoring. He had passed out. I thought of how the night before I had slept in his arms. How could love change to hate and fury so abruptly? What was wrong with him? With me? With us?

In the morning Monty insisted on talking with Steve first, to get his word he would not do anything to the kids or me. Then I walked into our driveway where Steve was working on one of our cars. He stared at me and said, "That was once." I understood: he would not let me get away with such behavior again. A few days later while Steve was flying, I kept an appointment with the priest. He assured me that nothing about either the incident or my visit to his office would appear in Steve's files. Years later I learned that many people were aware the kids and I lived with a tyrant. Some dropped by to make sure we were all right when I thought they were just being sociable.

Steve often discussed retirement with me and he debated about staying in another two years to make the 30-year mark. After he was passed over for promotion, he talked more seriously about retiring. Then 47 years old, he said he had no desire to fly more combat missions, especially in Vietnam.

Regulations stated that if retirement had already been applied for, to accept orders for overseas was optional. At the time of the Pueblo Crisis, there was great activity on the base as it was designated as a staging area for shipping troops on their way to South Korea. During that confusion, Steve told me he received orders for Southeast Asia but I need not worry because he had already filed for retirement. Months later he failed to complete his annual updating requirements by his birthday. All hell broke loose. He was accused of falsifying records and threatened with a Flight Evaluation Board (FEB). From the details Steve passed along to me, I thought he was being railroaded. One night after we were in bed, I asked him if there were anything I could do to help. He asked if I knew any senators. I had once met Senator Ted Kennedy during a fund raiser in my home state. "Would you write to him?" Steve asked.

I studied Air Force regulations and fired off a detailed letter to Washington which precipitated a Congressional investigation. A few heads rolled, but the findings also demonstrated that Steve had taken advantage of the Pueblo Crisis confusion by intimidating a junior officer into witnessing his signature on the retirement application that he had pre-dated to before his SEA orders arrived. I was aghast that my belief in my husband's word had also convinced a senator's crack staff and that now all of us had egg on our faces. I felt embarrassed, and angry. But as Steve's wife, I believed it was my duty to stand by him—"for better, for worse." He was grounded, extra flight pay ceased, and an FEB was held during which his peers as well as higher ranking officers reviewed the charges. He was found guilty. The grounding held. Although it was suggested he be stripped of his Command Pilot wings, nothing came of that, but his flying days were over. The Judge Advocate, a neighbor who contacted me privately, strongly suggested I not write any more letters. He alerted me to upcoming court martial proceedings and suggested I do my best to influence Steve not to fight but to accept the large fine and to speed up the processing of his retirement papers. A flight surgeon present at the FEB told me that Steve could have "won" had he apologized to the Board. "But he lied," he added, "and everyone knew he was lying. There were men on that Board who had been waiting years to settle old scores with him." Maggie had told me the truth about Steve antagonizing other officers and being fired. His retirement orders were expedited. While the packers were at the house, we attended a dignified but subdued retirement ceremony witnessed by a handful of officers, including the flight surgeon and the judge advocate and his wife with whom I am still friends. Steve was insulted because he was not honored with a flyover! After 28 years service, much of it outstanding, admired as a "pilot's pilot," but stained by his arrogance and dishonesty, Steve squeaked through with an honorable discharge.

With our furniture in storage and the motor home outfitted for a year of cruising the country until we found a place where we wanted to live, Steve, the kids, and our sweet dog, headed directly for a week's rest by the ocean at Salter Path, North Carolina. At midnight, when he officially became a civilian, Steve, the dog and I were walking the beach. He put his arms around me and thanked me for my support. Was his belief justified, that he was a victim? Could there have been a mistake? Logic told me he was guilty but my heart wanted to believe what he wanted me to believe.

I subscribed to an at-home tutorial program and held regular school hours with Liz and David. Their education was enriched by frequent stops at industrial and historic points of interest. We visited one of his brothers and his wife where he repaid their gracious hospitality by behaving abominably at the dinner table, hurling cruel remarks at the kids and me. His sister-in-law was aghast. In the morning Steve, all smiles and hugs, and his nephew set off on their mountain bikes. I returned Steve's waves and said under my breath, "I hope you break your fucking neck!" The next time I saw him was in the hospital. He had fallen off the bike and broken his collar bone. Close, but no cigar. I did not feel guilty. I felt disappointed.

Our plan to visit the Panama Canal, camp on the Baja Peninsula, continue north through Big Sur and then wend our way onto the Alcan Highway never materialized. We got as far as West Brookfield, Massachusetts to visit Mary Jane and Barny and stayed. We bought a place at the top of the hill, a nondescript farmhouse, magnificent barn, and a fledgling campground set on 103 acres of rolling land with a 30-mile view to the southeast and 50 miles to the west. We would begin a new life. Steve was enthusiastic. Campground ownership had been mentioned every time we brainstormed about possible post-retirement plans. With our best friends Mary Jane and Barny a mile away, I would have moral support. And should Steve get out of hand, I was sure Barny would set him straight.

Chapter 6

Owning and managing a campground was a great idea in theory but quite another in practice. We had very little working capital which meant a lot of gerry-rigging and long hours of our own labor. Gradually we made improvements and were pleased our efforts attracted more and more new campers and especially pleased with repeat business. All income was plowed back into the business; we lived on Steve's retirement salary. He suggested we ask Mother to make her home with us and give her the responsibility of keeping the books. He spoke of eventually persuading his mother and also Kenneth to come live with us. "We'll have a home for our own old folks," he said. Mom and Kenneth had no interest in leaving southwestern Pennsylvania where they had lived all their lives, but Mother was pleased to join us and her grandchildren.

Everyone had chores. Mine were to run the house, design brochures, write occasional publicity releases, and handle all correspondence. During the off-season we entertained, but during the six-month camping season, any entertaining was strictly casual because my additional responsibilities included supervising the campground store attached to the house and sharing the responsibility of monitoring and cleaning the restrooms in the barn and campground. Seldom did I prepare lunch and dinner for just the five of us. Serving ten or more became commonplace. Steve worked the kids hard, often Mother and I thought too hard, but he overrode our objections. He believed that work did not count unless it was physical. I learned not to let on how often I was tired. He carved a new road out of the woods, created new campsites. He said, "I work hard and I play hard." Many times he played so hard he wasn't good for much of anything the following day.

Steve liked visiting with the campers, sitting around campfires, talking and drinking into the night. There were evenings when both of us had a good time but others that went sour, such as the weekend a group of my former neighbors set up camp, and there was singing and drinking followed by talking and more drinking by Steve and some of the men—until dawn. Steve was still in a good mood. He was the undisputed center of attention all night. He flirted with the wives, and they with him. At first light, there was a low mist. We said our goodnights and agreed to postpone starting a few hours sleep by first taking a walk through the campground. I was slaphappy and feeling kittenish. Steve laughed. I tweeted like a bird. He said, "Don't do that again." I thought he was kidding and I tweeted again. He grabbed me by my coat sleeve and slung me through the air for 15 feet before I landed on a stone wall, half on my side; half on my back. The wind was knocked out of me. Steve came to me and said as much to himself as to me, "I didn't mean to do that."

I said, "But you did it." He swore at me, called me names, said I was no damn good; that I never did any work but just sat in the house all day, and he started to walk away. "Aren't you going to help me get back to the house?"

"Hell no! I hope you have to crawl back!"

I did not have to crawl but I could not stand up straight. I slept a while but when I got up, I could barely hobble. Steve said it served me right. The next day a friend insisted I see a doctor at the nearby military hospital. Steve refused to take me, so the friend did. I didn't care what went on Steve's record. I told the doctor exactly what happened. I was badly bruised but nothing was broken. The doctor prescribed a muscle relaxant, bed rest, and told me not to bend over, not even to open or close an oven door, and not to lift anything, not even a quart of milk. For the next few days Steve drank steadily and methodically. The incident was not referred to or ever mentioned. Sometimes I wondered if I had imagined it.

We were friendly with one of the camping families who left their trailer on its site year round. Steve could often be found at their site talking with Minnie while her husband, Gordon, was at work. A few times I found Steve and Minnie drinking at the trailer's dining table in late morning. I made no comment about the amount of time and attention he paid to her until some of the non-regular campers thought she was his wife. Late one afternoon while Steve ran the bulldozer near where there had been a swamp that we turned into a pond, I brought him a quart of cold beer and a glass. I told him campers were talking about him and Minnie and that I hoped he would stop spending so much time with her because I thought it was embarrassing for both of us. He became very angry, swore, and threw the beer bottle onto the ground. He yelled obscenities at me. He put the bulldozer into gear, and I walked away. He hollered at me. I stopped. He brought the bulldozer along by my side and told me I had a vivid imagination and he would do as he damned pleased and for me to stop acting like a goddamn fool. I was damned if I would let him know I was trying not to cry. He glared at me. I stared back. I resumed walking along the top of the beach by the edge of a fringe of saplings. He inched the bulldozer along beside me. I kept walking. He continued shifting and with every shift, he maneuvered the bulldozer closer to me and the woody area. I glanced up at him. His face was twisted with rage. He was trying to get the bulldozer in a position where he could run me down! I began running but I could not get ahead and away. The bulldozer was coming at me from a 45 degree angle. I crashed into the thicket, through the saplings, the roar and cranking of the bulldozer filled my head. I looked over my shoulder; he had turned the bulldozer into the thicket and was squarely behind me. I reached the stone wall and tried to jump over it but tripped and fell on the stones, scrambled, and landed on my back in the field. The bulldozer was stopped against a tree about ten inches thick. Steve stood at the controls, staring at me. I stared back. Our dog thought it was a new game and bounded over to lap my face. I did not move. Steve did not move. The bulldozer engine continued running. I thought, "That tree saved my life." I got to my feet and walked towards the house wearing one shoe. The other was some place in the brush. My knees and shins were scraped; there were scratches on my arms and hands. I was too scared to cry. I wanted to have Steve ordered out of the house, but what policeman would believe me? About an hour later, Steve walked into the house and said to anyone who might hear, "I'm married to a crazy woman."

I thought, "I'm about as crazy as he said Maggie was."

I felt more and more isolated from reality. I lived with fear more than without it, never knowing what might send Steve into a rage. I thought about running away, but how could I escape with my kids and Mother without Steve finding us?

Before the end of that camping season, Minnie and Gordon broke camp one afternoon and left the campground for the last time, pulling their trailer behind them. A violent argument had occurred between Gordon and Steve which I did not witness. According to Steve, Gordon threatened him with an axe and Steve told him he'd better make the first blow count. Somewhere in that bare bones story was the truth.

One of our cats or dogs was always pregnant, at least it seemed that way. The birthing of animals, no matter how many times it occurred, was a special event. David was interested, but Liz brought the concern of a midwife to each new litter. We were surprised to discover we did not have two male rabbits. One of the baby bunnies died, the other weakened. Steve deduced the mother rabbit had no milk, so he placed the bunny in with a new litter of kittens for the momma cat to nurse. One of our mother dogs sat by the box like a sentry. Steve told anyone who would listen that the reason three natural enemies cared about each other was due to my calming influence.

One evening, for who knows what reason, Steve became very angry with puppies that were still living out of a big box in the kitchen. He began to throw them about. The more I objected, the more abusive he became with them. He held one in each of his big hands—by the throat. He was deliberately choking them—slowly. We watched in horror. He stalked about the house. When a pup cried, he tightened his grip. "You're choking them!" I cried and he elbowed me aside. I whispered to Mother, "Call Mary Jane and Barny." Surely Barny would come and talk sense into Steve. But it was Mary Jane who showed up. Later she told me that when she told Barny what was going on, he said I was always getting hysterical and he refused to get involved. Mary Jane waded in and confronted Steve. I was amazed at her lack of fear.

"Steve, stop choking those puppies!"

He shot her a look of defiance. "This is my house!" he said.

Mary Jane stared at him and in a measured voice said, "And this is my town. The dog warden is a friend of mine."

Nothing was said for many long seconds. Then Steve tossed the puppies down. They scurried into their box, their mother after them. Later, after Steve passed out, I went around the house cleaning puppy excrement off the floors, even halfway up the walls. The next morning I put all three puppies into the car and drove into the city, crying all the way, "He'll never hurt you again. He'll never hurt you again." I left them at the animal shelter where I was assured they would be checked over and if okay, every effort would be made to place them in good homes. I cried most of the way home but I was dry-eyed and composed when I drove into the barnyard. Steve never asked about the puppies, and I never told him. Another time for no apparent reason, he suddenly and roughly picked up one of the mother cats. When she resisted, he began to choke her. She dug her hind claws into him, and Liz saw him slam the cat to the ground. She ran off and never came back. Steve said, "That damn Mittens scratched me," and the marks on his arm were an ugly red. Automatically I cautioned him about how infectious a cat scratch could be. Secretly, I hoped he would die of blood poisoning.

The effects of living in a combat zone within my own home affected me in unseen ways. I received permission from Steve (yes, permission) to take the kids to a young peoples' symphonic concert at Worcester's Memorial Auditorium. I eagerly anticipated the thrill of exposing my children to a special occasion there just as I had enjoyed many times while growing up. Thanks to never knowing when Steve would explode, we arrived for the concert shell shocked, survivors from living with a crazy, mean man. I looked around the vast auditorium and smiled at my memories of happy times and I was especially pleased to be there with my kids. Gradually members of the orchestra filed in from the wings, took their seats, and began practicing troublesome phrases, each musician playing something different. Soon the first violinist gave the pitch, everyone fine-tuned his instrument, and the conductor strode to the podium, acknowledged the applause, raised the baton, and the symphonic orchestra filled that great hall with music. I had a vague recollection of the tune and thought how nice that the first selection was something familiar. Everyone around us rose. Why? I felt like a country bumpkin come into the city. I got to my feet, and the kids stood. People were singing but I couldn't make out the words. The inside of my head was a honeycomb of fuzzy-lined compartments, all on overload. Not until half way through the music did I recognize our national anthem.

One evening while drinking beer and making some repairs in the kitchen, either the hammer or the nail slipped and Steve got a deep, jagged cut in his hand. I knew it had to be bad for him to say he needed medical attention. I drove him to the military hospital where the physician on duty said he must have surgery. Steve said he'd come back another time. The doctor pulled rank on him. I left hoping that by the time I got home there'd be a message from the hospital saying he had vomited while anesthetized and drowned. Instead, Steve phoned around two in the morning to tell me he was fine. "I didn't want you to worry."

Something dreadful was happening to me because I did not have one iota of guilt about having wished he would die. Even now when I remember the night he choked the puppies, when I see their fear and the excrement their fear squeezed out of them, my face contorts. Beyond one mental picture of Steve spanking David with a one-by-six, and my begging him to stop, and

Steve threatening to hit me, I cannot recall any specific incident of cruel punishment he inflicted on David and Liz, but I know he did. I am grateful I am spared the details of the pain and shame that accompany the guilt I carry because I was unable to protect them. Liz has since told me that he never struck her again after an incident in our house. One step down from the dining room was a library and in its corner between the dining room and the living room was an area we called the bar. Steve was scolding her. Liz said, "He kept pushing and slamming me into the built-in shelves of the library. He had not hit me. Yet. He just kept lifting his arm and making me flinch, banging me hard into the shelves. I was pissed that I was flinching from him whenever he raised his arm threatening to hit me. When I tried to get away through the living room, he grabbed me, and I grabbed the little knife off the bar, the one we called the 'lime' knife. It was small and had a curved blade, serrated on both sides. I have never seen another one like it. I told him that if he ever touched me again, I would slit his throat; and even if I had to spend the rest of my life behind bars, it'd be worth it. I also said, 'You have to sleep sometime.'"

A girl of 11 had more spunk than I.

Chapter 7

On our fourth wedding anniversary, it snowed so we ventured down the hill only as far as Mary Jane's. She and Barny separated the previous summer when he fell in love with a young mother 15 years his junior and they ran away together. Mary Jane, Steve and I spent a reasonably pleasant evening talking, laughing, and while Steve guzzled his drinks, Mary Jane and I sipped ours. When we left, Steve was drunk. No longer was a gentle snow falling but a full-fledged storm was in progress with blowing and drifting snow. Steve insisted on driving. Halfway up the hill there was a 90 degree left turn onto our road, and I could tell we were not going to make it because Steve had not swung widely enough. Through a series of drunken maneuvers, he got the car hopelessly stuck. He cursed me. A young man, a neighbor we knew, came along on a snowmobile and loaned his brawn towards getting the car back on the road. Even with me at the wheel and two men pushing, it was no use. The young man offered us a ride on his snowmobile. There was room for only one passenger and because Steve was not wearing a heavy jacket, I said I would not mind walking the remaining half mile back to our house. Besides, Steve was so drunk he could hardly stand. It was agreed, and I set off. When I heard the snowmobile approaching, I wondered if Steve might have conned the neighbor kid into letting him drive. I was afraid Steve might try to run me down. I climbed up and over a snow bank and hid behind a tree and watched the snowmobile go by. Steve was a passenger. I continued walking, enjoying the snowy solitude. Trees didn't yell.

When I walked into the house, Steve was in bathrobe and slippers. "Where the hell have you been?" he yelled. "You left me out in the snow to die!"

I thought he was kidding. He was the one who was warm and I was covered with snow. I removed my jacket and reminded Steve we had agreed he should be the one to accept the ride on the snowmobile. He denied this. I said I'd fix us something hot to drink. At the kitchen stove he shoved me; then he punched my arms and back. I tried to cover my face while the blows kept coming along with his non-stop accusations that I had left him in the snow to die. Through a large window that faced the road, I was aware of bright headlights coming up the hill. He continued beating me and backed me away from the cooking island towards the headlights, and then around a corner into the dining room doorway where he knocked me to the floor. He kicked me, again and again, all the while yelling at me to get out. During a pause, I spoke softly and carefully, "I will leave if you'll let me get up." I was afraid anything I might do or say would fan his rage to the point of killing me.

"Well, get up!" he commanded. I started to walk back into the kitchen. "Where do you think you're going?"

"I'm going to get my jacket."

"No, you're not. You leave just like you are. You see how you like being put out into the snow without a jacket and left there."

I was lucky to be wearing a heavy sweater, slacks and boots. When I stepped out the front door, a snowplow was parked on the road. A man's voice called out, "Do you need help?"

The headlights had belonged to the snowplow! At last, I had a witness. I feared Steve was watching. "Yes. Pick me up down the road."

When I climbed into the cab, the driver told me he had seen "the action" through the windows. I asked him to take me to Mary Jane's and to tell the local chief of police what he had seen and where I was.

Mary Jane washed the blood from my face. We both cried. Mother telephoned. Steve had gone to bed and was "out like a light." The next day, Christmas Eve, Steve came for me. Full of apologies, he professed his undying love. He begged my forgiveness, yet he could not remember about the snowmobile riding arrangements. I did not want to spoil the children's Christmas and I returned home with him. In private I assured the kids that I was okay. We got through that day and Christmas without more trouble. As usual following a rage, Steve was contrite and loving. He referred to me as his queen. He was the king. Any outsider looking in would have thought one was spying on a happy family. There were mounds of presents, plenty of food and lots of hugs. It was as if the other night had not happened. It had happened. There was a witness.

The day after Christmas, we drove the kids to the airport. As usual, they were spending the remainder of their Christmas vacation with their father, Brad, who had remarried and was living in Chicago. On the ride home, I talked with Steve about the two of us seeing a marriage counselor. I knew he would not agree to counseling for himself alone. His response was that there was nothing wrong with him; I was the one who was crazy and needed help. He also told me that if I wanted to talk to a shrink, I would have to see a civilian doctor and pay for it myself because he did not want anything like that showing up on his record.

The week went by; one tense day followed another. After lunch on New Year's Eve, my hair in rollers, I dressed in boots and heavy clothing to help Steve dislodge a tractor that was sealed in icy ruts in the barnyard. I stood in front and gave him directional hand signals. Just as the tractor broke free, I saw "the bulldozer look" on his face. The tractor headed straight for me. I moved quickly off to the side, and fell backwards. I heard what sounded like the whacking of a dead log against a tree. The sound was the breaking of my left leg in four places. Evidently the heel of my boot caught on a ridge of ice. Had the leg not broken, I might have fractured a hip or pelvis, or both.

I lay on the icy ground, totally helpless. Steve heard the awful sound too, even over the noise of the tractor. Perhaps the sound coupled with seeing me flat on my back snapped him back into sanity. He stood at my side and stared down at me. In a voice devoid of any emotion, I said, "My leg is broken." He bent over as if to move me. I commanded him, "Don't touch me!" He recoiled. For that precious moment, I found the strength to protect myself using only the tenor of my voice. He seemed confused. I instructed him to get packing quilts from the barn to cover me and then telephone for the volunteer ambulance. Mother came out with a glass of water and two aspirin. The pain had begun but I told her two aspirin wouldn't take it away. I told her what to pack for me. When the paramedics arrived, Steve did a lot of talking that made no sense. Could this be the same man who received survival training instruction throughout a long military career? We lived in a small town, and later the paramedics' reaction was relayed to me. They were convinced Steve was the cause of my injury. Also, they said I had my wits about me but that Steve "was as useless as tits on a bull." They fitted my leg with an airsplint, placed me on a stretcher and then into the ambulance. Steve followed in the car. En route, every seam in the road surface caused jabs of shooting pain. Yet, ever mindful of my appearance and the awareness that no lady ever appeared in public wearing rollers in her hair, I unrolled my hair. The paramedics got a kick out of that.

I was hospitalized for two weeks; the leg was re-set twice. When the kids came back from Chicago, hospital regulations prevented them from visiting me, so I stood at a window and waved to them. They were reassured I was okay. I returned home in a cast that rose up my leg all the way to my crotch. Steve said the crutches needed adjusting. He believed he knew more than anyone else, regardless of the subject. He changed the crutches to a height that caused sharp pains in my armpits. I spent most days immobilized, and Steve decreed that, therefore, I did not need more than a few hundred calories per day. He worked on projects around the house, so it was difficult for Mother to slip me extra food. However, he encouraged me to have wine or a martini before dinner. Steve's anger was apparent most of the time, drinking or not, but worse when he drank. He was often morose and stared off into space. While I became physically weaker, his hostility towards me intensified. One Sunday I asked him how long his mood was going to last. "Another two weeks," he snapped and left for a campground owners' business meeting 75 miles away. He would be gone at least six hours, long enough for the family and me to leave with a good head start. Mother urged me to leave by myself, to visit relatives in Maryland.

I said, "But what about you and the kids?"

Mother said, "He's nicer to us when you aren't around."

With Mary Jane's help, I got to the airport and with grim determination, hobbled up the steps and into the plane. At two in the morning while reciting my saga of woes to my cousins, Steve telephoned; his voice in his boots. That was the first of many calls in which he swung from being loving and contrite to vindictive and demeaning. I flew further south and visited friends at the military base. Then, two weeks after I left home—right on schedule—Steve's mood towards me changed. He wanted to drive the 1500 miles to get me. I told him that instead, I'd fly back to Washington and he could meet me there. He was as attentive as a lovesick suitor. Our reunion and the ride back to New England took on the qualities of a honeymoon. Almost two months had elapsed since we made love because he said the cast turned him off. His interest in sex had diminished before I hurt my leg, so I didn't pay any attention to what he said about the cast. Now however, we could start fresh—again. I nurtured renewed hope that the ugly past would not be repeated.

Inevitably, Steve's seesawing moods returned. In any given day I experienced kindness, sullenness, loving embraces, and bitter verbal attacks. He was an unreasonable disciplinarian, a stickler for perfect, adult-like behavior from Liz, then 11, and David, 10. Reasoning with him was wasted breath. He became paranoid and accused all of us at different times of deliberately doing things to hinder him; what things I never did figure out. He gave orders that only he could take the mail out of the mailbox and that he would distribute it after he looked at it. Atop a beautiful hill in central Massachusetts, part of the great United States, we lived under the heel of a dictator. We capitulated to his domination. I was married to a despot. I hobbled about on crutches, more afraid of him than ever. Sometimes I thought of the night I plotted to murder him and wished I had pulled the trigger. Only when the kids and I were alone could we laugh and be silly.

Chapter 8

I consulted an attorney and signed a blank petition for divorce because I knew that as soon as I had an opportunity to get us all out of the house, I would not dare squander precious head start time in an attorney's office. Spring arrived and with it a mid-thigh cast, followed by another that ended just above the knee, and then the final one that came to the knee. I had nightmares I might never walk normally again. Most of all, I wanted to dance again.

Steve left on an errand one day and phoned several hours later to tell me he was having supper with some campers, Janey and Bill. The previous summer, Steve flirted outrageously with Janey while her namby-pamby husband grinned and slurped beer. Steve wanted me to believe a convoluted tale of coincidences: that he ran into Bill 30 miles from their house and was invited back for a drink which led to another and then supper. My hunch was he deliberately sought out their house and simply appeared at their door, or he made arrangements in advance with Janey. If he managed to spend time alone with Janey was anyone's guess. The drinking part was true. I could smell liquor on him when he returned at midnight. He told me he had been so aroused by thoughts of Janey that on the way home, he pulled off the road and masturbated. "I've never done anything like that before," he said. This was his most bizarre poor-me victim story yet. Was he expecting me to extend sympathy? Our sex life was almost non-existent because Steve said he was sorry but he found the cast repulsive. Masturbation had become my way of releasing tension. I wanted to kick Steve with my good leg but I repressed anger and said, "I suggest you do not see Janey or Bill again." As far as I know, he didn't, and the subject was not mentioned again.

On a Sunday morning in June, a man banged on the kitchen door. From the direction of the campground, I heard a woman screaming. They were afraid their little boy had wandered into the pond. I phoned the police and hobbled into the bedroom to awaken Steve who drank heavily the night before. He reacted to the alarming news like he was in a daze. I dressed and hurried to the pond, perplexed that again when confronted with a physical emergency, Steve seemed incapable of responding. Almost half an hour went by before he ambled across the field to the pond. By then, the child had been fished out of deep water and resuscitation efforts were underway. They continued until a doctor arrived and pronounced him dead. The tragedy subdued the campers' usual Sunday afternoon high spirits. Information needed to be gathered for insurance purposes. Because Steve seemed detached, I took photographs and got statements from witnesses. Mother told me that after I had left the house and Steve did not appear right away, she went to the bedroom door and observed him trying to decide which clothing to wear. She said he seemed confused and changed his mind several times. She, too, could not understand why he hadn't pulled on a pair of trousers and headed for the pond the minute he knew there was a suspected drowning.

Love, hate, disgust, fear. I was dizzy from swinging from one emotion to another. Every time I decided, "This is it! No more!" and thought about divorce, I panicked. He'd never let me get away. He had told Maggie she would never know when a rifle was pointed at her head. I felt trapped. How many times did he apologize to me? How many times did he tell me, "I'm my own worst enemy." With such insight, couldn't he become master of his own soul?

An Air Force officer who outranked Steve found me attractive and desirable, cast or no cast. Flirting gave moments of lighthearted spice to my life; we corresponded through Mary Jane's address (after all, I was prohibited from using our own mailbox). He was married. We were two people with needs for emotional closeness and we allowed ourselves to enjoy the natural progression to sexual intimacy. Twice that year I concocted stories to cover reasons why I needed to travel to New York or Washington. I bet it never occurred to Steve I would find another man attractive, that I would be unfaithful to him, or that another man would not be turned off by the cast on my leg. The quality of the sex was excellent; I rationalized that I deserved the affection and I rationalized away any guilt I felt. I was married to an ogre, felt shackled to him. He chose to have intercourse with me sporadically but he also said he was attracted enough to another woman to masturbate. My infidelity fed my ego and insulted Steve's high macho opinion of himself. My secret gave me a feeling of control over one aspect of my life, a sense of empowerment, and a sense of triumph over Steve, the ultimate example of passive-aggressive behavior. I never let Steve find out. Nevertheless, I had the satisfaction of, in effect, spitting in his face. But all the other feelings for Steve did not change. I still loved Steve White but his other self I hated and feared.

Chapter 9

I thought I was aware of everything that went on in the household, but none of us was able to share all we experienced. We were bombarded by double messages—you are loved, you are hated; you're wonderful, you're no good. Our feelings network was haywire. We could not afford to be honest with ourselves. I could not permit everything I heard and saw to register in my brain because I could not tolerate taking on more pain. Therefore, I can recall only a fraction of what went on. Perhaps through hypnosis each of us could describe isolated incidents that would come as a surprise, both to ourselves and to one another. And I didn't help the situation. I'm sure I wore a martyr's face, and if I didn't make snide remarks, I thought them, which Steve could sense.

I can paint two pictures of Steve as dramatically different as the living Dorian Gray was from the realistic portrait of himself that he kept in a locked room. Steve was not all evil. He alternated between being a hero on a white horse and a villain capable of engineering diabolical plots.

Random recollections come to mind. He was tenderly solicitous of a stray puppy bloated with worms who wormed her way into our hearts, yet he confused this same devoted dog with harsh commands, swift kicks and beatings. He wept with me when she was struck by a car and had to be destroyed. Steve and Mother shopped for Christmas gifts together, hand in hand. While she kept a doctor's appointment, knowing how she hated to miss a particular soap opera, he watched and made detailed notes even though he had no use for such programs. When he surprised her with his report, it became clear he had watched the wrong soap opera. Tears of laughter ran down his face. All this, yet he threatened to break her arms and legs. On walks through the woods, Steve presented me with a single, perfect flower—many times. He waded into swamps to get cattails for me. He surprised me with a fistful of the first pussy willows. He had a florist leave a giant basket of daisies on the front steps for me to find along with a note in his handwriting, "Because I love you." He sang love songs to me; he chose half a dozen songs as "ours." In between lovely moments, he treated me with contempt, yelled at me, and told me I was no goddamned good for anything.

With unlimited patience, he instructed first David and then Liz on how to drive the tractor. He ordered .22 rifles for them, with consecutive serial numbers, and taught them how to shoot, stressing firearm safety. "Always assume a gun is loaded," he said. Occasionally he helped them with their homework. He praised David for a chore well done. He hugged Liz and affectionately called her, "Squat Blossom." He demonstrated to Liz, by snapping his fingers against her upper arm, that a little snap hurt far more than a silly old hypodermic needle until her tears gave way to giggles. At times he was a father to the kids in the best sense of the word. And he frightened them with his roars of unbridled anger over inconsequential childlike goofs. He declared, to whomever would listen, even the wind, that children, especially Liz and David, were no goddamned good. He inflicted punishments that far outweighed the crimes. He insulted them with sudden slaps across the face or a flat board across their behinds. He called Liz a pig, a goddamned female. He screamed at David, calling him lazy and stupid. The kids knocked themselves out trying to please him, we all did, but there was no way anyone could fathom which criteria Steve might be operating under, drunk or sober. Like that little girl with a curl on her forehead, when Steve was good, he was very, very good, and when he was bad, he was horrid.

As our family life deteriorated, each of us withdrew into ourselves; what we presented to one another and to the outside world was a facade. Moments of intimacy between my children and me became fewer and fewer until we rarely experienced closeness. I struggled with how to carry out my responsibilities as a mother while simultaneously trying to prevent setting off Steve into another tantrum. I was no match for him physically and so I relied on my wits. Some way, some how, I had to find a way to engineer our escape. Steve had convinced me that if I ever fled again, he would track us down and maim or kill us. I ruled out fleeing to another part of the country because I was sure

Steve would trace us through my Social Security number. I invested in him all the cunning of a career criminal together with the exceptional know-how possessed by both the FBI and the CIA. Surely there must be some way we could leave the country legally under assumed names. Using Mary Jane's address, I contacted the Australian Consulate. Travel costs were prohibitive. I felt trapped. I could talk with Mother, Mary Jane, and write long letters describing Steve's cruelty that were purple with self-pity. In return, I received appropriate exclamations of horror and disgust and sympathy. I desperately wanted to help my family and myself but no one gave me any suggestions, not even clues. The flight surgeon who had observed him in action on a few occasions and was privy to much about our home life volunteered his professional opinion: psychotic, with manifestations of paranoia and schizophrenia. He said Steve also had a drinking problem. Good friend that he was, the flight surgeon gave me a generous supply of Librium.

I believed Steve was mentally ill. How could any of us, and especially me, hate someone who was sick? I could and did and sometimes I felt guilty. His bragging, his grandstanding, his need to dominate any conversation, filled me with embarrassment—more for him than for me. I sensed people feeling sorry for me and part of me liked being appraised as a suffering but loyal wife. The other part wanted people to see how troubled Steve was and to give me a sense of direction. Their hand wringing combined with mine served to make a bad situation worse. I felt contemptuous of Steve when he drank and carried on; surely he must be aware he was making an ass of himself. But to my frustration, he seemed oblivious to spilled drinks, hogged conversations and making no sense. As for wetting the bed, he sloughed that off by saying he was so tired from having to do all the work that his brain could not rouse his work-abused body. One night in a motel after drinking steadily for hours, he awakened and headed in the direction of our bathroom at home and relieved himself on a floor lamp. Later that same night, he wet the bed. In the morning while he turned the mattress, he justified his behavior by saying he shouldn't drink so much when he was so tired.

My body reacted to the continuous stress by manifesting more and more colds. Splitting headaches were commonplace. Ulcer symptoms were ruled out after a complete gastro-intestinal series, upper and lower GI. But the sudden abdominal pains continued. I developed colitis and from time to time hemorrhoids. I put on weight.

Usually fights were followed by protracted periods of silence with neither of us talking to each other more than absolutely necessary. Often Steve did not speak to me at all. Instead, he spoke of me in the third person. During the punishment phase he laughed and joked with Mother, and they seemed to get along beautifully. Soon after we made up, Mother's standard comment was, "He's a bastard." I asked her how she could be so chummy with him when he was mad at me. "Because I feel it helps to take some of the pressure off of you."

Following one particular period of silent animosity, Steve stood with his arms around me and told Mother, "The reason we fight so hard is because we love each other so much. When two people love one another as deeply as we do, this is normal and expected." In the throws of pervasive irrationality, I was willing to explore the possibility of whatever had a speck of sense.

Chapter 10

By September I was free of all casts but still on crutches, but by then I had switched to forearm support crutches which gave me better support and easier mobility. All summer I'd had physical therapy twice a week. Healing progressed, but full healing would take more than another year. I saw myself as a semi-invalid and therefore even more vulnerable to Steve's volatile disposition. I went to extremes to avoid crossing him. I strained my wits.

When Steve planned a hunting trip to Colorado I anticipated the peace and quiet we would have during the month he was away. Then he shattered my fantasy by announcing I was going with him. I tried to convince him, with every excuse I could think of that he would enjoy his trip much more if I were not with him. With a bum leg, I feared for my safety more than ever. I was afraid I would not return alive; that I would never see my family again. I thought I was saved when I came down with a dreadful cold but, fever and all, he insisted I accompany him. Sitting up front with him in the motor home, I wept all the way across New York State and told him my sniffling was due to the cold. As we drove by Cleveland on a highway flanked by clusters of houses, I fantasized that everybody in those hundreds of houses was happy. I wondered what it would be like to change places with them.

He was cross with me several times because I failed to prepare a meal to his exact but unspoken specification or because I phrased sentences not to his liking. I thought how much easier it would be if he prepared a script for me to read: I could not read his sick mind. Fortunately, he drank moderately. He alternated between being sullen and annoyed. Only when he was having "a jar" before dinner—and while still at the wheel—was he sociable. Riding at sunset through the Platte River Valley with my own cocktail in hand, I absorbed enough Dutch courage to ask him if he had ever experienced a 24-hour period of sensuality. He said he hadn't. I asked him if he had ever made love for longer than five minutes, maybe as many as eight or ten. He didn't think he had, nor did he think it was important. All I dared to say was, "I think it would be nice." Thanks to the affair I was having, I knew foreplay paid huge dividends.

From Fort Morgan on, the Rockies were in view. With each mile, their majesty increased. By Denver I was in awe of them and braced myself for the next leg of the trip. Steve knew of my fear of heights and he fed into it by reminding me several times that we were going to go up and through the peaks. The higher we climbed towards Loveland Pass—what a misnomer!—the more tense I became. The "cockpit" of our motor home was located over the front wheels; there was no hood between the windshield and space, nothing to suggest even the illusion of a buffer zone. Above the tree line—two lanes, two-way traffic, no guardrails, yawning space and snowy switchbacks—VWs and trucks alike passed our heavily loaded motor home. With a caution-defying driver at the wheel, I was limp with fear. I breathed deeply through my mouth, trying anything to reduce my tension. I thought I was going to faint or throw up or both. I grabbed at a reinforcement roll bar Steve had installed, turned my head to the left and down. Steve laughed derisively but when he realized I was crying, he began brow beating me. He told me I was a sissy, no fun to have along, that I was ruining his trip, had no guts, was acting like a typical goddamn female, and if I kept it up, he would cancel the trip and take me home. "Either you shape up or I'm turning this thing around," he yelled. The last thing I wanted him to do was manipulate 30 feet of motor home through a 190 degree turn. To continue west on Route 70 seemed the lesser of two evils. As soon as the fainting scare passed—and Steve scared it out of me—I straightened up in the seat. His harangue continued. Eventually we began a descent and soon were back below the tree line. In a valley he pulled off into a deserted camping area. I unbuckled my safety harness, used our bathroom, and took a Librium. I filled the sink with warm soapy water and washed dishes. Having my hands in dishwater was wonderfully soothing. That, in tandem with the tranquilizer, helped me to center myself. When I could trust my voice not to crack, I apologized to Steve for becoming so frightened. I would have done almost anything to help abate his anger towards me. Soon we started out again, up and through Vail Pass, but it paled in comparison to Loveland. At least tree tops poked into view just off the edge of the highway, like miniature shrubs. Besides, the Librium was working and it was getting dark. What I couldn't see was fine with me.

There were signs advertising Glenwood Springs—lodging and natural hot springs. I hinted as much as I dared about stopping there. The thought of soaking in a hot spring was my idea of heaven. Steve did not slow down. The highway twisted along the edge of the Eagle River and later the Colorado. On the opposite side of the river was a railroad track and as a train snaked along, yellow light glowed in its windows. I wondered if Steve, who was going hell bent for leather, was racing the train. Once in Grand Junction, he pulled into a motel, turned on television, and mixed himself one drink after another. I had one before and another after a long soak in a hot tub, the water so high it sloshed over the edge when I moved. I snatched at any moments that offered tranquility, wishing I could store them for future reference.

We remained in Grand Junction two days while the motor home was in a garage for repairs, something about the brakes. I met the wife of one of Steve's acquaintances, and Steve tried to shame me by telling her how frightened I'd been in Loveland Pass. She said, "I've lived in these mountains all my life, but whenever we drive to Denver, as soon as we get to Loveland Pass, I crawl onto the floor of the back seat." I could have hugged her. She also said a tunnel through Loveland Pass was to be built. (It was constructed and named for Eisenhower.) Her testimony when coupled with the reality of a tunnel meant I wasn't such a scaredy cat freak after all. From then on when Steve told anybody about how scared his Eastern wife was in Loveland Pass, he added that so-and-so's wife in Grand Junction got on the floor of the back seat. At least I was off the hook on that weakness.

Our destination was a working ranch in Uniweep Canyon a few miles southeast of Grand Junction, a beautiful area dominated by the Uncompahgre Plateau. During the long days while Steve hunted, I read and wrote letters; and every day when he returned, I had his supper ready. He was solicitous and loving. But as his hunting luck continued bad, his moods turned surly. He had nothing good to say about anybody. He claimed that another hunter had stolen a shot from him. Everyone staying at the ranch bagged deer or antelope or both. One evening after savoring one of his favorite meals and while continuing to drink rum and coke, he thanked me for coming with him. He told me I was a good sport about staying alone in the motor home day after day and how much it meant to him to have me along. Then abruptly, with no warning, he barked, "Suit up! We're leaving!" I cleared the table as quickly as I could, placed dirty dishes and pans in the double sink and made sure the kitchen area was secure to travel. He shoved me. "Hurry up!" and then kicked my sore leg.

I said, "Do you realize what you just did? You kicked me in my leg!"

"If you don't move faster, I'll kick it again, hard enough to break it! Woman, get your ass in gear!"

He unhooked the water, electricity and sewage connections, mixed himself another drink, and within 15 minutes after speaking sweetly to me while we sat at the supper table, he turned on the ignition. When he swung by the ranch house to say goodbye, I was soundlessly saying, "Help!"

And so began a 2500 mile, four-and-a-half day odyssey of terror across the United States with Steve driving the motor home while embroiled in various degrees of a drunken rage. A few miles from the ranch, he deliberately drove across the road to hit a small animal. He knew this would bother me, but I said nothing. A few miles further, he stopped, grabbed a flashlight and one of his rifles, and disappeared into the woods, perhaps to jack deer. I heard a shot and soon he returned. I said nothing. He opened a can of beer and continued driving. At midnight he parked as close as he could to the rim of a cliff without going over the edge. The light and shadows of a full moon emphasized the steep canyon walls. My fear of heights gripped me. By then, there wasn't much I wasn't afraid of. I said nothing. Neither did he. Without undressing, he fell onto the bed and passed out. I was afraid the motor home might roll, or that he might get up and deliberately release the brake. In my mind I went over that cliff a hundred times before I remembered the Librium. I took two and feel asleep.

Before daylight he was at the wheel again, a fresh bottle of beer in one hand. I stayed in bed. He drove until mid-morning, not speaking, guzzling on one bottle of beer after another. In the heart of a Navajo Indian Reservation, he pulled off into a dirt area and went back to bed. I was very quiet while I washed, dressed, and checked my supply of Librium. I stood at the sink, eating a dish of peaches, watching Navajos in a pickup truck drive a few hundred feet to mailboxes and back to the house only to get into the pickup again and drive to an outbuilding and back. There were so many pickup trucks going back and forth on seemingly pointless errands that I chuckled to myself. "Here I am, stuck with a crazy man and surrounded by Indians." I dared not laugh for fear I might cross the line into hysteria. In Gallup where we took on fuel, I telephoned home. Steve listened and stared at me. I told Mother we were on our way. There was no point in saying more even if I could have. Why worry her? What could she do? Steve drank and drove all day. There was no conversation. That night between Albuquerque and Santa Rosa, moonlight bathed flat lands that stretched to the horizon where towers of clouds billowed up thousands of feet. A strong cross wind from the south buffeted the boxy motor home from side to side. Instead of slowing down for better control, Steve drove faster. The enormous clouds churned and boiled into grotesque turrets. Bright moonlight intensified the spooky dramatics of a restless sky. I was even frightened by the clouds. A semi passed us while we were going 70 mph. Steve sucked up to its tailpipe and drafted it for more than 30 minutes, the blunt front end of the motor home less than ten feet from the trailer, while maintaining a speed between 65 and 75 mph. Steve worked on another beer. He turned on the radio to an all-night music station broadcasting from Salt Lake City; the skip was on. Then he pulled out and tried to pass the truck. According to the radio time checks, we were abreast of that truck for a full 15 minutes, both vehicles at the mercy of the gusting wind which often brought their skins within a few inches of one another. There seemed to be an insane duel between the two drivers, one of whom I knew was drunk. I experienced the perverse thrill of a lifetime. I was too scared to pray.

Near Tucumcari, Steve pulled off at a truck stop and went into a roadside café. There were at least 25 trucks parked in the area, nothing smaller than a semi. I was sure his driving would kill us both. I plotted leaving the motor home and stowing away in one of the trucks. But because my mobility was limited by the healing leg, I knew I could not climb up into a cab without assistance. To help resign myself to whatever fate had in store, I took another tranquilizer and was seated dutifully in the passenger seat when Steve returned with a couple bags of peanuts. He drove almost to the eastern edge of Amarillo before stopping at a rest area for what remained of the night. The next morning he did not know where we were but insisted we were on the West side of town; that we still had to go through Amarillo. He soon discovered we were not and that I was correct. Ten years went by before I realized that for at least 150 miles the night before while driving at breakneck speed during dangerous wind conditions, he had been in a blackout.

By the time we reached the Ozarks, I was beyond fear. I was thankful to be back in rolling country where sunlight danced on leaves and little streams. Every mile brought me closer to home. Steve kept himself well fortified with beer and cursed other drivers. When he stopped to eat the lunch I prepared, he tried to pick a fight with me. He had his beer and I had my Librium. He cursed me. I told him, "I just don't care anymore." For a brief while, I crossed over into numbness. I overcooked a roast, and he complained about that for 50 miles either side of Indianapolis. He accused me of intentionally spoiling the meat. I said nothing in my own defense. Trying to talk sensibly with Steve when he was insensible from booze was an exercise in futility. He was mean and crazy, and drinking made him meaner and crazier. On our last night out while he boozed and barreled across Route 80 towards the Poconos, my heart was in my throat whenever he jerked the wheel to pass and then return to his lane. After midnight he parked in a rest area, had another beer and went to bed. The next morning he did not drink. Once we crossed the Tappan Zee Bridge and soon crossed the line into Connecticut on Route 84 headed towards Waterbury, I thought I might make it home after all. Mid-afternoon, after 117 hours of hell on wheels, we pulled into our barnyard. On a diet dominated by beer and peanuts, interrupted by a few martinis and only occasionally by solid food, Steve had averaged over 600 miles each day. The average was 800 on the trip out.

No one was home. I recalled that Mother was taking the children to the dentist. While Steve prepared a large country breakfast for himself, frying bacon and slicing potatoes, I made two trips from the motor home into the house with my toiletries and a few clothes. This took me some time because I moved slowly with crutches. After all those hours of no conversation, just verbal abuse and demands for routing directions, Steve began speaking to me while he continued cooking. I stood still and listened—and marveled—at a twenty-minute harangue in which he recounted what a miserable bitch I was, how I had ruined his hunting trip. He droned on and on and on. Finally he said, "And if you aren't going to change your attitude, you have five minutes to pack and get out of this house."

Here was the opportunity I longed for. He was relatively sober. My family was safe. I said, "Okay," and hobbled to the kitchen phone to call Mary Jane. In front of Steve, I told her I had been given five minutes to pack and leave, and could she pick me up? When I tried to re-enter the motor home for more of my things, Steve blocked my way and locked the door. I returned to the house and placed a few belongings in large grocery bags; the suitcases were upstairs and I had only so much time. I stood inside the front door waiting for Mary Jane.

Steve taunted me. "Look at that, a couple of sacks. That's all you have to show for living 41 years."

I said, "All I can say is that Maggie had a lot more guts than I have." He said

78

no more. When Mary Jane arrived, I got into her car with my two grocery bags and my favorite dog—I was afraid Steve would harm him. We drove to a crossroads where we waited to intercept my family. There I removed my engagement and wedding rings. With that act, I thought I divorced myself emotionally from a man I loathed and loved. The reunion with my family, after an absence of almost four weeks, evolved from joyous surprise into bizarre hysteria when I announced, "I've left Dad. I am getting a divorce." Three pairs of eyes looked at me incredulously. I showed them my ringless hand. Liz, then 12, hopped and jumped, half laughing, half crying.

David was 11. He looked at me with big, sad brown eyes. "Does this mean he will never hit me again?"

I felt safe enough to answer, "Yes."

He put his arms around my waist, and we hugged. Liz joined the hug. Tears rolled down our faces. We went on to Mary Jane's home but Mother returned to the house. "I pay board and room," she said.

The following day I saw an attorney and filed for divorce. I refused to talk to Steve when he telephoned to apologize. He packed up the motor home and told Mother he was going to visit Kenneth, his surrogate father, who lived 500 miles away. He said he'd be gone a week. The children and I returned home. Then I panicked. I was sure there was no way Steve would agree to a divorce. I believed that our physical safety demanded we leave. I prevailed upon a moving company to send packers at once. Two days later when we were within hours of being able to leave, the phone rang. Mary Jane's oldest boy had spotted the motor home coming into town. I called the town police who in turn alerted the State Police. Steve walked into the kitchen as I hung up the phone. Every room in the house was torn apart. Packers, packing paper and cartons were everywhere. Steve's face betrayed his shock and disbelief. He told the men to start unpacking. I told them to keep on packing. Steve commanded them to unpack.

And then the police arrived, one from the town and two of the biggest and tallest state troopers I had ever seen, bigger and taller than Steve. He had to look up to look into their eyes. Apparently someone had briefed them about our marital situation and Steve's temperament. They took all the bombastic starch out of Steve. He seemed to shrivel. "Why," I realized, "he's a bully."

Steve told the troopers, "I won't cause any trouble." Strangers were protecting me from the man I had thought would protect me. Mother, Liz and David witnessed the scene, perhaps the happiest of any scene they remember that included Steve. He said there was no reason why I had to move, that he would leave within a week, to give him time to pack and help me ready the house for winter. He said he would stay in the motor home. Looking up at the troopers' faces, he said, "There won't be any trouble, Officers, I promise."

The packers wondered what to do. Steve asked to speak to me alone. We stepped into the bedroom where he asked me, "Why?" I showed him my bare left hand. "Oh, no!" he said and began to weep. I steeled myself not to capitulate again to his tugs on my heartstrings. I told myself to remain calm. I verified he meant it when he said he would leave within a week. Then I paid the packers, thanked them, and sent them on their way. A minister friend and his wife offered to help us draw up a private agreement prior to any divorce that was witnessed and notarized. Steve was to sleep in the motor home and to leave within seven days. He agreed to seek psychiatric counseling and to send me enough money to meet all household and living expenses. In turn, I was to maintain the property and put a hold on the divorce until Steve and I reviewed our situation in six months. However, if he failed to honor the agreement, then I was released to proceed with the divorce. He agreed to accept the serving of divorce papers prior to leaving.

The first two days were riddled with barbed remarks and nasty innuendos. Now that I had some leverage, especially the knowledge the police were patrolling the house day and night, I longed to cut Steve down to size any chance I had. Reminders to myself that he was mentally ill fell on a deaf brain. I was vindictive. I behaved like an animal thrown into the same cage with a mortal enemy. Then he drank, got drunk and became a garbage mouth. Any sense of security I had evaporated. Terrorizing resumed. He stomped out the front door and into the motor home to mix himself another drink. I bolted the door after him and got my loaded .38. Soon he was back at the door, banging on it, yelling at me to let him in. I thought, "You bastard, you come through that door and I'll kill you!" When he got tired of pounding and yelling he went back into the motor home. But then he was back at the front door, kicking at it. I thought, "Please go away. I don't want to shoot you." After more noisy name calling he returned to the motor home. I sat down on the hallway floor, still holding the .38. After a long period of quiet, he was at the door again, this time dressed only in his underwear. The fear of rape flashed through my head—rape followed by murder. I stood and held the gun with both hands, pointed at the door, chest height. I prayed, "Oh Steve, please don't come through that door."

He called to me. "Donna. Donna." After a long silence, he said, "I won't bother you any more."

I watched him re-enter the motor home and then I resumed my sentry position on the hallway floor, the gun in my lap. I don't know how long I sat there, a couple hours I think, although it seemed like most of the night. I put on a coat and left by a side door and walked to the motor home. I could hear him snoring. I knew he was out for the night. I went to bed with the .38 on the floor beside me. In the morning Steve apologized. How weary I was of his apologies! He asked if we could declare a moratorium, at least for the days remaining until he left. Reluctantly I agreed. Certainly a cease fire would be to my benefit, too. With both of us on good behavior, and especially with Steve not drinking to excess, the days were remarkably pleasant, oft times enjoyable. I could feel my hatred abating and love returning. I knew I could not tear up the signed agreement; that I could not count on a few days free of strife to stretch into infinity because Steve had not changed, not from the inside out. That I needed to change too did not occur to me. With Steve out of our lives, our lives would be fine. Abracadabra.

The kids were staying with Mary Jane. Mother kept mostly to herself. Steve and I shared laughter, good memories, but any talk about the future was vague. He lived in the house during the day; we ate together, and at night returned to the motor home without any fuss. He took me out to dinner a couple times, and we allowed ourselves to bring out the best in each other. On the night before he was to leave, we embraced and ended up in bed together. For the first time ever, I felt Steve was making love to me. He relaxed some of his sexual inhibitions and was gentle, persuasive, and unhurried. I found it ironic that the pleasures of making love for more than eight minutes occurred on the eve of our separation. Before morning he returned to the motor home. "I don't want to get your mother all pushed out of shape." Our agreement to separate held. The goodbyes were painful. We said, "I love you," and cried. Still, when the last wave was exchanged as Steve drove down the hill in the motor home, I felt a sense of relief. David had come home to say goodbye to Dad. We hugged, both of us trying to deal with conflicting emotions. David and I loved the "White Steve" but hated and feared the "Black Steve." Liz hated him——period.

After he put 800 miles between us, Steve telephoned——collect. He was drunk. He told me he loved me and that I was a bitch. Nothing had changed. There were many collect phone calls during the next few months, most of them abusive. He did see a psychiatrist for a while but stopped. He never did send any support money. I exhausted what savings I had and sold the old bulldozer and later the small tractor. I also paid my mother for a loan Steve had gotten from her. Because he did not live up to the terms of our agreement, I told the attorney to get me into court as fast as he could, but I did not tell Steve. By the morning of my court date, early in February 1972, I was in agonizing pain from huge hemorrhoids and saw our family doctor en route to court. He hoped surgery could be avoided. Mary Jane went with me to court; she was my witness. The judge deduced that because Steve had not honored our separation agreement, he would not honor a court order to send me alimony. To my shock, the judge decreed that in lieu of alimony, all property was to be deeded over to me forthwith. I was staggered by the power of the court. Four months earlier I had returned from the hunting trip. Now I had a decree nisi. The divorce would be final in six months.

I returned home with a prescription for pain which provided no relief unless I also had a drink. I kept a log of when I took the pain medication and when I drank. I did not want to overdose. I lay on my stomach across the bed and wrote a long, detailed letter to Steve describing step by step what occurred in the courtroom. I mailed it to him in care of the psychiatrist because I thought he would need support when he learned I not only had a divorce but now was sole owner of all the property. He was bitter and threatened to take legal action but there was nothing he could do. From time to time we talked, but he no longer reversed the charges because I refused to accept such calls. I was property poor. His letters read like his speech—both loving and abusive—and I tried to make sense out of them. But I couldn't because there was no sense to be made.

Chapter 11

With Steve out of our lives, I anticipated a harmonious family life. Liz and David had suffered under a dictator, and I over-compensated for my guilt by letting them have their heads. I thought that after a week or so of freedom a sense of self-discipline would materialize. Instead, they acted out their buried anger towards me; I became a beleaguered figurehead parent. I knew we all needed help; we were walking wounded. I made inquiries and found a psychiatrist who specialized in family counseling. The children objected. I insisted. Our visits were a waste of time, something they discerned before I did. None of us, including the psychiatrist, could see that our inability to function within normal parameters was because we had endured several years of trying to adjust to rigid rules dictated by a tyrant who relied upon alcohol to escape his feelings. The psychiatrist could discern that the ex-husband and ex-stepfather was sick, we all knew that, but what none of us realized was that he had two diseases—mental illness and alcoholism—and we had been affected by both. Any questions about Steve's drinking were cursory. If I had been asked, "Is he an alcoholic?" I would have said no. I pictured an alcoholic as someone who staggers about swigging from a paper bag, sleeps on grates and pukes in doorways.

I took on a supposedly part time job in the city as editor of a small monthly magazine and let it consume more and more of my time because it offered a legitimate escape from the deteriorating situation at home. In a structured environment, I felt secure about my professional capabilities whereas at home, incident after incident underscored my failure as a mother, even as a daughter. I dreaded walking into the house because I was told immediately all that had gone wrong that day. Mother told me what Liz and David did or failed to do; Liz complained about Gram and David; David griped about Liz. I thought, "I'm living with a bunch of tattletales." I asked the family, Mother in particular, to please not dump on me until I had been in the house for at least five minutes. I wanted those minutes reserved for hellos, letting us feel good about ourselves and each other before the inevitable shit hit the proverbial fan.

A particular behavior pattern developed. If Liz was in a hostile mood, David was loving and cooperative. And vice versa. I recalled another pattern that had occurred while Steve was still living with us: when he was not speaking to me, he and Mother were very chummy; but once he and I made up, Mother let me know what a miserable person he was. I now know there is nothing unusual about such manipulative dynamics within any abused family, but the additional subtle nuances within a family that has also lived with mental illness and alcoholic drinking contribute another dimension to disharmony.

The kids went wild. David vandalized a camper's trailer, and Liz exploded with anger at me. One night in the kitchen, Liz and I lost our tempers. She threw a kitchen knife at me; luckily her aim was poor. Another time she made a fist and hit me on my back with enough force to send me to the floor. I still feared Steve might return to harass us and now I feared my daughter's wrath. Both kids were in and out of the principal's office; detentions became commonplace. Occasionally they skipped school. They lost their values concerning truth; if they felt guilty about any of their actions, they never indicated they did. They had reacted for so long to an adult bully that they would not accept and respond, except spasmodically, to direction from me, their grandmother or teachers.

Contact with Steve continued with phone calls and letters. By early summer, he asked me to meet him for a long weekend. I declined. But as the weeks went on and his letters and phone calls became devoid of abuse and recriminations, I weakened. Perhaps the sessions with the psychiatrist had helped. I said I would think about seeing him. Then I decided I would but not until after the divorce was final: I did not want to do anything to jeopardize the divorce. He sent me a classically beautiful long white dress. David invited me out to dinner, his treat, and insisted I wear the new dress. We had a lovely evening.

Early in September, one month after the divorce was final I accepted roundtrip air tickets from Steve and flew to meet him in Miami. As I walked into the terminal towards luggage claim, I felt a tap on my shoulder and turned to see Steve, his face naked of any guile. He offered me a soft, tentative smile. We kissed and then stood for a full minute with our arms around one another, the most loving single minute I ever knew with Steve. We spent a week in the Florida Keys where he was living out of the motor home, day after day of glorious sunshine, crystal clear waters, swimming, sunning, boating, shopping, being introduced to his new friends, and lazy lovemaking. While picnicking on a tiny, uninhabited key in the Gulf of Mexico, I skinnied out of my swimsuit and said, "There should be music while I do this."

Steve said, "You don't need any. You are music."

At noon in Key West while we sipped Bloody Marys in Sloppy Joe's Bar, Steve asked me to marry him. Back out on the sidewalk in the brilliant sunshine, he continued to propose. "We could get married right now, today," he persisted. How easy it would have been to say yes, to exchange my divorced single status in favor of all the benefits of being a married lady; the thought of financial security was strong. I still loved him. But I could not take the risk of putting myself and my family back into a hell. What I said was, "It's too soon. Let's see how things go." Besides, I felt like I was on a honeymoon anyway.

We decided that he would fly back with me to New England and spend a week with all of us. The night before we were to leave, he became ugly. I heard the same old routine coming out of his angry mouth, blaming me for wrecking the marriage, boasting how he was pulling his life together in spite of the way I had stolen his property from him, predicting I would have a life of misery because I divorced him. He launched into a litany of Liz's faults, David's faults, Mother's faults. He blamed them for breaking up our marriage. I excused myself and went into the bathroom and had diarrhea. I thought, "He's filled me with shit." In the morning he apologized. I said, "I can't take any more of that stuff." He assured me there wouldn't be any more. He said he had been upset because I was leaving and apprehensive about flying back to Massachusetts with me, and could he still come with me? He reiterated his love for me, how much he needed and wanted me as his wife.

We received a warm welcome from the family. David put his arms around Steve's waist and the tears rolled down his face. Steve complimented me on how nice the place looked and told me I had done a good job: the kids, Mother and I had worked our fannies off opening and running the campground that summer. On an afternoon while Steve and I lolled on the bed munching goodies and watching a football game he took a swig of beer and said, "Here I am, watching my favorite football team with my favorite girl." At the end of the week I did not feel as sad as I might have because we made plans for him to come back at Thanksgiving for an open ended visit. We said we would talk about remarriage then. So once again we kept in touch with long phone conversations and letters, reassuring each other of our love. But inevitably, Steve phoned and wrote when he was drinking, and my expectations of pulling our relationship together lessened. Once he called while I was out and he talked with Mother. She told me his voice was "in his boots," a telltale sign of drinking. When he called back, he accused me of being out with another man and of having Mother lie for me. I could not reason with him. On his next call, still drunk, he said he was going west to find a place to live, "that is, if I don't die on the way," and no, he would not see me at Thanksgiving or ever again. "Just forget the whole thing." After he hung up, I sobbed. Months later he telephoned from Utah where he said he had "found the perfect place to settle down, no thanks to you, because I almost froze to death on Christmas" but he added, "The people out here aren't cold-hearted like New Englanders, and they saved my life." My days were full with the campground and the editing job. I kept busy every minute which was the best way I knew to replace thoughts of Steve.

The kids became more unmanageable. They were careless with property, often heedlessly destructive, balked at doing chores, and had frequent run-ins with the principal. At times I felt I spent more time in school than they did. Liz's mood swings became more pronounced. I worried she might be suicidal. Years later I learned she was experimenting with drugs. David's temper came to be feared, the way he slammed doors, kicked furniture, and yelled. One evening the town policeman brought him home from a school dance—drunk. He had vomited in the cruiser's back seat. I was so addled from overload that hearing he was drunk barely registered. The kids lost no opportunity to tattle on one another. Mother alternated between making excuses for me to the kids and to me for the kids. We were all on a crazy merry-go-round.

One of my uncles who had developed a strong dislike of Steve, strong enough to say, "He should be kept in a compound surrounded by an electric fence and once a week thrown a chunk of raw meat," stopped by early in the summer to tell us he had just returned from a trip out West where he had seen Steve. "He's a changed man," he said. He also said that Steve still cared for me.

Now that I seemed to be the focus of any family squabble, I thought about what Steve said about Mother, my daughter and son. I could see what he meant about being trouble-makers because that was how they had come to seem to me lately. Was he right about Mother and Liz helping to break up our marriage? Connections I made between Steve's drinking and abusive behavior faded. I, too, wanted to place the blame on others. And if my uncle, of all people, said Steve was a changed man, then surely he must have changed. I wrote Steve a letter.

In return I received a long, lucid letter. He was happy, active, well and, yes, he still loved me, but he didn't see how it could work because of Mother and Liz. We corresponded all summer, and then he telephoned to invite me to fly out to visit for a few weeks. I was beside myself with indecision. I longed to escape the chaos at home, to spend carefree days and nights in big sky country, to seek adventure with Steve. I became incapacitated with hemorrhoids, the worst ever. Percodan did not cut the pain. I crawled about on the bed, on hands and knees, moaning, biting my mouth so I wouldn't scream. I persuaded the doctor to prescribe Demoral. I told him that if they did not go away within 10 days, I would agree to surgery. As far as I was concerned, they were caused by tension; so, if I could relax, they would disappear. I medicated myself with Demoral and vodka gimlets. I kept a written record of when I took what so I wouldn't overdose and cause respiratory failure. Even medicated with that potentially deadly combination, the pain subsided only just enough so I could bear it. One evening I had to leave my bed to search for Liz. I found her in a field with two older boys. Once back at the house, I vomited. Mary Jane was with me and saw what looked like blood. An ambulance rushed me to the hospital where a series of tests proved negative, and I returned home. Gradually, the hemorrhoidal swelling went down, and at the end of ten days, the doctor said I had escaped surgery. A few weeks later, clutching a donut pillow——just in case——I flew to Moab, Utah, to meet Steve.

I stayed three weeks and felt I was an intruder in Steve's life. He was in the process of moving from the motor home into a rented ranch house tucked up in the mountains. Some days passed without Steve scolding me. But then it began. One of his favorite expressions was resurrected, "I'm disappointed in you," and inside I shriveled. I wondered what I had done wrong and how could I live up to his expectations; sometimes I succeeded in pleasing him and other times I failed. I had no idea how I did either. He introduced me to a friendly, attractive woman he had dated and told me, "I asked her to marry me." He recited his sexual conquests. He insisted I read letters he had received from many different women. He often drank to excess. I suffered silently under the barrage of hateful words. One morning he stormed out. "I may return and I may not." There was no phone yet at the ranch and I was miles from the nearest town. I felt abandoned. Late afternoon he returned. I threw myself into his arms and sobbed. I told him I was sorry for whatever I had done to make him angry. He smiled. "Did you think I had gone off and left you?" I could only nod. "Poor little girl, my girl," and I eagerly accepted comfort from my tormentor. I was back into what is known as the Stockholm Syndrome, so named after hostages in that city bonded with their captors, the same emotional trap Patty Hearst experienced.

There were adventures. He borrowed a jeep and took me up and over smooth rocks until we could drive no further and we hiked, at one point having to climb up through a hole in the rocks. We set up camp for overnight on Spanish Rim; far above the lights of, I think, Moab. Under a small tent, we slept in sleeping bags; the wind howled. Another day I joined a group on a raft trip down the Colorado; my first experience with white water. When we put in for lunch, Steve arrived with the grub. I marveled at the spectacular view from Dead Horse Point, one I found more pleasing than the Grand Canyon. We canoed about 70 miles down the serene Green River, passing through two canyons—Desolation (correctly named) and Gray, camping overnight under a sky filled with stars. One of Steve's friends ran a steamboat on the Colorado and a few times I enjoyed the sunset cruise.

I dreaded returning to New England; most of the news from home was not good. Yet I knew I could not accept Steve's invitation to stay on for at least another week. Again, he talked about our getting married. We knew a personal liability suit had been brought against us and the campground by the parents of the drowned child and was about to reach court. Steve said he would come East for the trial if the insurance company paid for his expenses. And so, our parting was to be for just a short time. Once aboard the plane, I wept. God help me, I still loved him, but my uncle was wrong. Yes, Steve had changed—addresses. His moods were as mercurial as ever. I looked down onto the snow-covered Rockies and gave thanks that I was flying over them instead of white knuckling through Loveland Pass.

The trial date was set for late November. Steve's travel arrangements were cleared through the insurance company. I received letters from Steve and a series of photographs he and I took when we camped overnight on spectacular wind-swept Spanish Rim. On the back of each photo he wrote a few words. The ones of me said, "The right girl… At the right time… In the right place… Doing the right thing…" On the back of the one picture of him, he wrote,

"But with the wrong guy." In another letter he wrote about a week-long raft trip down the Colorado with a woman writer and a male photographer from major international magazines. I felt a pang of jealousy. Well I knew of Steve's attraction to anyone with prestige. Often he referred to well-known names as being "personal friends" when I knew he had met them while I interviewed them, and I did not consider them as personal friends.

David, Liz and I went to the airport to meet Steve but wondered if he had made the flight. Not until long after all the other passengers deplaned did he finally appear. He walked slowly; either he was truly reluctant about seeing us or he wanted to kindle feelings of insecurity and anxiety within us. There were few pleasant times during that visit. I tried to create and prolong loving moments but my efforts failed. We participated in pre-trial conferences with attorneys; we visited a few friends. I was embarrassed by Steve's super-macho demeanor, more pronounced since moving out West. Sometimes when I looked at him, I saw clothing stuffed with straw. There were moments however, when he brightened and extended himself to be congenial, even loving. I felt jerked about like a puppet.

During a trial recess, the parents agreed to drop their suit for a million dollars and settle out of court for a few thousand more than the cost of the child's funeral and burial expenses. On our way home, Steve stopped at a bar where he downed three drinks to my one. It was going to be one of those evenings—the night before Thanksgiving. We visited the minister and his wife where he wolfed down all of one of their Thanksgiving pies. He was drunk, argumentative, rude, demanding, and sarcastic. He did not argue with me when I said I would do the driving.

Thanksgiving Day epitomized Indian Summer, as balmy as a July day with temperatures in the 80s. Together we cooked, and our camaraderie felt genuine. Steve had a beer and then another and the atmosphere degenerated into guarded tension. He used the phone to call a woman in Utah and to others around the country. I made no comments but inside I seethed. Once all the food was prepared, he suggested we take a walk. While we stood in what we'd named Whistle Pig Field watching the sun begin to set, his arm around my waist, he told me to put the property on the market and then come west to join him. He talked about the house he would build for all of us to live in, the same house he had sketched with me at his elbow, the floor plans we had drawn, modified, and refined. He spoke of how wonderful it would be to be a family again. We kissed.

The dining table was set with the best china, crystal, and silver. Flickering candles flanked a centerpiece of fresh flowers. In the kitchen I stirred the gravy. Steve and I laughed and talked. He emphasized something he said by punching me on the arm. I said, "That hurt." He punched me again, harder. I turned and said, "That hurts. I don't like it. Don't do it again." His expression changed from one of mean playfulness into mean seriousness. He glared at me and punched my arm even harder. In a low but strong voice, I said, "Stop that!" I had spent two years in that house without Steve's abuse and in spite of the problems in my life I had managed to regain some of my self-respect.

Steve flew into a rage. "You can't talk to me like that!"

I refused to let him know I was afraid of him. With great control, I said, "This is my house."

What happened after that was a blur of sounds, most of them angry. Steve railed against me. The family came into the kitchen, and he railed against them, especially Mother and Liz. He announced he was leaving and told me to drive him into the city where he would get a bus. I said I was not going to drive him any place. He threw clothing into his suitcase, cursing all the while. In the hallway he continued his harangue. Mother went into the living room. David stood in the hall, watched, and listened. Liz stood on the stairs. Steve told her she was nothing but a goddamned female. She retorted she was as good as any boy. Steve said that as a female, she would never be able to do anything worthwhile, such as drive racing cars; that all the great inventions and leaders since the world began were men, not females. Liz swore. Steve swore. I pleaded with them to stop. Steve announced again that he was leaving, that he wasn't going to spend another minute in this goddamned house with all these goddamned females. To David he said, "I feel sorry for you." He told me I was to drive him to the city. I refused. "You come with me right now and leave those goddamned bitches behind. If you don't come with me now, this minute, you'll never see me again!"

Some part of my befuddled brain thought it might be possible to salvage the day and sit down at the festive table as a family and have Thanksgiving dinner. I hoped I could soothe waters with a quiet word. "You know I can't do that."

"Then I'm leaving," he said. He spoke to Liz and another battle of words began. I was afraid he would strike her. Mother stood near the foot of the stairs and tried to get Liz to hush. She would not shut up. She taunted Steve, demeaned him, cursed him, infuriated him. He tried to retaliate but Liz, then 14, bested him every time. "You're useless because you're a female!"

Liz shot back, "If it weren't for us females, assholes like you wouldn't be here!"

Again Steve announced he was leaving and ordered me to drive him. By now I was furious with him, too. He had given his claptrap about inferior females once too often. Although I wasn't doing the best job as head of a household, I knew I was not inferior to any man because I was a woman— woman, not female. He turned and went out the door. Soon he came back in and spewed more venom.

"Are you going to make me walk?"

"I am not driving you."

He cursed some more, cursed Liz in particular, looked at David and said, "I feel very sorry for you, surrounded by these goddam women. If you ever want to break loose, come live with me," and he slammed out the door into the darkness. I stood at the window in the unlighted living room and watched him lurch across the yard, into the road, and disappear down the hill. I was reminded of the night years before, the first time I saw him drunk, when I pleaded with him not to leave and stood at the edge of the property and watched him reel and stumble out of sight. This time I did not beg him to stay.

Liz felt triumphant. Mother and David looked stunned. We should have been at the table, all of us, as a family, giving thanks—all of us, including Steve. I was like a chicken that walks and flaps about after its neck has been wrung: I was programmed for a family Thanksgiving dinner. Everything had happened too fast. I began to wail. "I'll never see him again! He's gone!" I turned on Liz asking, "Why did you make him so mad?" I cried over loss and with relief. I was like the soundtrack of a movie that is out of sync with the action on the screen. I could not bring reality into focus.

Steve telephoned from a hotel in nearby Springfield. He said he hitchhiked, and I felt badly that such a proud man was reduced to bumming rides. He wanted me to bring his leather coat to him and drive him on to the airport. I refused. He cursed me and hung up. Late the following afternoon I had a hunch where he was. Through telephone information I got the number of the woman writer whom he'd met on the Colorado raft trip and phoned her, pretending I was a long distance operator placing a person-to-person call. Steve came to the phone and in his best cellar voice said, "Hello."

In a voice that dripped with sarcastic ardor, I said, "Hello, Lover," and hung up. Then I laughed hysterically. I savored the moment. I still do.

Mother laughed with me. "I would have loved to have seen his face," she said. I could visualize it. Liz chortled with delight.

David seemed shocked to think Dad had gone directly to another woman. "How did you know he'd be there?" David wondered.

91

A few days later I received a call from the woman writer. She had questions. I answered them and answered those she did not know enough to ask. I filled her in on Steve's background, his first marriage, his lies and lies and lies, his mistreatment of me and my children. For good measure I gave her names and telephone numbers of people she could call for verification including Maggie, the now retired judge advocate and flight surgeon, and two people back in Moab where he lived, including the woman he said he had proposed to. I thought, "This is one woman who is not going to be suckered in by his charm." Steve phoned the next night from a bar in Manhattan. He said he was confused but he knew he loved me. About a week later he called again, he said from Philadelphia. He said the woman in New York had called the cops on him, that she was crazy and had a lot of problems. He begged me to let him come back. He apologized for anything and everything he had ever done to me and the family. "I love you," he said, and said again. I told him he could not come back, that it was over. "I'll always love you," he said before hanging up.

Several weeks later the woman writer telephoned late one evening and kept me on the phone until dawn. Sometimes she excused herself to use the bathroom or to pour herself another Coke. She had called some of the names I had given her and became alarmed enough by what they said to change the lock on her apartment. When Steve reappeared and made a disturbance in the hall, she called the police. He insisted she had some of his possessions which included a book written by a famous man that he had received the day before from the author himself who had autographed it. He warned the police they would suffer severe consequences once the famous man knew how they treated him. The police realized they had a kook on their hands: the famous man had been dead for some time. They locked Steve up for the night, enough time for him to sober up. They told him not to bother the woman again; to leave the city. She had extra sessions with her psychiatrist who advised her, because of her fear, to leave her apartment temporarily and stay with a friend. Her employers hired Pinkerton agents to tail Steve. They stayed with him into Florida and later as far as the Mississippi and then verified when he returned to his home. She told me that when he visited her at work, a colleague asked her who the killer was in her office. She thanked me for letting her ramble on. She compared the process to a catharsis and then corrected herself: "No, it's more like an exorcism." She thanked me for tipping her off about Steve. She said, "I loved him." That I could understand.

I was recruited by a regional theater to be their public relations person, to begin when the current season ended. I accepted and put High View on the market. In March I found a buyer who insisted upon immediate occupancy. Steve phoned, he said from New York, to tell me he was coming with the brothers of his girlfriend to pick up things that belonged to him. He had already taken more than he was entitled to with the exception of his military records which I had boxed. I told him there was a warrant out for his arrest which was true, but I did not tell him it was for a registry of motor vehicles infraction. He insisted he was coming anyway; I alerted the local and State Police to be on the lookout for him. He never showed up. I waited a week to call one of his friends and learned he was back in Utah. Later he phoned to tell me to stop calling people, that I was upsetting them. More to the point, the calls were probably embarrassing him.

I wondered who the girlfriend was in New York, if even there was one, or could it have been the same woman who had talked to me all night. Steve had told her, as he had others, that his wife—me—had been blown up in a car. (He had seen *The Godfather* six times when he took me to see it.) He had distorted the truth about Maggie, and I chose to believe him and not her. What was to prevent another woman from believing Steve's twisted stories about me and believing I was crazy and he was the victim? Whoever the woman was, I wanted to take her hands as the base commander had once held mine and say, "You have my deepest sympathy."

Chapter 12

We moved into the city into a turn of the century Tudor home made of brick and stone and covered with English ivy. The realtor's listing described it as a "mansion." Hardly, but it was large, perhaps big enough to house four distinctive and strong personalities—17 rooms (counting store rooms) including eight bedrooms, five and one-half baths, four fireplaces, and a tunnel that connected the house with the cellar of a three-stall garage. I thought of the house as my new husband—strong, impervious to attack, solid, indestructible. In other words, safe. Gradually I developed an awareness about some of the facets of my love-hate relationship with Steve. I felt tremendous relief and thankfulness that the kids, Mother, and I got out with our lives. We survived, yes, but at a cost I would not be able to put into perspective for years. From that fateful Thanksgiving on, as nightmares and daytime fears became less frequent, I assumed that time would provide a full healing. What I did not realize was that the seeds of my infection had gone into hibernation. The fears, resentments, and defenses in our family were so firmly entrenched that until they were acknowledged, understood, and resolved, we were destined to create problems for ourselves and others.

When I reported to the regional theater's artistic director to find out what date they wanted me to start work, I was informed a man had been hired. I was stunned. I set up my own PR business and acquired a few clients. For the next three years between trying to stay afloat financially and floundering with my kids, I walked a tightrope. First Liz and then David became truant and eventually refused to attend school at all. They fought with one another, broke doors, smashed chairs, and one night they chased each other around the back yard—one of them wielding a log and the other a hatchet and screaming, "I'm going to kill you!" A neighbor called the police. Their bursts of violent rage filled me with fear. I thought divorcing Steve would end the fear!

During the years with Steve, Liz and David witnessed their mother behaving like a spineless coward. My daughter hissed at me, "I will never forgive you—never!—for not leaving Dad sooner." They saw me allow Steve to walk over me and over them too, so what was to prevent them from walking over me? They treated me with disdain, seldom with respect. They knew I was powerless in the face of physical or loud verbal intimidation. They repeatedly demonstrated they were determined to do their own thing, even if it included dropping out of school, becoming pregnant, shoplifting, breaking and entering, torching cars and being "leaders" of the peers they attracted, most of whom were their intellectual inferiors. I was aghast at the young people they brought into our gracious home—car thieves, drug users and pushers. I was in and out of Juvenile Court which turned out to be a cruel joke. On the court's advice, I took out a CHINS petition (Children In Need of Services) on Liz's behalf because I needed support and leverage to back up the values I wanted her to have. Instead I temporarily lost custody of her. She spent time in two foster homes, a painfully wrenching experience for both of us and which served to deepen Liz's resentments against me. Years later I learned both kids were experimenting with street pills as well as wine and beer, so it was no wonder their erratic behavior, their bullying, reminded me of the tyrant I had divorced.

The last thing I needed from well-meaning friends, I got—sympathy. But a Juvenile Court caseworker fed Liz facts about her rights to live on her own when she reached 17, albeit subsidized by the state. The woman implied to me that I had botched motherhood. I carried mountains of guilt for not being effective about protecting them from their stepfather. I went over and over in my head what I could have done differently and short of putting our lives in heightened jeopardy, I could not think of a thing. Occasionally David and Liz told me their own horror stories about the emotional anguish and physical suffering they endured during Steve's reign of terror. The enormity of Steve's meanness was so strong that I felt like he was not 2000 miles away but about to walk into the room and punish us all.

"Why didn't you tell me about this at the time?" I asked. The response broke my heart.

"We felt you had enough to handle."

I wept with them and alone in my room. I blamed Steve for all our misery and made excuses for the kids. They had lived with craziness, so why shouldn't they act crazy, too? By giving them my unconditional love, surely they would permit their innate goodness to dominate their personalities. I took hope when Juvenile Court referred Liz to a psychiatrist. He saw her once and according to Liz, I came out on the short end of the stick. When Juvenile Court recommended David receive counseling from a psychologist, I readily agreed, but as expected, David was a reluctant participant. Together we kept many appointments; and for one visit, Mother and Liz joined us. Little came of those sessions because none of us, even I who pushed for counseling, could be fully honest. Each of us held back. What we offered was distorted and incomplete; we could not expose our true feelings. We had become adept at repressing our emotions with the exception of letting fly with what we considered to be justified blame. The four of us were caught in a trap of self-righteousness. My stance as a hand-wringing mother was genuine—poor me, poor me.

I wondered if too much importance was attached to Steve's behavior. I wondered if the kids were making a career out of their hatred for him and their resentment of me. They gave the impression they deserved to be indulged, to have a good time no matter what the cost. My efforts to give them guidance, counsel, and sometimes even hugs were rebuffed. They found ways to let me know they believed I was continuing to botch motherhood. I felt rejected, not only as a mother but as a person. I felt helpless and defeated. I had lost their respect and I felt lost.

Bolstered by well-meaning friends who witnessed some of Liz's outbursts, who stated they would not stand for such blatant insubordination, gutter language, and breaking of society's rules, I decided to stop beating my head against a brick wall and instead look out for myself. I went to singles dances. I dated. I met men and women who seemed to have more emotional problems than I had. Some of the men, I realized later, were in trouble with alcohol. One already had been diagnosed with pancreatitis due to drinking excessively; others tried to control their drinking by skipping every other day or periodically going on the wagon.

And then at a dance I met Craig. That night when I returned home and stopped in my mother's sitting room, I said, "Tonight I met a man." He was well educated with wide-ranging interests, had left the corporate scene to become a consultant, danced beautifully, had been divorced for a few years, had two grown daughters, and I knew I wanted to see more of him. Within a few months we were dating, and my feelings progressed from falling in like to falling in love. About a year later, he said he wanted to have an exclusive arrangement with me. I was ecstatic. Most of our dates were dinners at his place: on the patio, even when it snowed, he grilled chicken or steak that had marinated all day while we sipped martinis and talked effortlessly about whatever we were working on or reading or questioning. Usually I spent the night, relishing the serenity, grateful to have a break from the constant upheaval at home. We talked about marrying. I dared to welcome a growing sense of emotional security. My kids' off-the-wall behavior was counter productive to fostering a relationship between them and Craig. He was accessible but they were hostile. The harmony Craig and I savored was jarred and then disrupted by his older daughter after she flew in from San Francisco to live with daddy. She was as stunningly beautiful as she was emotionally screwed up, and the moment I saw her I sensed, "Here comes trouble." Within months, our love affair disintegrated due in large part to the distorted stories she told her father about me, and the twisted stories she told me about her father. She played head games with Liz. She wanted her daddy all to herself. Her poison spread. She succeeded in keeping her father and me off balance. When the end came, Craig said, "I only told you I loved you because I figured that was what you wanted to hear." Even Steve, as diabolically mean as he was, never said he did not love me. David was furious with Craig for mistreating his mother and referred to him as "Gordon Goodshit" and "Dudley Doright." Saying goodbye to Craig broke my heart but simultaneously I was relieved to have at least that turbulence over. I forced myself to pick up the pieces, to put him out of my mind, but I was never able to move him out of my heart. Years later I learned that within two years, Craig told his daughter to move out. He removed her from his will. He never saw nor spoke to her again. Her behavior gave credence to the bad seed theory.

My family's mercurial ups and downs continued. Liz insisted upon seeing a young man of whom she knew I disapproved—a dropout and drug-user. Liz became pregnant and ended their relationship. She excelled in a school designed for pregnant, unmarried girls. She asked me to be her coach during labor and delivery, the first time in years that she listened and responded to what I said. With the arrival of a beautiful and endearing grandson, the acting out of repressed hostilities became more complex. Liz received her High School Equivalency diploma and attended college where she earned a 3.8 average. Meanwhile, David became angrier and withdrew more and more from the family. He refused to shovel walks or mow the lawn and when I hired others to do it, that made him angry. Mother spent most of her time in her own suite which consisted of a bedroom, private bath, and small sitting room. Liz spent half her time with Gram and the other half in her own spacious bed-sitting room, bath, and nursery. Mother and Liz complained to each other about David and me; Liz griped to me about David and Gram and let me know any time she thought I was off base; David griped about Liz and sometimes about Gram; and Mother let me know she disapproved of them and me.

When the baby was about a month old, I answered the phone one evening, "Hello."

"Say it again."

Steve. He said he was in Denver on business. He was surprised I was not dating anyone in particular. He asked me to meet him "any place you want—Paris, Big Sur, here, Florida, you name it." It would be a vacation, "no big deal, no strings." He said he was looking ahead to when David and Liz would be grown and out of the nest, that then we could be together again, because he believed we could make a go of it if the kids weren't around. He presented his case well. He said he wished he had listened to me, that I had been right about many things. He pressed me to give him a yes to his invitation, to meet him as soon as possible. I said I could not consider the idea, that we had our chance and blew it, that we were still basically the same people. He asked me to think about it and said he would call me again in two weeks for my answer. I told him he already had my answer.

Mother, Liz and David were upset about Steve's call. We all worried he might show up on the doorstep. David said if he did, he'd kill him. "I'm big now. I could whip him." David, now 16, had developed street smarts along with strong arms and scarred knuckles.

"You're not going to meet him, are you?" Liz demanded.

"Of course not," and I had to reassure everyone many times over.

But in the privacy of my room, I pondered Steve's invitation. My life was so awful, what difference would it make if I accepted and he pushed me off a cliff? If I had an absolute guarantee I would not feel uncomfortable in any manner while with him, would I meet him? Since such a guarantee was impossible, I knew meeting him was nothing to even waste time conjecturing about. I was tempted to flee the on-going tension in the household. How ironic to have escaped from Steve five years earlier through divorce and to fantasize about escaping to him from my own family. When he phoned two weeks later, I carefully phrased whatever I said to avoid irritating him. I thanked him for the invitation and reiterated all I had said when he first called. He was a good salesman but not good enough for me to throw all reason to the wind—not again. His last words were, "I love you," and mine to him were, "Thank you." Then the dial tone came on, and I cried.

I used dating as my means to escape. The hours spent away from the house were among the few times I could pretend I felt like I was a whole person.

Mother gave me some advice. "If you ever meet anyone you really care about, don't introduce him to your son and daughter. You have the worst acting children I've ever seen."

Chapter 13

In the middle of July, five and a half years after I divorced Steve, I met Harry, and the word "weasel" popped into my head: I should have paid attention. By turning on the charm, he sent "weasel" into temporary oblivion and instead I saw a tender, compassionate man, intellectually gifted, sophisticated yet old shoe, endowed with original and often irreverent wit. During our first meeting, he said, "I'm going to give you a rush the likes of which you've never known." The whirlwind courtship (there's valid reason why that phrase has become a cliché) began with flowers, and continued nonstop with lovely cards and sentimental notes, phone calls, leisurely cocktails leading to elegant dinners spiced with free-wheeling conversations that included both humorous and profound topics. In contrast to how I felt at home, with Harry I felt loved, wanted, desired, and respected. I was desperate to escape into happiness.

And escape I did. Six weeks after we met, Harry rented an apartment 15 miles away where we began living together. Those were giddy days. We were caught up in "the wonder of you" syndrome. At the end of our work day, we relaxed with vodka martinis before dinner and shared thoughts, ideas, and plans—always with interjections of Harry's topical humor. Belly laughs were common.

My family felt I had abandoned them. In the sense I removed myself physically, that was true. I continued to provide full financial support of the house, including food. Liz and Mother made regular contributions towards their board and room. I kept in almost daily phone contact and stopped by several times each week. Every ten days, I stocked up on groceries and also reimbursed them for any expenditures they had made. Some of my family's resentment about my leaving to live with Harry was verbalized to me but I suspect most of it was not. I wondered if they missed their whipping post. To my surprise, social workers and acquaintances I thought were straight-laced and would voice disapproval of me living in sin volunteered their moral support of my new living arrangements. One even said, "Let them devour each other." That sentiment fell in neatly with mine: I had switched from blaming Steve for all my troubles to blaming my family for many of them.

Harry's long-range plans for us automatically included marriage. Once again I loved a man who was separated but not divorced. I was confident everything would work out fine because our courtship, brief though it was, had proceeded as smoothly as if an unseen force were sweeping obstacles from the path. Living with Harry I bathed in tranquility—no slamming doors, no raised voices (except in laughter), no violent angry outbursts, no need to hide my wallet or cigarettes from petty thieves. I began a new journal:

How to describe this quietness, the absence of toxemia. The Puritan ethic would say it's wrong to be this happy, content, peaceful. In such an incredibly short time (seven weeks tomorrow). He asked me to write in here that he worships me. The feeling of acceptance he gives me in turn permits me to "Be". I feel as if I'm unlearning old defenses because with Harry, I don't need to be on the defensive— not about anything.

I did not know I was in a fool's paradise. Two weeks later on my birthday, he served me champagne in bed and gave me a lovely double pearl ring. He spoke of a diamond "at a later time." He wrote on the card: "My Donna, I wish you love, and give you the most precious of gifts—my total, complete trust, loyalty, compassion and my future." To say that words are cheap is to ignore how astronomically expensive they really are.

An incident occurred early in October that convinced me Harry was a find in a million. We were in bed enjoying a last cigarette in the dark before going to sleep. Our common ashtray rested on Harry's chest. I took a final drag, rolled towards him and cooed, "Goodnight, sweetheart. I love you," and began to grind out the cigarette. Suddenly he howled and jerked about. "What's the matter?" I asked. He kept making strange yelping noises combined with maniacal laughter. I was alarmed about him and concerned about setting the bed afire, so I made sure I stubbed the cigarette thoroughly. "What is it?" I asked.

Between laughs that convulsed his body, he managed to say, "You missed the ashtray."

I didn't know whether to laugh or cry so I did both. The more I said, "I'm sorry," the harder he laughed. I followed him into the bathroom while he examined his chest in the mirror. I had burned a hole in Harry. I scurried to the kitchen for ice cubes and insisted he apply the ice to his chest. He kept saying, "It's nothing," and laughing. I felt terrible, but he pooh-poohed me. He shrugged off any more first aid and still laughing, got back into bed. I caught up with him and slathered the burn with vitamin E. If I had burned Steve, I would have been slugged and sent through a window. And Harry thought it was funny! He said, "You did that with such classy sophistication," and he mimicked the arching of my arm and my words, "Goodnight, sweetheart. I love you," and threw in sound effects. "Ssst!" Our laughter began anew. "I'm yours now," he said. "You've branded me. I'm going to tell your mother what her daughter did to me." I drifted off to sleep in awe of Harry's unflappable disposition, the lack of violence in his character, and that obviously, he really loved me.

Not many days later, I got a glimpse into the future. Harry asked me for suggestions on how to handle an invitation he received from a woman with whom he had an affair. I said I wrote to a man I was seeing and spelled out my revised status. Harry became upset and told me he didn't want to hear any more, that he didn't want to think of anyone else ever having touched me. I said that as far as I was concerned, any experiences, intimate or otherwise, we had before we met each other happened for reasons, and the over-riding one might be so that we would appreciate one another that much more. This marked the first of many efforts to combat Harry's jealousy. I became aware that Harry drank four martinis to my two before dinner but I didn't recognize a hangover when I saw it; he called it flu. He described his symptoms as aching all over, especially his joints. I wrote in my journal:

He sleeps after a few choked swallows of warmed bourbon and fresh lemon to produce sweating, a ridiculous gesture inasmuch as he has no fever, but he does have something making him feel unwell.

In December, Harry formally asked me to marry him, which surprised me because his speech often included such phrases as "When we are married," or "After we're married." On Christmas Eve he gave me a diamond engagement ring. I wrote:

I figured he would not give me a ring—the ring—until he was legally free to do so. I am still trying to cope and I mean that. Too much has happened too fast. I am too scared, not scared as in frightened, but respectful of what is and what may be. We have weathered his jealousy, and I've weathered his correspondence and out-of-state trips, neither shared with me, and his gambling on baseball, basketball, and football games, and juggling of funds, but that's his money to earn and juggle and spend, not mine. We talk about honesty. Is he giving me the full honesty I give him? I wear his diamond, a pristine lovely. Is his commitment to me really total? Ah shit, Donna, no one has ever promised you a rose garden.

I was compounding my original mistake—not paying attention to a gut warning, just like when I overrode "weasel." In mid-January after living together almost five months, I made a long entry of profound significance:

Harry in bed, hopefully we have more than weathered another growth step. He does not feel well, temperature again today, and I feel very tired emotionally. Last Saturday he went out to clean snow off the cars and ended up sitting in his car for at least 50 minutes by the clock. He came in to tell me he needed to be taken to the hospital right away because he could hardly breathe. He looked ghastly. I feared a heart attack. While we waited in the emergency room, he said he would be dead within a week of kidney, liver, and lung failure. I was thoroughly spooked. X-rays, EKG, blood and urine tests were all negative. The doctor said his symptoms were "atypical, bizarre." Harry's recounting of recent medical history was inaccurate. He did not know the day or date. He could not count backwards by sevens from 100 accurately. He accused the doctor of being patronizing and added, "I have an IQ of over 160." He was incoherent and antagonistic. The doctor asked me questions regarding emotional stress. He had already tagged it an emotional breakdown of sorts. Between tests, Harry insisted I telephone two of his doctor friends and get them there and to alert his aged aunt. I reasoned with him and the calls were not made. It was as if he craved attention, sympathy, and carte blanche belief in whatever he said. The scene was filled with layered memories of both paranoid Steve and hypochondriac Brad. The hospital experience, the behavior change in Harry the last week or so, telescoped my years of marriages and shook me up plenty. Emotionally I lived again all those years of broken promises.

I was too addled to recognize that the future was foretold by the past.

I can cope with almost anything except dishonesty and/or bullshit. I refuse to use the overused female copout of how men are little boys in long pants. I've had moments of feeling suffocated by possessive love, of feeling as if my energy were being used to sustain another, and mixed in with all this were attacks of feeling disloyal. I have no excuse but I do have a reason: this has been a hell of a trip. Tonight Harry thanked me for sticking by him. Well, I'm no quitter. I'm a survivor, an optimist, and I trust and trust and trust, and once I know I've been had, I move. I've invested too much of myself in Harry these last six months, in our relationship, and I'll go 150 percent to make it work. I feel he needs rest, mega-vitamins, perhaps an antibiotic, and to assert himself logically.

He said the doctor told him "inner ear infection," but I don't believe that. Of course I did not tell the doctor of Harry's prediction he would be dead within one week. By then I felt as if I should be admitted.

He slept 12 hours that night plus a four-hour nap Sunday and about nine hours last night. He slept as if he were drugged. Then today, as he did last Friday, he said he was going out for a walk, that he needed to be alone, get fresh air, clear his mind, and he did not walk. I figure (a) he went to a public phone, (b) met someone, c) both. I forced a talk when he returned. He said he felt I should leave at once for my house ahead of tomorrow's predicted storm. I almost went but I figured if I did, the breach might defy repair. He said he had never and would never lie to me. He asked me to trust him.

All this recent shit is so out of his character as I know it. I walked into this relationship with enough growth experiences to choke a horse. I don't expect a life free of all strife, but with the man I love, any strife should not be of our making.

The emotional turmoil continued. On the following day I poured more into my journal:

Harry referred to his long walk and said he took a short one—a half truth. He said he urged me to go to my house because he felt we both needed space and that he was not up for a lot of questions. I contend no one indulges in so-called half-truths unless they have something to hide, ditto not answering questions. I sense copout. He also told me, again, that for years he was not able to tell the truth, that now it's so wonderful to be able to do so. That is almost word for word what Steve told me, and he was the goddamnedest liar. I think Harry is troubled by more than run-of-the-mill family problems, poor business outlook, and a dragging pre-divorce settlement. I feel it is either a female and/or financial indebtedness. I feel he has lied to me re events prior to our meeting, and that's OK—maybe—unless there's a particular aspect of his personal history I, as his next wife, should know about, e.g., heavy drinking, drying out—who knows? He doesn't know that by chance I discovered two lies weeks apart. It seems I need to get to know Harry better before I enter into a legal contract with him. How many women from his past does he still have to square away? Or is the pattern of fooling around so deeply etched that he can't change? Oh head, stop! stop! stop! There may be a greater chasm here than I want to admit. I first became uneasy before Christmas. Why? My intuition has never been wrong.

I do a few things such as empty the dishwasher, change the bed, shampoo, and come back to this journal. Am I being unfair to Harry to compare his words/actions with others? But, am I not supposed to learn from experience and not repeat errors in judgment? He's told me many times that he worships me. I'd need a calculator to tally the number of times he's told me he loves me.

What did he know that I did not know last Saturday morning to make him think I would leave him? He said he was upset because I told him I was in a funky mood and he did not want to come back into the apartment if I were not in good spirits. I can't buy that either. I feel he sensed that I was upset because of his change in behavior and further, that his own feelings of guilt caused him to be alarmed about losing me and that, still further, he worked himself into an emotional snit, complete with the hairy run to the hospital as a bid for sympathy and as a smokescreen. While the EKG was being taken, he tried to make me feel his condition was my fault because I had told him I was in a funky mood. Well, whatever guilt trip he's on is all his. I refuse to accept any of it.

I feel also that from time to time Harry has looked at this journal and if he reads all this he'll go through a turmoil of emotions. I want to be fair—to him and to me. Maybe I'm being too hard on him because I have weathered so much in my marriages and family and come out of it stronger and stronger, and I expect a grown man who held a position with full P&L responsibility, who deals now with individual sales in the high six figures, to be emotionally stable.

God! I don't want what we've known together to go down the tubes. It all seemed so right, so honest and open. He cheated on his wife all those years. But why woo and win me and then betray my trust in him? Steve was a chronic liar. He lied about anything, everything. He was unfaithful. He was also sadistic, masochistic, paranoid, and psychopathic. He could also wiggle out of a lie by straight-face eye contact and tell another one to absolve the original.

I go in miserable circles but I continue to reach the same conclusion: Harry has not told me what the real problem is; his actions are undermining the healthiness of our relationship. Perhaps I would be luckier if I were not as sensitive to what people communicate without being aware they are communicating.

I was ignorant about the symptoms of alcoholism. I had a stereotyped image of an alcoholic being a skid row bum when, in fact, only three percent ever get to skid row and then only a fraction remain there. Alcoholism is also known as "the disease of denial." What I wrote in my journal and what I chose to omit attest to the depth of mine: I omitted the ER doctor asking me, "How much does he drink?" and my reply, "Oh, not much, a martini or two," when I knew he often drank more. As we left the hospital, the doctor said to me, "Good luck," and he wasn't smiling. I could not bring myself to admit Harry might have a drinking problem because I believed alcoholism struck only weak characters.

Due to ignorance compounded by denial, I believed all alcoholics were bums, riddled with sin, unable to control their drinking because they were devoid of willpower—definitely inadequate people. I needed to perceive Harry as being strong. He had a fine job which he performed every day. Eventually I realized that he demonstrated remarkable willpower because morning after morning, sick as a dog with hangovers he described as ten cases of the worst flu strain rolled into one, he dragged himself out of bed and functioned. But I blocked out the reason behind the wild trip to the emergency room: on our return to the apartment parking lot, as I got out of the driver's seat, I saw an empty pint of vodka Harry had stashed under the seat. I couldn't tell that Harry was already drunk that morning thanks to swigging from that bottle. Only then did I begin to wonder—wonder!—if perhaps—perhaps!—this man I had come to love had a drinking problem. I could not bring myself to even think the word "alcoholism." And I certainly could not write such thoughts in my journal.

Denial is the single biggest factor that prevents recognizing the presence of the disease. It is estimated that an alcoholic sees seven messages about the disease before he/she seeks help; family members take an average of seven years before admitting another member is alcoholic and then take another two years before seeking competent help. Had I been receptive to the reality of alcoholic symptoms, I could have foretold the future just from re-reading the latest entry in my journal. It was all there—Harry's jealousy, untruths, fiscal irresponsibility, plays for sympathy, blaming me and others for his problems, excessive dependency upon a loved one—all typical offshoots of alcoholic drinking and thinking. My own enmeshment in the disease screams from those entries, particularly my growing obsession with Harry, what he thought and why and how, trying to worm my way into his head so I could figure out where I stood and how I felt and how I thought I should feel. The buried seeds of the infection I contracted while married to Steve were sprouting. Running through the journal like a thread of steel was my necessity to operate within the realm of mutual honesty and trust. Once aroused I could not make my suspicions go away. Also apparent is my inflated ego: I would give 150 percent; my previous experiences had given me greater and greater strength to emerge from crises as a stronger survivor. I even mentioned, "heavy drinking, drying out—who knows?" I was not ready to pursue such a frightening thought. I sensed Harry was violating my privacy by reading my journal. Yes, I was standing knee deep in a swamp of alcoholism and I would get in as far as my neck before I began to swim for my life.

I unknowingly reinforced other data: if the effects of alcoholism upon a wife of an alcoholic are untreated, the chances are greater than 50 percent she will marry an alcoholic again, often without realizing he is alcoholic. That Harry and I fell in love was no accident. He sensed I was unhappy and needy, that I was adept at comforting; in the alcoholism vocabulary, I was an enabler. As a loving, understanding person, I provided Harry with no incentives to take a hard look at what he was doing to himself and our relationship. Ergo, I enabled him to continue drinking. I had yet to learn that if left untreated, alcoholism is a 100 percent fatal disease and that death is often preceded by insanity.

Chapter 14

Before the month of January was over, I discovered what I thought was "fever breath" was actually the result of vodka. Harry drank faster and more heavily than I (I am still a sipper, thank goodness). Often he told me to "drink up" so he could fix two new drinks at the same time. Dinner was served later and later. During our first few months together, Harry became mellow, sometimes delightfully nutty, often sexy (many a time I was willingly seduced in the living room), never moody, and by mid-evening faded into sleep. Gradually the atmosphere changed; I felt less and less comfortable. Flashbacks of the years with Steve became common. My confidence deteriorated from walking with a firm step to tiptoeing on eggshells. I considered what I wanted to say about any given subject before selecting what I hoped were phrases that would not offend Harry. When he made sarcastic remarks, I felt both the sting of his words and the memory of the misery I experienced because of Steve's verbal abuse. Was booze changing Harry from a delightful companion with a beautiful disposition into a cynical, surly crank?

Even when we had only one round of drinks, the half gallon jug seemed to get lower just as fast. I observed this phenomenon for some time before I made a faint pencil mark at the edge of the label in line with the vodka level. Before our drinks were mixed the following day, I checked the bottle. Sure enough, the level was down the equivalent of two double martinis. I kidded Harry about getting a head start but he claimed he had not drunk anything other than a soft drink. His breath and the bottle said otherwise. Why would Harry deliberately lie to me about having a drink before I got home? Random phrases flashed through my head—drink alone; lie about drinking; alcoholism treatment. Eventually I confronted him. He denied drinking on the sly; then informed me I was not to interfere. He spoke with such force that I felt as if I had been slapped. He also told me he did not think much of my spying. Neither did I. I sought clarification in my journal:

I cannot talk about this with anyone because that would mean I was disloyal to Harry. Fear can attract precisely what one fears—self-fulfilling prophecies. I try so damn hard to quiet my thoughts. I'm scared about things getting out of control, like I'm trying to hold something up that is starting to collapse around me. Does he still have a roving eye? Can the gambling losses be the problem?

I delved deeper, searching for logical reasons for addictive behavior when the addiction itself is the answer. What was I doing or not doing that contributed to his compulsions? Did he drink because I was not attractive enough for him but too attractive to others, or because I was too overweight to suit me but too slender to suit him, or because dinner was served too early or too late, or because I was silent or lost my temper, or because in bed I was not aggressive enough or too submissive? He did not drink compulsively because of any excuse he offered such as family problems or money worries, but because of what I had yet to learn: Harry drank because he was addicted to the drug ethyl alcohol.

The social stigma of problem drinking kept me from talking with someone else; I didn't know where to turn anyway. I knew nothing about Al-Anon and that their hard-earned wisdom was as close as the phone book.

Harry confirmed my suspicions that he was reading my journal when he made references to people and events he could not have known otherwise. He left a note for me: "You have my word that I will never again violate your trust or these private thoughts." And it came to pass that he could not keep that promise either. My original journals began with the 8th grade, one day to a page. After I divorced Steve, my diaries became open-ended journals, big fat composition books with spiral binders; one day could be a single sentence or stretch out over a dozen or more pages. Sometimes I skipped writing my entries out in long hand in favor of pasting in typewritten passages. I had more than 13 years of journals spanning 35 years (I suspended writing soon after I married Brad and again after marrying Steve). In high school I knew that sometimes Mother and Grammie read my journals; occasionally I interjected a "Hi, Mother!" into a sentence I was writing. Not long before I met Harry, Mother confronted me about something I had written about her. After I moved in with Harry, Mother said she caught Liz reading a journal I had left in a bedside table. Years later Liz told me that my mother used to call her attention to some things I wrote in my journal. Thinking I was protecting my privacy, I packed all the journals in a box and brought them to the apartment. Harry said it was terrible for anyone to read my private pages.

My journals served as my confidante but beyond that, their purpose was paradoxical. Writing about happy events endowed them with permanence; any re-reading reinforced the original feelings and fed my self-esteem. I committed the hurt to paper to remove as much as I could from my system, give myself relief, and to help me put painful events into perspective and learn from them. In the journal I began after living with Harry, any insight I achieved was short lived because on page after page, the recorded pain was modified in only one way: it got worse. And here's the paradox. By putting pain into writing, the relief enabled me to accept more pain. In effect, the enabler of the alcoholic who was trying to climb out of a hole was digging the hole deeper. A healthy stranger could flip through the journal, skip whole months, and think he was reading a script for a slow-moving soap opera, throw up his hands in despair and frustration and exclaim, "Why does Donna put up with this shit? I wouldn't! I'd let that s.o.b. fall flat on his face and not pick him up." The unemotionally involved reader would be right. I read the words I wrote and felt schizophrenic: I remember how I felt and I am ashamed of myself for not walking away. Even though I know now that I lacked specific knowledge and perspective that would have empowered me, still I feel shame. I want to shake sense into that ninny! My goal in my first marriage was to become part of an existing family and then create one of my own. My expectation in my second marriage was to round out my family with a husband-father. When I met Harry, I despaired of pulling my children and myself into a viable family unit and so I ran away from the emotional chaos to what seemed to be the promise of a stable life. And I brought my journals with me.

Chapter 15

Mother and Liz became ill with the flu and I went back to the house for a few days to help care for them and the baby. I felt that I did not belong in my own house just as strongly as I felt out of place in the apartment with Harry. He telephoned several times, once to say he was afraid he had destroyed our relationship by reading my journal. He spent one night with me at the house, and we talked until the wee hours. He estimated his betting losses for the previous three months to be $800; probably they were more. He said he had been drinking heavily the past six weeks or so and that he had forgotten he had women's names, addresses and phone numbers in his wallet. He explained away staying at Neversink, a health resort in New York, by saying he and business associates used it as a substitute motel when attending a conference nearby. When I returned to the apartment, I found his car in the parking lot but no sign of him in the apartment. I waited and then went next door to a divorcee's apartment where her young son responded to my knock.

"Harry is here," the boy said, which didn't register at first until he added, "He came in and went in there," and pointed towards the bedroom area. I found Harry stretched out on Carol's bed. His greeting was hostile. He made no move to get up so I turned to leave. Carol walked in the front door. I declined her invitation to have a drink and returned to our apartment. Harry returned, went directly to our bedroom, peeled off his clothes and crawled into bed. He refused to tell me what was wrong other than to say it was me and for me to reflect.

"Write it all down in your fuckin' journal and leave me alone."

I asked him if he had been drinking; he said no, that he did not feel well; he had stomach cramps. I wrote:

For the next 12 hours he moaned loudly and repeatedly called me back from the kitchen where I was trying to fix myself something to eat. All I could make of it was he wanted me to feel sorry for him. I had empathy for his stomach cramps but the more childlike he behaved, the more contempt crept into my feelings. At eight o'clock I told him that, yes, I love him, but I did not love the way he was behaving, that I was not feeling that swift emotionally, and that I needed to settle myself down—do a crossword puzzle, eat—and I left the room. He made no more loud moaning and groaning sounds and slept about two hours.

The next morning he dressed and went to work.

I'm glad he's feeling better, but this emotional seesaw he's had me on the past two months is getting to me. He fixed coffee for himself this morning—what a poison for his stomach. He'd be better off to take it as an enema. He does not take care of himself. And I can't function as his keeper.

That afternoon he came home, napped, and fixed himself a martini and then another.

Assuming he made the drinks the way he usually does, he had four to my two. I knew I could not talk with him. He insisted he would eat a regular supper, which he did, but he got up from the table and went into the bathroom and gagged. He said he "barfed." Then he went to bed.

He complained about having a fever. I put a thermometer under his tongue, left the room, and walked back in to see him put the thermometer back into his mouth. The mercury was at 103, but his body was not hot.

"Harry, did you put the thermometer on the light bulb?"

"No!"

After I cleaned up the kitchen, I decided I had to get the hell out of here for a while. I said I was going out for a drive, not a walk, and that I might swing by my house. He became very upset. I tried talking with him but it was almost a repeat performance of the night before. Things went from bad to worse. He said he didn't feel like talking. I decided I'd spend the night at my house. But after I got into the car, I thought my arrival home would create a lot of questions, and my family's respect for Harry would diminish. I also thought that by leaving, I might create an impossible breach. So I came back in. Harry got up and took down a suitcase and said he was going to New Jersey for a couple days to run the office—run the office over a weekend?— and give me a chance to calm down. I countered with, "You don't feel well enough to talk but you feel well enough to drive to New Jersey." He agreed to talk.

It was not a talk. He either agreed with what I said or did not respond. I told him there were other ways to hurt someone besides using a bulldozer. He resented that and announced he was going to bed. By then I was consumed with frustration, very angry, and wondering what in hell have I gotten myself hooked up with?

We talked the next morning. Harry said he does not know what is bothering him, that he wishes he did. He said he will try to do his best re our relationship and he asked for a moratorium for three or four days. I agreed to that. The remainder of the day was without incident. He took two naps. He agreed, again, to take better care of himself and permitted me to serve him soft poached eggs. He had no martinis before dinner but instead drank white wine. He said he's not going to drink any vodka for a couple weeks.

Carol and I ran into each other while doing laundry. She told me Harry had one martini at her place but hardly touched the second. She wondered if he had already been drinking. He also told her when she asked if I were home that he did not know where I was. What bullshit. He knew exactly where I was. He always does.

There's a big problem here.

The following evening we had dinner with Karl, a business associate visiting from out of state. The two men explored the idea of going into business together in Texas. Karl said he had done some checking on Harry and the only detrimental comments he heard referred to Harry's "drinking problem." Harry calmly replied that such a comment had followed him for years and he told Karl, "I do not have a drinking problem." For the alcoholic, alcohol is not a problem; it's a solution. The alcoholic perceives those associated with him—family, friends, and often business associates—as the ones who have a problem. Alcoholism does not lack for gallows humor. The alcoholic says, "You're the one who has a problem with my drinking, not me!"

That same day I interviewed for a job as the editor of a proposed bilingual publication for the racially mixed city ghettoes. Although my high school Spanish was not much more than a hazy memory, I was confident I would be offered the position to train borderline illiterate young people in the mechanics of producing a newspaper. I told Harry that if we were going to follow through with our idea to take a mid-winter vacation, now was the time. Within hours we had reservations in the Florida Keys and for a two o'clock in the morning flight to Atlanta and on to Miami. Harry and Karl had started drinking martinis at lunch and by now Harry was happily "shitfaced." While Harry and I waited to board the plane, he kept telling me how much fun he was to travel with. My laugh was hollow. Fun? He was boring. Once airborne, he had two more martinis. Eventually he slept, more likely he passed out, hunched over with his head almost touching his knees. In Miami we rented a car, a deluxe model Cougar, and as we sped south with the windows wide open, Harry quipped, "I wonder what the poor people are doing!" Our week in the sun was, in the words in my journal:

Beautiful! I have never had such a vacation—never. Time flowed at a leisurely pace. The weather was ideal, and Harry was a dear, dear love. Old memories crept into the new ones being made but fortunately all my memories of the Keys are pleasant so there were no traumas. The glow we had about us while on the Keys, our contentment—it was like magic. Of course one can't expect to live in and on a high continuously, but . . .

And, of course, such magic could not last. Harry's alcoholism was progressing every minute and my confused emotions kept pace in tandem. One week after we left sun-bleached coral and returned to mounds of snow, I wrote:

Harry went to bed about 20 minutes ago without so much as saying goodnight, not that I think he's angry with me but that he is very concerned about his professional direction—compounded by drinking during the day.

Oh shit.

I almost never want to turn back the clock but yesterday I felt so much better than I do now. I came home from work as quickly as I could because I wanted to be with Harry, but within minutes I knew I was in the middle of another fucked-up scene. Twice upon query he told me he had not had anything to drink earlier but four hours later, he said he'd had a "belt" and on an empty stomach. He cannot tolerate alcohol on either an almost empty stomach and/or in combination with emotional stress. Ergo, I feel it is safe to say he has a drinking problem. I drank yesterday because I knew he wanted me to join him and tonight because I thought if he had not had a drink, he needed one to help slow himself down. His face was flushed. Now I know the heightened color was from alcohol.

He said he thought he should think about making a career change and he began placing long distance calls to professional friends. On one call he reached the man's daughter who said her father was out. Harry said his call was not urgent but in the next breath, he said it was. It was the emergency room scene all over again—the wild eyes, the short temper, ordering me about. I talked him out of making more calls because he was attacking what he called "seed planting" more like a starving man than an experienced farmer. Such erratic, illogical behavior frightens me. When we are at parties and he's happily affected by booze, I don't mind, but this alarms me. Each one of these episodes hits me harder and harder, and unconsciously I brace myself for perhaps the next. He said, "I'm fucked up today. It has to be." No, it does not have to be! He's intelligent, usually logical, clear thinking, and I hate it when his brain gets fucked up.

Living with an alcoholic who is actively drinking has been compared as second only to experiencing armed combat: no one knows when the shooting will begin, nor from where the bullets will come. There's one big difference, however: the enemy doesn't put his arms around you between battles to tell you how much he loves you, that he's sorry he upset you and promises never to shoot at you again—and then reloads. Harry's irrational, erratic behavior kept me off balance. I strove to keep up appearances.

The burden of getting out a newspaper is on my shoulders. The salary is low but it's money I desperately need to maintain the house. I feel I am the source of strength at work, at my house, and here. I don't like all that responsibility. I looked so awful to Liz when I stopped by the house that she phoned later to make sure I'm okay. Of course I don't explain why I am so tired. My limbs feel full of frustration—edgy, jumpy, nervous. I dislike and deplore these feelings. Fatigue is a big contributor and combined with mental/emotional anguish makes this whole feeling a real pisser. Help! I don't like what's happening to me, what I am permitting myself to do to myself. Poor health habits, less and less spiritual growth. I must live for myself. I learned that a long time ago. But it's so difficult for me not to try to please others, to be a helpmate, but by trying to be of help to Harry, I feel I sound like a nag. This pursuit of happiness, contentment, and enlightenment sure ain't easy.

Alcoholism is described as being a three-fold disease—mental, physical, and spiritual. Harry was going down the tubes before my eyes but only when I turned to my journal could I admit what was happening to me. By writing, "Help!" I acknowledged my powerlessness over my own ability to be good to myself. I, too, was caught up in a copycat non-alcoholism problem. Intellectually I knew I had to take care of myself, but emotionally I couldn't. The reality was too much for me to handle, and I resorted to my well-developed defense of ironic humor. Perhaps if I made light of the situation, it would not seem as awful. At the office I wrote:

This is a strange day for me. Although my body has no bruise marks or broken bones, my inner self feels it has been brutally pummeled. One part of me observes the beauty of this splendid spring day and another part functions as an editor. But the core that is me is comatose.

How can I go on as I have? The answer is: I can't, because to continue without drastic changes causing dramatic, positive improvements will contribute to an inner death.

How do I conduct myself now? The answer is: carefully, while I heal. I crave a

115

quietness to help alleviate my inner turmoil, a time in which I am permitted to move at my own pace within my own space. I need the freedom of privacy to unlock my thoughts.

I accept responsibility for my self. I am not responsible for any other person's self. I can give of myself only what I have to give. And before I can begin to give even a little, I need to replenish the essence that is me.

Soon afterwards I wrote in my journal:

We may have a breakthrough. Earlier this evening Harry got into bed and said, "I'm asking for help." He said he feels he needs to dry out and have counseling. He told me he wants me, does not want to lose me. He said he wanted to be honest about stuff he's been dishonest about, and I think he did the best he could at this point. For instance, he stayed at the health farm by himself, drove there drunk, and fasted four days. Certainly we cannot build our relationship into something fine and lasting unless and until he is honest with himself. His symptoms support a definite drinking problem (he had a belt at 8:30 a.m. today, has been consuming a quart daily since we returned from the Keys, and I suspect more than that earlier). So he knows I'll give him my love and support as long as he does his part. And that he is the one who holds the power of driving me away. I am one pooped cookie.

During the next several months, Harry was drunk but not as often, often sarcastic but not always obnoxious, and because I could see he was trying to control his drinking, I figured he was doing his part so I'd better do mine and hang in there. Not until late summer did he drown himself in a bender. He telephoned me at work to tell me he was making arrangements to check into a detoxification hospital. I hurried home to drive him to whatever place he chose which turned out to be Springfield's Municipal Hospital's detoxification center. I helped him into the car. He was so sodden with booze that he kept vomiting straight vodka and telling me, while his eyes slid around in his head, "I'm trying," and "I love you." Two emotions were at war within me—compassion and contempt. At the intake desk, he sat in a wheelchair and answered questions asked by the admitting nurse. I stood beside him.

"Were you ever in the service?" she asked.

"Yes," Harry said. He had never been in the service.

"What branch?"

"Air Force." Harry rolled his head up to me and winked. I bit the inside of my mouth so I would not laugh and locked my hands together so I wouldn't slap him. He asked me to call his house to let them know where he was. I did, and his second oldest daughter answered the phone. In a flat voice, she said,

"We've been through this before." I thought how sad that she was so unfeeling. Little did I know.

A counselor suggested I attend an Al-Anon meeting. I remembered a young friend married to a problem drinker who had gone to a few Al-Anon meetings and said they helped her. During the four days Harry was hospitalized, I attended three different Al-Anon meetings. I met gentle, loving women who nodded sympathetically, watched me dab at my eyes, told me they could not tell me how to stop my husband from drinking and handed me Al-Anon literature. Some of these women were still married to active drinkers after ten, 20, even 30 years. I thought they were either saints or masochists, and since I did not consider myself either, I did not see how I could benefit from Al-Anon. But I did read the pamphlets.

After Harry left detox, several days before the staff wanted him to leave I was elated because he discussed alcoholism and his drinking with me. He told me he was an alcoholic, that years ago he went to a treatment center and attended Alcoholics Anonymous (AA) off and on over a period of years. At his invitation, I accompanied him to open AA meetings and hoped no one there jumped to the conclusion I was an alcoholic. Following a few visits with an alcoholism out-patient counselor and more AA meetings, Harry told me he knew more about alcoholism than the counselor and that he could not stand organizations. He added, "I'm not a joiner." I did not consider myself a joiner, either. Based upon what little I had read and what I heard at AA, I believed I was intellectually capable of understanding alcoholism and my role in relation to what I thought was Harry's problem. I had yet to read or hear anything that emphasized the life-threatening aspects of the disease. I bought into Harry's denial of how ill he was and reinforced my own denial. Our unwillingness to stop massaging our inflated egos fed into denying the seriousness of the disease. Although I was experiencing the insidiousness of the disease, I did not recognize I was being adversely affected. I had yet to learn that everyone emotionally connected with an alcoholic develops behavioral changes. How can anyone think that trying, without success, to adjust repeatedly to un-adjustable behavior is not going to have an adverse affect on them? I was ignorant enough to think so. Based upon my limited exposure to Al-Anon and the memory of the loyal wives still living with professional drunks, I decided learning how to endure long suffering was not for me. Not joining Al-Anon was one of the worst judgment calls I ever made.

Chapter 16

Many restaurants post illustrated instructions on how to perform the Heimlich Maneuver, a procedure used to dislodge food trapped in the windpipe: stand behind the choking person, encircle him with clasped hands and make a sharp upward thrust just under the breastbone. Unless the blockage is removed or an incision made in the trachea, the unfortunate victim suffocates to death. Often this frightening event occurs because the person has had too much to drink and does not take care to put only small amounts of food in the mouth and/or does not take time to chew the food well before swallowing.

Harry frightened me several times by seeming to choke, but he always continued to breathe because the chunk of half-chewed food lodged in his esophagus, the food canal between the mouth and the stomach.

On a wintry evening, almost a year to the day he had me rush him to the hospital, I hurried home from the office to complete preparations for expected dinner guests and walked in to find Harry drunk. He informed me he had been drinking "all afternoon," "most of the day," and "a lot." I wanted to call our guests and cancel but Harry would not hear of it. He said he had been into my old journals again, and again he claimed he had read all of them. He told me that my old boyfriend, Nick, whom I dated just before Steve and I became officially engaged, had phoned three times. When the phone rang and I answered, Nick said a man had called his home earlier and left a message with his wife for him to call Donna and given my number. Nick wondered if Steve

118

were in the area which was not a thought to promote peace of mind. I played dumb and went along with the Steve hypothesis knowing only Harry could have placed the call.

Harry denied calling Nick and then admitted he had and said he hoped it had hurt Nick's wife.

"Why would you want to hurt her?" I asked.

"Because you did."

Harry was all mixed up. Back when Nick and I dated, we were both single.

Five minutes after Harry and I sat down at the table with our guests, he left the table for the bathroom where he threw up in the sink what little he'd swallowed but not chewed except for the something that was still stuck in his gullet. He swallowed water but the water came back up. I tried the Heimlich Maneuver which was useless because the obstruction was in the esophagus, not the trachea. He said, "I'm scared." With his approval, I phoned the police who arrived at once, appraised the situation and radioed for an ambulance. Their concern was valid: in his drunken condition, the food might come back up and be aspirated, sucked into the windpipe, and then there would be trouble. I followed the ambulance; alone in the car, I vented, mostly about Harry's obsession with my journals. At the hospital the ER doctor did not anesthetize Harry because, "He has enough in him." A solution of meat tenderizer was prepared which Harry was told to sip, but that came back up. A tube was inserted verifying the canal was blocked by food. The doctor administered the Heimlich Maneuver. Harry moaned. "You have just broken my ribs." Indeed, subsequent X-rays proved this to be correct. After hours in ER with no change, Harry was admitted; minor surgery was scheduled in the morning when he could tolerate anesthesia. Harry insisted I call one of his doctor friends who told me this had happened before because of too much booze and added, "He's such a great guy." I thought that yes, he is when he's sober, but when he's drunk, he isn't worth shit.

After midnight, I returned to the apartment. Our dinner guests had cleaned up the kitchen, washed all the dishes and put away the food. I wrote for a long time in my journal:

Earlier Harry said he doesn't see how he can make love to me any more, how I was in love with Craig and Steve and I can't ever love him as much. This relationship stinks. He said he feels I was used, made a patsy of, and I ask myself: what the hell is he doing to me? Because I believe anything and everything happens for the best and because this pattern keeps repeating ad nauseam, I ask: is it to demonstrate to Harry, graphically, that he must not drink? Or is it to demonstrate

119

it would be folly for us to marry? Maybe it's both. I have no desire, nor need, to cripple myself by knowingly becoming the wife of an out-of-control, non-reformed alcoholic. I have no wish to put in tenure a la his former wife—and I thought she had no self-discipline!

I'm at my wit's end. Tonight Harry said he wants out. Then immediately he said that wasn't true. Maybe out would be best for us both. I've loved him, loved being with him, but this seesaw is turning into a millstone. I have no desire to attend Al-Anon meetings for the rest of my life and be a brave (!) masochist. This situation stinks out loud. Either Harry (and I, too, perhaps) get counseling or else I'd better make other living arrangements. I am damn glad to be here alone right now. When Harry is drunk, or when he's into stinkin' thinkin' while technically sober, my energy is drained. No wonder I'm so inefficient at the office. It's a wonder I accomplish anything. He phoned me at the office to tell me he didn't want to lay any anxiety on me but he'd noticed something on the floor sticking out from my desk; it was an 8 x 10 glossy of Mark (a theater friend). Bullshit, he didn't want to cause me anxiety! Bullshit, he just happened to notice! Shades of Brad! Shades of Steve! Neither of them wanted me to do anything independent of them. What is this possessiveness crap?

I'm disgusted. I love Harry and yet I don't. I guess his actions are eroding my love. Brad's did. Steve's did. I might never know anyone who would give me more love than Harry, but the grief is beginning to eclipse the love. He says, "I'm trying." What is he trying? He's not trying to accept my right to a personal life prior to meeting him. He's not trying to understand his own origins of insecurity. He's not trying to remain sober. He's not trying to give me emotional security. I don't want to live in this kind of a mess. Why should I? Why do I? Am I afraid of hurting Harry? Is he concerned about hurting me? Hell no, he isn't. He throws up my past personal life to me continuously.

I'm truly sorry he's in pain. He brought it on himself. He can't drink.

I've had all the pseudo love I need with Brad, Steve, and Craig. I am a real sick cookie if I tolerate any more of this. Well, at least the entry before this said happy words. Last weekend with Harry was beautiful. He was sober.

We're in full moon. Oh whoopee, whoopee shit.

I have that awful dead feeling inside. I've given my love to Harry, and evidently he doesn't want it. He wants some other kind of love—a nurse-mother figure? Makes me sick that he called Nick and who knows who else. How terrible of him to invade other people's privacy; bad enough he's violated mine repeatedly.

What am I to learn from all this? I feel it's time I consider myself before I consider Harry. I don't want to live like this, not now, not ever again. I've put in my time and then some on this same miserable lesson.

By morning Harry was able to swallow. Whatever had been stuck had moved down to where it belonged. Before I drove to pick him up, I turned again to my journal:

I feel much less angry this morning than I did during the night, but there's still that dead patch within me. I remember how I used to start in all over again after each one of Steve's tantrums and redevelop some sense of love, trust, positive expectancy, only to be disappointed—and worse—again. I must not subject myself to this maddening pattern of being loved and being hated, of trusting and being betrayed. I know Harry is not responsible for his actions when he drinks or is on a dry drunk but I am always responsible. I don't have the same luxury of escaping my responsibilities through incompetency and the downright craziness brought on by booze or a dry drunk. I harbor deep resentments. Why does he persist in wanting to destroy our relationship? He isn't trying to preserve it. At the moment my feelings towards him are not as they should be. And that makes me feel lousy.

After I brought Harry home, we talked and napped. That night I wrote:

After lunch I told him I needed to talk with him. I've become an expert at initiating talks. I told him that unless both of us have counseling therapy, our relationship will end. He feels we can solve our own problems. I feel we are too emotionally involved and therefore lack the necessary objectivity. And when the no-sex statement was reissued, I asked, incredulously, "And you think we don't need counseling?" A little later he informed me he was going to have a drink and would sip it. All the Al-Anon objectivity went out the window. I can't stand being with him when he drinks. It's rained since early afternoon, mostly freezing rain, and so I felt really trapped. Besides, where could I go without having to offer an explanation? He ended up having a swig, maybe an ounce, he said.

Inside I went all dead except for the part still alive enough to hurt. God, I am so depressed. Harry asks me to remember all the good times; he claims 90 percent are good, and he feels only a few days overall in a year have been crisis ones. He's wrong. For every day of crisis, there are two additional days, at least, on either side. I am asking myself: how many crises have I caused? Am I at fault because he chose to read my old journals? He now says he read them all which took many, many hours. I feel as if I'm caught up in another tragedy and that it would be tragic of me to stay in it. There must be a positive change for me to remain with Harry. I had enough of the jealousy and possessive scene with Brad and enough of the erratic moods with Steve, and not much sex with either of them. I feel as if I'm in a time machine, and history—variations thereof—is being repeated. Is that my lesson?

By Sunday morning I was back into my journal, recounting and trying to sift through the words to find insight:

I asked Harry how I have contributed directly to the crises. He said I have not in any way. He also said he doesn't like himself very much. On probing, he said he probably never has. He said he doesn't like his looks; doesn't like an alcoholic; and doesn't like anyone who is floundering in his career. He said he respects me. How can he respect me and like me if he doesn't respect or like himself?

Subconsciously I feel Harry wants our arrangement to terminate. His actions say this. If I haven't contributed to the crises, then that means he has created them himself. In bed there's such a distance between us because of his no-sex feelings. I feel as if I'm where I should not be. He said he wishes we would de-emphasize the negative and emphasize the positive. I said I'd done so repeatedly but there had been no positive progress and now I feel it's folly to again sweep the reality under a rug. I will pursue again the need for counseling.

I go in circles re Harry's thinking. He volunteered that he's employing a double standard. He said the only difference between my history and his is that he didn't write his down. He spoke of a sexually stimulating and satisfying affair he had carried on, off and on, for seven years. He said she wanted him to shit or get off the pot but that he wasn't ready to, that he had dug himself too deep a hole—children, financial obligations. I'm in a financial hole, too, and I put myself in one twice before, but a financial hole is preferable to living like this. I should have packed it in a year ago, or last summer, but my positive attitude (translation: hope) kept me at Harry's side.

He's asked me to consider all the good times and the fact he has a positive attitude towards my family. Repeatedly I have taken all positive factors into consideration but now I've reached the point where they can no longer offset the reality of crises every two to four weeks. As I pointed out to him, Steve didn't mistreat me daily. And now that Harry has thrown in this no-sex thing… Aw come on, Donna, get smart!

The next entry was written later that same Sunday afternoon:

I forced talking again after a practically non-verbal brunch of waffles. He said he will do whatever is necessary to get his thinking in order and at same time to have our relationship continue. He has agreed to counseling. He said that although he is not aware on the conscious or subconscious levels of not wanting us to continue, he said the surface manifestations would indicate he is pointing out exit signs to me and to himself. He said he didn't know what he'd do if we parted; that under no circumstances would he return to his former wife; that he'd either lose himself in work or booze but doubted it would be booze; that there's no one else, not even in fantasies. I said he'd do as I would—go on.

He asked me if I love him. I told him I don't know, that I suppose I do. He's dragged so much of the past into the present, talked so disparagingly of my former friends, and belittled my acceptance of their statements that I'm all confused. I need counseling now as much as he does.

I feel as if I'm in a prolonged period of shock. Reality can do that. I feel as if I must be guarded now with Harry as a means of my self-protection, self-preservation. Why does he resent me? Why does he treat me now as have Liz, David, Brad, and Steve? What is this love-hate stuff all about? How do I affect the people I love to make them love and hate me simultaneously? What is there about my personality to cause this? Why do people I love, or have loved, resent me? Do these people resent the goodness I see in them which they are unable to live up to? I have many questions concerning myself. Why do I deliberately continue to expose myself to being rejected by those I love? With my immediate family, I am powerless to walk away. Am I masochistic? No, I'm not because I loathe being unhappy. Is my patience a cross I need to bear? This journal is a log of patience in action.

Chapter 17

Harry must have devoted great chunks of time to reading my journals. For me to read one slim volume, and much I skimmed, took me almost two hours. From his remarks, it was apparent he neglected to keep events in context—whether or not I was married, what was happening at home—because he singled out the sexually intimate moments and ignored everything else. I was reminded of a comment Grammie made to Mother years earlier about the Boston-banned novel, *Forever Amber:* "That's a terrible book Donna's reading. I opened it to several different places and in every place the same thing was going on." Harry questioned why I traveled three-quarters of the way across the country to spend time with Steve. "You must have loved him more than you love me." I could not understand why he tried to compare such an intangible as love which I thought was impossible and therefore a waste of energy. Sure, I had loved others to varying degrees based upon varying degrees of needs and wants and how I was feeling or reacting at the time. My love for Harry was the quietest and I thought the most mature and realistic, but I began wondering about the basis of my feelings for him. The more he threw up the past to me, the angrier I felt. I tried logic.

"How can you have expected me to be faithful to someone I had yet to meet?" Intellectually he knew I made sense but emotionally he remained somewhere out in left field. "I was divorced. You had affairs from the time you celebrated your second wedding anniversary."

"That was different," Harry said. "I never went to bed with anyone I didn't love. Besides, there weren't that many."

What I heard were double standards. We got nowhere. He arrived home before I did, drank, read my journals, pouted, picked fights with me, drank some more, and went to bed. When he became somewhat sober, he told me that as far as he was concerned, when he drank he became insane. In my journal I wrote:

Who in their right mind wants to live with someone who periodically becomes crazy? Not I.

I told Harry we could not go on unless we had counseling. Through contacts I made, a counselor was found, a personable psychologist on the faculty of a local college who also had a small private practice. I took pains to find someone who others, as well as the counselor himself, assured me had a full understanding of alcoholism. I should have checked out Harvey Dowd's credentials with an alcoholism clinic or council because my choice turned out to be another error in judgment which cost us dearly, over and above his fee. Social workers and therapists who are trained according to traditional psychology are effective with defined neuroses but when the nuances of alcoholism and/or other drug addictions are present, traditional counseling can do more harm than good. Bottom line: for any talk therapy to be productive, the client must be honest. An active alcoholic is incapable of telling the truth; even after a few years of total abstinence, he/she may think he/she is being fully truthful but the odds are the need to protect one's self remains. It is not uncommon for wives of alcoholics to be treated for depression through indiscriminate dispensing of prescription drugs. One young mother, divorced from an alcoholic, was prescribed first one tranquilizer, then a second and third to take simultaneously. Eventually she committed herself to a detoxification unit where she kicked one drug at a time and earned the wrath of the prescribing psychiatrist. I've heard other dreadfully similar stories and I am outraged, repeatedly, by misguided professionals who masquerade as Doctor God.

Two weeks into counseling, following one joint session with Harvey Dowd and a private hour between Harry and Harvey, I wrote:

I am experiencing another growth period in my love for Harry. We are both working at making our relationship consistently healthy, and we have outside help. During our initial joint session, I think Harry may have felt somewhat threatened because of the attempt I made to present my feelings, observations, and recounting of events in as unemotional a manner as possible. I doubt we'll have a long term need of counseling but it's OK if we do. We are now into our second week of contentment, devoid of any traumas.

125

Harvey Dowd explored Harry's childhood, trying to draw inference from the fact he was a soundly spoiled youngest child, and the only boy, and that there were few signs of touching in his family. Any guilt and fears I had concerning my children's lifestyles and my future with Harry were dismissed with the advice I cleave unto Harry. Dowd's intentions were honorable but his limited knowledge of alcoholism may have contributed to prolonging our suffering. Like many of his peers, Dowd had bought into the experiments in behavior modification conducted with alcoholics. He also espoused another study referred to as "The Rand Report" which, in effect, stated that alcoholism can be cured provided the psychological power of an identified catalyst is removed which had caused the need of the alcoholic to escape overwhelming feelings through alcohol abuse. Once freed, Dowd continued, alcoholics can become normal, social drinkers. Because I believed Dowd's credentials for counseling alcoholics were impeccable, I swallowed his theory. Harry and I singled out Lenora, his former wife, as the catalyst because she acted out her bitterness in hostile ways, such as through attempts to alienate their children from their father. In line with Dowd's adopted theory, once the emotional dust settled from the divorce, Harry would be a cured alcoholic. (Much later after prolonged exposure to Harry's alcoholic behavior and I had expanded my knowledge of the disease and how it affects the family, the anger I felt towards his former wife was replaced by compassion for what she had endured and the sincere hope she and the children would break through the denial about how they were affected and seek help.) Harry had spent enough time in AA to know there was no known cure for alcoholism, nor a consensus on what causes alcoholism in one out of nine drinkers but not in the other eight. In my presence, Harry got what he wanted: official permission to go on drinking. Five weeks into counseling, he resumed heavy drinking. I painted this picture in my journal:

Another plummet on the seesaw. My head goes in circles—again. I feel I am less the object of Harry's love and more an obsession with him, that he wants to possess me. I am back to walking on eggshells just as I was with Brad and Steve. This morning Harry told me, supposedly sober but still manifesting some of his drinking quirks, that I have no idea how much anxiety I cause him by things I tell him about. For example, the man at the Civic Center who mistakenly used the ladies room when I was there; the workmen at the health club when I and other women were measured and tested. I remarked it is becoming increasingly obvious that I must censor what I choose to tell him. He said I mustn't do that because then the relationship would end. But if I share openly with him, I put what he calls "anxiety trips" on him. So I'm damned if I do and damned if I don't. Although he apologized this morning for his behavior last evening, he continued in almost as belligerent and hostile a manner as last night. Because of his eyes and a couple expressions he used which now I recognize accompany drinking, I believe he drank during the hour he was out this morning, which he denied, but he cross hatches accounts of alcohol consumption to me with one contradiction after another.

Counseling an alcoholic who is actively drinking is a waste of time because he is going to protect his need to drink at all costs. Therefore, he cannot be honest which is why many psychiatrists have written off alcoholics as hopeless. On the two occasions I contacted Dowd after we stopped seeing him, he stated that Harry was a pathological liar.

The issues remain the same—my previous relationships, my doing anything other than working and/or visiting my family without him, and I'm not so sure about that, either. He can't see why I have to make a "cause celebre" out of his drinking, that yesterday was yesterday and today is today. I said that means it's OK for him to call the shots and then Donna just trudges along obediently. He said, "You have a point there."

Last night when he was so verbally abusive, telling me I didn't know what I had done to him the past few days while I was away on a business trip, I asked why he was punishing me. Today when I phoned Dowd for an extra appointment, his comment was, "He's punishing his mommy for going away and leaving him. Alcoholics have very dependent personalities." Harry was not happy I called Dowd. He said I've always needed help from someone. He cited my inability to sustain a relationship since divorce, even with my kids.

I am depressed—again. Each time this happens, I sink lower faster. The contrast between my life with Harry when he's sober and when not drinking/drunk is like day and night. He contends I want euphoria all the time. How untrue! I'm no longer a romantic girl. I deal with realities. I am willing to make concessions, compromises, but I feel as if he has me on a leash, complete with muzzle.

Harry said he was no longer thinking about yesterday but of our marriage, when and where, our future home. I don't know if our marriage is being postponed indefinitely—yes, I know it is because I will not incorporate these problems into a marriage contract. He said that while he was thinking about marriage, I was probably thinking about the next man in my life. How wrong! If the relationship with Harry can't be pulled together into something consistently healthy, then I cannot foresee any man in my life, not with the luck I've had.

Recently the big, beautiful house had sold, and Mother, Liz and the baby moved into an apartment. I no longer had an escape hatch.

A small apartment just for me would be fine, and I'd work during working hours for others and then during my own time, I would indulge my interests at a typewriter. Sure I might accept social invitations, but the idea of a boyfriend and sexual relations turns me cold. I don't want to be encumbered with the far-reaching responsibility of augmenting someone's happiness. I called Dowd today because I needed beneficial feedback. I can't talk with family or friends because their responses would be, "Get out of a relationship with an alcoholic."

The following demonstrates how wrong my impression was of Al-Anon:

I refuse to attend Al-Anon because they advocate ignoring the alcoholism and creating a life of one's own. If I did that, I'd be sentencing my life with Harry to falseness, and he'd be more disturbed if I resumed my independence.

And I muddled on, getting deeper and deeper into my bottomless well of self-pity:

I feel like chattel and I despise the feeling. Harry seemed pleased to tell me today he'd been drinking and then pointed out how he vacuumed. Last night he grudgingly acknowledged he'd been drinking and then made a big deal out of preparing dinner. It was like he was saying, "I'm a naughty boy but see how good I can be, too."

Had I been attending Al-Anon, I would have learned that by making an issue out of his drinking, I was giving him an excuse to justify his drinking. I was helping him to kill himself.

Some days Harry phoned me several times at the office, happy calls, and I looked forward to getting home. One day I found beautiful flowers in the hallway outside our door and then walked in to find Harry in happy tears. Then I realized he had been drinking and my happiness sank to my feet and through the floor.

I suddenly felt so awful, so betrayed, that I refused his commands for me to nap. Then, a bundle of hurt and confused thoughts, he ordered me to go to bed. I asserted myself about taking a bath first, and he insisted upon washing me. All I wanted was to be left alone to soak. Then he refused to let me put on a pajama top and insisted upon rubbing me with blended oils—too hard, hurting and insisting he wasn't hurting me. When he drinks, he is not gentle, and I feel awful. I hated myself for feeling as if I were at his drunken mercy, knowing (or feeling) I couldn't go anyplace for refuge. I was filled with loathing and contempt of him and myself. I felt trapped. Finally he left me, and I went to sleep only to be awakened by him about an hour later, tugging and pulling at me because he wanted to hold me. Shit! So he got angry and left but came back, got into bed, left me alone and went to sleep. We were two strangers in a bed that has been warmed by our love and chilled by our hostility too many times.

His statements today included that heretofore he's been willing to take 95 percent of the blame but now he'll take 65 percent. I did not create the alcoholic! I did not create his low self-image! I did not create his dependency on me! Therefore, it seems to me I need to rely upon myself to maintain as best as possible, my sense of perspective. Long ago I learned that self-reliance is the answer, to wit, me and God. So, why did I run to Dowd on the phone? A stopgap measure, help for restoring this fucked up relationship to at least a quasi-healthy basis until it can become truly healthy? Or was I acting out the role of a victim? Or a combination of both?

Harry contends I left my old journals around because I wanted him to read them, so that he'd accept me regardless, so I could start off with him with a clean slate. I suppose there might be some truth to that. It might also be that rather than testing his love for me I was testing whether or not I can have personal privacy with him. I've thought again about removing the journals, boxing them, storing them at Liz's. But why should I have to? Am I to protect him against himself in order to protect us? That seems stupid to me and very false.

Why does he get so upset about sexual experiences I had with others when I don't get upset with his? Why does he write off, in effect, his continuous infidelities while married and sit in judgment of my affairs when I was single? Is sex dirty to him?

Dowd suggested I wrap a chain and padlock around the journals. I did but it was like locking the barn door after the horse had been stolen. If I mentioned any man I had once known, Harry asked me if I had fooled around with him. I became so disgusted with his obsession about my sex life before I met him that I told him to just assume I had slept with every man I ever knew regardless of their age, marital status, or whether or not they were relatives—anyone, including cab drivers, animal trainers, my kids' teachers—in short, all men. On a business trip when I was bumped in Indianapolis because of bad weather and along with the other passengers I spent hours in the airport, I mentioned that another passenger bought me a drink. Harry said that was being unfaithful to him. He speculated about what if the man had put something in my drink. He said that in all his years of business travel and being stranded, he never asked a woman to have a drink. I wondered how truthful he was and furthermore, I wondered if he were projecting his guilt as an unfaithful husband onto me. I rose to the bait. I pointed out I was hardly an innocent young thing but someone who had traveled, often alone, and met all walks of people, that I am gregarious and talk to strangers but only within what I feel are controlled situations. I recounted that a good friend had once remarked I was the only person he knew who carried on conversations with toll booth attendants. Harry said I had to be careful because they might take the conversation as an invitation and trace the car's registration.

Harry went on another bender while we were still seeing Dowd. On Friday morning when he could hold no more, he told me to cancel our plans to spend a spring weekend with friends on Cape Cod. I thought I would go anyway but Dowd, who had responded to a call from Harry for an immediate appointment, phoned me at the office. He told me Harry really needed me, that he was hurting terribly. For me to have gone ahead with my plans was the correct decision; by remaining with Harry, I helped ease the pain of his drinking. He belonged in a detoxification unit but he made arrangements for us to spend the weekend by ourselves on the Rhode Island coast where he was not only lovingly attentive but sexually passionate. Drinking did not seem to impair Harry's ability; in fact, it seemed to enhance his ardor.

In recent years I had amassed knowledge about the benefits of optimum nutrition and I was aware of specific nutrients depleted by alcohol abuse. I prided myself on getting Harry back on his feet quicker than a professional detoxification center. (How's *that* for ego!) And I waited for the magic moment when he would no longer be driven to drink excessively by the so-called identified catalyst. I might just as well have been waiting for Godot.

Harry made it through the summer without any major benders. I took on renewed hope. But on a fall trip to San Francisco that included a drive through Napa Valley and visits to several wineries, Harry sampled the wines, and his personality changed. He thought our week on the West Coast with excursions to Monterey, Carmel and Big Sur—and wine at lunch and dinner—was wonderful. I felt like I was vacationing with a time bomb.

But there were some nutty fun moments, such as the evening we dined at a small French restaurant in Monterey-by-the-Sea. The interior was starkly elegant—less than a dozen tables, polished floor, chalk white linen, and a full complement of heavy tableware. The atmosphere was calculated to impart exclusiveness but we saw calculated pseudo-poshness. Only three tables had customers. Best behavior influenced by phoniness was too much for me. Between courses, I slowly and quietly said to Harry, "I have an irresistible urge to dip my finger in this butter," which I did as I spoke, "and then to place it on your nose like this," which I did, right down the center.

Harry's expressions did not change. He spoke in a slow, low voice, "That is interesting because I, too, have an irresistible urge to dip my finger in this butter," which he did, "and place the butter on your nose like that," which he did. There we sat with butter smeared on our noses from the bridge to the tip. Neither of us smiled.

I spoke, still in a low voice, "I now have the desire to dip my finger in this butter again," which I did, "and to ..."

But I never did because two tables away, a couple who appeared to be in their sixties and perhaps from the Midwest, unbeknown to us had observed our foolishness. The woman said, with mock seriousness, "If you two children don't behave, we shall have to send you to your room." Harry and I burst out laughing; they laughed. We cleaned off our noses. And the four of us agreed the restaurant was pompously boring.

After we returned home, Harry announced that he could drink California wine with no problem. Within a month he was going through 18 proof cream sherry like it was soda pop—his other drink. The verbal abuse resumed. He phoned me mid-afternoon at the office to ask me several times if I was all right. His voice struck alarms in me but I knew he had been fighting a bug, so I figured that was what I heard. I arrived home to find him in bed. He moaned and I went to him. Later I wrote:

I am so stupid, so blind! All signs indicated drunkenness but I couldn't believe he'd drink. He said he'd had one glass of wine. Later he amended that to three or four "and one more swallow than I could handle." Sarcastically he told me about all the bottles he drained and threw out into the trash bin. This is a double heartbreaker because he was so sure he had overcome the problem, removed the catalyst. He's had his divorce since March, but I decided to postpone marriage plans until the water remains smooth for a full year. Is it that he can go no more than five or six months without alcohol? He so wanted to believe he could handle wine. He could, if he'd be moderate.

There was so much about alcoholism I did not know! A heavy drinker may be able to cut back without succumbing to out-of-control drinking but an alcoholic can never, ever drink safely.

He was very angry and defensive with me. I asked him what the catalyst was this time. He said it would be me if I continued talking the way I was. While I was in the bathroom, he left at 8 o'clock, an hour ago. This is a miserable night, rain and wind. I wish I knew whether or not he's coming home tonight. It's creepy not knowing. I dread it if he does. I'm supposed to leave when he does this but I resent spending money on a motel room when I pay half the rent. I can't keep bouncing back from his moods. Every time there's a crisis, he kills off some of my love for him. Just when I start to feel happy towards him again, after a healing interval, he gets ticked about something or other. And so it goes.

Harry returned at two in the morning. I had left a note on the floor inside the front door. "You left. Please bed down on daybed. Thank you."

He wrote a retort: "Know why I left? You are abrasive!" I responded by jotting this comment: "As good a copout as any other."

He was out of bed less than two hours that day. He could not eat more than a few swallows of soup and half a piece of toast. He said his throat hurt, that he had a terrible headache and ached all over. I wrote:

I don't know if he's ill from a bug or alcohol. How can he sleep so much? Is he sodden? Is he genuinely ill with a virus? I don't want to take over where his former wife left off—a nursemaid to a drunk who ran around. God only knows where he was for five hours last night. I don't like feeling I'm being played for a chump. Tonight in the mirror, I looked haggard again just as I did when I was having so much trouble with Liz and David. I'm disgusted and losing respect fast for myself.

After he sobered up, I let Harry know I was seriously considering moving out and why:

I covered a lot of territory. I told him I did not want to go through another roller coaster type holiday season. I was open, frank, blunt. No more games for this lady. He's a big boy. I am not his protector. I don't believe I ignored any grievance. To err is human; to air is divine!

Harry cut back on his drinking but the mood swings did not stop. Without any rhyme or reason I could detect—because there was none?—he zinged me with sarcastic barbs. Compared to what the previous weeks were like, our time together seemed like heaven. I refused to recognize the progression of the disease. I did a good job at it, too, because early in January, I wrote:

I am pleased to note that the holidays went well; I experienced the most continuous happiness with Harry yet. I have felt close to him and very much in love with him. He remarked he's been feeling particularly close and in love with me. I have more positive than negative thoughts about marriage. If this closeness endures, then marriage will be a natural event.

Living in an apartment complex became too confining for us. Each of us had been homeowners for more than 25 years, and the restrictions of an apartment grated. We found a unique home for New England—a flat roof, no cellar, contemporary redwood ranch shaped somewhat like a boomerang, set on two secluded acres with beautiful views of the Berkshire foothills. The interior with its redwood paneling, brick and glass gave us esthetic pleasure. There were two bedrooms at opposite ends of the house; one would double as Harry's office. He wanted not to have a laundry ("because if Liz has problems with her washer, she'll come here") but instead to turn the oversized, pine-paneled utility room into my office, which is where I wrote the first draft of this manuscript. The price was right; I used the money from the sale of my house as the down payment.

There is no record in my journal of the following event, and that in itself is significant. I became confused enough to think I could demonstrate my total commitment to Harry and our upcoming marriage by destroying all my old journals. Surely such an act of sacrifice would give Harry comfort and put an end to his snide, jealous remarks. I removed the chain and padlock and tore the pages from their bindings and then into small pieces. In the apartment's cellar storage bin, I dug out others from packing cartons Harry had not discovered, leafed through the pages, randomly read passages, and tore them apart. I threw all those bits and pieces of my life into the dumpster. I refused to permit myself to feel anything. But now when I write this, if I were to draw myself, I'd color myself gray; and between the shoulders and the pubic bone, there would not be a solid torso but a hole, like a donut. Finally, 25 years later, I can let myself weep. And curse.

Chapter 18

On an April afternoon in their apartment, Liz married Mike, the father of her second child. She had turned 21 a few weeks earlier. They said their vows with tenderness and tears. Liz looked lovely in a soft blue dress, white and blue daisies woven through her long hair, and she carried a matching bouquet. Most amazing of all, she remained in her wedding finery for several hours before changing into corduroys and going barefoot.

The physical self-improvement campaign Harry and I began a year earlier still held in spite of drinking interruptions. I worked out at a health club three mornings each week, and every day we jogged and walked. About six weeks prior to Liz's wedding, we put ourselves on a strict diet—less than 1000 calories—fresh fish, fruit, and many raw vegetables. By her wedding day, we were lean—and hungry. We agreed we would not drink any champagne. Harry threatened he would not attend the wedding because Brad was giving the bride away. Then he said he would attend for only one hour to take pictures. Harry and I did drink champagne on practically empty stomachs and we were the last to leave. We sent out for pizza. The champagne got us tipsy and it humanized Brad. He and Harry had long conversations and discovered they liked each other. Brad and I had a brief, private talk and ended up in tears as we hugged. I felt the past hurts we shared were put to rest as much as possible at that time.

When Harry and I finally left, we were silly, giggly, and flying high. We were in separate cars; I followed him. First he stopped at Baskin Robbins for two giant ice cream cones. The next stop was a package store for champagne, like we really needed more. Harry parked at a seedy looking bar in a small mill town. He said he had driven by the place hundreds of times and wondered if the sign in the window was to be believed: "Exotic Dancers." The trauma of my daughter's wedding was history, and I was as eager as Harry to release pent up energy. Slumming felt like fun. It was also eye-opening; my first exposure to exotic dancing. I condensed our 40 minutes in the bar this way:

Exotic? Sure, if cellulite cells are in and class is out. But, amusing.

Next we went to a disco lounge, another first, where I talked the proprietor out of socking us with a cover charge. We ordered wine but never touched it. Instead we danced non-stop, actively and inventively, for over an hour. We were the oldest people there by at least 20 years; we got a kick out of the young adults who danced no more than 15 minutes before taking a rest. In spite of all the champagne, I did not work up a sweat which I attributed to the aerobic dancing I was used to doing. The strobe lights and monotonous beat became boring, and we left to find a place with a live combo that played a variety of music, from swing through rock and disco. We could not remember where, in the huge parking lot that also served a large shopping center, we had parked the car. The more we hunted, the more hilarious the situation became. I suggested Harry go one way and I the other. We found the car. The next lounge several miles up the expressway was too jammed with people to stay. By then it was after midnight, and we were starved. Off we went to a Chinese restaurant where we could not decide on a choice. We made it simple and ordered their dinner for two. The egg drop soup was a godsend. Whatever we ate in between that and the coconut ice cream tasted fine. At an all-night convenience store, Harry bought a pint of honey ice cream which we enjoyed devouring after we got into bed. In my journal I wrote:

We have no idea what time we got home. Sunday we dragged our way through the first welcome day of Daylight Saving Time and laughed about our good time the day and night before. We're still enjoying it. We earned the private party, our good time together, our silliness. I have marvelous fun with Harry when he isn't being a pain in the neck which, fortunately, is becoming more and more rare. So now that we've passed papers on our own home, we are planning our move and at the same time, making plans for our wedding day.

I did not write in my journal again until mid-December, eight months later.

Chapter 19

Our whirl with the champagne and the breaking of our diet did not set a precedent. We resumed eating healthful foods and abstained from liquor. The fact that the champagne binge did not set Harry off on a drinking spree proved to me Harvey Dowd had been correct: Harry's alcoholic drinking was no more since the catalyst's vindictiveness had calmed down. I anticipated that long-desired ride into the sunset—first the move into our exquisite hideaway followed in six weeks by our wedding. We would be married on the third anniversary of the day we met.

In his eagerness to secure a divorce, Harry not only depleted his financial holdings in lieu of alimony but agreed to a child support agreement which, according to Harry, was the equivalent to many people's annual income. The down payment for the house came from the last of the proceeds from the sale of my house. Harry determined it would be financially prudent not to hire professionals but to rent a truck and hire some young men to help us move. Liz helped me with the small stuff, and we made several trips with loaded cars. Harry made three trips with the truck and both were loaded—the truck and Harry. Rather than move the liquor, he drank it. According to the Holmes-Rahe stress scale which rates the degree of social readjustment required following such events as divorce (73), marriage (50), and buying a house (31), Harry had earned a cumulatively high stress score. His excuse for drinking was that he hated the process of moving and the best way to get through it was to be smashed. I assigned all three to "temporary catalyst" status and wove them into the fabric of my denial that a real drinking problem existed. Harry drank heavily for almost three weeks until, as usual, he could not down any more booze and keep it down. His hostility towards me increased and intensified. I knew I should cancel the wedding plans. But how would I feel about our joint ownership of real property without being married? The thought scared me because if anything happened to Harry, what kind of a mess would I be in? So I let financial security take precedence over emotional stability and nursed Harry through the days and nights of detoxification. Loving tranquility resumed. We worked in the yard during daylight and puttered around the house after sunset. There was no drinking. Three weeks before the wedding, I mailed invitations to immediate family and close friends. Even a small at-home wedding required attention to many details. We were busy and happy.

My dear friend Martha and her new husband Joe flew in the day before the wedding from their home in Texas. We met them at the airport with chilled champagne and drank socially that evening without incident. Harry's delightful disposition was enhanced by their company and the martinis. I was disappointed, however, that just before our two o'clock ceremony, Harry had a drink. "I was nervous," he said. So was I: Liz was detained at the hairdresser's and arrived several minutes late in a breathless, apologetic whirl with cornbraided hair. The same Justice of the Peace who officiated at Liz and Mike's wedding conducted our ritual with dignity and warmth. Harry and I incorporated much of our own writing and favorite Biblical passages into an otherwise traditional ceremony. A simple reception followed—plenty of champagne, shrimp, raw vegetables for assorted dips, beautiful cookies made by Harry's sister, and a wedding cake of rectangular tiers I designed and baked and that Liz and my son's girl, Laura, decorated. With the exception of Harry's two oldest children (the other four chose not to attend) everyone seemed to enjoy the festivities. Although I respected his daughters' loyalty to their embittered mother, I did not know and therefore could not appreciate then the depths of their other feelings.

Two days later after saying goodbye to Martha and Joe, Harry and I headed for a brief honeymoon on Cape Cod Bay. The weather was glorious; we swam, sunned, made friends with a lively couple, and continued to party daytimes with champagne and before dinner with martinis. All was bliss.

Two weeks later, Harry turned on me. He resurrected his jealous talk about men he had read about in my journals while standing on the very spot where we said our marriage vows, in front of the brick fireplace wall. I was furious. After he went to bed in a drunken snit, I decorated the fireplace wall with a dozen pieces of 8½ by 11 paper on which, with bold magic marker, I quoted him. The language was foul. Once I had spent most of my anger, I got into the far side of the king bed. In the morning Harry took down the "crazy decorations." Two weeks later after another eruption brought on by alcohol abuse, I wrote this to Harry:

To my husband,

I am tired, tense, but otherwise rather numb. These outbursts of yours are sharp, uncalled for, undeserved, unbecoming to you and insulting to me. I refer to last evening circa eight o'clock, when after approximately six hours of steady drinking, you informed me: "I'm pissed at you. Fuck off!"

I am disgusted with your return to alcoholic drinking. Yes, that is the way you drank yesterday. And your seven o'clock martini was a throat burner. Then you had the gall to tell me that the soda was soda and ice only, that you had started to pour vodka into the glass but changed your mind because you decided you'd had enough. Such a statement made me think I hadn't observed you correctly, but when you left the room, a quick taste of the "soda only" verified I had seen and heard correctly. That soda was loaded.

And so were you.

Again—oh again!—I will tell you that when you have exceeded your metabolizing limit and start feeling sexy, making overt or thinly disguised sexual advances to me, I am totally turned off by your touch. This is a fact, and it is unchangeable. Sharing a bed with you under such conditions is a revolting experience for me. You thrash, swear, and your breath reeks of vodka. The entire room stinks of it.

When you are drunk, I can only do my best of tolerate you. I withdraw because I do not care at all for the person you change into. After a certain point, you are not the happy, loving drunk you like to think you are. You are obnoxious.

Last night was the second time in seven days you have lost control and turned on me. This time I had the good sense not to attempt—vainly—to reason with you. When you lose control, you exemplify the contempt which pervades the expression, "fragile male ego." Your ego is quite healthy when you are sober and/or in control but otherwise you behave like someone who has no ego —— like a bully.

The aftermath of another episode is compounded today: I wonder in what condition you'll be upon your return today. This is a lousy way to spend a day—and all of last night.

You can drink normally, but it's up to you. You have the power to exercise self-control if you want to. To hell with the theory about the needing of an outside catalyst. The catalyst is within you.

I have tried to point out to you how to drink normally. How dumb of me to try!

Your progression the past three weeks to drinking stronger and bigger and bigger and more drinks has played hell with my feelings. This lightheadedness of mine is directly related to emotional stress.

You need to ask yourself some tough questions and then shut up and listen to the answers. To wit: why do you want to undermine our relationship——our marriage, for God's sake——and if left to continue like this, to destroy it? Because as sure as I'm sitting here, totally frustrated, that's what will happen. You are unrealistic if you think I can survive and continue to respect myself in a schizoid scenario. You could create a point in time when it will be redundant of you to tell me to, "Fuck off!

This letter signals that I was beginning to waver between accepting what therapist Harvey Dowd told us and what I had read in AA and Al-Anon publications. I was on target when I wrote, "The catalyst is within you," but I was deluding myself to think Harry could drink normally——"but it's up to you. You have the power to exercise self-control if you want to." This is what an active alcoholic does not have——self-control, the ability to drink normally.

The stage was set, the props were all in place; the script was old and worn. And in the tradition of both the theater and alcoholism, the show went on. And on.

Chapter 20

My letter may have helped in a negative sense to provide Harry with collateral for borrowing time: he managed to control his drinking and outbursts. I was ready to buy back into the catalyst theory.

Labor Day arrived and with it the unspoken farewells to summer. Neither of us cared about battling holiday traffic; besides, our home was as serene as any destination we might afford. Our perspective changed when we received an invitation to attend what was billed as the annual neighborhood picnic. That conjured up hectic, brittle scenes of adults determined to have a good time, laughing and whining kids of all ages, and a lot of pesky dogs. How could we stay home and avoid the party without sending the message we did not care to become friendly with everyone within hollering distance. We stewed for days until Saturday morning when we located a motel on the Rhode Island shore with a vacancy, packed and headed out.

We spent the afternoon on a favorite beach—a couple miles long, no concession stands or bathhouses, not at all commercial and never crowded. Hours later we returned to the motel to shower, dress for dinner, and enjoy a mayonnaise jar of martinis that Harry mixed before we left home. Following a mediocre dinner at an overpriced restaurant, we drove into town for an ice cream. Because the night was wonderfully warm, we decided to return to the beach for a quick swim. We changed into jeans and sweatshirts, period. Our swim would be in the nude.

Swimming in the ocean was out of the question because the surf was too high. We walked back through the dunes to a large salt pond. The night was black, almost no stars. As we shed our clothes and placed them in a neat pile, I looked across the pond to lighted cottages and took a fix, using three lights, so we would be able to find our clothes. Then we waded into the warm water which was just inches deep for 30 feet and did not reach waist high until we were 100 feet from shore. With each step, our feet stirred up phosphorus, and with each exuberant outburst from Harry, I cautioned him to keep his voice down.

"Haven't you ever been skinny dipping before?" I asked him.

"No, not with a girl."

"You're kidding!"

He was a quick study, and we laughed and fondled each other, swam lazily, kissed, swam a little more and all the time I kept reminding Harry to be quiet, that voices traveled easily across water. We enjoyed the silkiness of the water on our nude bodies for some time and then made the long return wade to shore. We literally could not see our hands before our face. I looked across the pond for the three lights but they had been turned off. We walked along the narrow ribbon of sand searching for our clothes. I suggested we walk in opposite directions. I walked with my head down for several feet and stopped. I sensed something ahead. But there was nothing. I took another few steps when suddenly, directly in front of me, a flashlight blinded me and a man's deep, husky voice said, "Welllllll....hel-LO there!"

I wheeled and ran into the pond, the flashlight following me. Frustrated because the water came only half way to my knees, I flopped down on my stomach. The voice behind the flashlight, now crisp and authoritative, said, "Come out of the water. I'm a police officer."

I would have quicker believed him had he said, "I'm a pervert." I said nothing, and he spoke again. "Lady, come out of the water!"

Harry had heard the splashing and a man's voice and, still nude, walked towards the flashlight that beamed out into the water. Harry had severe myopia and without his glasses, which were with our clothes, his vision was extremely limited. Nevertheless, Harry figured I was in trouble, and he was coming to my aid. He walked up to the man and said, "What's the problem?"

The officer swung the flashlight onto Harry in all his natal glory and said, "What's going on here?"

"We went for a swim and can't find our clothes."

Harry, naked as a jay bird, stood almost toe to toe with one of Rhode Island's finest while I remained belly down in less than a foot of water. My bare bottom was above the water line. The flashlight swung from Harry to me and back again, depending upon which one of us the officer was addressing. We were informed we were trespassing, that the area had closed an hour or so earlier, and that he could arrest us for both trespassing and nude swimming.

I've got to hand it to Harry: he was quick on his feet even when naked. He said, "Aw, come on, officer, have a heart. We're on our honeymoon."

"When were you married?"

"Two weeks ago."

I thought, "Oh God, we've been married seven weeks and if they check, they'll add giving false information onto the other charges."

The officer shone the flashlight back on me. "Lady, come out of the water!" I did not budge. He turned back to Harry and said, "Let me see some identification." I wondered how much more identification he needed to see.

"My wallet is with my clothes."

The flashlight shone on me again. "Lady, come out of the water!" I remained still. The officer said to Harry, "I'll help you find your clothes." Our clothing was no more than a couple feet from where they were standing. While Harry pulled on his jeans, the flashlight beamed on me again. "Lady, come out of the water!" He sounded annoyed.

Harry said, "It's okay. Come on out."

The flashlight was on Harry again. "How old are you?"

I thought, "Please, Harry, don't try to pass yourself off as being in your forties." The week before he was not thrilled about celebrating his 52nd birthday.

Harry answered, "I'm 52."

That's when I became righteously indignant. I stood up and declared, "Yes, and I'm almost 50!" and with the flashlight full on me, I strode towards the beach, adding, "And I have two grandchildren!" At the time I thought it was one of my finest moments. Come to think of it, I still do.

I joined Harry, the officer and the damn flashlight. "Lady, get dressed." I didn't move. "Listen, lady, put your clothes on! There are some other officers coming."

"You lower that flashlight, and I will." He did, and I pulled on my jeans and sweatshirt.

Harry said, "I can't find my glasses."

Two other officers came along the beach. "What's going on here?" they asked.

The first officer replied, "He can't find his glasses." So everybody got into the act of hunting for Harry's glasses which Harry found with his foot: he had been standing on them. The two officers disappeared into the blackness, and the first officer escorted us to our car. By then I was oozing dignified charm, anything to prevent him from taking us to the station and booking us. At the car he wished us a lot of happiness, we thanked him, and drove off. Half a mile down the road, we burst out laughing.

"I can't believe that happened," I said, still laughing.

Harry said, "I wondered which one of our kids we'd call to come bail us out," and the irony of having the tables turned sent us into another laughing fit.

I said, "When you owned up to being 52, and I stood up and said I was almost 50 and a grandmother..."

"You were quite a sight."

"Yeah, like Venus rising from the waves."

"I bet that policeman thought he had stumbled onto something he could fool around with because you don't look like a grandmother." I loved Harry a lot for such kind words. I was thankful I had lost weight and toned up at the health club. "I bet they're having a good laugh back at police headquarters."

But none of them could have laughed harder and longer than we did. We laughed going to sleep. We awakened in the night laughing. When we told our kids, especially the boys who knew what it was like to be busted by Rhode Island policemen for sleeping on the beach; they laughed with us. While reconstructing this adventure for these pages, I've laughed. When I was writing the first draft, Harry came to find out why I was laughing; I told him, and he laughed.

I don't know what part, if any, alcohol played in our flirtation with arrest. We had baked in the sun during the afternoon, polished off a mayonnaise jar of martinis before dinner, sipped wine with dinner, then had ice cream cones. Given the same conditions again only without the liquor, I think Harry and I would still have gone skinny dipping in that salt pond after dark, provided we didn't know what we came to know: the area closed after sundown and was police patrolled.

Chapter 21

By the time Christmas carols dominated the air waves, the deterioration in our relationship filled me with dismay. Harry's attempts to control his drinking failed time and again. What helped to keep me going was the health club where every Monday, Wednesday, and Friday mornings I tried to regain my integrity and identity. I drove to the club quickly but poked getting home because I did not know which Harry I would find. Often his gentlemanly manners were replaced by rudeness and crudeness. He seemed to resent me. I thought of advice I received in a private meeting with Harvey Dowd: "Break with him. He's a loser. You have too much on the ball to be saddled with him." I learned it was folly to attempt rational communication with him on any subject, drunk, semi-drunk, or temporarily sober. Most of my opinions I kept to myself to avoid verbal confrontation. He was strongly opinionated, prejudiced, and very negative. Yet he could be loving and kind. He was good to my family but often bad-mouthed them and then always added, "But I love them." I thought he used the word "love" indiscriminately.

The ugliest incident occurred six months after we were married during a pre-Christmas house party hosted by friends. Harry was very drunk before we arrived and continued to swig down vodka martinis. Forty guests milled about the old rambling farmhouse. I was relieved to have Harry wander off and conduct his own socializing. However, I was careful not to chat more than a few minutes with any man because I did not want to precipitate any subsequent jealousy attacks. I was aware of Harry devoting attention to one woman. Eventually I joined them and was surprised to discover she was someone I had known casually years earlier. She threw her arms around me and ignored Harry. Soon he was talking to another unattached woman and after a while, introductions were made. We three women shared common interests and formed a conversational trio. Harry referred to himself as a professional gigolo. We laughed. Harry wandered about. Late evening a guest arrived, a professional pianist, and the party took on new life. I stood by the piano. While growing up, I studied piano but in recent years, seldom played. When the piano player took a break, I sat down and played a little. He returned and joined me on the bench. He resumed playing and I ad-libbed on the upper keys. I felt alive, inventive. I was having fun. I lost track of time until I realized that most guests had left. I thanked the piano player for the good time and joined Harry who was seated on a couch within sight of the piano. He and the host were talking. I felt happy. I smiled at Harry and our host. "That was such fun!" The host, also a musician, made some gracious comments about my playing. I said to Harry, "We're the last ones here. I think it's time to leave before they have to invite us for breakfast."

Harry said, "Why don't you fuck the piano player?"

I was sure I could not have heard him correctly. "What?" I said.

In a louder voice, he said, "Go ahead and fuck the piano player. You know you want to." I wanted to pass off his words like they were a bad joke but Harry continued. "Go on. Fuck the piano player. That's what you want to do. Fuck him!"

In a blur of embarrassment and shame, I retrieved our coats. We thanked our hosts and stepped out into softly falling snow. Halfway to the car, I turned around, re-entered the house, and told the hosts, "I'm sorry. I apologize for what Harry said." The piano player was there, too. "I'm sorry," I said.

The piano player said something like, "That's all right." The host and hostess smiled, and the host said, "Don't worry about it." That was our last invitation to their annual holiday party. Years later I learned that Harry made a pass at the hostess.

Harry drove and launched into an abusive harangue. Among other names, he called me a "cunt." The snowy roads were treacherous. Once I thought he deliberately steered towards an oncoming car. When this happened a second time, I insisted he let me drive. His verbal abuse continued. He dropped a lighted cigarette onto the floor and fumbled to retrieve it. I stopped the car. He could not find the cigarette. He opened the door, got out, and turned around. He bent over and collapsed on his knees, his face on the floor of the

145

car. He said, "I can't get up."

I was engorged with fury. I commanded him, "GET UP!" He crawled back onto the seat.

The following day we had separate family commitments and did not see each other until he returned at 6:30 pm, drunk and carrying a pizza. I continued eating the dinner I had prepared for us and went to bed. An hour later I got up. He was writing a note to me. He said he had not finished. I went back to bed and soon thereafter heard him leave. His note said:

To my Donna—
I love you!
But, I can't stand the poison
Love —
I'll be back
Sometime!
s/H.
P.S. Must have time to myself!

This was one in a series of inebriated, exclamation point scrawls. Operating on only a total of 14 hours sleep in three nights, which was about par during his drinking bouts, I had no difficulty falling asleep. I awakened around three and wrote in my journal:

I am thoroughly enjoying the absence of the aggravation he causes me. Yes, drinking—again, still, yet. I am so sick and tired of him being sick and tired that a long-term separation, even a divorce, seems like a heavenly idea. Since we married, there have been 2.8 occasions per month of communication breakdown (translation: fighting). All 14 times were directly related to his inability to handle alcohol. I love the sober Harry but the sodden-brain Harry is no one I can even respect, and pity is on the wane. I marvel at what his first wife endured. In the past week, he and I have spent only 1 to 2 hours per day together when he was awake and sober. I've come to feel like a prisoner in my own beautiful home, having to tiptoe while he sleeps during his daytime naps, and he's in bed before 8. As of last night he refused to take vitamins, another masochistic display of rebellion and self-destruction. This morning he tried to con me into believing all the ugly things he said to me at the party were just kidding. Of course, he was still semi-drunk. I don't feel I am loved but rather possessed. I've told him I refuse to let him transfer his guilt trip onto me, the 23 years he cheated on his first wife. She warned me he was an awful liar. He's lied about eating when he hasn't, tells me different versions of the same conversations. I no longer believe anything he tells me. I wouldn't be surprised if he's shacking up with someone right now—and I don't care! I've lost interest in having an annual Christmas letter printed. I want to cancel our New Year's Eve party because I don't want to subject friends to embarrassment.

I suspect Harry does not have it in him to be faithful or dedicated to anything very long. His attention span is short. He is a 52-year-old spoiled brat, demanding, and I am reaching the point of exhaustion. I am appalled at the messages he used to get me to fall in love with him, getting me to perceive him as he'd like to be. Is he, after all, a weasel? I am embarrassed to have made another mistake in judgment. Aren't there any men who have their act together? Why are they so immature? He's forever looking for sympathy. God, what a child. He's the most adept procrastinator I've ever known. He talks a good game.

I am painfully disappointed; disillusioned with our marriage. This is not how I want to spend my sunset years. I'm feeling defeated. I dread the continuation of this debilitating scenario for even one more day, and yet I know there are going to be many more "one more days" to endure, not enjoy, before anything is clarified. I feel I was suckered into marriage, and with marriage, Harry felt he no longer needed to work at fostering a loving partnership.

Oh, how lovely and peaceful it is here with him not around! How great it is to be able to breathe freely! But this is only a reprieve just as are his hours of being sober before resuming alcohol. I'm facing the fact I'm caught up in a real mess. I don't like myself very much for being in it, for permitting myself to be trapped, hoodwinked, conned, duped. How much initiative can I, should I take?

The most rewarding part of my life, the most exciting, takes place within my head. My retreat and solace is what I find within me. How much more fulfilling my life could be if I could share with a kindred spirit rather than someone who gets his spirits from a bottle.

One enormous burden is my lack of financial independence. I wonder where he went tonight? Which bars? Which motel? It must be great to be able to spend money indulging oneself the way he does. And he keeps on increasing his personal debts. God, what a farce all this is! I'm returning to bed, to enjoy peaceful sleep, no moaning and groaning beside me, no demands to roll this way or that. I could become very used to this blissful solitude. It's like the good feelings one has after a headache goes away.

Harry returned mid-morning, drunk and begging for help because he again admitted he was alcoholic, a fact he denied when sober. I took pleasure in telling him I enjoyed not having him here, that if he could afford to drink and stay out all night, he could afford to drink and dry out someplace else. But he was so pathetic; I could not bring myself to insist he leave. He was obviously ill from the booze. I did not know how and where he spent his long night, but he said he filled the car just before he checked into a motel and that he had not showered and not slept. He made up for it: he slept two full days and nights.

While he slept, I went through his wallet. I found two telephone numbers. The first one did not answer. The second was answered by a giggly girl who said the name Harry meant nothing to her but she'd ask her friends, and I heard them say, "No." A couple days later I tried the first number again. A woman answered. I had a hunch the number belonged to the old acquaintance Harry flirted with at the party. I asked, "Does the name Harry mean anything to you?"

"Who is this?"

"This is his wife," and she hung up. I dialed again. "Please, don't hang up. I'm not calling to bother you. I just want to let you know that my husband tends to be flirtatious, especially when he's drunk, and not to take anything seriously."

"I don't know anyone named Harry," and she hung up. Her agitation convinced me I had not called a stranger.

Later Harry mentioned he had looked up her number in the phone book and found two listings for the same name. He said he wanted to apologize to her for coming on so strong at the party. He told me he thought he might have given her the wrong impression about our marriage and he wanted to correct it. I did not believe a word, but all I said was that he did not have to bother calling her because I already had. He did not seem pleased to hear that. Apologizing to the hosts did not occur to him. I wrote in my journal:

I think Harry has been unfaithful to me and I'm having difficulty dealing with this. When we got married, I ended my verbal gift with, "I hold you in love with an open hand," because I know it's impossible to hold anyone in love any other way. I do not know what I've done or not done to make him feel it's necessary to seek out other females. Or, I ponder, has it nothing to do with me per se but some need he has, the ego-builder. In any social situation, he is very solicitous of other women; it'd be called flirtatious if I behaved in a like manner, even seductive. I know he's lied to me, and cheating in any form whether or not sexual intercourse is involved is a form of deception. So it boils down to being untruthful which, to me, is like spitting on the bond we may have had. I say "may" because now, in retrospect, I feel unsure about anything. The drinking is so unfair. I suffer when he drinks and after he stops. Alcoholism is a very selfish, self-centered problem. I am not giving him the nursing attention I have before because I can't bring myself to demean my integrity again. It's a matter of self-preservation. I don't see how Harry can successfully attack his very real alcoholism until he admits freely to others—family, friends, strangers—that he is an alcoholic. Those who have recovered have done so inside and outside of AA meetings. He has to stop playing games with himself. During the past months he has said (1), he's not going to drink any more; (2) he's not going to drink for a month; (3) he's going to drink on weekends and holidays only; (4) he's not going to drink vodka; (5) he'll only drink when he has eaten. Ad nauseam.

I wrote in here that I don't care where he went, even if he were shacking up with someone, and much of me doesn't care, but the residual part of me that still loves the "real" Harry is curious. But what is the real Harry? The womanizer, sober or drunk? The liar? The one who tells me he could never be unfaithful to me, has no desire for another woman; the one who couldn't bring himself to perform with anyone else? I've thought that he doth protest too much.

I told Harry I am going to voice my opinions, not keep my mouth shut to preserve the peace. Let him get angry! I've been permitting myself to be intimidated and manipulated by a spoiled brat. I doubt his proclaimed love for me. As I told him, after 12 drinks, he tells any woman he's "totally in love" with her. He's all mixed up but there's no reason why I have to become neurotic.

Just before Christmas I wrote:

It's a terrible feeling not to be able to believe what he says. How did Lenora stand it all those years?

His dear elderly Aunt Bibi phoned after Harry visited her one day. She said that "in past crises, he's always been weak and has turned to drink to get him through, but I know he'll be all right because he is coming home to you." I thought: I'm no saver of souls!

When I asked Harry about how and where he spent his time the night he was away, he was evasive. "Why do you want to know?"

"Wouldn't you if the situation were reversed?"

I wrote:

It's just as fruitless for me to pursue truthful answers from him when he's sober or semi-sober. I have no reason to believe he's going to make any serious effort at long-term sobriety. He pleaded for help and understanding from me Sunday, Monday, and Tuesday when he felt so hung over and ill. But on Wednesday and Thursday, he deliberately took in alcohol. There's little difference between a wet and dry drunk. His thinking is all screwed up. He contradicts himself. He creates holes in his stories big enough to drive a semi through. I am sick at heart. I can't turn him around; only he can. He finds excuses to drink, justifications. How do I cope with this and keep my equilibrium? He owes an apology to our friends about the piano player, a written apology, but I doubt he makes it. I'm smoking like a chimney.

149

Whoopee for me. This journal is a log of unhappiness interspersed with brief moments of fun and renewed hope. I was a fool to marry. I believed in him, gave him credit for strength of character he evidently has never had. I love him and resent him. A lot of positive changes must occur and continue non-stop for this marriage to be pulled together. I can't tolerate lies and womanizing, which are one and the same. In all my Christmas card notes and letters, I've made no comments about being happy. I couldn't because I am not. I am discouraged and yes, angry as hell.

Chapter 22

And then we had two months of feeling happy and close—no drinking, no problems—until the evening Liz phoned. She had married into a family riddled with alcoholism, and her husband Mike's drinking and irresponsible behavior were escalating. Liz and Mike supported alcoholism data: 60 to 90 percent of the children from alcoholic families, if left untreated, will marry and/or become alcoholic and/or other drug addicted. The disease has become so widespread that it is estimated one of every ten school children comes from an alcoholic home. Liz and I saw "the problem" as belonging solely to the problem-causing drinker.

Liz asked if she and the children could spend the night with us to create an empty environment for Mike when he returned home. Knowing his dependency on her and his need for a family, she figured the show and tell of an empty nest would jar him into being receptive to counseling. Harry agreed she could come and added, "What choice do we have?" Between her call at suppertime and when he went to bed at nine, Harry presented only the darkest scenario. He resented the invasion of our privacy; Liz had made her bed and should lie in it, that he'd say that to any of his kids. He did not know how much more he could take of work pressures and tensions with my family. He said he couldn't promise me what might happen, "as much as I love you." He said he did not want to start drinking again or have a heart attack. After he moved his car to make room for Liz's, he said he thought about where he could go while she was here, some place I would not know about; and how when he moved his car, he wanted to keep on going. He talked as though Liz's overnight visit were a forerunner to her moving in with us. He said to tell her that if Mike showed up and created any kind of a scene, that one of two people would leave—Liz or himself. In the next breath he told me not to tell Liz how upset he was. Thanks to Harry's manipulative skills, I felt caught between a rock and a hard place.

That morning Harry had said how much he loved me, loved being with me, married to me, how much he admired the manner in which I handled problems with my children. Actually I didn't handle their problems at all; I filed them between layers of flannel, anything to create buffer zones between reality and anxiety. To receive unsolicited verbal support from Harry in the morning and to have it withdrawn, rescinded, and cancelled hours later jammed me with confusion. He equated Liz's visit—her escape—to the end of our marriage. I did not see why a marriage could not co-exist with outside problems. Nor could I understand Harry's lack of compassion for Mike's drinking because he had been there too. And Harry had not lain in the bed he made for himself, well, not exclusively. Not counting the affairs while married to his first wife, Lenora, he had stayed with Aunt Bibi and twice lived several months with an old school friend. It struck me that Harry did not want to share me; maybe he felt I loved him less if I gave love to my children. In fact, I loved him more when he gave me his moral support. The irony was that after she arrived, Liz told me she knew there would not be any problem with Harry about her spending the night because he would not mind, that the real problem would be with me. A year later I learned the basis of her reasoning. During cookouts at our house, Harry usually told Liz not to hurry home. When she hesitated because she felt we wanted to be by ourselves, Harry told her, "Oh, you know how your mother is. She wants me all to herself."

Harry gave me double messages about my children. He said he would take David any place because he made a good appearance, had good manners, spoke well. He said he got a kick out of Liz, her irrepressible wit. He said he loved them both but did not particularly like them. I was not asking him to like or love them but to accept them as individual human beings. Heaven knows I cringed at their lifestyles and the holes they dug for themselves. David had spent another couple nights in the police lockup for traffic violations that were alcohol related. David phoned: unless he came up with paying a $25 fine, he would be put in jail. I did not feel I could or should help him. Harry had told me we had a choice of helping the kids or canceling our vacation plans, that we could not do both. After I turned down David's request, I cried, "Oh God, did I do the right thing?" Harry told me to tell David to get $30 from my mother—$25 for the fine and $5 for gas—and we would reimburse Mother.

Harry said, "I'm doing this because I don't want David put in jail because of $25. It relieves my conscience to make this offer. I'm doing it for you and also for his father because I know Brad would not want his son to go to jail."

The year before I had loaned David $300 so he could wipe out his court fines, pay his car insurance and other debts and start off a new year with a workable budget, which included repaying me. I received $20 towards repayment of the loan. Twelve months later, he conned Brad into loaning him $1500 for the same reasons. In the meantime, he increased his debt to Mother by $1000, owed me an additional $130 for clothes he charged with my permission to my account, and he also owed on the diamond he gave Laura, $400 to a friend, $90 to his landlady, and who knew what else. What all this said to me was the help David received had not helped but instead crippled his initiative.

Mother talked to me, again, about her final arrangements, reminding me as she had since I was a young girl to keep her burial costs to a minimum—no calling hours or funeral but a memorial service. A minister friend was her choice to officiate, and she told me to make sure that first I mixed him one of his favorite Manhattans.

Money! Money! Money! There seemed to be no end to worrying and talking about it. The month before Harry had borrowed $1000 from me to help him over some hump which left me with only $1000 of my own. Harry made it clear he did not want me to work outside the home; he said I had worked long and hard enough. He wanted me to pursue my painting or writing or both. I did not feel up to doing either. I was devoid of any creative urges. I felt as though a net were closing around me. For the first time in many years, I did not have an income of my own. I was financially vulnerable. I felt like I was being absorbed by Harry. My money was used for the down payment on the house and with the exception of three pieces of furniture Harry brought from his former home, the entire household was furnished with my things. And we had no wills. Every time I mentioned having a will drawn up, Harry procrastinated. But then, Harry procrastinated about almost anything.

Liz and the children spent the night. As she predicted, Mike made an appointment with a counselor and begged her to come home. Harry told me he was sorry he had upset me.

Chapter 23

In late February we vacationed in the Virgin Islands with Martha and Joe. Harry was still on the wagon, often testy, but he conducted himself well for someone fighting the incessant desire to drink. During the seven days, Martha and I snatched private girl talk moments for a total of 30 minutes. She said that somehow we would make plans to meet—just the two of us. Early in May she invited me to join her in New York for a couple days of theater and uninhibited sharing. I feared Harry would object but he said he was happy I could go. He added, "When you're in New York, don't call your old boyfriend," referring to Dane, whom I had loved and lost during high school. My sense of fidelity to Harry was too strong for me to even entertain such a thought. Off I went to the Big Apple and relished a sense of personal freedom I had not experienced in years. Martha had tickets to the Broadway opening of "The Little Foxes" starring Elizabeth Taylor. Rather than have us hassle with taxis while wearing long dresses, she hired a chauffer driven limousine for the evening. We giggled like Cinderellas. The next day we played tourist, even had our picture taken atop the Empire State Building. And we gabbed nonstop. I also enjoyed sipping a martini before dinner and wine with dinner without feeling I was misbehaving. Casual, social drinking with Martha was just that—casual and social. I don't know if Martha knew it but while we vacationed in the Virgin Islands, Harry correctly pegged Martha's husband, Joe, as an alcoholic.

Martha compared Harry with my former husband, Steve, and stated categorically, "Harry is obviously so much in love with you that he would never carry on with other women the way Steve did." I liked hearing that, especially from a dear and trusted friend who had the advantage of emotional and geographical distance. I chose to believe her assessment and not my contrary suspicions. I returned home tired and exhilarated.

Harry met my train, his face flushed and puffy. He complained of aching all over. He said two business friends had spent the previous afternoon at our house, "drinking up a storm," and that, "even the smell of vodka turned me off." He proceeded to sleep most of the weekend, sometimes complaining of fever, his classic post-drinking symptoms. Two weekends later we entertained a couple who, by process of elimination, had become the only friends we saw locally—Cara and Wally. Harry was quick to refill Wally's whiskey and water and to push champagne refills on Cara and me. As the lazy afternoon wore on, I thought Harry acted as though he had been drinking too. When I discovered that more than half of a half gallon of Colombard had disappeared, he admitted he had been drinking and that an earlier denial was due to what he called "conditioning." The following day he had flu-like symptoms but denied they were alcohol related.

Midweek when I dropped him off at the airport to attend a three-day sales meeting, I tried to crowd out the impression he was eager to get away and kick up his heels by remembering the many times he told me, "I hate to be away from you. I'll be glad when I get home." When I met his return flight, I thought I detected the aftermath signs of boozing. He said he tasted wine on a winery tour and some beer "but no more than two ounces all combined." However, later he said he had "had a few." The next day he announced he had begun an experiment while away and he was going to have a martini. "If it begins to cause a problem, I'll stop because I'm not going to put you through that again." He drank two martinis that day and the next, but on Sunday he abstained "because tomorrow is a working day." Monday he came home hyper, as if he had been drinking, and had two martinis before dinner. Immediately after dinner, he insisted we go jogging—the first exercise he had done in over a year—and I cautioned him about overdoing, especially with so much alcohol in his system. He pooh-poohed me. He set the alarm so we could jog before breakfast, but then he reneged "because it's raining." Wet ground and a slight drizzle did not stop me. He talked repeatedly about quitting smoking and quitting soda pop. We had both stopped smoking for a year but resumed during the bender at the time we moved. He was off soft drinks for several months too. Once he spoke of being "on a collision course with death." As far as I could tell, Harry was his own worst enemy.

I opened the telephone bill which was less than usual and looked over the itemized long distance calls. During my visit in New York, he made several calls after business hours to numbers I did not recognize. "While I was away, you were a regular chatty Cathy. Who did you call?"

"I don't remember," he said, which I did not believe because Harry seldom forgot anything. Later while having a drink before dinner, I said, "I need to talk about the phone calls."

"Can't we just forget it?" he asked.

"No, I can't."

He owned up to calling one of his old girlfriends, Sherry, a woman he had an affair with before we met. He said he called her "to close the door" because he continued to receive Christmas and birthday cards from her at his post office box address. He said her son answered first and said Sherry was out. Because years earlier he told me he didn't like Sherry's son, I doubted he spent 11 minutes talking with him. He said he called again five minutes later and talked with Sherry for two minutes. Another call for five minutes he said was to an old high school girlfriend to let her know he would not be attending an upcoming reunion. He had no explanation for calling another number three times and another one once. He said the telephone company must have made a mistake. His overriding reason for calling Sherry and the old high school flame was because he was "slightly snockered." Then he told me no business friends had been at the house while I was in New York; he had drunk—and a lot—by himself. He used a liar's typical ploy: by volunteering unsolicited information (bogus, it turned out), he deflected further query about the phone calls. The screaming irony, which I did not mention, was he had told me not to call my old boyfriend while I was in New York, yet he called two of his old girlfriends and who knew who else. Years later I learned Sherry had been his guest that weekend, in our home, in our bed.

The following day I checked with the telephone company and verified the calls had been made from our phone. The names of the people called were given to me. I phoned the number assigned to the name of Lambson first; the one Harry called three times. A man answered with a laid back, "Hello out there!" I was so flustered, I hung up. I called the other number and reached a woman who said the name Harry meant nothing to her and she added she was the mother of four children. That seemed odd information to volunteer. Then I called the Lambson number again. When I said, "I'm not sure I have the right number," the man quickly said, "Please, don't hang up!" He said the name

Harry meant nothing to him but suggested I call his wife who worked at a convenience store around the corner and he gave me her phone number. I was surprised at how friendly he was. Mrs. Lambson said the name Harry was not familiar, and she was exceptionally congenial. She volunteered information about herself. In addition to the convenience store, she said she also had a part time job selling cosmetics, how full her hours were, and implied she just did not have time to know anyone named Harry. I did not believe her, her husband, or the woman who said she had four children.

That evening while Harry took his daughters out to dinner, I phoned Sherry. When she answered, I said, "Hello, Sherry. I'm sorry to bother you but I need to talk with you. This is Harry's wife." She thought I was Lenora, his first wife! She did not know about his divorce and remarriage. He had told her we were roommates, just good friends, and it had been convenient for us to buy a house. He told her I was manager of a radio station.

When I asked her the purpose of his recent call to her, she said, "Why don't you ask him?" Sherry was not about to volunteer information.

"I have asked him, but he seems to have some problem with being completely truthful."

"Yes," Sherry said, "it would seem he has."

Although we talked for two hours, I did not learn the nature of his first and second call. She said she had contacted him six months earlier because she had a problem; they drove around in his car, she said, and he was not wearing a wedding ring. They had met three years before I met him because Harry answered an ad she placed in a singles magazine. He'd told me they met by chance in a restaurant. She said that for three years they saw each other every week, never exchanged a harsh word, and she was very much in love with him and still was. She was shattered for a year after he wrote her that his wife was about to have a mastectomy and therefore he felt he should be with his wife and would not be seeing her again nor would he talk with her or answer her letters. That date corresponded with shortly after Harry and I began living together. Lenora never had a mastectomy. Sherry was shocked to learn Harry talked about marrying me from the beginning; that he gave me a diamond that first Christmas, and she wondered what I had that she didn't. She asked me questions about my appearance, our lifestyle, what type of person I was who had "won Harry away" from her. She had felt she could believe anything Harry said because he had told her, "I never lie; I always tell the truth." She had prayed for him to come back; she had been waiting for him to tire of Lenora and return to her. This well-spoken woman with a cultured voice had

157

been in love with Harry for seven years. He had told her, "We'll have the rest of our lives together." She was wounded, even crushed, and I felt badly he had not made a clean break with her, been honest with her. She spoke often of how much she loved him, would always love him and treasure the wonderful times they shared. She repeatedly said she was disappointed in him because he had been so untruthful with her. I continued talking with her long after I could have ended the conversation because I felt the roles were reversed: she was now the one who needed to talk with me. I felt sorrier for her than for myself. I was too angry with Harry to have room for self-pity. Sherry assured me she would have no further contact with Harry because, "His place is with his wife."

I had barely enough time to somewhat compose myself when Harry returned home. I asked him, "Do you want this marriage to work?"

"Do you?" he countered.

"Do you?" I shot back.

"Yes, but if you're going to talk in that tone of voice, I'm getting into the car and leaving." Once again, Harry had launched his winning-through-intimidation technique. He was angry when I told him about calling the phone company and then about the people I called and what they said. He insisted he had not made the phone calls. "So it's no wonder no one knows anyone named Harry."

But when I dropped the bombshell I had talked with Sherry for two hours, he was furious. He denied what she said and called her a liar. He said he would never remove his wedding ring. He took the offensive. He called me a bitch, a lousy housekeeper and more: Harry was out for the jugular. He said what I had done was sneaky and he was disappointed in me. Now he agreed with Steve about women. He said my detective work was far worse than his reading of all my journals. "As far as I'm concerned, you've blown the marriage, and I just don't care anymore." I was not about to argue with someone who had been caught with his hand in the cookie jar. "I now think you hate men—all men—and that you'd like to be working and living alone." From now on he would leave the house at eight and not return until five, if that's what I wanted. He would surrender our mutual funds so I could have some cash of my own and set up an account just for myself. This was ludicrous since he was the one with all the free, unsupervised time and the one with his own private checking account. "I refuse to give in to alcohol. I'm determined to beat it if I can, to become a normal drinker. I began experimenting earlier but I did not tell you, not because I was trying to keep something from you but because I did not want to tell you." I found the semantics interesting.

I knew I was not his keeper regarding alcohol or any phase of his life. Therefore, if I was not his keeper, neither was he mine. He expressed surprise when I told him I could not write effectively if I was always being interrupted; all my attempts at creative writing were aborted. Even when I typed letters while he watched television, he resented my not being with him in the same room.

Our fighting wore down. I said, "If you were calling Sherry 'to close the door,' then I guess my call locked it and caused the key to be thrown away."

Harry said, "I guess I should thank you. I never had the balls to tell her." He put his arms around me and said, "It means a lot to me to know you care enough to have called her. If the situation had been reversed, if there had been an 'Arthur,' he would have ended up a soprano. I don't want to lose you."

I wrote in my journal:

I feel like I'm a fulcrum for a seesaw; like an actor in a play that isn't complete waiting for the next couple pages of script to come from the playwright so I'll know what my dialogue is.

I'm asking myself over and over how I feel about the trust being broken and how am I going to deal with that now and in the future? In the same breath I remind myself I knew his faults before I married him—the alcohol, womanizing, lies, unfaithfulness—so my marriage was based upon a calculated risk. Therefore, I can't react with shock and I am not, but I'm trying to search out answers to what his needs are and why. He might prefer an open marriage—open for him but closed for me. I told him long ago and more than once that I feel what is sauce for the gander is sauce for the goose.

Our relationship has moved to a different plateau, not a higher one, sort of a lateral move. I can't define it because I still can't bring my thoughts together. The numbness that nature provides when hurt is in force. I suppose I'll get angry, but what good will it do? My rational approach is a waste of breath when countered with evasive statements.

Do I apply my logic in the manner of a balance sheet, debits and credits, pros and cons, and total the columns, and weigh the good against the bad? Do I count the number of good times and subtract the others? Do I spend every day from now on wondering what flirtations he may be fostering on the QT? Do I speculate when he recounts stories as to which parts are factual? Do I simply acknowledge the goodness that is within him that is within all human beings and become a patsy? Do I wonder, when I get a vaginal itch as I did a few days after returning from NYC, if he slept with some other woman, the same thing that used to happen when Steve did? Why in hell can't most men be faithful? What insecurities propel them? When do men complete puberty? Should I return to work? Should I create an independence, separate my identity from his? Tune in tomorrow, folks...and buy that soap!

Without realizing it, I was deep into my own alcoholism related illness. Rather than allow myself to feel the pain of Harry's betrayal, I took refuge in intellectualizing. Logic, I thought, was my ally. Logic, it turned out, almost sent me over the wall into full-blown insanity.

The next afternoon when Harry returned at three o'clock, supposedly directly from working, he immediately said he wanted to talk with me about not cheating on me, how he would never, and how he would never lie to me about such a thing. Then he made an odd statement. "I could look you right in the eye, right here and now, and tell you, 'I just got laid,' and that wouldn't be true." What a peculiar illustration of honesty! The date was June 11th.

That evening we went out for pizza and danced to country and western music in a country inn. Harry was in loving, high spirits. I drank with him. Back home, both of us tipsy, we made love. He had two ejaculations only minutes apart. I felt as if there were another woman in our bed.

We made another decision to stop smoking and to drive to the Maine coast for the weekend. In the morning he was in good humor but after he returned from checking his post office box mail, he was glum and touchy. On the long ride to Maine, he complained about how boring it was, how bored he was. We checked into an ocean front motel and went out to dinner. Neither of us had smoked since the night before. He ordered two rounds of martinis and jumped on anything I said. When we got into a discussion about politics, he said, "You don't know what the fuck you're talking about." When I asked him to repeat something I had not understood, he barked, "What's the matter with you? Are you deaf?" Back in the motel room, he got into one of the double beds and assumed a posture that prompted me to ask if he preferred to sleep alone. "Might as well. There are two perfectly good beds here." This was the same man who 24 hours earlier held me in his arms and made love to me as if he could never get enough.

The next morning after he walked and I jogged along the beach, we checked out and found a room in an enormous old inn, a wooden monstrosity that in its heyday 75 years earlier was a watering spot for the wealthy and their entourage. Our room had a splendid view of the frigid ocean. Over fried clams at lunch, Harry called me "Sherry" because he felt I was dawdling over my food, an annoying habit he said she had that drove him nuts. He was terribly hyper. I thought he was just existing between drinks. Sure enough, he found a place that served steamers, beer and wine. As far as I knew, he did not like beer, but he drank beer. We poked in and out of gift shops. When I saw a wind chime made of brass seals, he hesitated about purchasing it because it cost $14. He spilled more than $14 on every bender. We chose a highly recommended restaurant for dinner and arrived so early that Harry suggested we have a drink first in the lounge. We had two there and then when seated, he ordered another round. One section had been given over to a wedding party. The contrast between their joy and the miserable scenario going on between us tore me apart. I could not hold back the tears. No matter how much I dabbed at my eyes and swallowed, they ran down my face. Harry squirmed. "What's the matter with you?" he demanded.

"I feel I have lost my marriage. You've broken my heart."

Harry became furious. He told me to stop making a scene. He asked for the check and mumbled something to the waiter about his wife having a crying jag. Back in our room, we changed into jeans to walk the beach, but once outside, he played dumb games, wandering off, not answering me, and we never did walk together. He became more and more angry. We returned to our room. "You're spoiling the weekend," he said, and insisted he was going to drive me home right then. Suddenly it was ten years earlier, and I was with Steve in Loveland Pass. I told him I was not going anywhere with him because he was too drunk to drive and I wasn't about to ride with him. He got verbally ugly. For once, I gave him a small taste of his verbal medicine. He did not like having me speak up. Nothing was accomplished except we both became angrier. I left the room and sat on one of the sweeping verandas for almost an hour. We slept in separate beds. In the morning he said he was not up to jogging, and I jogged alone. We began the return trip and stopped at another scenic spot for brunch where we were civil but not communicative. Little was said on the return trip. He said we would go out to dinner and asked me if we could have a moratorium Over two martinis, I selected what I hoped were safe subjects. He went to bed early, and I stayed up another couple hours until he was sound asleep. I wanted no physical contact with him, certainly no intimacy. We had accomplished one thing: we weren't smoking. And we made sure our bodies did not accidentally touch during the night. The next day I assumed he worked and I went to the health spa where I felt like a zombie. I wrote in my journal:

Every time he drinks, it's worse. The breach gets wider. He asked me with such tenderness, "What's wrong?" and I told him I'd already told him Saturday night, that I feel my marriage has been blown. He said he didn't feel he could give an accounting about Sherry until he knew what had been said which, of course, was a dumb slip on his part. I said, "You don't have to know what anyone says. All you have to do is tell the truth." And there's the big rub. I don't think he can because for some reason he's a pathological liar. His personality splits. I knew we'd not get anywhere talking with martinis. For every one of his barbs, I tried to counter with a retort. He hated that. We received a spur-of-the-moment invitation from neighbors to come swim in their pool—their first invitation—and I declined. I did not want to go any place while we were on the outs. But Harry went. When he returned and without any preliminaries announced he could not stand being under the same roof with me another minute and he was leaving then for a city downstate where he had an appointment the following morning.

I churned inside. He was about to pull his disappearing act again, spending money he did not need to spend on overnight accommodations, leaving me to cool my heels at home in an non-air-conditioned house during a heat wave. He was very drunk, and I was just high enough to become aggressively assertive. I said, "I insist upon 'per diem' for me." He looked blank. "I want equal pay for equal time and money you spend on your pleasures when away from me and away from home unnecessarily. I want $100 to match what you spent last December when you took off and $100 for tonight. I want a check on your account for $200." I suppose Harry may have thought that if that was all the grief I was going to give him about taking off, then $200 was worth it. I followed him to his desk while he got out his check book. I asked, "How long do you expect to be gone?"

"Two days."

"Then make the check out for $300."

He did, threw clean clothes into an attaché case, grabbed a suit on its hanger, and left at 8:30—very, very drunk. I was relieved to have him gone. I hoped he would not cause an accident. I do not know how I would have felt if anything had happened to him. At 3:30 in the morning, he phoned from a Holiday Inn, the next town over from his appointment. A one to two hour trip had taken him over seven hours. He went to elaborate measures to account for his time. He said he had taken the wrong turn and wound up in a terrible section (probably, I thought, a red light section), became lost, and been stopped by the police who advised him to get out of the area. I did not believe one word of his cock and bull story. He also said he was not feeling very good about himself. That I could almost believe. Maybe he had done something for which he was ashamed.

In the morning I drove to a branch office of his bank, cashed the check, and got signature cards so the account could be changed to a joint account. Next I drove to a different bank in town and opened a checking account with the $300. As a new customer, I was given a brief case. Mother phoned to tell me Harry had tried to reach me at 1:30 pm while I was still out and told her he was having lunch with some men; that he'd made a $100,000 sale, and he did not know when he would be home. He phoned her again at 4:30 and said he couldn't reach me (I was at home) and again said he didn't know when he'd be home. Mother said his voice was thick and he sounded terrible. He pulled into the driveway at 8:30—smashed. He said he had not eaten since supper 24 hours earlier, only had coffee that morning; that he and a vice-president had drunk their lunch. He referred to it as "an old time hard sell." Yet at 1:30 he had told Mother he had already made the sale and was lunching with some men—plural.

In my journal I wrote:

I guess he was giving me more bullshit to cover unexplained time. I suppose he got his rocks off once or twice on that trip; he gets so horny when he drinks. And he carries on about how long it's been since we made love—four days—yet sometimes one, two, even three weeks go by and he shows no interest; in fact, he's indicated a lack of interest. Does this mean he's been getting sex on the side? After we went to bed, he tried to fondle me. I could not tolerate his advances. He repulses me when he drinks—a geek—and the only way I can begin to tolerate being around him is to drink too.

In the middle of the night, I looked in his wallet and found a stub headed by four imprinted letters and below that, an imprinted sequential number. On lines for name and date, Harry's name had been written and that day's date. Then these words were imprinted: "Yearly members every tenth visit 50% off on all services." As I held it in my hand, the words "massage parlor" came into my head. I replaced the stub and then thought better of it. Harry had come home so drunk, he might not remember he had put it in his wallet, and if he did look for it, he might think he had forgotten he had thrown it away. I wanted the stub for evidence—once I determined how he got it.

I saw myself as a victim. I ruled out counseling because Harry thought he was smarter than everyone else. Every day for four days he asked me, "Are you going to divorce me?"

I think he wants to be punished. He knows what he's guilty of, and I intend to know. I refuse to be put off by his protestations of innocence. He insists his three calls to that telephone number were not made from this phone but are a computer error.

Has he been fooling around ever since we began living together? I don't believe he's capable of being faithful. Why, if I mean as much to him as he's said I do, does he want to destroy everything we have together? He looks terrible. His posture gets worse and worse—round shoulders and stomach tire—deep creases in his face. From the back he looks 25, but full on, he looks 65. All the years of heavy drinking, smoking, and "fast living" have a way of catching up. I wonder if my loving him causes him more pain than happiness? My love has not made him feel better about himself. I'm beyond being heartsick. I'm numb, yet conversely, I'm angry. And oh my, but I am truly frustrated.

In the days that followed, Harry gave me eight different versions of those 24 hours away from home. He varied the events, their sequences, the time elapsed. Now I realize his drunkenness had a lot to do with his confusion but not all of it. One day he hollered to me from his desk. "What's this entry in the check book for $300?" He had no recollection of writing the check. I made it easier for him. I filled him in on the details. "Oh yeah, I remember." He did not ask me what I had done with the money. Not then.

Chapter 24

Harry seemed keenly interested in the personal ads placed in *The Advocate* a weekly regional tabloid. I'd looked at it years earlier and found some ads humorous, others shocking, even repulsive. To glance through a copy every six months was enough for me, but Harry brought various editions home every week. When I asked him why he continued to read the ads, he said, "I find them amusing." I was sure he had more than a passing interest.

The Friday night following his Monday all-night escapade, Harry was a happy drunk and said, "Let's go dancing!" In the car he spoke of how proud he was of me, proud to be seen with me, and exclaimed, "I am totally in love with my wife! You don't know how good that makes me feel! My wife turns me on!" I rejoiced in dancing and exalted in the release of physical tension.

The next morning while Harry slept off his hangover, I snooped in his office. At the back of his briefcase, I found a different publication, a small magazine filled with nothing but personal ads, a veritable cornucopia for randy swingers. The ads were grouped according to location and ranged from blatantly suggestive to sexually explicit. One woman's ad read: "Attractive, sexy, horny. Can travel anytime. Seeks men of all ages for swinging partner. Answer all."

Under the heading for the town where Harry kept his post office box, I found this ad:

"W/M has good news, girls. Free, erotic, loving massages, by safe expert lover, in privacy of your home. You'll adore the back rub and more. Travel southern New England. Discretion assured. Orgasm guaranteed."

My stomach turned over. I sensed Harry had written the ad. I checked the magazine's lexicon. Safe meant sterile. Harry had a vasectomy during the first year we lived together. It was his idea; he said he was doing it for me. Now I wondered.

I left the house and jogged. Tears ran down my face. While Harry continued sleeping, I weeded the garden—thinking, puzzling, feeling betrayed, and often bending over double because my belly hurt. With every weed I pulled, every dead marigold blossom I broke off, I tormented myself with questions—and answers. There it was in black and white: my husband had more than a drinking problem. But there was an outside chance he had not placed the ad. How could I find out? To ask him point blank would invite lies as well as give him ammunition against me—the fact I snooped in his briefcase. Until I could compose myself and verify his connection with the magazine, I would have to remain silent. By the following evening, I was beside myself. I wrote:

I am so tired that I ache, want to weep, and feel as if I'm going out of my head. Possible titles for this saga: "My Husband is a Pathological Liar" or "My Marriage is Dying: Disconnect the Life Support System." And, "The Woman Who Learned How to Lie."

Later I crossed out the last title because I suspected Harry might be reading my journal even though I changed its hiding place frequently. I did not want him to suspect I was about to assume an alternative identity—Mata Hari.

I feel ill, depressed, and despondent. Yet, I've had sex with him and tried to follow specific love-making instructions, something he's not verbalized before. My sixth sense has yet to be wrong. I've not been sleeping at all well, shallow sleep, awake often, mind in a turmoil. His jealous tantrums make sense now.

Then I wrote a pathetic question, blaming myself and thinking I had the ability to change the situation:

How do I pull myself, him, and the marriage together?

At every opportunity, I poked through his desk and into his briefcase. I made furtive notes. I kept track of what time he left and returned and made neat notations on index cards that I hid between books. I composed a letter in response to Harry's ad, suggesting we meet in the reference room of the public library where I could position myself and observe—without being seen—anyone who walked through the door. I dared not write it myself because I doubted I could disguise my handwriting enough to fool Harry. I elicited help from the one person I knew I could trust, and I hated to ask her—my mother. We followed the magazine's instructions. We put the letter from "Elly" in an envelope, sealed it, wrote the magazine's code number for the ad in the upper right corner, "Elly" in the upper left, and placed it, along with $20 and a stamp, in an envelope addressed to the magazine. I guessed it would take about a week to reach Harry's post office box.

Harry tossed his charge receipts into a desk tray. I went through them one by one and found a receipt for a $17 meal at the Venetian Restaurant on June 11th. I checked the calendar. Harry and I had not dined out that day; therefore, it was lunch for two people. Sometimes he took customers to lunch, but the Venetian was far removed from the area where he conducted business. Then it hit me: that lunch was on the same day he came home in the afternoon and said he could look me right in the eye and tell me, "I just got laid," but added he would have been lying. Could he have been telling the truth? I put the receipt into my wallet and had it copied. I visited the local office of *The Advocate* and placed an ad to see if it would attract Harry's attention and response:

WMF, svelt, shapely 45, committed to sexless marriage desires lighthearted afternooners with professional WM, 40-55. No strings. Discretion essential. Sense of humor helpful.

I was paving the way to move in for the kill. Without the benefit of being addicted to alcohol, I had developed some of the same symptoms displayed by Harry; and now I, too, was becoming a liar, losing my sense of values. Like the alcoholic who lies and cheats to get money to buy his fix, I rationalized the end justified the means.

While sitting on the patio drinking martinis, I made up a story. I mentioned to Harry I had received an anonymous phone call almost two weeks earlier from someone who told me they had seen him having lunch with a woman at the Venetian. His first words were, "Do you have any evidence? Do you know anyone who works there?" He denied being there, ever being there, and added he did not know where it was.

I said, "Well, I know you never pay cash for luncheons, so if you were there, it'll show up on one of the charge card statements," and I changed the subject. At his earliest opportunity, Harry went into his office. A glass covered picture on a right angle wall acted like a mirror: I could see Harry rifling frantically through his cache of charge slips. I gloated.

I used the martinis-on-the-patio time to elicit information from Harry, but I waited until he was visibly drunk. I remained reasonably sober: when he excused himself to mix his third drink, I poured most of my second into the sink and refilled my glass with water. One tidbit I seized upon was Harry's statement it would be possible to explain away his wedding ring as a Masonic ring to someone who did not know better because of its distinctive design of three bands in one. I guess he had tried that with success.

Towards the end of June I wrote:

During the last two weeks, I've swilled a lot of watery martinis and listened to a lot of declarations of deep, faithful love for me. He has told me repeatedly how much he loves me, worships me, that I'm his Donna, his precious wife, that he wants everything between us to be perfect. He has told me he does not care about anyone else, is not interested in anyone else, and does not read singles ads for such purpose and, in fact, does not know of any such publications. What is so weird is our lovemaking—six times in one week which is usually the total for five weeks. It's as if he's kicked inhibitions or he's trying to prove to me what I mean to him. But, I'm not a Pussy Goddess. The mind still means more to me than the genitals.

I was told secondhand that Harry said he had been having an affair "for some time" with a secretary. Later when he was asked how it was going, he said, "Donna found out. It's all off." By then I was waiting for the letter from "Elly" to reach him and also for *The Advocate* to publish the ad I placed.

So one afternoon while we were having sex and Harry was coaching me on techniques—an abrupt departure from his usual behavior—I interrupted the heavy breathing to say, "Do you realize you're being fucked?" He laughed. I laughed. Never was a double entendre more loaded.

My ad was published. Harry asked me if I had placed an ad. I denied doing such a thing. I hoped I came across as a better liar than he did.

Our martinis on the patio continued. I relished the first drink, eagerly awaiting the sensation of slight mental numbness. The only way I could bear being with Harry when he drank was to drink with him. While he drank straight vodka and I switched to flavored water, I maneuvered conversations to include why anyone would advertise for a sexual partner and why anyone who ostensibly had no physical need for another partner or partners would deliberately copulate with a stranger and why some men seemed incapable of monogamy. I listened with great interest to Harry's comments. He said that such a person might be experiencing an identity crisis with a need to reinforce his concept of his own masculinity, even to cancel any doubts he might have about latent homosexuality. He said such a person might be always wondering if the next she or the she after her would give him "the ride of his life," forever seeking the ultimate sexual high. He also said the person might have deep, psychological problems requiring psychoanalytic help. My racing brain wondered how much of what he said could be related to him personally. I believed any or all of it could apply. I believed that drinking, beyond lowering inhibitions, had nothing to do with rampant promiscuity.

Attempts to promote what I considered non-threatening philosophical discussions failed because inevitably Harry made them pointedly personal. Often he retorted, "That was a dumb, stupid fucking statement." Once I contended that everyone has a price even if it isn't measured in dollars and cents. That subject was too close to the bone but I persisted. I walked a tightrope, playing Mata Hari while simultaneously trying to figure out what I could do differently that would help save the marriage. To the other records I kept, I added a new one—a notation of every time we made love.

I asked Harry if he would like to have me go away for a while. His reply was a vehement, "God, no!" I did not know where I would go but I was prepared to give him time to do his thing with whomever. He told me about a business associate who was unhappy with his wife but would never cheat on her. I wrote:

I bet that was a helluva conversation. I think men are worse talkers than women. God, I am so tired and look it—the martinis every night, the impaired sleep. Ah, hey, Donna! Grow up! Put your g.d. integrity off to the side. Accept reality and get on with it.

I persuaded Harry to take a walk after dinner. Suddenly he turned to me and said, "You've never had it so good," and then went on to tell me what a good husband he was to me, how no one ever loved me so much. Those were the same words Steve said to me years before. Steve had also said, "You'll never find anyone who loves you as much as I do," and I had thought, "I hope not." Harry exclaimed over "how good the sex has been." I smiled but I wanted to scream. I was performing like a whore, pretending to be enamored of his lovemaking. I was another person while in bed with him but amazingly enough, that other person still had orgasms. I was caught up between hate and lust and loathing myself because I still loved Harry. What was wrong with me?

Harry talked a lot about money and budgeting. We were going further into debt. His solution was to cash in a small mutual fund we both contributed to. He said he kept nothing back from me regarding money and asked me what

169

I had done with the $300. After I told him, I was angry with myself. Why should I tell him when he had yet to tell me where and how he spent his nights away from home? He claimed the $300 was the cause of the current month's budget problems. That was ridiculous. The problem was due to debts dating back to before we met, child support payments, and what he spent on liquor and other pleasures. We got through the long Fourth of July weekend with martinis, flareups, defenses at the ready, over-eating, over-smoking, marking time. My searching brain never quit.

On Monday morning while Harry was still trying to get going, I left ostensibly for the health spa. Instead I drove directly to his post office box for which I also had a key, and there was the letter from "Elly." I put it in my purse. Yes, Harry had placed that awful ad in which he guaranteed orgasm. My journal entry that day was brief:

Kaput. Finis.

The next night I wrote:

There's a strong element of boredom setting in. I'm bored with Harry's unwarranted jealousy, his fragile ego. Disgusting scene Sunday night. Something went "click" within me, but not at the time. He prefaced his remarks by saying he was "stone cold sober," which was a pretty good trick after four martinis and four beers. And that's something else I'm bored with—his alcohol. He stated, "I will never make love to you again," which he amended to, "but it'll never be the same." The idea of him not making love to me has almost a refreshing essence. Today when I questioned him as to what marriage means to him, he said, "Fidelity. Trust. Cooperation." I asked, "Mutual?" and he said, "Yes." He said he has never spent money on anything other than legitimate business expenses or us or the household. He suggested we use $100 of the cashed in mutual funds to celebrate our first wedding anniversary on the Cape "or for a divorce lawyer." I am not numb but I wish to God I was.

The Northeast smothered under the blanket of a Bermuda high; the relentless heat and oppressive humidity accentuated our misery. Midweek Harry re-iterated his faithfulness to me. I was weary of listening to his lies but told myself, "So be it," and hoped we could spend a bland evening. Then he said he wanted to explain all he admired about me and the new facets about me he had become aware of. Instead, he tore me apart, telling me not to interrupt. I made notes, partly for rebuttal, if given the opportunity. He criticized my family, my friends when I was growing up, the few people I still saw occasionally. When he wound down, I took a cool water bath and suggested he have a tepid shower to bring down his body temperature. He picked another fight and left; I hoped he was gone for the night. He returned within half an hour to say he didn't want to go anywhere else. I wrote:

He said he couldn't take any more, that I'd blown it, and he wants a divorce. I said, "OK." He said I could have the house and everything in it but quickly added, "I want a relationship with you." He started tearing me down, telling me I'd never sustained a relationship with anyone, not even with my kids. I agreed with everything he said—how he has friends but I haven't, how I can't handle my liquor very well. It was all very boring. In the morning he was gone long enough to pick up his precious mail. I spent most of the day doing nothing but aching—forearms and joints. He offered to rub my feet, and I let him. He also offered to fix a spaghetti supper, and I let him. Why not? I'm all worn out because of him. At 3:30 pm he said he wanted to talk but first he was going to mix himself a drink. I said if he wanted to talk, then to talk before drinking. He said that was one of the things he wanted to tell me—that he's decided to cut back on his drinking. So, he started in at 3:30. He said he was sorry for all the things he said last night, that he didn't mean any of them, that he was angry and, "I love you." I've had almost four years of too much booze, stupid jealousy, dumb scenes, and empty apologies. I've had too much tension and catering to a moody, spoiled brat.

The following afternoon I picked up replies to my ad at *The Advocate's* local office. They were coming in by the dozen. I glanced quickly through the envelopes and there it was—a reply from Harry. As I read it, I felt like a spear had been thrust into my heart. It said:

Hi there Pretty Lady!

Would love to meet you. Have you ever seen those ice cubes with holes in them? Well, I married one! Am 5'11", 170 lbs., professional, have all my hair and teeth, etc. (50 yrs. young). How about dropping me a note with a phone #?

Thanks.

s/Harry

I brought all letters to Mother for her to open and read. At age 87, Mother received a crash education in the amorality of swingers. Over 500 replies came in until I stopped bothering to pick them up. Over 500 men panted for adulterous afternoon encounters including physicians, surgeons, and psychiatrists, lawyers (even an attorney general), professors, media personalities, and the gamut from business executives with their expensive stationery to semi-illiterates who scribbled on scraps of paper. The deluge of mail, some from as far as 400 miles away, most of whom claimed their wives did not understand them, deepened my contempt for my own husband. I felt great sympathy for those trusting women and wondered how many were also married to a drunk. Surely, I reasoned, these men were mentally incapable of distinguishing between right and wrong, but I, who placed the damn ad, was above reproach and in full command of my values and faculties. Such irony escaped me during the progressive throes of my living hell.

I fantasized about what my life might be like after the divorce, how I would re-enter the mainstream. In my head I composed another personal ad: "Chronologically 51; to the eye, 45 tops; but thanks to life's experiences, older than Methuselah. Would like totally honest friendship with healthy, energetic man, 45-55, with wide interests, who has completed puberty. Not interested in husbands whose wives don't understand them or alcoholics, womanizers, the fiscally irresponsible, bigots, or macho chauvinists. I've got my act together and won't settle for reasonable facsimiles. I'll answer all replies—all two of them." And I giggled hysterically. What was so crazy was that I sincerely believed I did have my act together. What a self-deluding act!

Mother called my attention to two letters she thought I should read. One from a physician said if we didn't hit it off sexually, he could at least give me a free pelvic exam, and he included a five dollar bill for me to buy myself a drink. Another was not from someone who wanted sex in the afternoon, but a freelance writer who wanted to know what had prompted me to place such an ad. I almost replied to him but then thought: why should I give away a good story idea to another writer? I did not read any of the other letters. The last I knew, Mother catalogued them by professions. I still have many of them stored in a box.

During that hot week, I worked on our budget and drew up one that was accurate. I informed Harry that his budget with all the deficit spending looked like it had been devised by a Democrat. As a life-long Taft Republican, he chuckled, but our finances were no laughing matter. With Harry's deteriorating health, I worried about him losing his job. I worried about finding work that would pay enough to support the two of us and the house. I feared that if he died, most of the insurance money would be used to clear up his debts. That idea made me angry—not that he might die but that I'd be in one hell of a lousy financial situation.

And then the weekend of our first wedding anniversary arrived. The weather was a carbon copy of our wedding day. I felt terribly sorry for myself. I made myself feel worse by constructing a shrine of sorts. In front of the fireplace, on the carpet, I placed flowers, a Bible open to a passage from the Book of John that was read during the ceremony, a hand-lettered and framed scroll I had made and given Harry of a quote from Corinthians, the top tier of the wedding cake which had been frozen, and I flanked the collection with candles—artistic self-flagellation. Everything represented Harry's mockery of the wedding vows. I could not cry. I thought about the beautiful sunlit hours 365 days before. I hoped the collection would make Harry feel unbearably guilty. Instead, when he walked into the living room, he exclaimed, "Oh, how beautiful!" and immediately took several photographs.

I composed a response to the letter Harry wrote to my ad and suggested we meet for lunch on a Wednesday. After I knew he had received the letter, I played more head games during our patio cocktail hours. I asked him what kind of a week he had coming up, and he outlined Monday and Tuesday, and as for Wednesday, he said he would probably be making calls down near the coast. In past summers, he asked me to accompany him when he went near the ocean and sometimes he made it a half day of work and we spent the afternoon on the beach. I suggested this as a possibility on Wednesday. He scrambled for excuses. I overlooked them. Finally he burst out, "You don't know how I depend upon you going to the spa on Monday, Wednesday, and Friday!" I thought: I just bet you do.

My schedule was predictable. His was ultra flexible. He could cover 50 miles in an hour and say he had spent two hours 50 miles from where he actually was.

From day to day, sometimes moment to moment, I felt as if I were waiting for the other shoe to drop.

I consulted the same attorney I had talked with during my marriage with Steve. I gave him a rundown of the whole lousy mess, including potential courtroom exhibits of the raunchy singles magazine, "Elly's" letter I had intercepted, and Harry's response to my ad. The attorney roared when he learned how many replies my ad generated. When I described Harry's jealousy about my life prior to meeting him, how I finally destroyed my old journals hoping that would end it, he said, "Oh Donna, how sad—all your writing gone." With compassion, he asked me if there were any chance Harry would agree to counseling. "Never, not a chance." To establish Harry's interest in sexual diversions, I was advised to try to trace the membership stub I found in his wallet. The procedure of a no-fault divorce was outlined, what I could expect a judge would approve as a fair settlement. There was no question I would get the house because of the money I invested up front. I was advised to ask for a lump sum which would mean any lending institution Harry turned to would have to sweat out the payments and not me. I left the attorney's office with a sense of direction I had not felt in some time.

The second I held the membership stub in my hand, I had felt it came from a massage parlor. I contacted a detective agency located in the area where Harry spent his overly explained 24 hours and sent them a copy of the stub. Drawing on the account I opened with the $300 "per diem" deposit, I wrote a check for the detective's retainer.

I needed my own copy of the singles magazine. I pulled into the parking lot of an adult bookstore and prayed no one would recognize my car. It was mid-morning and the summer sun shone with a fierce brightness. I wished it were dark, but I would have been afraid to visit such a place after dark. Until my eyes became accustomed to the dim artificial light, the interior looked like any small store that sold books, magazines, and tapes. There was already another customer, a man—so early in the morning! I swallowed hard when I comprehended the rows and rows of magazines. The smut relegated *Playboy* and *Penthouse* to a minor league. This was hard core pornography with full-color covers exploiting sexual preferences ranging from plain old heterosexual couplings between consenting adults to sexual kicks spiced up with black garter belts, handcuffs, and more violent variations of sadomasochism, sex-starved teeny boppers, gays and lesbians, sodomy, even little kids—children for God's sake! And there amid this trash was a row of dating magazines including a copy of the same small issue I'd found stashed at the back of my husband's briefcase. I held it in my hand while I walked around the center island, past the displays of vibrators and dildos of various lengths, the rubber vaginas, and about then, I suppressed gagging. I stepped to the checkout counter, paid the $3, and fled.

Chapter 25

During the wee hours of Saturday, a week after our anniversary, I wrote:
I've wondered when all this slime would hit me. It has today, progressively. Watching "Mr. Roberts" movie tonight, the scenes where Ens. Pulver pulverizes the laundry with his homemade firecracker and all the soapsuds fill the gangways, I laughed until I cried. It was as if the physiological effects of the laughing were the same as crying, as if the locks were broken on the fortified doors I made within, and when I realized the intensity of my crying, I quickly went into the bathroom so I could derive beneficial release from the sobbing. Then I returned to the living room but I was careful not to let myself really laugh again. If Harry noticed, he made no comment. When he said goodnight, he added, "I love you, very much." I just looked at him. At my insistence, he is sleeping on the daybed in his office. I doubt we will share a bed again. I expect that a week ago, our first—and only—wedding anniversary is to have been the last time we ever make love, or to express it more correctly now that I know my husband has been unfaithful to me, have sex. Harry is not only an incorrigible alcoholic and chronic liar but a lecherous womanizer. This evening I could "see" him presenting his body for hedonistic pleasures, and I felt sickened at his degradation and the insult to my trust and—the egomaniac—my intelligence. I'm hearing the same old tapes, the alcoholic reformational promises, even received a four-page letter of beautifully phrased half-truths and lies as explanations of previous lies. In turn, today I typed a four-page response in which I told him repeatedly that I do not believe him.

Events have overlapped. He claimed he suspected my ad was mine when he first responded to it, and really thought it was when he wrote the second letter suggesting lunch at Maurice's. I wonder! What clinched it was he found one of the replies to my ad in my car; he must have been searching to find it. He spent three days hounding me to confess, calling me a liar—so full of righteous indignation—feeling so superior, that I snapped, lost my steely cool. Once he confronted me with the letter (that he had opened), I owned up and immediately said, "Let's talk about your lunch at the Venetian." He still denied it, then said it wasn't a woman, and he'd get a statement proving that it was a man, and he was livid when I told him a copy of the restaurant receipt was in a box in Springfield ("That's sharing!") and he wanted to read the letters "Elly" had received (even I have not read them). He was drunk. Such ugly scenes. Finally I said, "Your presence is not enjoyable." He made me repeat, twice. After several false starts, he packed some underwear in an attaché case and left at 9:15. I phoned Liz and asked her if she would like to spend the night with me. She never hesitated to say, "Yes." I was so glad to have her here. I told her about the drinking only. We sat up until quite late and then went to bed. Once she put her hand out and took mine. There was such love and comfort and compassion in that simple gesture. I've never loved or appreciated my daughter more.

Harry returned mid-morning, claiming he slept in the car in Granville State Forest eight miles from here, but I wonder why the odometer read 36 miles after he got gas? What a liar he is! He was not wearing his wedding ring, which I pointed out to him. He returned to the car and rummaged in the glove compartment and came back into the house wearing it. He said he had been so angry when he left that he threw it in the glove compartment.

A master charge statement arrived and on it were charges of $83.86 to a place using initials only. The charges were made during the 24 hours Harry was away the month before. He says it was a restaurant, what it cost to take those two men out to lunch to cement an order. Now he's back to saying two men, not one. Now it was steaks all around, not just Harry and a vice president drinking their lunch.

Harry was not pleased Liz was with me and less pleased when she and I left together for the city. I dug through the box of "treasures" at Mother's and, armed with a fresh photo copy of the master charge bill and the membership card stub, I verified there was no such restaurant in that little mill town. After calls to the Town Clerk and librarian, I confirmed my suspicions: the initials stood for the incorporated name d/b/a "The Near East"—not a restaurant but a massage parlor. Whatever hurtful feelings I had, I quickly buried under feelings of superiority: I had proof Harry had lied and lied big, and I had found the source of the membership stub before the private detective agency. Liz wondered why I was not crying and screaming. "I would be," she said. It was as if my skin had been replaced by tubular steel. I would let nothing more penetrate.

Liz also said, "If I ever need any detective work, I'm going to call on you." My ego was receptive to anything that remotely resembled a compliment.

When Liz and I returned to the house, Harry called me to one side and said, "I want her out of here!"

"I've invited Liz to stay for supper. I am through responding to your every demand."

For the first time in years, I had marked the vodka bottle before I left. Harry had consumed nine ounces from that bottle while we were out. He also stashed bottles in his car, the tool shed—the two places I knew about. While he drank during our absence, he wrote this letter to me:

My Donna,

The only way we can survive as a team is for me to get my act together and start acting like a mature, sensible person.

I plead insanity—booze related.

It is more urgent than the temporary (I pray) strain on our marriage. If we were to catalog every problem that our marriage has suffered, only those pages headed "Harry drinking" would be filled.

So, this will be the last day I ingest any form of alcohol. I plan to have a drink or two before dinner this evening, the last ones ever. And I will keep this promise.

When I drink (controlled? nonsense), I am a different Harry. The cork goes back in the bottle and stays there. Also, everything suffers—my logic, my job, my attitude, everything.

In addition, I will never, never lie to you again. You are the most beautiful person I have ever known and you do not deserve my drinking insanity. You are my wife; I am proud of you and I want desperately to put our marriage in A-1 shape, in every way.

Counseling is not needed, nor is detox. The absence of alcohol has solved every problem of the alcoholic. Yes, I'm an alcoholic!

I am profoundly sorry for having caused you so much pain. If I may have your forgiveness, charity, if you will, I shall strive to earn it.

The drinking started a couple months ago in a sales meeting. My alcoholic logic said, "Hey, shithead, you don't want them to think you can't drink, so have one and prove you're normal." God, what a bunch of crap. It continued while I was away when I lied to myself by saying, "Shit, Harry, you can handle this, just like anyone else." I can't.

AA is not all bad; their Second Step states "Believe that a Power (God) greater

177

than ourselves can restore us to sanity." And I say (with Sanskrit help):
Yesterday is but a dream
Tomorrow is only a vision
Today with your love makes
Every yesterday a dream of happiness
Every tomorrow a vision of hope.
Therefore, live today.
One drink is poison to the alcoholic mind. It leads to ultimate death.
I only want three people in my life—God, you and me.
So, as God as my witness:
1. I love you. Oh! I love you!
2. I have lied to you.
3. I have not had any sexual contacts with any person/human being since our having met.
4. The stinking thinking (alcoholic) prompted me to invite Adelia (don't even know her last name) to lunch. A total disaster. She had so many problems it would have taken an Atlas to find the real person. Nothing happened. I met her at the Mall, struck up a conversation, and the old boozer said (to himself), "What the hell, no harm in lunch." P.S. She was a two bagger.
5. Sherry and I never connected sexually. She's a desperate 58 or 59 year old gal, a nice person, even a friend, but never a lover. I am very sorry that El Boozo (me) ever opened that line of communication. It's dead, past—please! let's bury it. She is capable of being untruthful.
6. That other ad in the newspaper—it was not mine. I am sorry for the person who placed it. Probably an alcoholic. But it wasn't your husband.
7. Lenora lied to me several times. Enough said.
8. The telephone calls. Another lie. I can't remember her first name, Mrs. ? Lambson. Probably 65 years old. Very pleasant. Stopped there at the convenience store most mornings for cigarettes. There was never any lust, never anything but kidding and joking. I liked her. She's funny, witty, and we swapped Henny Youngman jokes. She also has warts and is about as sexy as Prime Minister Begin. You were away, I called her (twice, I think) to tell her jokes and B.S. Had the Henny Youngman book in my hand at the time. But, I lied!
9. The other phone calls. I have no idea as to what person or persons are exhibiting this cruelty.
10. I am not involved with anyone, any group, any anything. Despite my fucked-up illness, there is no one, nor has there ever been, nor will there be.
So, my love, I am grateful for you, grateful to be living in a day and age when an

178

alcoholic is treated for what he or she has, i.e., a curable [sic] disease. I am grateful that God has given me the strength and courage to continue, to love you, to wipe the slate clean with truths.

I cannot, nor will I tolerate alcohol mentally or physically.

I am grateful that my conscience is now CLEAR. Thank God I have not been unfaithful. I have made a searching and fearless inventory of myself. I don't like the printout. But I can change this. I can be your Harry. I care about us and where we're going.

I am more appreciative of my wife than ever before. With your help, I'll live the way of honesty, unselfishness, and faith. I love you!

There were lies in the letter. If visiting a massage parlor didn't fall into the category of sexual contact and unfaithfulness, what did? Harry's statement, "I will never, never lie to you again" was broken in the letter and I expected would be many more times. Considering how full of vodka he was while writing the letter, it is a minor masterpiece. It helps to demonstrate how lucid alcoholic insanity can be, how an alcoholic can switch back and forth from sincerity to hogwash as quickly as strobe lights flash. An alcoholic also lies to himself; of all his deceptions, that is the most lethal.

Liz gave us a barbeque for our anniversary, and that evening we initiated it. Harry continued drinking—another 10 ounces. Liz left early. With more booze in his system, Harry was in no shape to talk. We exchanged verbal barbs. He kept referring to his letter as if it had value. He wanted me to give him a hug goodnight.

"I wish I could but I can't."

"But I can hug you," and he tried to put his arms around me.

I squirmed and bent over. "Please. Please."

He left me alone. I went into the bedroom and locked the door. I recalled how easy it was for Harry to spout good intentions, even definite plans. Deciding to quit drinking while drinking was like deciding to quit smoking when the system was saturated with nicotine. The next morning I wrote to Harry:

This is in response to the letter you wrote to me yesterday afternoon, the longest letter I've ever received from you. I have read it thoroughly at least ten times, and some passages more than that.

I would like to believe your letter is factual, truthful, but I cannot.

I cannot accept your theory that alcohol is the root of your personal problems and the force behind the breach in our marriage.

I feel you know intellectually that alcohol creates problems, distortions in your personality, affecting your ability to think clearly, to work effectively, to have unimpaired health and energy.

I feel that intellectually you know that one method for controlling alcoholism is to keep the cork in the bottle.

I don't feel that because you state you know what the problem is (alcohol ingestion) and further that you know how to overcome it means that your interpretation and your method will be effective. I base my belief on the irrefutable facts of your history: you have stated repeatedly that you know how to control your alcoholism, but the fact you know how intellectually has been demonstrated repeatedly not to be enough. I contend that until you connect with your problems (that is plural) emotionally and physically, physiologically, your problems, including drinking, will continue to manifest themselves.

In the meantime, you are in effect saying, "Do as I say but not as I do."

In other words, you've had enough exposure to AA and to detox-related counseling to be able to spout "the party line." You talk a good game.

I am not suggesting I know what the approach should be for you to pursue to become a wholesome person. I do know, only too sadly, that all your good intentions coupled with your method(s) of self-rehabilitation have not endured. This tells me that if it is your intent to start again at ground zero and follow the same course, within 6-12 months you'll be making renewed resolutions at a new ground zero.

When after great soul-searching and examining the facts as I knew them I finally agreed to become your wife, I did so knowing full well that you were (1) an alcoholic and (2) that you were blatantly flirtatious with other women, and especially in a party situation. I also knew that in the past you had lied to me, but I no longer thought that would be a problem because you had led me to believe your lying was alcohol related.

I felt I could cope with occasional falls from the wagon and outrageous flirting.

I knew I could not cope with lying. And I can't. I won't.

I contend that much of your letter contains more lies. The only one of your 10 points I can believe is number two: "I have lied to you!"

Your #4, about inviting someone you call Adelia to have lunch with you at the Venetian, adding she had many problems and was a "two bagger"—do you really expect me to believe you struck up a conversation by chance with a "two bagger" and subsequently invited her to lunch with nothing else on your mind except sharing her company in a restaurant?

Your #5, re Sherry. You did "connect sexually;" maybe you did not experience "the ride of your life" with her. But you have yet to be completely truthful about your contacts with her since you and I have known one another and particularly since we've been married. You write, "She is capable of being untruthful." Anyone is capable, given provocation, but I do not believe Sherry lied to me. Yes, I am saying I believe Sherry before I believe you.

Your #6, re the ad, I continue to believe you placed in the weekly newspaper because saying someone thinks "sex is a number between 5 and 7" is your kind of mean, sarcastic, black humor.

Your #7, re "Lenora lied to me several times—'nuff said." If Lenora ever lied to you, I contend she had a damn good reason. I have no reason to believe Lenora ever lied to me. Again, I am saying I believe another person before I believe you.

Your #8, re the calls to the Lambsons is a blatant example of you trying to wriggle out of one lie by telling more lies. If your association with the Lambsons was as innocent as you want me to believe, then you had no reason to deny making the three phone calls to their home, nor to the dairy store where she works and where you want me to believe you had your only contacts with her, but to her home. Further, if your contacts with her were so innocent, why would she deny knowing you? If you "stopped there most mornings for cigarettes," then you got to know one another, to know one another's names, and to know one another well enough for you to know her home telephone. You must think I have an IQ of about 10 to believe your explanation of your three phone calls to the Lambsons of North Mountain Road. Her husband, Ray, is a winner.

Your #9, re the phone calls coming into our home, the innuendos and smut that have been purposefully directed to my ears about you. I'm sure that if you did know who was behind it you would do what you could to stop it.

You have obviously made some contacts with other people who are, to put it politely, questionable.

I contend that Adelia and the Lambsons and the Dehaneys down state represent only the tip of an iceberg. I rule out Sherry because she struck me as being too refined and because I feel that subsequent to my phone conversation with her you had somehow placated her with convincing untruths or half-truths.

Your #10, re "I am not involved with anyone, any group, any anything. Despite my fucked-up, illness, there is no one, nor has there ever been, nor will there be."

I don't believe you.

Consider this fact: you began your career as a liar when you were a child, long before you and alcohol declared war on one another. Ergo, your lying is not necessarily alcohol related.

A couple weeks ago when I asked you what marriage means to you, you responded, "Mutual fidelity, mutual trust, mutual cooperation." The person who has manifested fidelity and trust in this marriage is I, not you, and I am the one who has repeatedly worked at keeping lines of communication open whereas you have spouted your zingers and then walked away.

I don't know where I am, I don't know where you are, and I sure don't know where our marriage is. For me and for my feelings about our marriage, I guess I would have to say I think I and my marriage are in limbo.

Even if your account re Adelia and the Venetian lunch were true, you were not behaving like a proper husband to me. You took her to lunch and spent $17+ after we had initiated our concerns about our finances.

Last night you chastised me about having a "lack of initiative," about not being a "self-starter." I agree, and I'll tell you how this has come about: I feel drained by you.

You experienced less than one week of suspecting I was "Elly" and only two days of knowing I was. I've endured six weeks of knowing my husband was lying to me and being sure that if he were lying to me about a few things, he was lying to me about a lot of things. I have never felt more emotionally tired in my life. I have never felt more hurt or betrayed or used or mentally frustrated. I feel devastated. I have an absence of a sense of purpose. I am trying to ward off sinking into a full depression. But every day, I have less energy.

You say that you love me. Perhaps you do, to the best of your ability. But if love is what I have experienced from you, then that is a love I want no part of. That love is destructive.

I truly believe that until you really, truthfully, and completely wipe your slate clean, face yourself and your transgressions honestly, that you will continue to dwell in a private turmoil and the breach in our marriage will become finite.

In the meantime I have to look out for Number One—me. I have never felt so emotionally and financially insecure. I have never needed love and reassurances more than I do now, and the one person above all others I should be able to turn to— you, my husband—I can't.

Two days after he stopped drinking, I wrote in my journal:

I've spent time re-reading sections of this journal. What a colossal ass I've been! He has repeatedly conned me. It's a sickening feeling, the mendacity of it all. He refused and rejects any suggestions of counseling, not that I think counseling could help because he cannot be truthful. He'd con the counselor. He thinks he's so clever, so smart, and all he's doing is outsmarting himself and losing a once loving and devoted wife in the bargain. It's a relief to know we are coming to the end of our relationship-marriage. I'm in for some difficult times financially and I have a tremendous amount of healing to go through. But it'll be such a relief to have the burden of Harry with all his chronic problems off my back and out of my life. The sooner, the better. He has not improved, not grown at all since we met, and I have deteriorated. Today he was really hung over and I did nothing towards nursing him. He can go fuck himself—perhaps one of the few he hasn't.

My head reels from the sweet words of garbage he has mollified me with. Each husband has had more problems than his predecessor. Each relationship—ditto. It would seem I am not to have what I've longed for—a healthful, loving, stable home. I must be working out one horrendous karma. Maybe this is the life experience when I'm getting all the losers.

I won't be able to tolerate being under the same roof with him much longer. I don't care to converse with him because words are such a mockery. I cannot believe a thing he says! Poor Lenora! His poor kids! The wakes of unhappiness he's created for so many people to flounder in! His sickness is contagious; he drags others down with him. He has been an incessant drain on my energy. This time when the Phoenix in me rises from the ashes, I will rise without the albatross he personifies.

Even the compassion I've had for him is negligible. He's been the boy who cried wolf too many times—and I've had "only" four years of him. What a destructive person he is. He wants to blame all his problems on alcohol. What a copout! Unless he went directly from the breast to the bottle—the alcohol bottle—he was a liar from childhood on.

I revel in having the privacy of a bedroom to myself behind a locked door. I long to have sustained peacefulness. God! I have so much of myself to heal!

One half hour has gone by. Harry knocked and said he wanted to talk with me. More denials. He even went so far as to answer my question with, "No, absolutely not," when I asked him if he had ever placed himself in a sexually compromising position. He added I could not come up with any proof because there is none; all I could possibly do, he said, was to get someone to lie, and he added he didn't think anyone would do that. It pains me to be with him, to be reminded of how I trusted him, believed him and was played for such a chump. He says his drinking this time did not get out of control—true, he hadn't started drinking before 2pm. He feels there were no "big hassles." Hell, there were continuous hassles. He speaks of my cruelty, never his own.

Earlier today he reiterated his spiel on alcoholism, the alcoholic thinking, that alcoholism is a thinking problem. He said he'll take the four, five, six days to let the "poison" get out of his system and then another two weeks of adjusting before he makes a decision as to what he's going to do re his alcoholism.

Today I purchased a half gallon of vodka, one gallon of wine, two six packs of beer. All those months when I occasionally would have enjoyed a martini and did not have one out of deference to his feelings, and he was sneaking more than booze on the side. Makes me furious. I'm still sipping wine, about half a quart so far. Fuck him!

After dinner tonight, out by the tool shed, I had those awful abdominal pains that double me over. Eventually I went around to the back of the shed, out of sight, and sat on the ground crying. The only words that kept coming out of my mouth were, "The fuckin' bastard! The fuckin' prick!" In view of his other lifestyle, these words felt most appropriate. I've actually slept good sleep, three to four hours at a time since I've not been sharing a bed with him. This is the fourth night. He refers to sleeping in his office as "a rat hole."

I'm sure he doesn't understand why he received from me the "most loving he'd ever had," referring to the remarkable frequency of our lovemaking a few weeks back. He doesn't know I felt like a whore. But now I know of his shenanigans, I could not even act like a whore with him. He said tonight he never had any reason to seek sex elsewhere "until now." My withdrawal, antisocial behavior, he says, is, in effect, driving him nuts. What in hell does he expect?

Earlier today I said, "I would think your mind would be spinning, wondering, 'What else does she know?'" He replied he doesn't wonder at all because his conscience is clear. I told him no jury in the world would believe he was innocent, with nothing to hide, and still have denied the phone calls. He said, "A jury of one would," meaning, I assume, God. We evidently do homage to different deities.

He keeps trying to shift guilt onto me—for calling Sherry, the Lambsons. He said my initial questions of him re the phone calls were "entrapment." Hardly! I didn't know the answers to my questions—not then.

Harry was into his third full day of alcohol withdrawal and awash with righteous indignation. A fury burned within me. I was determined to break through his denial that all our problems were booze related, but more important to my peace of mind was to have him stop denying he had ever in any way been the least bit unfaithful to me. I burned to have him stop lying and tell the truth—any truth, but the truth.

I submitted a typed catalog of most of the blowups between us that occurred during the previous 15 months. They averaged out to 2-1/2 awful fights per month; I figured it took me a minimum of three days to recover from each one. That meant at least 10 ten days out of each month for a year I was in a state of turmoil, 33 percent of the year. Although Harry accepted the figures, he reasoned that the other 20 days were fine with no problems. That was not true. After the full gale abated and there was a cursory mop-up, it was the height of denial to pretend maggots were not hatching in the debris.

I told Harry that his gesture of signing over the stock purchased with my money felt like he was trying to buy me and that a better way to have demonstrated his concern about his "precious girl" would have been not to spend money we could not afford on other women. He said, "You're babbling." My frustration erupted. I gave him the finger. He shot me a look of such superiority, as though he were an infallible god-like creature, and in the voice of a disapproving parent, he said, "Class. That shows a lot of class." I wanted to ram a hot poker up his supercilious ass. He told me I was sick, paranoid, and that I should talk to a counselor. And how he chortled about me losing my cool. I wrote:

If he knew how much of my cool I'm operating on, he'd freak out.

I was filled with anger; actually repressed rage. I mixed myself a normal size martini and wrote him another note which began, "You want me to believe I am making a mountain out of a molehill. Can you prove I'm wrong?" and I countered his accusations of me about holding grudges and my attitudes towards money. Much to my surprise, he agreed and said he had been pretty selfish and confessed he did not know why he flirts.

"I'll have to work on that," he said. He said he was not a womanizer. Although I did not say so, I felt he was a whoremaster and that he had womanized me. Back in my journal, I poured out my feelings:

I don't know how he could have behaved as he has knowing my bottom line re lying and infidelity, not if what I thought we shared was of value to him. I suppose the smart aleck in him figured he could have his cake and eat it, too, without detection. He was so gleeful about calling me an amateur for leaving an ad reply letter in the car, yet he has directly contributed to his own exposure through lies and carelessness. He said again today that he feels sorry for me. He was undoubtedly trying to make me feel I didn't have a leg to stand on. There are unconnected moments when I feel sorry for him but most of the time I am consumed with contempt. He invited me to go ahead and pursue my suspicions but added he hoped I wouldn't hurt any innocent people in the process. A couple weeks ago, in bed, he said he felt good about his body. I sure wouldn't believe what any hooker said.

Chapter 26

In honor of Mother's 88th birthday, I invited her to have lunch with me. Although a creator of many savory meals, Mother no longer liked to cook; eating out became her preferred source of luxurious entertainment. Not until we were in the car did I tell her our first stop would be the massage parlor. Her eyes sparkled with excitement. She was wearing the same black and white print dress she wore to our wedding. Her softly waved and slightly teased white hair provided a suitable cushion for the invisible crown she always wore: regal bearing, five feet two, diamonds on her manicured fingers, still smashing legs, Mother was not referred to as "The Duchess" for no reason. Like her mother before her, the indomitable Grammie, Mother was ready for adventure at the drop of a hat.

It took us over an hour to reach the hot, dusty mill town with its mishmash of small store fronts, many boarded up, a town not in contention for an American Beautiful award. The massage parlor was near the end of the dreary main street, sandwiched in between two small dirt parking lots, just before the overhead railroad tracks. With its board and batten front, it looked more like a bar than the actual bar across the street. A few hundred feet further on where the street, scarred by pot holes and tar patches, curved into a lazy "J" was a large off-street dirt parking area. The surroundings were bleak, ominous. In my frame of mine, I saw the portent of danger and evil in any direction. I felt uneasy about leaving Mother in the car. I left the key in the ignition so she could activate the electric windows and I made sure both doors were locked.

As I crossed the street, my heels sunk into the pavement softened by days of hot sun. I walked along a cracked and broken sidewalk, acutely aware of how out of place I looked and felt. I was dressed appropriately for a dignified birthday luncheon, not for schlepping around a seedy neighborhood as a self-appointed gumshoe. I minimized my self-consciousness by imagining I was on the set of a B movie. What was a nice girl like me doing in a place like this? What possible reason could Harry have had to feel a need to use such a place? Could he be into kinky sex? My determination to establish beyond any reasonable doubt that this indeed was the massage parlor he visited overcame my trepidations about walking through the recessed doorway. Once inside, I turned to the left and passed through a beaded archway to reach what I presumed was the reception area. The room was cramped and dimly lighted. No one was about. There was a small desk and behind it on the wall was a large chart outlining what the massage parlor offered and the prices—The Polynesian, Sue Lei, Geisha, and Samurai. My God! Old stories Mother had told me about nice girls kidnapped and sold into white slavery, old movies featuring Sidney Greenstreet—how vulnerable was I in a place like this? I was attractive, looked younger than my years, but I reassured myself that a middle aged lady was no one any pimp would want for his stable. On the desk were small stacks of printed material. Reading them upside down (wasn't it fortuitous I had experience reading slugs of type during my newspaper days?) I recognized a card with a perforated division between it and the stub, and the stub was identical to the one I found in Harry's wallet. Yes, this was the place.

A mulatto woman entered through another beaded doorway. She appeared to be in her late twenties. I smiled and made it freeze on my face. She smiled, revealing a mouthful of white, even teeth. She wore a mid-thigh black satin dress accented by a wide shiny belt of flaming pink. Her full lips were coated with layers of glossy lipstick a few shades darker than the belt. She seemed to hesitate a moment, perhaps surprised to find a middle aged woman who reeked of middle class suburbia. I broadened my smile, doing my best to ingratiate myself, not wanting her to think I was an advance scout for a raiding party. I had to admit she was attractive in a cheap theatrical way, voluptuous—my first known encounter with a working prostitute. I was fascinated by her; my old interviewing skills ached to be used. What string of circumstances brought her to work in such a place? I could not feel superior to her because she sold her body, not in view of my recent bedroom performances of feigned desire for Harry which I equated with whoring. What else did she and I have in common? Had we had sex with the same man? Had my husband paid $83.86 for her? How had she caressed my husband's body? What did she know that I didn't? Probably plenty.

I tried to exude amiability and hoped I appeared to be a high-spirited woman on a shopping spree. I addressed her as though she were a knowledgeable clerk in a fashionable boutique. I gave her what I hoped sounded like a warm hello and quickly added that I hoped she could help me. I said I was looking for an unusual birthday gift for my kid brother, and did she have anything on the idea of a gift certificate? Through a series of questions and answers, I learned I could buy a membership for $3 for my brother and then purchase one of their specials for him, and she pointed to the chart. There was nothing explicit enough in the descriptions to satisfy my curiosity. I could not think of how to ask about details that would not make me sound like a dirty old lady or what I really was—a jealous wife insane enough to visit a whore house. I did not want to be patronizing because I felt compassion for her. The last thing I wanted was to arouse her suspicions causing her to push a concealed button that would signal a bouncer—because surely there must be one on the premises beyond that beaded curtain doorway. I told her I had a terrible memory and needed to make notes so my brother could tell me which of the specials he wanted and then the rest of the family could pitch in on the cost. I asked her for a piece of paper. She excused herself and disappeared through the beaded curtain doorway and I helped myself to a business card, and from the middle of the deck a printed card, which I quickly dropped into my purse. I hoped there were no closed circuit TV monitors. What a disgrace to be caught pilfering in a massage parlor! She returned with paper, and I copied down some of the descriptive information while vainly trying to elicit more specific information from her, and mentally tallying various combinations of prices trying to match $83.86—and what was the 86 cents for? Obviously other delights were offered at a negotiated price.

I purchased a membership for $3 for my imaginary kid brother, who was becoming more real to me by the minute—such a high-spirited, elusive bachelor! When she asked for his name, I thought fast and gave my son's because if she wanted identification from me, I still had a valid driver's license in my former name. Then to my dismay, she tore the membership card, explaining she had to keep the longer portion on file for him to sign when he came in. Into my hand she placed a stub identical to the one I had found, the differences were the sequential number, and the name and date she wrote in. The handwriting appeared to be the same as on the stub Harry brought home. With another exchange of smiles—she had such a wide mouth; where had that mouth been on my husband? I thanked her and left.

I returned to the car and announced to Mother, "That's where he was. Look!" and showed her the membership stub. We were in full agreement: Harry was a no good bastard. Mother spoke of the proper but inquisitive lady, Mrs. Meade, wife of Dr. Meade in *Gone With The Wind*, who after being told her husband was with Rhett Butler and loyal Confederates at Belle Watling's "sporting house," asked her husband, "What did it look like?" And off to lunch we went and then visited Harry's Aunt Bibi. We said nothing about our adventure. Bibi doted on her nephew.

The next day I phoned a private detective near the mill town and told him I wanted to know exactly what went on in that massage parlor so the $83.86 could be reconstructed to the penny. He was a former policeman who referred to the place as "the pits" and said he did not like to be seen going there even on official business. He was shocked when I told him I had already visited the place. He told me there were strong speculations that part of the ownership was shared by members of a motorcycle club similar to Hells Angels and that the term "massage parlor" was a euphemism for "house of prostitution," and that in order to operate, the owners managed to buy protection. Of course, for a fee, he would visit the place and get the information I wanted. I mailed him a check drawn on my equal opportunity account. His written report satisfied my intellectual curiosity but it played havoc with my emotions. I swung between a type of voyeurism and nausea. Within any given minute, I could think about the report and what it signified with detached professionalism and almost simultaneously feel disgust, betrayal, and yes, compassion for Harry.

The credit card charges were supported:
$3.00 Membership fee
35.00 Polynesian package, 1 hour
40.00 Tip for additional services by hostess
78.00 Subtotal
5.857 2 % surcharge for credit card
83.85 Total (the massage parlor miscalculated and overcharged by one cent)

It was easy for the massage parlor personnel to assure the private investigator that Harry had come in alone because middle aged patrons who visited there accompanied by one or two "guests" were the exception. The charges of $83.86 were for one person only. Membership was required only if the customer was going to participate in a sexual encounter, either physical or verbal. By signing the membership/registration card, the customer disavowed he was there for entrapment purposes. If a person brought a guest and he, himself, was not going to partake of their services and he wanted to put his guest's expenses on a credit card, he could do so without having to take out a $3 membership for himself. In other words, only those who walked into the back through that beaded curtain doorway had to sign a registration card with the waiver. Harry had signed the membership card which was how he got the stub. Also, full payment was not made until after the customer had completed his visit.

The Polynesian, Sue Lei, Geisha and Samurai packages automatically included erotic massage which meant being masturbated ("hand job") by the attendant (hostess). If the customer desired additional sexual services, he negotiated directly with the hostess, usually after they became "acquainted." But first, the customer selected one of the packages and a hostess from the available girls on duty, then showered before entering a room with a massage table and/or bed. The lower cost programs had a massage table only. During the massage, the customer could touch the girl. Then once a "rapport" was established, the hostess asked the customer if he would like something in addition to or in lieu of the standard "hand job." At that point a price was negotiated, called a "tip." The minimum tip was $30 but some attendants had a personal minimum of $35, $40, even $50. Usually the $30-$40 tip was for fellatio ("blow job") or cunnilingus ("going down" orally on the hostess); $40 to $50 for anal penetration and/or intercourse.

"Light bondage," such as being tied up and slapped was indulged but requests for so-called "water sports" (urination, also called "golden showers"), and enemas were usually not fulfilled. A manage de trois ("harem") cost more. Use of a waterbed was also extra. College kids might get away with dropping $50 per visit, but the average income per customer ranged between $135 and $175. The world's oldest profession represented big money. That sleazy massage parlor in a blighted mill town, after deducting for overhead which included payroll and protection and taxes on what wasn't skimmed off the top, netted an annual income in the six figures. The girls who worked there— white, black, brown—were young, most no more than 25, none over 30. They were not required to submit to periodic medical examinations; any checkups they had were voluntary and done on their own time at their own expense. Therefore, the possibility of contracting venereal infection was high. I phoned a gynecologist's office for the earliest appointment available for a complete checkup, including smears and blood tests.

I was bombarded with almost unbearable images of Harry—my husband!—naked, deliberately presenting a freshly showered body to that young mulatto prostitute in order to experience a sexual pleasure he felt he could not experience with me, caressing her body as he had done mine a few days before he was there and again a few days afterwards. I told myself she was not my superior in any department except for having a body approximately 25 years younger than mine, and she undoubtedly was familiar with erotic "moves" it might behoove me to learn. There were moments when I felt he cheated himself more than cheated on me. Did not this kind of sexual encounter focus on genital eroticism? The sexual coupling became an entity unto itself, the participants were objects, what Erica Jong in "Fear of Flying" described as "a zipperless fuck." There was no sharing of mutual respect; there were no emotions short of lust. Certainly there was an absence of love. There were no shared concerns about car repairs, what's for supper, vegetables growing in the garden, political disagreements, and none of the little private jokes two people accumulate by sharing their lives.

I thought of our lovemaking from the first time—in a blur of too many martinis—through just days before Harry visited the massage parlor, and since. But the time I remembered as being profoundly special was the first time we made love after we were married. That joining together of our bodies seemed to transcend the purely sexual and, for me, a spirituality pervaded. I wept afterwards with a joy stemming from a reverence for an unnamed power greater than us—God, I think. Marriage meant far more to me than a piece of paper on file in the Town Clerk's office. With Harry's subsequent unfaithfulness, I felt the bond we established was not simply broken but torn and shredded. I felt used, deceived, and betrayed. And yet, how could part of me hate him, feel contempt for him, and another part of me think of him with compassion and love? What was wrong with me?

Chapter 27

I learned more about Harry's ability to speak out of both sides of his mouth almost simultaneously. Cara told me that two weeks before we set our wedding date, he said, "I'm not in love with her. I can't stand her family. I don't know why I'm getting married." During that same time period, he told Mother, "From the moment I met Donna, I wanted her to be my wife." All the while I hesitated about marriage, he pushed for it. I learned from Liz that during her family's infrequent visits, Harry told her she should come out more often, that we didn't see that much of her and the kids; whereas to me, he groaned and complained about their visits—before, during, and after. Cara told me that her boyfriend did not like Harry very much; that they continued to see us because Cara did not want to lose my friendship. None of these people had any more understanding about alcoholism than I did. Our consensus: Harry was mentally sick.

One week into not drinking, I invited my family to a cookout of leg of lamb, corn on the cob from a nearby farm, green beans and tomatoes from our garden, and rich ice cream. That morning Harry said he would not come home while they were still there because he did not want to experience my barbs.

"Besides, with me not here, you can all reminisce to your hearts' content about the campground and Steve and Brad. And I'm apprehensive about what kind of condition I might find you in because you can never get through a visit from your family without champagne."

I said, "If you feel that way, why bother to come home at all?"

"It's still my house, too," he replied, "at least a small part of it is," referring to his office and the daybed where he was sleeping.

That night I wrote:

When it was almost 5 o'clock, I felt schizoid—the habit of happily anticipating his arrival and the dread of it. I became very sad. He phoned at 6:30 from the center of town and asked how much longer they would be here. I didn't know. He said he didn't feel up to coming home while they were still here but he rolled in about a half hour later and privately said to me, "I can remember how happy you used to be when I came home."

I can't continue like this much longer or I'll be as emotionally goofed up as he is. I've given him repeated opportunities to recant, but he's sticking to his story he's done nothing wrong, no infidelity, and that I'm blowing the marriage over "a lousy lunch." He's defied me to go ahead and try to find any proof. I said, "What if I presented you with some"? He replied, "I'd be shocked." When my suspicions were still suspicions, I could cope, pretend, but once they were verified—a week ago tomorrow—I snapped.

It was my custom to wave good bye to Harry, from the kitchen window during bad weather, standing in the doorway or the driveway itself in good weather. I continued to wave but once I figured he could not discern detail by looking in the rearview mirror, I changed a five finger wave into one. By flipping him "the bird," I experienced a perverse sense of control. Then I went directly into his office to rummage through his desk drawers, the briefcase and the shelves of business literature and stationery supplies. I also pawed through his office wastebasket. Many days at noontime, I shadowed the parking lot at the Venetian and other restaurants in the same general area. I also checked out cars at nearby motels. Every time he reiterated to me what I knew were lies, I waited impatiently until he left and I could run to the phone to report his latest words to Mother or to Cara. Before I left the house, I noted exactly how I left certain things so I could tell when I returned whether or not he had been in the house during my absence. I was particularly aware of how I made the bed. I suspected he would take advantage of any block of time he knew I would be out of the house by bringing a woman home and into our bed. Not even Sherlock Holmes was more aware of details, including the positions of the telephone cords. I looked for fresh tire marks. I noted if bathroom towels were used. I was feeding into my obsession with him just as he did with alcohol. The difference was that I did not have the relief of an alcoholic pain killer. My pain was slowly killing me. I was stark, raving sober.

Chapter 28

The night after my family visited, Harry instigated talking—all about alcoholism; all I had heard him say many times. He said it meant a great deal to him when I attended Al-Anon three years earlier, that he'd never forget it, how I didn't write him off but tried to learn so I could be of help to him. He snapped at me a few times and told me I should do some reading. I resorted to writing him another letter because that was the only way I believed I could capture his attention and receive specific feedback. He returned it with marginal notations. He agreed the incidents I was concerned about were so recent he could remember everything about them. He noted there was nothing he had not told me about which I could get upset. This, of course, underscored his untruthfulness. To my statement that I believe alcoholism to be a symptom and not the problem, he wrote, "Alcohol = Insanity."

The next day, one week after Harry stopped drinking, I joined two libraries and checked out all the books I could find about alcoholism. Two were valid—*Alcoholics Anonymous* affectionately referred to as *The Big Book*, written by members of AA, and *I'll Quit Tomorrow* by Vernon E. Johnson, director of The Johnson Institute, an alcoholism treatment center in Minnesota. Harry surprised me by reading the first two chapters and said it was the best book on the subject he had ever read. All the books I had checked out had one thing in common—they emphasized the necessity of the alcoholic to come to grips with his rationalizations, defenses, and to get in touch with his innermost feelings so he could then no longer be manipulated by them but could make them work for him. The overriding message was the alcoholic must be honest. In my journal, I wrote:

I've been pushing all along for him to get in touch with himself, not just intellectually but emotionally. It's his only real hope for breaking his destructive pattern. (Boy, aren't I smart.) (Bull shit.)

We talked again the next day for a couple hours. Harry wanted me to believe that somehow this time his resolve not to drink was different, "but I'm not ready to tell you how or why." I smelled another con job. He also said he did not know what course he would follow. He rationalized a lot. I was able to establish that he had never really tried AA because he had skipped their Fourth and Fifth steps—taking a self inventory and then admitting the wrongs to another person—and the Ninth Step of making amends to those who had been hurt. Harry contended that only two of the Twelve Steps had value—Step One, admitting one is an alcoholic and powerless over alcohol; and Step Two, admitting there is a power greater than oneself to restore one to sanity. I countered by saying AA itself states an alcoholic can't make it without taking the inventory and doing all the Steps. He became annoyed with me for doubting his words and good intentions. I then read aloud a few pages from *The Big Book* and *I'll Quit Tomorrow* to support my statements. Harry told me, again, that he had been totally honest with me about everything, and that for any suffering I had experienced, his was ten times greater. I awoke the following morning feeling very depressed. I cried and then sobbed in the bathroom. I wrote:

Perhaps it was a combination of the months of tension and then learning about "the pits" and all the crash reading I did last night. I wasn't feeling sorry for myself but scared and awfully frustrated with Harry's stubbornness.

After we exchanged a stilted good morning, I said, "I'm very depressed this morning. I have a pain in my side."

Harry said, "My shoulder is killing me." He paused. "I want to know when I'm going to get my wife back."

I saw red. I pulled off my wedding rings and cried, "Do you want me to remove my wedding ring the way you do?" and slammed my rings on the counter.

"What the hell is the matter with you?" he demanded.

I wanted to scream at him about his raunchy ads and the massage parlor; to expose his lies to his face, but I wasn't ready—yet. I was saving those things for leverage toward getting a good divorce settlement. I went jogging. I left the rings on the counter for a few hours and then suspended them in a jewelry cleaning solution. Harry noticed I was not wearing the rings, as I hoped he would, and asked, "Are you going to leave them off?"

"I'm cleaning them."

"Oh, I didn't notice."

At noontime, I put the rings back on. I felt zapped. I took a bath, put on a fresh nightgown, and slept deeply for almost two hours. During the remainder of the day, we talked a few times and twice I put my arms around him. At once I had tears, like flicking on a switch; they started that quickly. I said, "I want to be your friend."

"You are," he said, "my best friend." Then he looked at me and laughed, "My only friend." I appreciated the wry humor and managed a wan smile but I could not laugh. Probably being his only friend was more truth than poetry.

I continued with my reading and began having doubts about how superior I was emotionally to Harry. I wrote:

I read passages about the effects of alcoholism on people close to the alcoholic. Typically, I may be almost as neurotic as he is. I remember what a wreck I was when Brad and I separated and I began seeing the psychologist to re-establish my feeling of self-worth. I'm not sure if I have that problem to anywhere near as great a degree now as then, perhaps because I determined then that I'm rather normal. I don't feel crazy, but I'd be crazy to remain in a no-win situation. Unless he somehow gets enough courage to face himself, it'll be a no-win.

I also learned through reading that it was not necessary for the situation to remain status quo. I wrote in my journal:

Vernon Johnson writes of "crisis creation" as an effective means for breaking through "the almost impenetrable defenses characteristic of the disease." Maybe that's what I'm leading to. I think on Monday or Tuesday I'll try to make contact with knowledgeable AA people for advice.

Finally I was having a few rational thoughts. But, by the end of the next day, I was as confused as ever. I had written Harry a strongly supportive letter, telling him I appreciated the searching, reading and thinking he was doing. He made no reference to the letter but seemed to be more cheerful. Oh, I knew he had read it; its position on his desk was changed. Several times during the day he indicated both verbally and physically that he'd like to have sex with me. I could not think of coupling with Harry as making love. When he did not force the issue, I told him I appreciated that and added I was not trying to punish him; that such was not my intent at all.

"Regardless, the result is the same." Then he added, "I don't believe you're trying to punish me because I know you miss it as much as I do."

196

I couldn't tell him about my fear of him exposing me to a venereal disease; I was particularly concerned about herpes. That evening, 60 *Minutes* featured a segment on herpes, and I could have screamed.

We went for a ride and Harry suggested we explore a nearby gorge. We walked into the woods and along a path that skirted the edge of a dramatic drop into a boulder-strewn river. The natural beauty was marred by picnic trash and hundreds of broken beer bottles. We met few people. He suggested we move on to another parking area further up river. There the path was very steep. I became frightened. No one was about. Maybe he had guessed I knew about his ads and the massage parlor and valued preserving his reputation enough to harm me, perhaps kill me. We heard voices. Harry said, "I don't care about going down there. There are people down there. I can hear them. Let's come back another time, during the week."

That night I wrote:

I don't want to go back. Treacherous. I'd rather go there when there other people there. I am spooked. My own thoughts spook me. Suppose Harry is not sincere about his alcoholism reading; suppose——whatever——is a ruse, a deception to allay my concerns. Am I involved now in a cat and mouse game? Am I getting paranoid? I know he's very troubled, but how troubled is he?

The next day, Monday, at the Municipal Hospital detox offices I saw Stan, the same out-patient counselor Harry had seen three years earlier and that he wrote off because Stan was not an alcoholic. I briefed Stan on the events of previous months and that now Harry contended this time he had stopped drinking for good. I filled him in on Harry's lies. I asked if it would be alright for me to confront him with his lies. He said he believed I could handle it well. I reviewed my demands with Stan——that Harry attend AA and have counseling. We explored my alternatives in case Harry refused.

"Can you make it on your own?" Stan asked. I believed I could. Stan gave me his moral support and said, "Stick to your guns." I left his office resolved to follow through and scared to death. I kept reminding myself I had all the ammunition, that finally Harry would be trapped in his own lies. I stopped by Mother's where Harry caught up with me by phone. I told him I had just seen Stan.

"If he's the same counselor I saw before, your visit was a waste of time. He never had a drinking problem. I wrote him off." This was not the moment for me to remind Harry one doesn't need to have had cancer to operate on it. Instead I listened to Harry's seductive voice. "I feel pretty good about myself. I'm not ready to talk to anyone yet. I can work it out. I have so much going for

197

me. I quit on my own. I understand the mental gyrations, the defense mechanisms and repressions. It'll take time—months, years, the rest of my life. I need mental surgery on my mind. If I talk with anyone, I want it to be someone who's been sober 15 years, who was in the same position I've been in."

He switched to salesmanship. "I feel fantastic about everything except you and me. When you saw my note in the middle of the night, I thought you'd come in and get me, tell me to come to bed with you, and we'd hold each other and make love. Then this morning you were down, and I felt down, so I have an idea of what you've gone through, that 94 percent may have been caused by my problem, but you have a tendency to over-react sometimes. When and if I have doubts about my sobriety, I'll go to New York or Boston with you, and we'll see someone who is really good. But I'm not ready yet."

Next he mixed God with more lies. "We're really never alone. I have already gone through the first Steps. I've admitted I'm an alcoholic. I've told you everything there is to tell—everything. Believe me."

I re-read Johnson's chapter about Intervention, an involved and sensitive technique requiring the cooperation of many people close to the alcoholic to recite as unemotionally as possible the effects of the alcoholic's behavior on them, the people most important to him—spouse, child, parent, employer, friend—with the purpose of helping the alcoholic realize for himself the scope of his problem and the need for treatment. Buttressed with Stan's moral support, I would try to pull off a one-on-one confrontation. I figured I had a right to feel scared.

After dinner while seated in the living area, I asked Harry to recount in outline form the events of the 24 hours he spent down state. He refused because he said he already had several times. I said each accounting varied. He still refused. Then I told him I had traced the charges of $83.86 on his master charge statement to a massage parlor called The Near East. He was furious. He said he had taken two men to The Near East to help land that big order; that he had to pay the $3 membership fee for himself so the cost of their visit could be put on his master card. He said he never went beyond the reception area. He said he left the men there and he paid for "no tips." He said he would never pay for sex and he would never, never expose me to anything he might contract in such a place. He said my efforts to reconstruct the $83.86 were futile. I sat on the couch and listened in total amazement. Never had he sounded more sincere or convincing. I was flabbergasted at his ability to invent even more lies.

He reiterated how this time his sobriety was different, that he couldn't explain it, but that it definitely was different. He asked me to consider all the good times we had shared, all we had—a beautiful home, a good income, how my kids were getting better, growing up. He said he loved me, how he took responsibility for the majority of my sadness but he pointed out I could be difficult to live with, too, because of my moods. He said I hadn't had it so bad, not like other women who were married to alcoholics. He said, "I want us to get on with our lives."

I longed to believe him, that somehow "this time was different," but past performances reminded me: keep all this in perspective. Therefore, I ticked off the lies associated with the massage parlor, stated my feelings of betrayed trust and apprehensions about the future and announced my terms: he had the choice of attending AA and seeking informed counseling or I would file for divorce. I said no more and waited. I did not want to file for divorce but neither did I want to continue as we were. I knew idle threats were a waste of time. Harry had already boggled my brain by denying the incriminating evidence. There was more to come: in response to my conditions, Harry took me on a dizzying, verbal rollercoaster.

He accused me of being judgmental, convicting him on inaccurate and incomplete circumstantial evidence, of not being a Christian because I did not offer forgiveness. He alternated between sounding sincere and being on the attack, from speaking like a loving husband to sounding like he could hardly wait for me to get out of his life. He told me I was emotionally sick, paranoid, that I should see a therapist, that he felt sorry for me. He called me a spoiled brat, a would-be Scarlett O'Hara, an alcoholic unable to handle my liquor, a whore. He told me I was incapable of sustaining any relationships and responsible for blowing the marriage. It was a virtuoso performance. He tried to project onto me the feelings he had about himself. He ended his diatribe by telling me I had 24 hours to think it over.

I thought, "I'm going mad," but what I said was, "Listening to you, I think I'm going mad."

He asked, "Which one of us is calling a realtor tomorrow about putting the house on the market?" I knew I would not sign anything until we had either an agreement prior to a no-fault divorce or I had a decree nisi. He referred to the office where he was sleeping as "a cave." When I picked up Johnson's book to resume reading, he said, "I hope you're not going to make an obsession out of all this. I want to talk about other things besides alcoholism." I just bet he did. The evening ended with a bitter exchange of sarcasm. So far I had not acquitted myself as an adept student of Johnson's intervention procedure.

Harry's response was typical. Alcoholics do not like to be confronted with facts and more often than not, they do not want the spouse to become knowledgeable about the disease. Even after years of sobriety and a lot of AA meetings behind them, some recovering alcoholics prefer to have their families remain ignorant about alcoholism so they can continue to wield control over them.

As we neared the end of the 24-hour thinking period Harry had given me, we were again seated in the living area. I had my nose in one of the books I found that day in the third library I joined. Harry asked me, "What's your decision?"

I told him that through Stan, I made contact that day with another counselor, a Luke Pennington, who was a recovering alcoholic with seven years of sobriety, a therapist with a Master of Divinity degree, an ordained minister, whose own marriage was once in trouble because of his alcoholism. I said, "My conditions remain unchanged: attend AA and seek counseling from someone such as Luke Pennington." Harry said his position was unchanged.

I said, "Well, I guess that's that. I have no choice but to file for divorce," and I resumed reading. My attempt to stage a one-on-one intervention had failed. Feelings of sadness, anger, and frustration vied for prominence but mostly numbness won out. The silence grew heavy. Harry reopened the dialogue. He said he was not ready for counseling yet, but I pushed for beginning as soon as we could get an appointment. Knowing his attitudes towards groups and counseling and the impossible state of our marriage, I thought receiving joint counseling would be a satisfactory compromise. My convincing persuasions were that Pennington was neither a psychiatrist nor psychologist—two more of Harry's pet peeves—and the fact Pennington was an ordained minister signified he probably had come to terms with some form of spirituality. Harry had been making a lot of noises about his own new-found spirituality. Pennington met all of Harry's requirements including attendance at AA. With reluctance, Harry agreed to my conditions but added that only if counseling was financially possible and we would not stop going until we were both in agreement. He also volunteered that should he drink again, he would submit himself to intensive alcoholism therapy at a "first-rate residential treatment center." I had no sense of victory; rather I sagged into a feeling of relief. He volunteered he had been going through a personal inventory mentally, admitting things to himself, and how relieved he was to discover there was nothing more he was hiding from me. I said, "What you're saying is that you've never been physically or sexually unfaithful to me since we've met and that you never made any attempt to be."

"Yes, that's right."

I knew counseling and AA couldn't begin soon enough. That night I wrote:

When I got into bed just now, I felt as if the bed had been used today while I was gone. A little while ago, sitting on the couch, Harry said goodnight to me, we kissed, and at once I was crying, then sobbing. What happens? Sustained tension, stress, but why do I cry when we touch? My arms were around him, I felt as if I could cry forever, but he separated himself from me and said, "I don't want to make you unhappy. I love you," and he left the room and went to bed in the office. I cried another minute or so, and then the tears all dried up as suddenly as they began.

By agreeing to my conditions, I was committed to support his efforts to get well. Yet I knew we were both encumbered by his continuing deceitfulness concerning the greener grass evidence. All alcoholism authorities, and that includes recovering alcoholics, agree that recovery is contingent upon being totally honest. How could I be a helpmate knowing there remained a breach in trust? I had documented facts; he denied the obvious. I felt I was in the midst of madness.

I awakened the following morning and wished I hadn't. I faced another day of living with lies. Before Harry left the house, he let me know, in his words, that he was "so horny I could burst, and that's something I wouldn't have told you before," meaning that before he stopped drinking, he wasn't open.

I said, "My appointment with the gynecologist is still two weeks away. And it takes one week after that for the results of the blood test."

"That's so foolish," he said. "I'd never expose you to anything like that. I love you too much." I knew he had exposed me.

Soon he was whistling, almost hyper, and my suspicious mind wondered if he were anticipating something pleasurable.

"I'm not hyper. I feel good," he said.

How could he feel so good and I feel so miserable? My head kept telling me his extra-curricular pursuits had not stopped, that although dry, he was as drunk as ever. Or he was a pathological liar.

When I called Stan to let him know what happened, he asked me which bothered me more, the sexual infidelity or the alcoholism, I said I could not differentiate. All I could speak of was the broken trust, the lying and worse the lies on top of lies while swearing he had nothing more to hide and how good he felt about that. I hurt so badly that I alternated between staring into nothingness and pacing. Each minute dragged. So much around the house needed attention. The bathtub had needed a good scouring for days, but I could not summon up energy to perform such a simple, three-minute task. I lit one cigarette after another. I wrote in my journal:

I feel like I am going crazy. If I don't talk with someone, I will be a certified madwoman by noon.

I knew I had to get off dead center. I was afraid the chaos within me would burst through my skin and bits and pieces of me would splatter everywhere. I dared not cry. I spent the long hours not crying, not screaming. Madwomen cried and screamed. Somewhere there had to be help and since help was not sashaying up to my doorstep, I had to search for it. But where and what? I was positive; I knew what my husband needed to do to get well. There was AA for him. But what about me? The books I was reading mentioned Al-Anon. Stan asked if I would go. I was annoyed by my recollections of those sweet, long-suffering ladies I met three years earlier in Al-Anon meetings. I wasn't sweet and I sure wasn't going to be long-suffering. I didn't belong with people like that. But a voice inside me said, "The books all say you need to go to Al-Anon." The books were written by alcoholism authorities. I swallowed my pride, my swollen sense of superiority, and turned to the Yellow Pages. I called the Al-Anon number and got a machine message telling me to leave my name and number and my call would be returned. I hung up. Soon I called again but left a message. Every half hour I called and left another message. The hours dragged by and no one returned my call. I was frantic. I called the AA number and explained my difficulty in contacting Al-Anon. I was given another AA number to call. The lady who answered said she had permission from an Al-Anon member to release her number. "Her name is Anita," she said. I dialed the number praying Anita would be home. A soft voice answered.

"Is this Anita?"

"Yes."

"Anita, AA Intergroup gave me your number. My name is Donna."

"Oh, hello Donna," she said, just as if I were a long, lost friend. The genuine warmth in her greeting traveled throughout my body. As briefly as I could, I described my home situation and the decision reached the night before to attend AA. I babbled about the lying.

Anita said, "They lie because they have such guilt. Yes, they're lying, but they think they are telling the truth." I wondered if even that could be true, but I told myself Anita must know what she was talking about because her husband was about to celebrate his eighth year of sobriety. "He lives for AA," she said, and that alarmed me. I wanted sobriety in our house but I didn't like the idea of being tied down to a bunch of reformed drunks for the rest of our lives. Anita said she went to a weekly Al-Anon meeting and sometimes accompanied her husband to AA meetings. She told me, "One day at a time for you, too." She told me there was an Al-Anon meeting that evening geared especially for newcomers. "Just keep it simple," she said. I never had such a surge of love for another human being in all my life—a voice at the end of a phone. I thanked her for talking with me, and *she* thanked *me* for calling her. Incredible.

I scoured the tub and felt that simple task the equivalent to scaling Mount Everest. I cut up cold chicken for salad. Then my feeling of being immobilized returned. I believed if Harry really leveled with me, we could both get on with our marriage; that the lies were rendering me useless. I could feel what I thought was acute depression coming on and I didn't want that to happen. Before Harry came home, I wrote:

There's nothing wrong with me that his real honesty couldn't have prevented. If I can just hang on a couple more hours, I'll be okay.

When I told Harry I was going to Al-Anon that evening, he tried to talk me out of going. "There isn't anything troubling us that we can't handle ourselves," he said.

I thought, "The hell there isn't!" Aloud I said, "I'm going for *me*."

It is said that a drowning man sees all of his life flash before him. On the drive to the Al-Anon meeting, I would have welcomed remembering the happy times in my life. Instead, I could think of nothing except my husband and how he and his damn drinking had given me the worst summer of my life and three lousy years before that and what a fool I'd been to marry him and how stupid I'd been not to recognize soon after we met that he was a loser. I did not drive a car to that meeting. I drove an eight cylinder pity pot fueled by anger.

At the Al-Anon meeting, I was one of more than 20 people, women and men, who were beside themselves because of another's uncontrolled drinking. I listened to wives, girlfriends, husbands, boyfriends, mothers, fathers, sons and daughters, and from each of them, I heard bits and pieces of my story coming out of their mouths: the details were different, but the feelings were identical. I did my share of garbage dumping, too, and I felt comforted knowing whatever I said was understood. The two Al-Anon members conducting the meeting spoke of how sick they had been when they attended their first newcomer's meetings. "We were as sick as the alcoholic." Whoa, wait a minute: my head spun from lies and verbal abuse but I wasn't addicted to booze. Then again, if I were as sick as the alcoholic, wouldn't I also receive sympathy and understanding similar to that bestowed on the alcoholic? Did I not want and deserve TLC? So, if accepting I was as sick as the alcoholic, I gained acknowledgment as a hurting human being, then I would go along with the label. When in Rome... And since Al-Anon was the only game in town, I dealt myself in. The two members spoke about what it was like before coming to Al-Anon and what it was like now. One had been in Al-Anon only three months, and she seemed calm. Their experiences imparted strength and a sense of hope. By listening to everyone there who wasn't too traumatized to speak—a few never opened their mouths; one had a facial twitch; a few blew their noses, a lot—I learned first hand about the many symptoms of the disease and how universal its effects are upon other people.

I asked, "What do you do when you know the alcoholic is lying?"

"You accept it," and she recited *The Serenity Prayer*: "*God, grant me the serenity to accept the things I cannot change, the courage to change the things I can, and the wisdom to know the difference.*" For a split second, I grasped the essence of the prayer but then my mental confusion took over. Accept Harry's lies? Never! No way! But I came away from the meeting willing to give at least lip service to the possibility I might be sick. I needed to perpetuate the impression I was emotionally sound. Even with the internal conflict of, "I'm sick," and "No, I'm not sick," I had more positive feelings about myself. I knew I was not alone in my misery which verified the cliché, "Misery loves company." I concentrated on keeping alcoholism in perspective, accepting that it is a disease and has been recognized since 1955 by the American Medical Association as an illness that affects the whole family. I was surprised to discover I felt genuine compassion for my husband; I had no difficulty accepting the fact he was sick. I heard the standard Al-Anon chant, "Keep coming to meetings," and I committed myself to follow their advice: to attend at least six consecutive meetings because, they added, "If you don't like us, we will cheerfully refund your misery." I scooped up a handful of free literature. I returned home with a prayer of thanksgiving and a smile on my face. I had taken one step towards moving myself out of a victim mentality; I was helping myself. I felt uplifted, maybe if Harry could make it, I could make it, we could make it. I looked forward to sharing an embrace with my husband, and the hug was better than I anticipated. I asked him if he wanted to sleep in the bedroom. Fortunately he made no sexual advances because I do not know how I could have handled them. Before he went to sleep, he said, "Tonight when you returned, I received the most wonderful gift I've ever received—the smile on your face when you walked through the door."

As tired as I was from an emotionally draining day, I became increasingly tense as I lay in bed. For two weeks while sleeping alone, I had gone to sleep easily. Part of my brain said, "You wish you could scream," but I knew I wouldn't. I agonized about what my body might be trying to tell me, why I couldn't relax into sleep. I knew my head might lie to me but never my body. Had I, at the Al-Anon meeting, bought into a con job? Was I feeling too great a responsibility towards trying to help another human being and it was going against my grain because the process was damaging me? Did I know what I wanted? Could I ever really accept the lying on all terms for whatever reasons? That question I could answer: I couldn't, not yet, maybe not ever.

I was at it again in the morning. I told Harry he was an accomplished liar but that he was no good at his coverups. I gave him a slip of paper on which I wrote:

-Clandestine—*secret or hidden, especially for some illicit purpose; surreptitious; furtive; underhand.*

-Illicit—*improper*

-Surreptitious—*done, got, made, in a secret, stealthy way.*

-Furtive—*done or acting in a stealthy manner, sly, shifty.*

-Underhanded—*deceitful; not open or straightforward, unfairly.*

All of the above, including clandestine, I have felt you were guilty of. But you tell me such feelings are groundless, and particularly now that you have embarked on a program of total honesty, including totally honest self-evaluation.

Harry said, "You're right. I am guilty of all those things."

When nothing more was forthcoming, I said, "Yes, I know that. When the day comes, if it ever does, that you tell me about them, I'll know progress is being made." What I did not add was that I needed to find out if his lying was the result of alcoholism or if he were a pathological liar.

That morning he made a phone call to a nearby hospital where alcoholism was treated and found out they had copies of the AA meeting list. We made plans to pick it up. I semi-joked, "Can you leave me there?" I referred to a treatment center in New Hampshire where he said he'd go if he drank again. "Can I go to New Hampshire?" I spoke of a hilarious scene in *Harvey* when the psychiatrist, Dr. Chumley, and the problem drinker, Elwood P. Dowd, swap roles briefly, and the psychiatrist reclines on the couch and says, "I wish I were in Akron with a cold beer, and someone sweet was stroking my head and saying, 'You poor, poor thing.'" I was ready for sympathetic stroking. I was ready to climb inside a bottle of my own.

When Harry left at noon to begin his work day, he asked, "Do you fool around?"

I said, "I've been known to."

He seemed happy, almost ecstatic. "It's so good to have my wife back."

Only I wasn't back, not wholly, just a small fraction. Not making love was a deprivation for me. I got no hey-hey out of masturbating. But I was fearful of making love with him and not just because of fears about infection. I would have to tune out my mind, my real emotions, and go with animalistic feelings only. That seemed to me like I'd be using him. That night at Harry's suggestion, we slept apart again. He said, "I don't think you're quite ready for me." He was right, and I felt badly about that.

Stupidly I asked him, "Are you seeing someone else?" and received vehement denials.

"If I ever do, even for 20 minutes, I'll tell you and pack my bags because I'm not going to play a double role with you."

Although I felt down that whole day, I did not feel as badly as I had the day before. I gave many thanks to what I refer to as my guides—others sometimes use the term guardian angels. I had not talked with God in a long time; not so much because I had lost my faith but because I felt too oppressed to practice it, like, what's the use? I also felt I was not worthy of being listened to. That night I wrote:

I received a low blow of information today. That sick ad Harry ran in that awful singles magazine was placed before Christmas—eight months ago. I need to have The Serenity Prayer tattooed into my whirring brain.

Chapter 29

I did not recognize the recovery process had begun. Harry was drying out, reading AA's *Big Book* and he asked me to accompany him to an open AA speaker meeting two nights after I attended Al-Anon. I read Al-Anon and AA literature and was particularly impressed by an Al-Anon pamphlet, *A Guide for the Family of the Alcoholic* by the Reverend Joseph J. Kellerman, former director of the Charlotte, North Carolina Council on Alcoholism Inc., in which he wrote: "The place to begin in helping an alcoholic recover is with self. Learn all you can. Put into practice, not just into words."

I read, *Marriage on the Rocks* subtitled, *Learning to live with yourself and an alcoholic* by Janet Geringer Woititz, Ed.D, which detailed what happens to people like me who are affected by the alcoholic's behavior. She wrote of the related sickness we develop, sometimes referred to as "near-alcoholism." Harry read some of its pages and said he did not like it. That did not surprise me because the book wrote of the family's pain. *Off The Sauce* by Lewis Meyer, a recovering alcoholic with almost 20 years of sobriety, presented amusing anecdotes through which were woven AA's philosophy. The author's sense of humor appealed to Harry, and I enjoyed reading a lighter touch about a serious problem. In the dozen or so books I read, even the ones I considered less than first rate——the ones that hinted at cures for alcoholism——I learned more about the illness that had affected me.

There was one book that both saddened and frustrated me, a narrative written by the widow of an alcoholic who had died from alcohol-induced cirrhosis of the liver. Barbara Mahoney's eloquent *A Sensitive, Passionate Man* demonstrated the tandem progression of "both" diseases—his alcoholism and her co-alcoholism—and I found it a skillfully written primer on what not to do if either wished to become well. Neither she nor her husband availed themselves of Al-Anon or AA; indeed, her account indicated none of their doctors recommended the programs to them. She presented heartbreak without hope. I wept while I read it. I identified, repeatedly, with her saga of horrors; and I gave thanks I had broken through my denial enough not to follow a similar self-defeating path. One passage about their sexual intimacy struck such responsive chords in me that I copied it into my journal; her description connected with the conflicting emotions I was experiencing. Ms. Mahoney wrote about "willingly" copulating in answer to sexual hunger and afterwards feeling "depraved." She wrote about catching glimpses of "the former tenderness" which caused her "to sink into post-coital tristesse." I wondered as she did: who was the more "hurt and confused," my alcoholic husband or me?

By accumulating knowledge about the disease and especially by attending just one—so far—good Al-Anon newcomer's meeting, I could feel stirrings of compassion for Harry. I could accept the fact he was powerless over alcohol; I wanted to believe what both he and the books stated, "alcoholism = insanity," and to write off his philandering to the effects of the disease. I did not doubt he loved me; and by fighting to preserve the marriage, I demonstrated to myself that anger and resentments notwithstanding, I loved my husband. So in the middle of the night following the first Al-Anon meeting, I wrote a note and left it on the floor of the bathroom for Harry to find:

If you would like to join me in bed, I'll make room for you.

We made love wordlessly. After the orgasms and climaxes, I felt choked with sobs I couldn't let go.

The next morning I was given a painful gift: while barefoot I whanged the little toe of my left foot into the chrome base of a kitchen stool. The waves of real physical pain for the next several days made it possible for me to focus on something other than Harry for a few seconds at a time. I could not tolerate shoes without limping and wincing. I thought nothing could be done for a fractured toe, and it was three weeks before a friend told me to tape it to the next toe. I believe those weeks of physical discomfort helped to preserve what little sanity I had left.

Harry and I resumed sharing the bedroom. Sometimes the coupling was an act of love and other times it seemed perfunctory, and I doubted Harry derived any more emotional satisfaction than I did. I said that when he was drinking, he appeared to be more interested in sex, sexier, but he disagreed. He did say that sex was better when sober.

For the week following the confrontation, I was not as depressed or off the walls to the same alarming degree but I was far from stable and happy. I had pervasive feelings of numbness and then despair. I was aware of how precious time tick-tocked away. I continued to be bloated, a sure sign of my inner turmoil. When I kept an appointment with Stan, I unloaded my feelings of confusion. He assured me my feelings were normal and advised me to just go along—albeit in limbo—because the initial weeks of not drinking were known to be difficult. "There are no quick resolutions," he told me. I wanted everything to be right as rain yesterday. He reinforced what I had read by telling me that just because drinking stops, the alcoholic thinking and behavior continues; therefore, I could not expect honesty from Harry because the structure of denials and rationalizations persisted. I said I felt I would not be able to make any positive headway either until Harry became honest and truthful. He told me I might not be able to believe everything Harry said for a full year. I wondered how anyone could not be truthful for a full year. Well, why not? Harry had not been truthful with me for four years. One year was better than four. I continued to write in my journal and to hide it in different places, but I had no assurance Harry wasn't snooping. I did not have a leg to stand on in that department because I was all over his office the minute he stepped out the door. I went through his pockets. I looked in his wallet. I was doing everything short of physically climbing inside his head.

I told Stan about accepting Harry's invitation to accompany him to a couple of open AA speaker meetings—hour-long gatherings where two or more recovering alcoholics spoke extemporaneously about their experiences while drinking, how they came into AA, and what their lives were like now. One speaker dwelt upon how he had rationalized everything more and more during the years he drank. I was so glad Harry heard his words. But then Harry began looking at his fingers, his watch, around the room, and when I remarked about this later, he denied he wasn't listening. Stan said that perhaps Harry was hearing stuff he did not want to hear or accept. Stan concurred that Harry's reactions to *Marriage on the Rocks* was because it was unpleasant reading about the profound side effects of alcoholism on a wife and children. A few days later Harry referred to the book and said he had not realized the effects on me, how he had thought he was the only one suffering, and he remembered how he had accused me of being overly dramatic. I made no comment because his words did not ring true; I thought he was trying o convince me of his awareness.

I harbored such unexpressed rage and resentments about Harry's extracurricular activities and coverup lies—mostly the cover up lies—that I could not apply the Al-Anon philosophy of minding my own business, concentrating upon myself and my recovery and letting him run his own course. I set myself up to reinforce my suspicions. I noted which mornings he dressed with greater care and one particular morning, I said maybe I should tag along with him. Time was when he would have exclaimed, "Come on!" Instead he equivocated about the heat, too hot to sit in company parking lots waiting for him. I felt rejected, which I interpreted as further proof he was still into personal meetings. I stood in the driveway and at the last moment waved a "no-class" finger. Then I went into my usual act of rifling through his office. When he returned six hours later and said he made seven calls, I thought he was too vague about time to be believed. Another morning he told me I looked pretty and asked me if I had a boyfriend, if I were meeting anyone else. I said no, of course, but as he got into his car—with the latest copy of that damned weekly *The Advocate* on the back seat—I smiled sweetly and said, "But one of these days, I'm going over to the Mall to see if someone will pick me up and take me to lunch."

This riled him, as I hoped it would, and he gave me a steely, "Goodbye." I kept smiling and returned what I interpreted were his reluctant and perfunctory waves with mine—punctuated by one finger.

Three weeks after his last drink, the day of our first appointment with Luke Pennington, Harry expressed negative feelings about seeing the counselor. "I've never known any who were any good. Seeing him could undo what I'm accomplishing in AA." I reminded him of our agreement and the fact that detoxification centers combine AA meetings with on-on-one counseling, and he shut up.

He took back the five dollars he had insisted I have in my wallet the day before and told me I could get money during the day if I needed it. I interpreted his remarks as an indirect reference to the $300 I had coerced out of him. Contrary to all Al-Anon teachings, I deliberately provoked him my saying, "I can always go down to the center of town and sell my body." I was pleased to see anger flash in his eyes.

"Every morning you send me out of here with a zinger," he said.

"Like you say, Harry, the AA meetings remind the alcoholic of his problem, and all I'm doing is reminding you of how stupid you behaved while actively drinking." It was my turn to go for the jugular. "We don't want to forget those two-baggers." After he left for work, I wrote in my journal:

He said the AA closed discussion group he tried to attend last night had disbanded and so he attended an open speaker meeting. He'll make no progress until he gets involved. I'm coping better with the awareness I can't believe most of what he says, but this is no way to run a railroad. I am going one day at a time. Now to stash this journal again…

I was not "going one day at a time." Into every new day, I dragged all the previous days of our four years together. I finally demonstrated some self-honesty that night when I wrote:

Who do I think I'm kidding? I'm not coping worth a damn. I proved that to myself during our visit this afternoon with Luke Pennington. I said my reason for being there was to get our marriage on solid footing, based upon mutual trust. When Harry stated he had always been faithful, I brought up The Near East and all the supportive details demonstrating he visited alone, did not pay for any guests, and used the facilities himself. He denied it. He said he sticks to his story, that The Near East is not run that efficiently. Pennington pushed me for what I need in order to proceed. I could not answer and told him I couldn't. I felt blocked. Harry said he almost said I was right about The Near East in order to have it settled once and for all but that he couldn't do that because he'd be lying. He said he was protecting the two other men and that he'd do the same again and lie about it again. I suppose nothing short of subpoenaed hostesses and receipts would get him to change his story. My contention was that honesty cannot be selective. He and Pennington agreed he has to re-earn my trust. The thing is, he had my trust before. I even mentioned how he had told another person he was fooling around with a secretary. Harry said he never said such a thing and wanted to know who said that as he'd like to confront him and cited how something said can be distorted in the retelling.

I also brought up the ad I put in The Advocate and described how Harry acted like a Cheshire cat over catching me. I still don't see why a non-guilty husband would have a passing thought his wife had placed an ad. He also said that what's more important is his sobriety because unless he maintains it, he'll die and I'll have less than nothing. That sounded to me like he was saying I'd not be able to make it without him. At one point I lost a grip on my composure; my damn voice cracked and my eyes got watery. I felt so trapped, thwarted, and incredulous and terribly frustrated. (So what else is new?) I said, "Then my only recourse is The Serenity Prayer and that doesn't help me."

I was dumbfounded by Harry's story as to why and how we happened to be there.

"Donna made the appointment and I'm glad she did." He ducked the question, "Why didn't you go to AA meetings as soon as you stopped drinking? Why did you wait two weeks?" When Pennington mentioned he's an Episcopal priest, Harry said he'd been an Episcopalian most of his life. That was news to me. I thought he spent more time in Christian Science. I had the feeling Harry came out of the meeting feeling he had scored, was on top of the situation, vindicated and unjustly accused, and that I had been diminished, even discredited. I came away feeling that surely Pennington could see through Harry's maneuvers, surely he knew he was lying about The Near East.

Now I ask myself what the hell difference does it all make? I refer to what feels like an exercise in futility. We didn't talk much on the way home. Well, he said he liked Pennington.

During the night Harry moved into the daybed because he said I was very restless. I was not surprised because my dreams included tidal waves, medical experiments and nightmares about our big white cat being changed into a huge white bull that fell on its back, was decapitated, but it took a few seconds before the head died and of my being trapped in an elevator going between the first and 13th floors with Harry and a white haired man who complained he had a heart problem, and of Harry, while I slept, moving furniture about, crazily, creating a chaotic mess.

Harry accused me of a frontal attack in Pennington's office and told me he did not like surprises; and that the informer who tattled about the secretary could be only one of two people. That subject ground to a halt because I did not feed into it.

I took the weekly newspapers out of his car and could tell from turning the pages one by one which pages he had looked at because they were the ones that were no longer connected by tiny perforations: he had looked at the personal ad sections only. I wrote:

Why is his honesty about the past so important to me? Until he's owned up to the past, how can I believe the present? Why did he throw away two pages of his credit card telephone bill?

Pennington said that in a year's time, Harry might say, "About The Near East, you were right," and I still might not be able to believe him. I feel if he ever owns up, he'll be telling the truth. Harry said he asked himself if he wanted to continue being married to me, had searched his soul, and very quickly decided yes, that he wants no one else, but he added, "There are a lot of women out there." I picked up on that but said nothing. (There are a lot of men—more than 500 responses so far to my ad. I told him that last weekend. He wants to read the letters, but I don't think that would *be wise. After all, I promised discretion; at least I implied it.) During counseling I felt, again, that Harry wants to avoid painful issues. I'm the one who brings up problem areas, e.g., my family and those interactions. I think Harry wanted to give the impression there are no problems now that he's stopped drinking (four weeks today). He cited the number of AA meetings he's attended. I mentioned we went to church, and he injected, "That was my idea," like he was trying to win approval (see what a good boy I am). I was moved by the church service. We're going again. Harry feels Pennington is another Harvey Dowd, "a nice guy, but I don't see what we're going to get out of it." Thing is, you can only get out what you put in. I'm candid, open. I wish he would be and perhaps in time he will be. Recovery is laborious. I'm getting help from Al-Anon, others' input and mine because I think I'm contributing, so that helps me, too.*

Harry told me that a good psychiatrist who has an appreciation for alcoholism will tell a patient to go to AA for a year and then come back and see him. He cited remarks made by a speaker at an AA meeting, that the reason psychiatrists have had such a low success rate is because alcoholics lie. Perhaps our counseling is premature, that the alcoholic thinking has yet to run its course? Of course the alcoholic thinking was still going on. I expected Harry to change his attitudes, but I had yet to change mine. I was behaving like a self-righteous prig.

I met a woman in Al-Anon, Nanette, whose husband stopped drinking about the same time Harry did. She, too, was counseling with Pennington who recommended she become a Family Patient for a week-long program at Spofford Hall, a new alcoholism treatment facility in New Hampshire. When I learned her insurance would cover all her expenses, and without knowing a thing about the place, I urged her to attend. I did not need X-ray vision to know she was miserable. She looked drawn, seemed listless.

Harry and I celebrated his birthday on Cape Cod—a sunshine-filled weekend of walking the beach, taking a whale-watching trip and eating like pigs. He was in good, stable humor and only occasionally seemed preoccupied. He was affectionate. The night we returned home we switched on the Jil Clayburgh, Alan Bates movie, *An Unmarried Woman* which we had first seen in a theater when I felt secure of Harry's devotion to me. During the first minutes of the movie, I already knew, of course, the husband was cheating. I exclaimed aloud, "He's such a prick," something I wanted to say to Harry. I wrote:

It's not surprising Harry chose to go to bed rather than watch. I'm still watching it, and the damn film is tearing me apart and putting me back together—ha. I'm far from being together, the Me of I. I've got a handle on alcoholism. Period.

A week later on Labor Day, I wrote:

Where am I at? I want to operate/function on/at one comfortable level yet I'm stratified, like Saturn's rings, wanting to develop spiritually but trying to follow Al-Anon's detachment modus operandi which means, in effect, having to sublimate my feelings and not being really honest. This means that a part of me gets better—or does it? In one piece of their literature they say not to let the alcoholic think he is getting away with anything less than honest, yet we're also advised not to push for feelings. Harry hides his feelings, a lot of them, many of his thoughts anyway which he may think would be injurious to our relationship. Yet until he gets in touch with his inner self, where is he and where are we? I don't understand his continuing fascination with the personal ads. He picks up two different editions of The Advocate. He looked at the local one three times today. Most, if not all, are ads placed by men. Is he still looking for the elusive sexual high? I don't ask because such a question would only compound my anxiety because I would not get an honest response.

At last week's regular Al-Anon meeting, the subject was honesty. I identified with two women's responses. One spoke of her need to learn all she could about the clinical facets of alcoholism and furthermore, that for her, without trust, there can be no real relationship. I learned later she has divorced her husband. Another woman said she was going through a particularly difficult time because she doesn't feel her husband is being honest with her. I'm in a position of trying to pretend that I trust my husband in the hope that if I take such a positive approach, it will be so, that by eschewing negative actions and reactions, I won't project negativity. There's even a saying for that: "Fake it until you make it." So rather than working from the inside out, I'm working from the outside in, and my sense of honesty has a problem with that. Late yesterday afternoon I developed a headache, the kind with sudden, piecing vibrations, like shafts of electricity. I took three grams of vitamin C at a whack several times which helped but occasional stabs continued, even through the night in my sleep. All day the headache has threatened to break through. Why? Simple. It's my anxiety about Harry's honesty.

At church yesterday, a communion service, the words spoken by the minister coupled with the fact it was the first time in ten years I'd taken communion affected me deeply, emotionally, and I was powerless against suppressing tears. I heard him say that voluntarily taking communion meant I was acknowledging the past but putting it behind, not absolving transgressions exactly but not clinging to them, not wiping the slate clean but of trying to be a better person—more loving, forgiving— of not planning to repeat past mistakes. I am unable to remember what else I heard, or what it seemed to me I heard, nor can I identify every thought and feeling I had which caused my tears and my sense of a spiritual attunement, albeit transitory. Certainly I've experienced an unrelieved succession of intense emotional experiences during the last ten years. I know that yesterday most of this awful summer came back to the surface, the worse summer I ever remember. I sat there between my husband and my mother, in a beautiful church, and how I longed to weep. This morning I cried a little tiny bit when Harry and I hugged, but he didn't want me to cry, so I stifled it. It only went inside, and unspent feelings seem heavier when they're driven back down again. Last evening I tried to talk with him about the communion service, my feelings, what he felt, but all I got from him was that he didn't feel the way I did and how Catholics confess and take communion and then repeat the same transgressions all over again. So I learned nothing about his feelings and I never seem to. Instead he doesn't so much talk about a subject but talks away from it. To the many long, revealing letters I've written to him, he's responded with stuff like, "I agree with you. You're right. I love you." I come away feeling empty, cheated.

Tonight I spoke about people who feel they are in tune with the cosmos and listening to our inner voice, and he said he's never heard any inner voice. Does this mean he's devoid of a conscience, is amoral? I hear an inner voice from time to time, and many times in recent months. I've felt I was being directed to certain things at particular times, especially when I was off the walls and had trouble thinking logically at all. I've felt my guides were very close. And I've thanked them and God, and I've felt more comfortable about turning to them for help. (I've got to ask more often and harder.)

In The Language of Feelings by David Viscount, M.D., he writes: "Without honesty there is no freedom."

Well, I've lived a life in which I've been painfully intimate with pain and joyously intimate with pleasure. So if nothing else, I can always say, "I lived." But if I were to have a grave and marker, I'd want it to read, "She loved."

So, where does all this fall in relationship to Al-Anon? And our counseling from Pennington? Am I forced to accept time and more patience? I feel as if I'm marking time, still in a limbo, as if I'm doing the right thing but wondering why it doesn't feel right.

I thought of Sally, a counselor at an alcoholism clinic, someone I talked with the year before when Harry thought he might go into a detoxification unit. I wrote:

I just talked at length on the phone with Sally. I seem to get more concrete help from non-Al-Anon philosophy, that is, alcoholism professionals are more graphic and definite. Not that I don't value the Al-Anon philosophy; come to think of it,

Sally was espousing it but doing so in non-namby-pamby verbiage. In essence, the word is for me to look out for myself, to make my own life. Yesterday I finally returned to the health club and today I have multiple good aches. I'd used my broken toe as an excuse for not going. In actual fact, I held off going because of something Harry said before he stopped drinking last July when I tried to wangle an invitation to accompany him a week hence on a business trip to the shore area. He had many reasons why I couldn't go and finally he said, "That's a Wednesday—health club day." I said, "So I won't go to the club." He said, "You don't know how I depend upon you going to the club on Monday, Wednesday and Friday!" So what I've been doing is playing a game, trying to thwart his free time, perhaps hoping to catch him being unfaithful, or at least making it more difficult or less easy to cheat. And, so what? He'd only deny anything anyway and in the meantime, I'm depriving myself of feeling and looking better.

That "game" is the stock in trade of a controller. There was no difference between my trying to thwart Harry's escapades than it was drawing a line on a vodka bottle to determine how much he drank on the sly. Al-Anon and family therapists frown on controlling behavior. And no wonder: it is soul-consuming.

With my 51ˢᵗ birthday only days away, I'm forced to recognize most of my life is behind me. And what's still to come, I want to be quality. It bothers me that recently while having sex, I have to resort to fantasizing to arouse myself, whereas before I knew he was unfaithful, I didn't. This clashes with my integrity. Sally suggested I tell him because by remaining silent, I'm carrying garbage and building resentments. But with Harry's fragile ego, especially regarding sex, I'm sure if I said anything, that would end our sexual coupling. So, I've opted for heterosexual coupling with fantasies over boring masturbation. Sally's philosophy, "If you're handed a lemon, make lemonade." But I don't like myself for doing so. Talk about a catch 22.

Recently we watched a TV interview of Bo Derek, 25, and husband John Derek, 54. I envied the free wheeling honesty of their marriage. We also watched a NOVA special about Dr. Linus Pauling, now elderly and still obviously in love with his wife and she with him whose open communication of depth emphasized what's lacking in my marriage. Sally pointed out the dilemma of alcoholic thinking, the inner turmoil Harry is going through. He's spoken of how worried he is about money. The rigid consensus is for me not to help him by selling any of my stock. That $1500 is all I have left. He's spoken of negotiating a loan. I feel he must take the responsibility. He did not talk with me at length about taking out the loan initially, and he "borrowed" $900 from me in January which he never repaid. He's secretive, which he wants me *to believe is due to worries about the economy and lack of business. Yet he doesn't seem to put in full work days.*

He wants all to be just as it was when he had his cake and eating who knows who besides. I pointed out to him he has an ideal setup—his own hours, own post office box, even an answering service. He said he will go to his grave denying he was ever unfaithful to me, that he couldn't be. All and more he told me when he was seeing others.

My inner turmoil was relentless. Three days later at midnight, I wrote:

Does the fact it is full moon give me the right to think crazy? To think maybe I might be crazy, paranoid, and then at once feel I am perhaps crazy to doubt my thoughts that send me in crazy circles? After our appointment with Pennington, Harry asked me, "When are you going to trust me?" I answered, "I don't know." I am so tormented by memory fragments dating back as long as four years, including his putdown remarks about me and to me (and to others about me, it seems) and then his "I'm only kidding," and his infidelity denials all along—and I ask myself, "Am I crazy to hang on, not to make a decision? Is Al-Anon helping me, can it when I'm so hung up on needing him to be honest with me for my sanity? How much can be attributed to alcoholism? Has he really admitted Step One?" I've acknowledged Step One. I feel, still, although I seem to be better than I was a month ago, that I'm hanging on to whatever with my fingernails. I'm tired physically yet I could not get to sleep so am up after giving myself an hour in bed. I feel terribly agitated. My gut feelings are that Harry is playing some kind of game with me. He tells me he loves me, has resumed calling me his precious girl, that he's sure of one thing: I mean everything to him, I'm all he wants. One night he went to AA and I to Al-Anon and we went together to two AA meetings; another evening to an Al-Anon anniversary meeting where we heard a wife (Al-Anon) and husband (AA) speak. Today we went to church; although it was his idea initially, I've been the one pushing to go ever since.

I saw Nanette at a meeting. She was glowing. Gone was the rasp from her voice, the dull eyes. She had spent a week in a treatment center in a program geared for family members. "They talk a lot about feelings," she said. "I hope I can hang on to what I got." I rejoiced in her new-found serenity and decided I wanted what she had.

"What did you say the name of that place was?"

"Spofford Hall."

During our next session with Pennington, I heard again how painful it can be for Harry to get in touch with his feelings. I spoke of how painful it was for me at the end of my first marriage, and I wasn't an alcoholic, but the

217

psychologist did not let me off the hook when I rationalized or threw up defenses. My greatest and most valuable lessons came out of pain, not pleasure. Pennington said I was ahead of Harry with my feelings.

My suspicious mind could not still itself. I thought of a young woman I befriended during the spring and at her request helped her write a speech for a large conference that focused on adoptees searching for their birth parents. During that period I saw a lot of her; visits at her place and mine were common. I had not seen her since mid-April nor had she phoned. When I called in May, she sounded preoccupied. In June I left a note at her house but there was no response. She had not struck me as someone who would take advantage of another's skills and then drop out of sight. My suspicious mind wondered if Harry contacted her and so ruptured the friendship. I think he did because years later I learned he made advances over the phone to several of the Al-Anon women who called me on a regular basis.

The new issue of the raunchy singles magazine was published that included the two ads I made up months before to entrap Harry. I knew it had been published because I found the plain envelope used for its mailing in Harry's wastebasket, but I could not find the magazine. I returned to that awful bookstore and bought a copy. My ads read:

W/F, 48, too old for an affair of her life? Trim, slim, curvy. Bored with fumblers. Want great sex not relationship. Your place or mine. Will answer all with SASE.

W/F, 30, with great body, looking for older man 45-55 with mature know-how. No candlelight and wine required, just sex filled fun. Daytime preferred. SASE guarantees an answer.

One night that week after we went to bed, Harry asked me, "When are you going to trust me?" I reiterated all I had said before, including my fear of his infidelity history being repeated. He spoke of how my ad in *The Advocate* bothered him, "the deceit of it."

I said, "All I was doing was fighting fire with fire."

He stated, voluntarily, he had not advertised at all; he did not know of any publications for singles advertising; had not seen any. But he wondered if I might have come across any and was advertising. I guessed he was suspicious about the ads I wrote in the latest singles magazine. I went along with the game. Why not? Games seemed to be our specialty.

"Has some ad in a recent issue of *The Advocate* made you wonder if I placed it?"

"No, but I just had a gut feeling you might have placed another ad someplace, and I wondered how reliable some publications might be about honoring confidentiality."

I had wondered if Harry and the publisher were in cahoots and now I wondered if maybe they weren't, and so he was worried about being found out. I said, "I think if they disclosed advertisers' identities word would get around in a hurry and people would stop advertising."

He talked about related subjects but kept returning to the same question. "Have you placed any ads, other than the one we both know about?" He wove the question in three or four times, and each time I lied and said, "No."

"Don't ever lie to me, Donna," he said, which struck me as the height of irony.

Again he declared he had never been unfaithful to me. We talked about the numbers of husbands and wives who are unfaithful.

I said, "Even if a wife does not have concrete evidence, she can often know something is going on because she senses something is being taken away from the marriage."

He brought up how I had originally denied running the ad in *The Advocate*. "But I finally did admit it, even before you confronted me with evidence. I didn't try to wriggle out of it by saying I'd been helping a friend, letting them use my address."

"Which is what I would have done," he said.

"Why, all of a sudden, are you asking me all these questions?"

"Oh, no particular reason. I just had this gut feeling. I'm tired of games; I don't want any more."

I could understand that. I was just discovering how tiring game-playing is, and I was a novice at it. I relished knowing he was beset with doubts about my honesty. I hoped he felt tormented as hell. I was nagged by the thought he had been playing games when he pushed for our marriage. "Did you really want to marry me?"

"Yes. Fortunately I had enough periods of sobriety not to get my thinking fucked up about how I felt about you. I'm proud to be your husband; I'm proud of you. I love you. I love our lovemaking. You're my precious girl."

We kissed goodnight and were quiet. My brain raced. I would not be able to begin trusting him again until he owned up to all I knew and also tore down the smoke screens surrounding episodes I sensed were way out of line. The next morning I wrote:

It was like he had compartmentalized his life—his life with me that he valued, did not want to lose, and the romancing Romeo life he dabbled in. He wondered if I'd follow through on my threat, "...sauce for the goose, sauce for the gander." I told him I was not interested in anyone else; that all my energy was going into our marriage. That was an understatement. He said the women who answer ads in The Advocate are probably hookers and he'd be concerned about the old badger game. That didn't make sense to me because men needn't spend money advertising for hookers.

Last night's Al-Anon meeting was a downer, a big meeting, perhaps 60 people. The subject was The Serenity Prayer, and I got tired hearing what sounded like banalities. Also, I get depressed being among so many who are continuing to endure the abuse of alcoholism. I can't help but view them as masochists.

Chapter 30

In the movie *Gaslight*, the husband (Charles Boyer) deliberately tries to make his bride (Ingrid Berman) think she is losing her mind by telling her she has not seen or heard what she believes she has. Finally when his plot is exposed and he is trapped and then roped to a chair, he begs her to cut him free with a knife. She has been so long under his demoralizing influence that audiences fear she will succumb to his desperate pleas and protestations of love. As she remembers how he has tormented her, she taunts him with the knife, saying that although it looks like a knife, it can't be a knife; she drops it and pretends she can't find it. Then she informs him she will not help him and that her decision is made "without a shred of pity, without a shred of regret." It was not unusual for audiences to break into applause.

Harry did not set out to drive me insane; nevertheless, I suffered through a "gaslight syndrome." He contended most of my illness was created by the physical violence I experienced with Steve. He spoke of how he had never laid a hand on me, that his drunkenness was sporadic, not constant. Steve's moods changed abruptly from loving to verbal abuse and/or physical brutality, and once his initial rage was spent, he nurtured hostile silence anywhere from hours to weeks. Steve was either Jekyll or Hyde, never both almost simultaneously. However, Harry's attitude towards me swung between loving attention and verbal invective laced with lies and lies, all within a matter of minutes. While Steve was full of apologies and worked overtime to get back into my good graces once he returned to rational thinking, Harry delivered his cover-ups with the righteous conviction of a wrongly accused man until my mind vacillated between knowing I was right and doubting my facts. I do not minimize the input Steve made into my co-alcoholism, nor do I discount the interim years of coping with my emotionally scarred, angry children. What I weathered contributed to diametrically opposite effects: I was made stronger, yet my mental stability was compromised. I believe Harry's mind games were an entity unto themselves, and his prolonged attempts to deny he had broken the trust brought me to the brink of madness. That I did not dump Harry once he verified much of what I believed to be true reinforced what I told him during our first weeks of knowing one another and restated time and time again: "I can stand almost anything as long as I am told the truth."

Although I was obsessed with Harry, I had not assimilated what I read about alcoholism and post-drinking behavior to appreciate the horrendous confusion surfeiting him. He was sober; I was hurting. It is a wonder I did not drown in self-pity. I thought of myself as a once bright leaf that gale winds—created by Harry—had wrenched from a branch and whirled down onto the ground to be stepped on—by Harry. All his talk about loving me, wanting only to make me happy, I heard as empty talk. His betrayal of our marriage and his persistent lying to me and now to Pennington as well—surely he knew this was neither love nor how to generate happiness. But Anita said alcoholics in early recovery lie believing they are telling the truth. The whole damn disease generated crazy-making!

I moved like a corpse within a tangled sheet of conflicting emotions. I picked up objects and then wondered why I held them. I was unable to concentrate on any subject beyond the attention span of a small child, with one glowering exception—my husband's past, present, and future behavior. I castigated myself for feeling white anger towards him because intellectually I knew he was a victim of a disease that gives license to irrational actions. Because I was schooled to believe that to hate was to commit evil, I tried to suffocate the hatred with layers of guilt. To feel anger was too painful; to feel my guilt about the anger was too painful. To feel love, even compassion, was too painful because loving re-exposed my vulnerability. My emotional board was overloaded, and I tried to rewire my feeling network so the needle would barely move. I wanted to become numb. In numbness there would be peace.

I did not, could not, permit myself to act out my inner turmoil in obvious ways. I did not scream out loud. I choked back crying every time I could because I thought Harry equated crying with weakness and I did not want to give him additional power over me. Besides, he often displayed anger when I cried. I had received all the anger from him I thought I could take. I tried to cry only when I was alone and often nothing happened, like dry heaves, so when tears did wet my face, I felt victorious. I had a desperate need to hang on to the image I wanted to project—rational, fair, truthful, assured and the whole jumble of stereotyped components of what society had educated me to believe constitutes a good wife. I was enslaved by that enfeebling question: "What will other people think?"

Anything I did required tremendous effort—personal grooming, basic household tasks, placing and returning phone calls, opening mail and answering it, preparing meals, even going to bed. My sleep pattern deteriorated. Many nights I got up and brooded in the dark. Other nights I paced. On warm nights, I walked about our property. That made me feel spooky and slightly mad. I was too old to play Ophelia. I felt swamped by despair, defeat, and oh, poor me, that I had been so badly manipulated. I hated my lot, fate. I longed to pray but my feeling of being unworthy of help had deepened and all I could say was, "God, why?" My conceit was so acute I felt my problems were at the center of the universe.

I was consumed by my burning need for full disclosure from Harry. I felt smothered by his emotional dependency on me, his need for me to center all my attention on him. I felt trapped—by my marriage vows; by alcoholism; by Al-Anon's "goody two shoes" message. The emotional conflicts within me worsened. I was torn between trying to salvage the marriage and bolting. My desire to flee begged my sense of responsibility for permission to chuck it all.

I found it difficult to adjust to an absence of drunkenness. What I had loathed, I missed because I had acquired methods of coping with unpredictable behavior. I no longer had a script to follow because overt alcohol abuse was not the pivotal character. I even missed being snarled at, ridiculed and browbeaten because when verbal abuse was in full flower, I could justify my anger and contempt. Contrary to Al-Anon's philosophy of live and let live, I baited Harry and deliberately tried to keep the pot stirred. Yet part of me wanted the cancer eating away at my insides excised, that voracious growth that made me feel I deserved to be demeaned.

Paradoxically, I experienced isolated periods of feeling better. I sensed some of the Al-Anon philosophy connecting when I felt a release from tension—fleeting foretastes of that elusive state of serenity, Al-Anon's pot of gold at the end of the rainbow. I did not want to crawl or walk into serenity, I wanted to run into it, charge at it with all barrels blasting and claim it as my own. And I wanted to do it my way. Consequently, I remained mired in grief for the loss of the person I had been, the loss of what I hoped my marriage would be, the loss of trust. I wrote in my journal:

But how do I work through this grief, when every day I'm living with the fucking corpse? I can't buy alcoholism as the master excuse. At some point, parts of Harry stopped maturing. I say he's saddled with a character disorder. I'm forcing myself to get to the health spa. I have to start with myself someplace. Inasmuch as I can't seem to deal with my splintered emotions, I'll work on my body. There are bound to be fringe benefits, like keeping me from going crazy or copping out with a breakdown because such would only prolong my dependence.

Chapter 31

In the tenth week of not drinking, Harry wrote a long letter to me. It began:

My Donna,

It is time for me to grow up, start acting like and being a real person, a loving, trustworthy, deserving husband and take Steps 4 and 5. The Big Book suggests this be written down, and I agree continual review is necessary—for both our sakes.

You've said you would know and recognize the truth. I hope so. I am now turning my life over to God. Living as I have will destroy us both.

He listed 21 characteristics he considered to be wrong with him. That was followed by, "Things that bug me," and he listed 17. Before continuing, he wrote:

This ain't easy, none of it. Comment: I have been wronged, too, probably 2:1 or more.

The next section he titled, "Step 5—To God, Donna (my choice as another human being) and myself, the exact nature of my wrongs)." This was what I had waited for; I read with eagerness and hope. He made passing reference to the hurt he created during his first marriage, and then he itemized the issues that had been consuming my energy. As far as the Lambsons were concerned, he stated, "There was nothing to this whatsoever." He wrote he had never seen her outside the store and no longer stopped there; that sex was the last thing on his mind where she was concerned; and that "I was wrong (and smashed) to ever call her at home. Maybe I thought I was lonesome.

Who the heck knows what my alcoholic mind was—thinking." The hitherto unexplained call to a number downstate was to a former date to whom he had lied about being single. He felt he had treated her badly and "my drunken motivation was to straighten things out." A man answered the first two times he called and the next time he tried, the phone had been disconnected.

As for Sherry, he stated he had not had contact with her since he stopped drinking. "She's probably glad. I know I am." He wrote that the night in December he was away all night he lied when he told me he stayed in a motel. He said he slept on her couch. The night in July he was away 12 hours, he wrote that he drove to Sherry's but did not stay. "I did spend the night in the car and damn near froze to death." He injected:

At this point I should confess that heavy drinking has made some sequences foggy but I know basically what transpired. Also, that this is very painful, but I'm holding nothing back. Further, alcohol in excess does render me impotent. A few drinks, getting slightly smashed, hasn't affected our sex life—am amazed at that—but prolonged drinking does and has finished me sexually.

And then I read:

The massage parlor episode. I lied. I was alone, stinkin' drunk and got conned and "screwed." I was told (as I foggily recall) that a $50 tip was normal for the full treatment. I said, "Fine, put it on the slip," which I signed. After a shower I was given a massage by a mulatto girl and she began to play with my genitals. Nothing happened. I mean nothing. I got up and left. The drinks and shame were too much. It was a disaster—God, how I've suffered over this. My ego wouldn't let me tell the truth—until now. She's probably still laughing at this middle-aged fool.

As for the time I was in New York, Harry wrote he lied about any men being here, a story he invented to cover up all the booze he drank.

About Adelia, he wrote that he had responded to an ad she placed in the swingers magazine; they talked on the phone, and he kept a luncheon date with her where he discovered she was fat and 50. He wrote that he went through with the lunch, nothing else, no sex, and that he had not seen her since. The two issues of the swingers magazine, he wrote, were mailed to him but he did not know how he got on their mailing list. About his own advertising, he wrote:

I did place an ad months ago—so stupid—done more out of alcoholic curiosity. I did not get a response—no replies. Thank God, as I am, was, and will always be incapable of this type of thing. As a swinger, I'd make a good paper hanger. There are no ads anywhere now.

It took Harry six hours to write the letter. He concluded:

I have no double life. I am seeing no one, anywhere. I am not looking for anyone. I want my wife back and no one else. We must start anew, with love and trust. I will do my part. There is no shit hidden—anywhere. I am sorry for the hurt I've caused you. I am capable of being sober and honest. If you'll have me, share with me, I'll work hard to be a good husband and make you proud of me.

Although I had no concrete evidence to the contrary, I sensed Harry's confession was incomplete because he addressed only the suspicious incidents I had belabored. In other words, he lied by omission. Even so, I sensed some of those explanations also contained fabrication. But because he owned up to his visit to the massage parlor, which must have been difficult for him to admit, I accepted what he wrote as a step in the right direction. However, my overall impression was Harry had again demonstrated his ability to practice selective honesty. I responded with a lengthy letter in which I referred to incidents that continued to trouble me, e.g., his drunken flights for long, unexplained hours, even over night, during the time we lived in the apartment. He did not elaborate. His association with Sherry was vague and incomplete; my hunch was she was his houseguest during the time I was in New York because otherwise why did he bother to tell her buying the house was a business arrangement? (My hunch turned out to be correct.) The Lambson explanation was full of holes. What I needed—even more importantly, what *he* needed, a complete "fearless and searching moral inventory" of what he had done that was unfaithful to his expressed commitment to me, before and after marriage, had yet to be written. I felt I had no choice but to try to begin rebuilding my trust in him while still harboring doubts about his honesty. I would try to do what Sally suggested: "When you're handed a lemon, make lemonade."

Chapter 32

Thoughts of Nanette, the Al-Anon member who spent a week at Spofford Hall, kept intruding into my consciousness. Her appearance alone told me she had benefited. I heard another woman in an Al-Anon meeting speak and I admired her gutsy attitude; she had also spent a week at Spofford. I knew that if possible, I would avail myself of their treatment. I wrote to Spofford requesting information. I summed up our present situation and wrote, "My gut tells me we could be doing more."

Instead of a reply letter, I received a phone call from the first Director of the Family Program, Sandra Cohen-Holmes. We talked at some length. For the first time since going to Al-Anon, I knew I was talking with someone who new exactly where I was coming from; however, Mrs. Cohen-Holmes displayed a depth of understanding that surpassed any I had encountered at Al-Anon and from Pennington. I learned that every Sunday morning Spofford offered a free orientation lecture open to patient's families, prospective family patients and the general public. I told Harry I wanted to attend the Sunday program and asked him if he would like to accompany me.

The hamlet of Spofford, New Hampshire, is roughly midway between Brattleboro, Vermont and Keene, NH, neither of which is exactly a teeming metropolis. In 1981, Spofford Lake was dotted with summer cottages, a typical small lake duplicated throughout New England. We rounded a corner, and the visual shock of Spofford Hall hit us—an elegant complex with one large section low to the ground and an attached wing that resembled any first-rate three-story motel. Well landscaped grounds shaded by tall Norway pines complemented the modern architecture. The lawns sloped directly to the water. The spacious reception area could have doubled as a lobby in a fine resort—four separate conversation areas. All furnishings, including the wall-to-wall carpeting were in complementary earth tones. Fine paintings and prints hung on the walls. I discovered attention to esthetic harmony prevailed throughout the facility. The large dining room was ringed with windows that looked out onto the lake; the vast, dramatic living room with its curved outside walls also offered window after window of water views. Each sleeping room with its own bath, two twin beds, modular bureaus and writing desks also included a separate round table flanked by armed occasional chairs. An indoor pool with an attached whirlpool, separate exercise areas with sauna and steam rooms attested to Spofford's concern with the total well being of its patients. Dependent and co-dependent patients were provided with a dignified setting for their recovery.

A soft-spoken young woman Carol, a therapist on the staff, conducted the two-hour orientation lecture. Spofford's philosophy included recognizing that alcoholism is a family disease; that affected family members are entitled to patient status equal to the alcoholic; and most important, the family is not used to "get to" the alcoholic but receives treatment for their own part of the illness so they may become whole human beings. We completed a True-False questionnaire which was then discussed and we received an answer sheet for enlightened discussion.

The Orientation's most fascinating segment was responding to the request that we call out symptoms of alcoholic behavior which were then jotted down on a large free-standing blackboard until all the space was filled. Next we were asked to call out what we, the so-called non-alcoholics, had felt or done. With the exception of being addicted to a mood-altering drug (such as alcohol), the symptoms were identical.

In her paper, "Conflict In The Hallways: Better Here Than Home," presented by Sandra Cohen-Holmes to the National Council on Alcoholism Forum held in New Orleans in April 1981, she stated: "The symptoms are the same because unsuccessful attempts to control either drinking or drinkers bring about the same results. Spofford Hall attempts to treat them for what they all have: acute and chronic alcoholism. Family patients have identical symptoms because they have the same disease. Treating them or their disease differently or separately is like watering half the garden and hoping the other half gets some rain."

Part of me wanted to accept her belief, the part that wanted to receive the same deferential compassion as the newly sober alcoholic who had to fight off the withdrawal demons, but another part thought our similar symptoms were due to coping with the unpredictable, bizarre behavior of an addict out to protect his degenerative lifestyle. Frankly, I resented being characterized as cut from the same cloth as someone whose addiction/habit was the catalyst for destroying families and committing other crimes against humanity. However, I figured that even if I could not swallow this same disease concept, becoming a family patient would be to my advantage. I was impressed by Carol's lecture and especially by the knowledge and compassion with which she conducted the orientation.

Before I made a reservation, I wanted to check out their food. On a long serving island flanked by shelves along which to slide a tray was a Sunday dinner buffet worthy of a fine restaurant. There were salad ingredients, rolls, butter, soup, vegetables, leg of lamb, and a variety of desserts. Also available were coffee, tea, milk, and water. The quality of the food was excellent. After enjoying all we could eat, Harry and I visited the Admissions Office where we learned our insurance would cover 100 percent of my treatment costs. Harry pressured me to make a reservation right then and there. I resisted because I was tired of feeling he controlled my life and because I was not sure if it were too early in his recovery for me to be away. I wanted to talk about it with Pennington.

Chapter 33

I looked forward to our next appointment with Pennington because with so much now out in the open—Harry having admitted what he had denied—our joint therapy and particularly help with our inadequate communication could get underway. My anticipation crashed when Harry suggested I keep the appointment by myself. "Right now you have more problems than I have," he said.

When it was time for us to leave, he agreed to go with me. Renewed hope returned. But as we walked through the corridors to Pennington's office, Harry said he hoped there would not be a lot said about the past he had admitted to me, particularly the massage parlor, the personal ads, Sherry and Adelia, the issues I had insisted were real and he had denied in front of Pennington. My expectations were we would share the facts but not the details so Pennington would know my accusations had not been false, that at least in one area I was not a crazy paranoiac. By acknowledging his dishonesty to me to Pennington, I would be validated. Not only did I feel cheated but I felt Harry was manipulating me and trying to control the tenor of the counseling. During our previous visits, my ability to communicate with Pennington was marginal at best. My impression was he looked upon me as the albatross around Harry's neck, that he had no appreciation of the torment I endured as a result of Harry's bizarre drinking behavior. I felt Pennington attacked me with a whip and coddled Harry with kid gloves. I could not follow much of what little Pennington said because he was maddeningly laconic, and

I needed to hear full sentences.

Unbeknown to Harry, I phoned Spofford Hall the day after we attended the orientation and made a reservation for two weeks hence. During our session with Pennington, both men stressed it was important for me to go to Spofford. I said, "I am definitely going," but I preferred not to say when because I thought it would be easier for Harry and me if only one of us knew when I was going until a few days ahead of my departure. Pennington said that too often people would say they were going for treatment but unless they made a definite commitment, would end up not going. I looked straight at Pennington and repeated, "I am definitely going to Spofford." When our abbreviated hour was up, I could hardly wait to get home and mix myself one hell of a martini.

Harry sympathized with my frustration but from the standpoint that Episcopalian clergy tended to be chauvinistic. My feeling was that because Pennington was a recovering alcoholic, he identified more with Harry's recovery than with mine. I was reluctant to give full vent to my feelings in front of Harry because I did not want to inadvertently give him any excuses to decide—again—that counseling was for the birds. But very early the next morning after being awake for hours, I wrote to Harry:

I am filled with angry feelings. Why?

I looked forward to our meeting with Pennington yesterday. Although very tired, weary, I felt more positive and hopeful about our marriage than I have since you wrote Steps 4 and 5 ten days ago—and loving you more than I did ten days ago.

But being asked not to belabor any points about old garbage, to keep Steps 4 and 5 between ourselves and God put me on the defensive. You asked me not to make a big deal out of the massage parlor as it had caused you enough pain and embarrassment already.

You were pained and embarrassed about the massage parlor visit itself and then further by sitting in Pennington's office denying my accusations. How do you suppose I felt? I sat there knowing facts and being told I was wrong, that I was imagining things. Those things included my disbelief about how you met Adelia, to say nothing of the personal ads crap.

What would it have cost you to own up to Pennington that you were guilty of making me out to be "super-imaginative"? Instead you made an indirect statement about "needing to get rid of the garbage" so you could get well.

It feels to me like you ducked, avoided, the painful and embarrassing repercussions of your pain and embarrassment at the expense of mine. It also seems to me that by avoiding making a statement of apology, that you cheated yourself out of the full value of growth to be derived from the Steps. So as I sat there, I felt like I was still coming across as a woman who can't differentiate between truth and fiction.

And the pressure on me to go to Spofford Hall began while we were still in the Admissions Office. You wanted me to make a reservation right then. On the ride home, although you disclaimed trying to influence me, I got the opposite impression. This was reinforced yesterday in Pennington's office.

I had good feelings about going to Spofford Hall. My intent was to get my own thinking and feelings worked out, exposed and understood, so that I could then make positive contributions to our marriage; so that by being closer to complete within myself, I could be an asset to your continued recovery and to the viability of our marriage.

My feelings now after what transpired yesterday with Pennington is that if I go to Spofford Hall—if and when—I'll go FOR MYSELF; and then as far as your recovery and our marriage are concerned, let the chips fall whatever way they fall.

It's been stressed by Al-Anon and you that much of your recovery can be affected by my attitude. Therefore, I've been thinking in terms of the full picture— you, me, marriage.

I don't have a feeling of your real support. I feel that my attitude is my full responsibility, that I have to work on me independently of you. I don't get any sense of there being a team effort. I got the feeling yesterday that somehow I may be considered as being an enabler of your alcoholism and/or alcoholic thinking—like, hey Donna, what the fuck is the matter with you?

About my hesitating to be away seven days, I wanted to explore this with Pennington, not re the possibility of you hitting the bottle (that did not occur to me) and re you fooling around in my absence (you'd already assured me, voluntarily, that in my absence you would be a "faithful, loving husband"), but rather would being "alone" for seven days be too much of a strain for you during this early recovery period.

Instead, the whole subject degenerated into making me look like a jealous wife. When he asked me what I was afraid of, he supplied the answer before I could get my thoughts out (and by that time, I was completely addled anyway). He said, "You're afraid he'll drink and live it up?" or something like that. And regarding any feelings of the possibility of you fooling around, he said, "So what?"

That "so what" struck me as callous. I wonder if a woman counselor would have been so flippant. My feeling is that women, wives, may have stronger feelings than men regarding men's marital infidelity.

I can't seem to get across how much I value marriage and particularly ours. And why what has transpired has so devastated me. I feel like I'm being patted on the head, being patronized—"there, there"—and my frustration is acute—chronic, and now acute.

Did I see you as a knight in shining armor when I left my home and joined you in the apartment? Had I not worked through the emotional turmoil of the previous five years and so went from the frying pan into the fire—and now the burns are being manifested? I sure as hell don't know.

But I know what I feel. I feel like I'm getting double messages from you. I feel you love me but at the same time you want to belittle me, to make me appear less and you appear to be more. I don't sense a pervading spirituality. I feel you resent me.

I feel lousy.

I went back to bed and slept through Harry's departure. He left me a note:

My love,

Read your note and am able to understand your anger. You should bear none of the blame: it was my behavior that caused our problem.

I love you.

s/H.

I phoned Sally, the counselor, and recounted the session with Pennington. She helped me understand what Pennington was probably trying to accomplish: because it takes the alcoholic longer to sort through post-alcohol confusion, counselors like to have the affected family members get well quickly so they can then assist with the alcoholic's recovery. I felt a flash of anger. I had spent years while sober trying to adjust to Harry's alcoholic demands, whims, and aberrations. I interpreted her interpretation of Pennington's objective to mean I had to continue putting Harry first. I suppressed my anger because as a woman and wife, I was conditioned to being relegated to second-class consideration. My anger was healthy.

Spofford's orientation and the reading I did emphasized my need to have treatment for me. Because alcoholism is a fatal disease, that death is a certainty unless the alcoholic abstains from any and all alcohol, counselors understandably want the non-dependent spouse to get help, too, because there is a 50 percent chance the alcoholic will relapse if the spouse's attitudes remain unchanged. I resented what I perceived as two recovering alcoholics ganging up on a squirrely wife.

When I told Sally about Harry wanting to censor what I might relay to Pennington about his written 4th and 5th steps, she said, "Oh-oh. That sounds like he did them more at the intellectual than emotional level, so he's feeling uncomfortable because probably he is still carrying a lot of guilt." Her assessment coincided with mine, but I was not cheered by it. She reminded me it took a long time to create garbage and it would take a proportionate amount of time to undo it: spending six hours one afternoon writing did not constitute the creation of a clean slate. Healing time was required for both of us, and we could not heal from the inside out unless we purged ourselves of our emotional poison.

After we talked, I wrote again to Harry and couched some of what I gained from Sally in what I hoped was diplomatic and not inflammatory language, but still specific enough to stimulate his thinking. In part I wrote:

I see nothing amiss in your ego and therefore I don't see any need you may have to present yourself other than exactly who you are because I believe you to be a basically fine, decent person, definitely worthwhile and valuable and important in your own right. Any time I feel you are stating something that is not factual, I am going to mention it. I would expect you to do the same with me.

I chose the letter as my way of letting him know I had made a reservation at Spofford Hall.

Pennington's "So what?" probably also meant: "So what can you do about it?" I'd already covered that should there be any further extracurricular activities I would terminate the marriage. But the "So what? If you should not be a loving, faithful husband while I'm gone—well, I can't do anything about that. I can't control you and/or your actions. Except when you were on a bender, you were not away during the evenings. And while I'm home, you're away during the days. So my being away for seven days and nights does merit a "So what?"

I'm going to Spofford Hall for me. If it turns out the benefits I receive can also be incorporated into building our marriage and facilitating your recovery, then that'll be so much gravy.

I've worked out the anger I came away with yesterday. Your little note helped tremendously. I love you.

Much of my love for Harry was not healthy. I wanted to own his thoughts, to direct his recovery, to make sure he was doing all he needed to do. I did everything short of physically climbing into his head. When an AA speaker said something I felt was important for him to tune into, I repressed the urge to nudge him; instead, I tried to expand my peripheral vision. Whatever Harry shared with me about meetings he attended alone, I listened for clues about his recovery progress. I wondered how well he was connecting others' words to what I felt were issues germane to his recovery. As far as I was concerned, his talk about his new-found spirituality did not jive with perpetuating half-truths. I told myself that anyone who used the words "honest" and "truth" in conversation about themselves as Harry did was being neither honest nor truthful because an honest and truthful person does not feel the need to talk about their integrity: they live it.

I limited my Al-Anon meetings to one or two a week. I continued to read voraciously but I did not use the telephone to call other Al-Anon members with the exception of Anita: I called her a number of times. Although I still did not have a handle on the Al-Anon philosophy, I sensed Anita did. Many of the others I met in meetings projected inner tension whereas Anita exuded calm. I read the Al-Anon Steps and Traditions and half-heartedly practiced them in my head: I thought they applied more to others less intelligent than I. I was all pushed out of shape about Harry's ego, and mine was big enough to choke a horse. I wondered why I was not being transformed into a model of serenity. The answer was simple. I was selective about what I used of the Al-Anon program, exploring only those areas which I felt I could master easily. No one in Al-Anon challenged me. No one got on my case. Consequently I became more and more obsessed with the recovering alcoholic, and my co-alcoholism progressed.

I was a walking and talking arsenal of information pertaining to alcoholism. Intellectually I had an in-depth understanding of the disease and its effect upon us both. I no longer felt any stigma attached to the terms "alcoholic" or "co-alcoholic" because I saw them not as labels but as diagnoses. My self-image was not going to keep me from seeking treatment. I knew I was emotionally troubled. In my mind I had all the answers. But I was unable to translate the intellectual knowledge into emotional understanding because I was being eaten away by resentments over my husband's behavior. My recovery regressed.

Two nights before I was to leave for New Hampshire, Harry told me an AA friend intimated he and his wife were not getting along too well. The friend said he thought the spouse could be more sick than the alcoholic. I interpreted the remark to mean the alcoholic husband was trying to present himself in a more favorable light. Harry didn't help by saying, "After all, you have the same disease." I did not like what he said or the way he said it. I was not a boozing drunk! I was an emotional drunk.

I learned from Mother that David told her a doctor had confirmed that his girl, Laura, was pregnant. Because David and Laura had assured me they would let me know as soon as they found out, I felt David was rejecting me—again. That hurt.

Liz visited and together we froze a bushel of broccoli. I wrote:

How I love that girl! I thoroughly enjoy her company, her insightfulness, wit, perception. And my heart goes out to her over and over again because of the hole she's dug for herself. She doesn't have two dimes to rub together and is hoping she's pregnant.

On her own Liz went to a few Al-Anon meetings and also some with me. Her husband Mike's problems from drinking and smoking pot were escalating. But Liz decided that the Al-Anon meetings she attended were enough.

It was three months since Harry stopped drinking. I was shocked by my reflection in the mirror. The eyes that stared back at me reminded me of the eyes of a wounded hunted animal. I was face to face with my own pain and fear. I felt pain with the fear and fear of the pain. I wondered what I would learn about myself at Spofford Hall. I told myself I didn't care how much emotional pain was involved if feeling more pain could release me from pain.

Part Two

Intervention at Spofford Hall

Chapter 34

At six in the morning on the day I left for Spofford Hall, I wrote to Harry:
My love,

Such foolishness, being awake the past two hours. We've cuddled, you've rubbed me (and me you), I've counted numbers—and I've thought about You and the Septic Tank; You and the Wood; You and the Cats; You and Keeping Warm; You and Eating Breakfast; You and Taking Vitamins.

I've also thought I'd better pack my warm cloche (hat) and mittens and long underwear tops because could be damn nippy jogging/walking at 6 a.m. in New Hampshire.

And of course I've thought about "Sleepy Hollow," wondering what really goes on there and will go on within me. Hoping that assuming I am assigned a roommate that (1) she sleeps soundly so my sounds don't disturb her; (2) she has a sense of humor (re #1 and other reasons).

I haven't projected much about the drive itself except I want to take a can of V-8 with me in front seat, maybe an apple. Stop for cigarettes. And should I drive to the Admitting door and disgorge all my gear on sidewalk and then park the car? Anyone would think I was going on safari.

I've thought about your meeting with Pennington, how if my attitudes re trying to communicate with him are brought up that you'll express yourself to him as you have to me, i.e., that you understand my frustrations.

And, because of the difficult experience I've had with Pennington, I hope I don't have problems communicating with whomever at Spofford Hall. It's so seldom that

I can't get on with someone; I think that's a needless apprehension.

Leaving you is not easy. I get weepy thinking about it. I love you, Harry. I've hated the crap that came into our lives, true, but as disgusted and frustrated I became, I never stopped loving you—the basic you that has so much goodness and compassion.

I feel good about how far we've both come in three months. I rejoice that I feel better about being able to talk with you vs. talking to you or having you talk to me. I feel the chords of response now that I've wanted, longed for, and I feel I'm only occasionally walking on egg shells. I'm feeling more loved by you, and oh Harry, I want your love.

I'm glad I'm going to NH now and not a few weeks ago because I am going to understanding and not running away, and that's such a positive feeling. I am literally wrenching myself away from you as I in one breath hate to leave yet in the next I know it's necessary. Oh, everything would probably work out OK if I didn't go, but the process could take longer.

About worrying about you while I'm away. I've voiced my fears as they've surfaced. I don't think I'm worried about you having a slip. I'm believing you about your fidelity to our marriage. Please forgive me for momentary attitude slips of my own, and I'm expecting greater understanding about this through my efforts at Spofford Hall.

I'll have you with me every moment. How can I tell you how important you are to me? Hell, I'm getting all weepy. So I'm going to do my sit-ups and leg raises.

Have a good week, a really good one. And take good care of yourself. You are precious to me. I love you with all my heart.

A few days later I received the note Harry wrote to me soon after finding my letter:

My love,

Thank you for your beautiful note. I cried like a baby. You've been gone a half hour and I miss you so.

10,380 minutes, 622,800 seconds and you'll be home.

I know that your going is as much for me (maybe more) as it is for you, And I am very grateful to have you for my wife.

Donna, I could never be unfaithful to you. You are my precious girl.

Enjoy! I love you.

s/H.

On the back he drew two faces, one sad for how he felt that day and one smiling, how he would feel when I returned home.

A few diehard leaves still clung to branches when I set out on that gray

October morning for Spofford Hall. My thoughts and feelings blended, separated and meshed only to splinter again, as if they were in a food processor that kept blowing fuses. I felt both sad and excited as I said goodbye to Harry. I choked up when we held each other, but better than half of my sadness feelings were dictated by guilt: I was far more eager to be away from Harry than to stay with him. I felt guilty because I did not feel as sad about leaving him as I thought I should and not as sad as he indicated he felt about my leaving. I felt I was being selfish to go away by myself, for myself, leaving Harry at home for a week with the cats, wood to split, and a septic tank to uncover so it could be pumped out. I kissed him goodbye and felt another wave of sadness and guilt because he looked so forlorn. I reassured him I would telephone every evening. Relieved that the parting was over, I got in the car and headed for New Hampshire.

The further north I traveled, the landscape became less like fall and more like winter. Naked trees were silhouetted against a lowering sky. Midway, I drank from a can of V-8 and was annoyed when some spilled on the front of my white sweater. A makeshift first aid kit in the glove compartment included alcohol preps, and I dabbed and swabbed until only a hint of pink remained and I reeked of alcohol. The irony of arriving at an alcoholism treatment center smelling of alcohol forced me to smile, but I felt uncomfortable about meeting other family patients while wearing a blemished sweater. I consoled myself with the thought I would check into my room and change. More than twelve hours elapsed before I had time to shed that sweater.

I was eager to get to Spofford. From reading library books and talking with Sandy and Nanette, I knew that for alcoholism-affected people, group therapy was more effective than one-on-one counseling. I knew that deep inside me were smothered feelings I had to air. I was not afraid about what I might find out about myself because I already knew the worst and carried heavy guilt because of it——how I had failed to live up to my maternal responsibilities, not protecting Liz and David from Steve, not being an effective parent in the years following the divorce. I wore my guilt like a hairshirt, adopting them only to rob them of a father figure when I divorced Brad. To remember them as vulnerable babies placed in my arms by foster parents, innocent little human beings who were given up by their birth mothers in favor of a better life, was to feel a pain no anesthetic could alleviate. I had not lived up to my expectations of responsible motherhood and far worse, I had disappointed and hurt my children. I grieved for the injury I had done to them.

I talked aloud in the car. I tried to pray and hoped I sounded sincere. "It's in Your hands," I said. I felt closeness with the spirits of Grammie and Daddy, sensing they were giving me moral, loving support. I sent words out into the ether to four of my cousins who were dead. The first was killed in France during World War II; the second was killed a few years later while piloting his plane; the third was killed two years earlier while crossing the street in front of her house; and the last one, the one I was the closest to, had died the year before because he stopped wanting to live; learning years earlier he was an alcoholic filled me with sadness. However, I was relieved that with his death, the pattern of sudden accidental death was broken because my superstitious mind was reassured my chances of living to a ripe old age were improved. By talking to my beloved Grammie, Daddy, and my favorite cousin, I created a supportive, but unseen, family to accompany me through the doors into Spofford Hall. I needed more than Harry and Mother rooting for me.

At 10:30 am I placed my luggage in the switchboard room, a half hour earlier than I was told to arrive. One case held vitamins which I had cleared with Sandy that I could bring provided they were still in their original containers. Transferring the 23 bottles into a cardboard box created what I hoped would be only a minor and short-lived sensation. I had to leave the vitamins at the nursing station. My anxiety level was rising but I told myself everything would work out.

Polly was the next family patient to arrive, a tall, slender woman with beautiful blue eyes, wearing a well-tailored tweed suit. I thought her appearance epitomized sensible Boston chic. Later I learned her household had been in terrible deficit spending crises for years and that the suit was a hand-me-down gift. Polly joined me in the front lobby. Words shot out of her mouth with the rapidity of a machine gun. She neglected to finish sentences, even idiomatic expressions; I marveled at her verbal shorthand. She referred often to God and being in God's care, and I wondered what it would be like to have such solid faith. Polly's openness was endearing. Her confusion and emotional exhaustion were alarming. I hoped we might be roommates, but the fact I smoked and she didn't ruled out that possibility.

We new family patients came together for the first time in a room dominated by a large rectangular conference table. We straggled in and sat down. A self-conscious silence pervaded. I glanced at each woman for a clue to her personality. Penelope, who became my roommate, was pulled as taut as taffy. I felt she wished she could be anywhere but where she was. She was the only one older than I. Joann was tall, and her ample girth eclipsed Penelope's brittle thinness many times over. Her thick mass of wiry curly black hair accentuated her brooding expression. The youngest, Connie, only 13, had begun the metamorphosis from child to young woman. Her liberal use of eye makeup in conjunction with residual baby fat and developing breasts reminded me of how impatient I was at her age to appear grown up. Her shoulder length white-blonde hair, as frothy as early morning sunshine, framed her pretty little face. Connie was accompanied temporarily by her mother who was winding up her four-week stay as a chemically addicted (CD) patient.

Fifi, christened Bridget Siobhan in honor of her Irish-Scottish ancestry, had brown Orphan Annie hair, was of medium height and trim except for a rounded belly. She reminded me of a floppy rag doll that had been trained to sit straight. Madeline was the last to enter the room and took the empty seat at the head of the table. She was impeccably groomed in a casually elegant suit, long shapely legs encased in what I hoped were real silk stockings, fine leather pumps, and she carried a proportionately costly leather bag. I admired the professional artistry of her makeup. Every manicured inch gave the impression of a fashion magazine's idea of a modern executive woman. How appropriate that she occupied the chair denoting power. Her glamour triumphed over her air of bone-tired weariness.

In the presence of Madeline, I felt like a slob. I broke the silence by gesturing to her and saying, "Just what I needed——a Sophia Loren look-alike."

Fife quipped, "Yes, but can she type?"

I laughed with appreciation of Fifi's quick humor and thought, "Oh good, there's a least one other nut in the crowd," the other one being me.

Madeline looked surprised. "I can't type but my secretary can," and I thought, "Oh dammit, I hope she isn't going to be stuffy."

We wrestled our luggage to the second floor and found our names on the doors. My room faced the parking lot. I was reminded of the parking lot views from the apartment Harry and I shared, and the memories were unpleasant and claustrophobic. I longed to be across the hall with a window that looked out onto the lake. Water views soothe me. I took solace in one advantage: I had a room to myself. We had no time to unpack before we were herded to the nursing station to receive our hospital-style wrist bands. Those of us who drove our cars there were relieved of our car keys. No question about it: I was a bonafide alcoholism-affected family patient quartered in a rehab facility.

While we ate our delayed Sunday dinner, Irene, the last of the eight family members, arrived and was introduced by an admissions staff member. I wondered why she arrived two hours late and since I considered tardiness a sign of discourtesy, I had reservations about liking her. She was of medium height, and gave the impression of having a large frame. I felt intimidated by the physical power she exuded. Because her short brown hair was shot through with gray, I thought she was about my age. Actually she was ten years younger.

The eight of us were there because we were affected to varying degrees by alcoholism in our families. The fact we ranged in age from 13 to 58 became insignificant; none of us reflected our chronological age. We came in different sizes and shapes and from different backgrounds. Our differences were eclipsed by what we shared in common—emotional pain. Like pioneers who circled their wagons to strengthen their defenses, we banded together, creating a bond that intensified throughout a week jam-packed with concentrated efforts to focus on ourselves. Unlike the westward ho travelers, our primary enemy had moved from the outside world to within ourselves.

Four had family members in the 28-day program for chemically addicted patients. There was Connie's mother, Pat, and the husbands of Fifi, Joann, and Madeline. One of Penelope's adult children who had completed the month-long program had persuaded her to become a family patient. Polly was urged by her psychologist to attend. I think Irene and I arrived by similar routes to our decision to check in. We were eight troubled people who somehow still had a spot of healthiness within us strong enough to accept direction and ask for help. At first we reached out to one another in tentative, subtle ways, but as the week went on, most of us craved feedback from each other and stated our needs clearly.

Spofford Hall's seven day residential program for families and other concerned persons repeatedly emphasized that we were patients in our own right and not appendages to the alcohol and/or chemically dependent whose eccentric conduct had automatically earned them center stage attention. I was there to rehabilitate myself. The family program was designed to help me recognize the effects of another's alcoholism and drug addiction on myself and to accept help for my own problems inherent within this affliction that, like pancake batter, poured into a hot skillet overtakes anything else trapped within its rim. They offered me in-depth knowledge of alcoholism and drug addiction. They helped me identify my defenses and inner feelings and assisted me in learning new communication patterns. They hoped my week would make me want to choose to change the role I had developed from coping with the skewed family dynamics and would help me discontinue enabling behavior that serves to fuel addiction. Throughout the process, I began to rebuild my self-esteem and accept responsibility for my own well-being. The more than one hundred alcoholics and other addictive patients had their programs for rehabilitation; I and the other affected family people had our own. Although dependents and co-dependents shared many of the same symptoms, my confusion, hurt, anger, inadequacy, frustration, and fear were my pain to resolve.

Carol, the same soft spoken therapist who conducted the orientation program Harry and I attended two weeks earlier, caught up with us after dinner as we started to unpack. When she discovered I had no roommate, she said that was not allowed; everyone must have a roommate. The smokers and non-smokers were identified. Polly moved out of Penelope's room, and I moved in—into a room facing the lake. Polly and Irene teamed up; Joann and Connie, the two youngest, shared a room; and Fifi and Madeline became roommates. I apologized in advance to Penelope about my snoring; both Harry and my kids teased me about it. Penelope had brought a stack of magazines not realizing we would not have a minute's time or inclination to indulge ourselves in escape reading. In addition to my Al-Anon *One Day At A Time* book (the *ODAT*), I brought several Al-Anon pamphlets, Vernon Johnson's book *I'll Quit Tomorrow*, and a thick novel with convoluted syntax that was beyond the capabilities of my churning mind. I later returned it to the library unread. I also brought a new journal for keeping a running record of the week. I wrote in it twice—that morning while waiting in the front lobby and that night.

There was not time to finish unpacking before our 45-minute orientation. We grabbed the blue multi-ring notebooks issued to us earlier—and our pocketbooks. Female family patients were easy to identify by the pocketbooks they carried at all times. I can't speak for others, but during the drinking years my purse was my mini-survival kit: I was prepared for flight on a moment's notice. Orientation included familiarizing ourselves with the physical layout and Spofford's strict rules and regulations, none of which struck me as unreasonable.

Next, in an hour-long Group Introduction, we were told to select another person, find a quiet spot, and ask, "Who are you?" and to listen carefully to the response because when we reassembled, each of us was to share what we had heard. We had five minutes to talk about ourselves and if we hesitated, our partner was to ask again only the one question, "Who are you?" Connie and I sat on a couch in the front lobby. I discovered how shy she was, how difficult it was for her to express herself. To describe the exercise is to render it as being deceptively simple. Actually, I found it one of the week's most difficult, perhaps because it was the first and also because I was asked to open up to someone I had met only hours earlier and to a teenager who was almost 40 years younger than I. But the real kicker was discovering I no longer had a defined idea as to who I was.

During the next hour, a different family therapist talked to us about "Alcoholism/Drug Dependents." This was my introduction to Alena, a short young woman with cropped, glossy black hair, a pretty face dominated by large dark eyes, thick lashes and heavy brows, and mannerisms I found annoying. She bobbed her head after making statements, like she was affirming what she had said. Sometimes she responded to a question or statement by cocking her head and saying nothing but prolonging eye contact with silence. Among former family patients, this was known as "The Alena Look." She could be curt with her responses. In my vulnerable state, I also found her abrasive, especially when I felt she was deliberately picking on me. As the hour wore on, I perceived her as a pushy bitch. I hoped I would not see much of her because I felt uncomfortable in her presence.

Before we broke for the evening meal, we were asked to choose a group representative for our morning Community Meeting, someone through whom to channel any complaints or needs we might have. I was chosen and wondered why it was that ever since I was a young girl, although I seldom was elected to any office, my peers singled me out to be the spokesperson for disagreeable issues. We were also told to select someone to awaken us at six the following morning. Madeline volunteered because she said she would be up much earlier than that to wash and blow dry her hair. These responsibilities were supposed to rotate but for whatever reasons, one being that Madeline and I satisfied the requirements, the group agreed to have us keep the assignments.

After supper I telephoned Harry, and then I sat at the round table in my room with Penelope. We concentrated on completing a 94-question "Psychosocial Evaluation." The following excerpts reflect exactly how I felt that first exhausting evening at Spofford Hall. In response to what effects friends' or family's drug or alcohol abuse had on me, I wrote:

Have you ever seen a wreck walking? (If the musical parody was missed, I sketched a couple of notes.) *During active drinking, I felt anger, resentment. Detested illogical speech. Bored!* (*I'm referring to my husband's drinking.*) *I felt sexually turned off to drunken advances. But the worst was the absence of*

248

honesty—the deceit, the amorality.

I described my relationship with Mother:

Excellent—great role model—a true friend (with only a few exceptions, all of which I understand). Very supportive of me.

When asked about any family members who might have mental health problems, I wrote:

My children and I suffered during my second marriage. I thought I had resolved my feelings, but my kids still carry strong resentments, including against me for (1) marrying him in first place and (2) not divorcing him sooner. I left at the earliest opportunity I felt we'd all be safe.

In the section called "Vocational Assessment," I had some fun. When asked if I were presently employed and if so for how long, I wrote:

"No. Two years."

I responded to the question about where and what type of job:

My husband and I formed a publishing company (tax write-off) and have published three pieces for mail order. (He doesn't want me to work; feels I've worked enough.)

I was asked the approximate salary of my job and wrote:

Funny!

That was followed by a question asking me how I felt about my job:

Hysterical. Seriously, I've supported myself, off and on, for 30 years, mainly through writing.

Asked to describe my relationship with my boss, co-workers and/or employees, I couldn't resist stating:

We sleep together.

I had no difficulty becoming serious again when asked if the chemical problem in my family had interfered with my job, job performance or attendance:

I've not been able to do one damn bit of creative writing since June—and only sporadically before that. Looking back, I've not enjoyed any prolonged contentment for 25 years.

In the section, "Current Emotional Status," I was asked to describe my moods and/or emotions during the previous month:

Erratic. Easy to cry. Emotions on the surface.

I was instructed to check off any words that applied to how I had been feeling and I checked all of them—joy, fear, depression, anger, numb, guilty, tired, bored, hurt. I crossed out "hopeless" and I amended "cheated" to "cheated on." For my choice of an additional feeling, I wrote,

"Grief."

Was there one feeling I had experienced more frequently than any other throughout most of my life?

Fear of being left. Began with fear my mother might die and I'd be an orphan. Transformed into fear of rejection by those I love.

When asked if I prefer to be alone frequently, I wrote:

Occasionally, yes. I like to collect my thoughts. I was an only child and got used to and then savored privacy, but not all the time.

In response to if I felt most people understand me, I wrote:

Yes. This current marriage counselor (Pennington) has me stumped. My daughter seems to be developing a better understanding of me. She's been a marvelous friend.

Do I have any fears?

Yes. Other than fear of rejection—and this is really the same thing—that my husband may be amoral again and maybe he didn't really want to marry me.

Without hesitation I responded to what was the most important thing in my life right that moment:

To get my head and my act together and feel good about me and contribute positively to a healthy marriage and my husband's continued recovery.

Asked what I would be doing if I didn't have these problems:

What I want to accomplish! If single, I'd be working—writing. I'd like to be a successful creative writer, finish a book.

The final question concerned what completing the form had done for me:

Given me writer's cramp, smarting eyes (fatigue)—and made me realize that the spectrum is bigger than I thought.

I headed some additional writing I did that evening with "Addendum," but I have no idea what it was an addendum to. It reads:

I'll know I've changed because it'll be like lights have been turned on in various rooms; I'll look better, especially my eyes—they'll have life in them again. I'll have a sense of peace, serenity, calmness, as once I did.

I have two major concerns or problems which I feel could interfere with my total involvement in my rehabilitation program. The first is tonight when I phoned my husband; he said he'd not felt that hot all day, and he didn't think he was ill, but due to my not being there—missing me. The rainy, windy, cold weather interfered with some of his outdoor plans, but he didn't tackle his desk as he thought he would, just sat and rattled around. He did not feel like attending an AA meeting.

One of my major concerns about coming here now was that it might be too early in my husband's recovery for me to be away—not that I was concerned he'd have a slip—and I think I got over the concern he might decide to fool around with someone. But when I tried to discuss this with our marriage counselor, he told me (I'm paraphrasing what I understood him to say) that I needed to come to SH for myself; that I could not control my husband. And so again I felt a subject I was concerned about was not adequately explored. When asked, my husband said he was in favor of my coming here. At home he said he wished it were already history. So, I'm concerned about my husband becoming too lonely, getting depressed, down in the dumps. Hopefully his regular AA meetings on Monday and Wednesday nights will be beneficial. Originally he told me he'd be "living" at AA while I was away.

The attitude here re letting me take my vitamins after assuring me three different times—prior to making a reservation and at time of reserving—that as long as I brought them in their original bottles, there'd be no problem.

Just like most M.D.s have had only 2 ½ hours of education re alcoholism while others have studied the disease, so have most M.D.s had only 2 ½ hours of nutrition, and I've studied and read and talked hours and hours and hours re nutrition and mega vitamin therapy. I am concerned with prevention of illness, not crisis intervention at which M.D.s are skilled. I subscribe to research performed by Abram Hofner, M.D., e.g., and others – Passwater, Cheraskin, Williams, Pauling, et al.

As to how I enable, I learned a little from attending Al-Anon meetings and reading many pamphlets three years ago when my husband was in detox. Such helped, but not enough. However, I did NOT try to control his drinking. Unless I'm missing the point, I don't believe I'm an enabler—UNLESS you count my mood swings and my need to understand, to know all that affected me, get everything out. And if that's what you mean, then I'm an enabler of his disease. However, it's imperative for me for me to get well!

Then I wrote to Harry, the first of four letters:

9:30 p.m., Sunday

My love,

Just completed filling in the Psychological Evaluation—94 questions. You can tell I have writer's cramp. My eyes burn. But, I got to take my vitamins and so can rest easy tonight anyway.

It hurt to call you tonight, to hear your voice. It hurt good and it hurt bad. Good because I love you so much. Bad because we're apart. I may soak in the tub tonight and in the morning. I feel as if I'd been up for days. It worries me to know you haven't felt well today. Please make an effort to keep busy. I think it's unthinking of this place to admit family people on a Sunday, but when would be a better day?

Sweetheart, I'm too pooped to write more. I feel you with me every second and I like the feeling.

251

I love you. Hurrah for us!

More than an hour later, I wrote in my new journal:

Finally in bed. Soaked in a hot tub. Was able to get my vitamins for tonight. We were in session until 6:40 pm then finally released for supper. Sat at table with Irene, joined later by my roommate Penelope, very pleasant. All the members of the group are nice and all at various stages of hurt and pain. I phoned Harry 7:30 pm or so, and he sounded lonely. I was disturbed to hear he's not felt all that well today, aching, and a cold rain, lots of rain, so he stayed indoors, didn't even tackle his desk. I tell myself I must not worry about him. They (Carol) told us that if we're distracted, we won't get full benefit from this week. But I can't turn off loving and loving concern. I spent hours filling in a Psychological Evaluation, only 94 questions, re marital history, family, physical, sex, identity, fears, effects of alcoholism—a draining query, especially at end of a long, grueling day. Just tried to work on a crossword puzzle but too tired. For a few minutes I thought: I don't care if the subject of alcoholism never comes up again. Penelope next door gabbing. There are a couple night owls in the bunch. Poor Polly, so sweet, compassionate, and admittedly thoroughly confused, went to bed some time ago, exhausted. This bed is good and firm and narrow so its width will probably help me not to miss Harry quite so much. I mustn't worry about him! He put two sweet notes in my suitcase; brought tears to my eyes. I left a note for him in silver pitcher plus a dozen or so little ones hidden around the house. Wrote him a brief, scrawly note. Too tired to think or even try to any more. Wish I had the stamina to stay up and bullshit but I'm reveling in being alone and quiet for a few minutes.

Harry and I were compulsive note writers. Whoever left the house last or went to bed before the other returned, left a note as a welcome-back greeting. I did not want Harry to have a full week without notes; every evening during my week at Spofford when I telephoned him, I told him to look in the teapot or under a cushion or some other place for a note I had hidden. They read as follows:

(1) *My love, I wish we were doing the New Hampshire scene together. s/Your love.*

(2) *Hiding notes around the house is kinda silly—but it sure beats personal ads! I love you!*

(3) *I love sleeping with you, and I know even the single bed I'm in seems empty— because it's empty!*

(4) *Every one of these little notes represents postage saved. I love you.*

(5) *Dumb expression: "When all is said and done..." Nothing is ever all said and done. Proof: I keep writing you silly notes.*

(6) Sweetheart, "How important is it?" Well, taking your vitamins is important. (I love you.)

(7) Probably by now, my head is coming apart at the seams—along with my fat stomach. Consolation: just think of how much more there is of me to love you.

(8) I can cope with being an "alcoholic by proxy," but loving you long distance is a pain in the ass.

(9) When I grow up, I wanna marry someone just like you. Will you wait for me?

(10) Please make at least mental notes of "your" week. That way I won't feel as if I missed everything by being away from you. (I love you.)

(11) Hiding notes for you to find is a game. You don't like games. But are you enjoying this one, just a little? I just wish I could think of funny things to say.

(12) This looks like just another note. Right? Wrong! This is a GIANT hug in disguise. I love you!

(13) OK, my love, almost time for me to come home. Get ready!

The two notes from Harry I found tucked into my suitcases read:

My darling, I love you. Here's to a strong bond and a beautiful life together. Have a good week. Your, Harry

My love,

Everybody loves you – MOSTLY ME! I am only yours. I love you. H.

Chapter 35

Madeline roused us from our beds at six o'clock, and within the hour we were eating hearty breakfasts. I relished not having to grocery shop, plan, and prepare meals. Our housekeeping responsibilities were light—make our own beds and strip them on Wednesday if we wanted clean linen. At our first Community Meeting following breakfast, I passed along requests for more soap and towels and requested the confusion surrounding my vitamin intake be clarified. There was no problem about the soap and towels, but the vitamin request went into a holding pattern.

We were advised that the best way for us to benefit from the program was to concentrate on ourselves and to keep any outside contacts to a minimum, especially for the first few days. I mentioned that Harry and I planned to talk via phone every day and that to change this plan might add to any discomfort he might have directly related to my absence.

"You aren't responsible for his feelings," I was told. That struck me as a harsh copout. "Has he been in a program?" implying if he had, he would understand. Harry had gone to a treatment center 15 years earlier. His descriptions of their therapy compared to Spofford's sounded like trying to compare high school with post-doctoral seminars. To renege on my promise to call him daily plus the run-around I continued to get about my vitamins caused me to take advantage of free time before the 9:30 lecture to write in my notebook:

To whom it may concern—Carol? Julie? Alena?

From Donna

I am having a great deal of trouble handling two issues which were avoidable had a pre-admission fact sheet been sent to me or read to me, and if my questions had been answered factually.

A. Although I was told by a former family patient here and our marriage counselor that this week was primarily for me, there was no suggestion, intimation, or directive that I curtail contact with my husband (who is at home).

Yes, I know I am not responsible for him, but inasmuch as we both expected we would have daily phone contact, it troubles me now to be put in the position of having to tell him that for me to derive maximum benefit from this program, I need— in effect—to cut myself off from the outside, and that translates to not talking with my husband.

I may not be responsible for my husband but I feel I have a responsibility to him.

Like many alcoholics in early sobriety who after years of bouncing around AA and detox places has just taken Step One and is dealing with emotions, feelings, issues he previously anesthetized himself to, he is more sensitive than ever—raw nerve endings—and mine are pretty raw, too.

(All I really want to do right now is cry. This is due in part to emotional fatigue compounded by not enough sleep and ACUTE frustration re Spofford Hall's lack of organization/communication. How ironic that my number one resentment now is with the very place I've eagerly come to for help to get well!)

B. This damn vitamin fiasco! Three people, including a nurse, assured me in advance of my arrival that as long as I brought my vitamins in their original bottles, there would be no problem.

Now this morning, I was able to select a few items from what I usually take after breakfast but not all, and I'm told I must talk with a doctor here re what I may/may not have. Had I known that earlier, I could have had a physician knowledgeable about vitamins as a means of preventing illness write out a prescription.

The anxiety this issue is causing me is severe. I know my body. Vitamins are not prescription items! They are not drugs! It blows my mind that I could ask for aspirin or a laxative—both of which dump poison into the body—but that I am denied taking concentrated foods!

With everything else going on in my life—and being here on my own volition for constructive therapy – I do not have the energy nor the backup of enlightened physicians – in person – to take on the medical establishment.

C. I feel I am being unnecessarily manipulated and that these issues could have been avoided had Spofford Hall personnel been organized and knowledgeable re the program demands and "medication" procedures.

255

Next I wrote to Harry, condensing what I had already ventilated on paper, and continuing:

They want our heads here to be as free of outside concerns as possible. Thing is, the concerns I have are of their creation—not setting guidelines prior to admittance (pre-information) and not clarifying this g.d. vitamin fiasco.

My roommate is equally pissed—same reasons but not same issues.

I'm reminded of the health spas that woo customers—the almighty dollar/greed syndrome—and then let one flounder.

My emotional fatigue is now compounded by lack of enough sleep (five hours) and these totally unnecessary frustrations.

I saw Carol on my way to the lecture hall and described the hassle about my vitamins; that it was interfering with my therapy. I had endured the skepticism and sarcasm of certain staff members. I felt totally frustrated because I expected people who had taken the initiative to know more about alcoholism than most physicians would also have explored the fallacy of a so-called balanced diet being adequate in today's world where crops are treated with herbicides and pesticides, animals are fed antibiotics and hormones, and the efficacy of water and air are violated by pollutants. Later that morning I was told I could take my vitamins at the nurses' station—morning, noon, evening, and bedtime. I received permission to do what I was told prior to arrival I could do. I was elated and wanted to tell my group in a way that would demonstrate my relief that the aggravation was history. To compare the nurses' station and the Spofford establishment to City Hall seemed trite. I decided in favor of ridiculous hyperbole, one I thought would elicit at least a chuckle.

"I have stormed the Bastille!" I announced. "I can take my vitamins!" No one laughed, but three in the group who seemed pleased for me smiled. I was silly to think everyone would appreciate the humor and foolish to think the others really gave a damn whether or not I got to take my vitamins.

The first activity every weekday was an hour-long lecture given by various staff members and attended by all patients—alcoholics and/or chemically addicted, and affected family members. That no-nonsense Alena gave a powerful and cohesive presentation about the totality of addiction, how everyone in the family is affected. If Alena had notes, she seldom referred to them. Staff members knew their subjects inside and out.

Each affected person was represented by a "doughnut"—a circle within a circle. The larger circular band was reserved for defenses, and within the inner circle were the hidden feelings. Among Alena's first words were, "No one in a dysfunctional family feels okay." To survive, they mask their feelings with defensive behavior. No one wants to look at the truth. The so-called "troublemaker," the alcohol dependent person, demonstrates defenses of anger, charm, work dedication, rigidity, perfectionism, aggression, righteousness, grandiosity, perfectionism, and intellectualizes. Whereas inside, his feelings include guilt, fear, pain, hurt, loneliness, shame, rejection, and a sense of inadequacy. They display Jekyll and Hyde attitudes. Alena had just described Steve and Harry.

The "chief enabler," usually the spouse, becomes addicted to the "troublemaker." Their defenses include affecting powerlessness to do anything and playing the martyr. Other defenses include self-blaming, fantasizing, self-pity, seriousness, manipulation, and becoming super-responsible—taking over responsibilities shirked by the "troublemaker." Their inner feelings are also anger, fear, guilt, pain, hurt, loneliness. I did not like listening to Alena expose me, and at once my defense mechanism of self-righteousness told me, "Donna, you earned your feelings. You really are a nice person." And sure enough, Alena pointed out that outsiders give the enabler sympathy ("Poor you, what a wonderful person you are to put up with all this"). But her next words did not get me off the hook: as the enabler's personality changes because of using survival techniques to cope with the "troublemaker," outsiders may also say, "If I had a wife like her, I'd drink, too," because outsiders often see only the charm exuded by the "troublemaker." As time wears on, mates lose the person they married, a sex partner, happy home life, and friends. Extramarital pursuits by either spouse may be symptomatic of a problem not related to addiction but due to the inability to communicate, an art not learned before addiction set in. The affair(s) may soothe the ego temporarily but they don't help the person to feel better.

Alena stated, "I am a miracle. I come from an alcoholic family." Bitchy or not, I had to admit she seemed to have her act together and I took renewed hope for myself.

The characteristics of children in an alcoholic family were described—the Hero, a super-achiever; the Scapegoat, a rebel; the Lost Child, who never makes waves; and the Mascot, who offers amusement. Because I was an only child, I could see some of myself in all categories. I did not determine which slots best described Liz and David because they took turns trying them all; but I had no difficulty seeing the roles Harry's children filled.

From the lecture hall we went into an adjoining room for an hour and 45 minutes of Group Therapy. Alena was the facilitator, and I hoped I could become invisible. I might just as well have wished the earth were flat. The subject in group was always the same—feelings. I found our first exercise easy: draw a picture of our principle fantasy. I sketched idealized figures of my family playing croquet. From left to right, I drew David and Liz standing close to one another, holding mallets. In the center Mother was bent over about to hit a ball through a wicket. Next were Harry and me, watching, and then Liz's two little boys horsing around. All of us were smiling, but by the time I finished the sketch, I felt sad and defeated. I was sure the fantasy was beyond the realm of being fulfilled. As each of us described our pictures, I recognized that our longings were identical—a life of harmony.

The subject of anger was brought up, then hatred, even to the point of wanting to kill. I was so wrapped up in my life with Harry that I did not remember the night I plotted to murder Steve nor the night I sat inside the front door with a loaded gun in my hand ready to shoot him if he tried to enter. It came my turn to say something. My response was garbleygook but it included, "I believe thoughts are things." I wanted to get off dead center and into philosophizing. Fifi sat next to me and laughed and scoffed in the same breath.

"Oh, really? You don't really mean that!" I felt she was trying to push me into changing my statement. I was too flustered to explain where I was coming from, that I meant thoughts were things in the sense that sometimes our fears could become self-fulfilling prophecies, that we become what we think. My intellectual defenses were firmly in place. However, Fifi continued to speak directly to me; I felt like she was hammering at me. I wanted to punch her in the face. I thought, "Who is this self-styled therapist? Where does she come off presenting herself as being superior?" Unfortunately I kept my thoughts to myself. I had not learned how to say, "I feel angry because of what you are saying and the way you're saying it." Instead I silently disliked Fifi and took pains throughout the week to avoid crossing her and having her sharp tongue directed my way again. In defense of Fifi (who would have been the first to say she needed no one to defend her), she was trying to get me to admit that I had been angry enough to have the thought of murder cross my mind. I had not accepted the fact that feelings are neither good nor bad; they are either comfortable or uncomfortable. I had spent years holding myself up to my own judgment and listening to others' judgments of me, and if I did not know how others perceived me, I imagined I did. To admit I entertained thoughts of murder was more than I was ready to do. I did not believe I could take on any more guilt. I felt terribly self-conscious, all eyes focused on me, and angry with myself that I had failed—first time out in Group—to acquit myself well. After my failures of having my words understood at home and in sessions with Pennington, I was afraid that I would not benefit from Spofford's therapy.

I was relieved when the focus shifted from me to others. Joann said very little; Connie squeezed out a couple of monosyllables and otherwise shrugged her shoulders to connote, "I don't know" or "I guess so." Penelope and Madeline responded only to what was pulled from them. Polly went a mile a minute. It was Irene who impressed me because not only did she voluntarily open up and share some of her fears, she actually cried. I admired her for being able to cry in front of people she hardly knew. How could she trust herself and the rest of us to let down her defenses to the point of actually crying?

I had a hard time differentiating between thoughts and feelings; I sat quietly for a large portion of the Group. Irene noted that at the end of the session I, with tears in my eyes, asked whether or not Group would become easier to participate in. Alena was quick to perceive that I felt my needs had not been met during our first Group meeting.

After the session ended, Alena informed me she had been assigned as my Case Worker. Talk about fear becoming a self-fulfilling prophecy! How could I possibly cooperate with someone who had such a knack for making me feel uncomfortable? I considered requesting a different Case Worker but then decided I had already distinguished myself negatively enough by pursuing the vitamin issue. So I fell back onto the Serenity Prayer: "God, grant me the serenity to accept the things I cannot change, the courage to change the things I can, and the wisdom to know the difference." And I reminded myself that everything happens for a reason. Therefore, since she could zero in on me so well, then she was the best one to help me get myself well. She made an appointment to meet with me at 5:30 pm.

At one o'clock, I continued writing to Harry:

Have bolted a good lunch and am changed into swimsuit covered by running pants and sweatshirt. Exercise in pool next. We dash from one thing to another. No rest for the wicked!

I have my vitamins! That is, I can go to the nurses' station and get them on demand. They bring a box to me, I select and swallow there, except for one "C" I squirreled away for two hours from then. What a relief! All that anxiety.

Group session this a.m.—in tears (not alone)—will be most difficult aspect of program for me and what I want and need most. Knew this ahead of time.

Just found your letter. Made me feel sad, but I rejoiced that you cried. About time. I hope you are able to cry a lot, about anything. As pointed out today, some feelings are more comfortable than others but there are no bad feelings. Off to pool.

We had Activities Therapy every day except Thursday and were joined by some of the 28-day patients. The program varied. On some days we did easy exercises at poolside and/or in the pool. One session included an exercise in trust. Each of us had a partner, one of us was blindfolded, and without touching, the seeing partner used only verbal commands to guide the blindfolded partner through a maze of obstacles—chairs, tables—scattered around the pool. First I guided Polly, and then she guided me. I had no problem with that exercise because I trusted Polly completely. I knew she would rather die than inadvertently steer me into the pool.

Another day we all got in the pool and were told to make a large circle and then walk as quickly as we could in the same direction. Within a short time, we created a strong enough current so that walking became effortless and we were sucked ahead. Then we were told to reverse our direction. The initial steps were extremely difficult because we bucked a strong current. We were told to persist. Before long we created another whirlpool, and this time we were permitted to enjoy the effortlessness of being swept along. The instructor gave us the moral: it requires only a little effort to get caught up in the disease of alcoholism, its progression, and when we decide we want no more of it, it requires great effort to change our ways of thinking and doing things. But if we persevere, recovery can become a way of life we can enjoy.

Creating first one whirlpool and then changing directions and struggling to create another whirlpool made a profound impression on me. To create the first whirlpool was easy, and to be swept along by the disease had seemed to happen against my will. There I was in an indoor heated pool, within an alcoholism treatment center, struggling to free myself from the pull of the disease, bending against the current, laboring to put one foot ahead of the other in an effort to break my addiction to the old whirlpool, to create a new way of seeing myself and living. The sense of exhilaration I experienced when we were permitted to literally go with the flow of the second whirlpool underscored the fact that by working at recovery, I could look forward to a dramatic easing of tensions. My determination to get well was reinforced.

On another day at poolside, a physical therapist extolled the virtues of biking. I couldn't have cared less about bicycles and peddling over hill and dale but I appreciated the purpose of the presentation—to acquaint patients, particularly those who were there to break their chemical addiction, with outlets for their new time freed from bellying up to a bar. With all due respect for the lecturer, I laid back on a chaise lounge and felt myself dozing off. I prayed I would not give myself away by snoring (I didn't.).

Afternoons from 2:30 until 4 was Communication Group for us family patients and four others—the husbands of Madeline, Fifi and Joann, and the mother of Connie. Carol led the group. "Our outer defenses protect us so well that they prevent us from getting what we need." We were told to draw a "doughnut," the outside circle for defenses and the inner for feelings. We were to print what we thought of on our own and write what occurred to us while listening to others as they described their "doughnuts."

The defenses I thought of were smiling; creating a laugh; affecting poise; withdrawing; writing; talking to someone; and blocking out unpleasantness. By listening to others, I was able to add: think too much, deny anger, escape through sleep; focus on other people; mood swings; procrastinate; perfectionist; and underachiever.

The initial inner feelings I printed were: fear of rejection; dishonesty in others; lack of trustworthiness; anger; hurt. I added: financial anxiety, and exposure of my feelings. I was intellectualizing my feelings out of existence. I feared others' dishonesty because such represented a feeling of loss. My defense mechanism of blocking out what I did not want to feel prevented me from including "guilt" among my feelings.

Carol compared anger to a pressure cooker, cautioning us to let out the steam a little at a time otherwise the beans could end up on the ceiling. As for feeling guilty, we were told that guilt keeps us stuck.

I was particularly interested in an interchange between one of the wives and her husband. He said he liked, wanted and needed to feel he was the center of her attention; and when they were joined by others, he felt her attention was diverted from him. I knew about that only too well as I felt drained by the attention Harry demanded I pay to him. I quoted in my notebook what Carol said about trust:

"It takes a lot of time to rebuild trust."

And within brackets, I wrote:

"H – please say, 'I'm sorry.'"

Throughout Monday, each of us was paged to report to the nurses' station. From there we were directed to a small office for psychiatric evaluations, medical history, and physicals. I was pleasantly surprised to meet a psychiatrist who was warmly friendly, who smiled easily and had eyes that twinkled. During what felt more like a conversation than interrogation, I later discovered he learned a great deal about me in less than a half hour. He noted that during the years I mentally adopted myself into families, I chose those

261

with a good, strong father; but when I chose a man for myself, I was not as careful, with the exception of Harry whom I married after a great deal more circumspection than I practiced before marrying Brad or Steve. Even with two divorces and a third marriage, he realized I had all along valued marriage, which he correctly interpreted as my deep need for a sense of family, wholeness and company. He found this thread which had influenced my life-long search "fascinating." He was perceptive in recognizing that Harry had many positive qualities, but that active alcoholism made it impossible for him to respond to my needs consistently. The fact I felt depressed, shattered, anxious—sometimes to the point of walking out of the marriage—he described as a real mixture and gamut of opposing feelings and conflicts. There was no hiding the truth: I was on an emotional seesaw.

Each of us found the psychiatrist charming. Polly said, "He asked me how I was, and I didn't stop talking for the full time." Then she smiled. "The poor man!"

At 5:30 pm I reported to Alena for our scheduled half hour and became increasingly anxious as the minutes ticked by and she didn't appear. She sent word she was delayed, for me to wait, and although I appreciated her courtesy, I was concerned about not getting into the dining room before it closed. Actually, Alena's delayed arrival worked to my advantage. We talked for a while in the office where I stretched out on the couch and cried a little as I went through my litany about Harry, his morals and new soberness, my children, Mother, and how I had defined myself according to roles—wife, mother, patient, and earlier by what work I did. I admitted to Alena that I was totally out of touch with who I was and what I was feeling. Only through indirect means was I able to express my feelings of fear, confusion, inadequacy and insecurity. She referred often to the 94-question "Psychosocial Evaluation" I had completed the night before. There was much to cover, and she suggested we go along to the dining room and continue talking there. Consequently, I ended up having three times as long with my Case Worker as scheduled, and in the process, I discovered Alena was not really a bitch but a warm, loving, caring woman. She was a bitch only in the sense she could see through me and read me like a book. I took comfort in knowing I was in good hands.

I discovered that Alena and I shared a love for literature and we were hypersensitive to strident and/or loud noise and to harsh colors. I confessed I oft times had difficulty hearing the message behind sentences spoken by individuals who had not mastered proper grammar; my train of thought was momentarily jarred, interrupted. Alena noted that I was bright but that I seemed to let my head get in the way. This she found particularly evident. Because I could not grasp the fact I focused on my husband indicated I had a controlling attitude. Therefore to break my confusion, fright, and being almost totally unaware of myself, she gave me two assignments. I was to keep a 24-hour "feelings diary," to note every hour how I was feeling with one word, and if I was feeling nothing, to note that, too. I was no longer to speak of Harry in any Group session or, for that matter, at all. Her dark eyes danced merrily when she added, "You're not to refer to him, not even euphemistically!"

That lovable bitch! "Not even euphemistically?" I asked.

"Not even euphemistically," she repeated. She also cautioned me to keep an eye on my intellect, especially as to when and how it impaired my communication. "Accept responsibility for your self," she told me. Although the assignments did not sound difficult, I discovered they were ball busters.

Ten minutes later I made my first entry in my Feelings Diary—"Encouraged"—and continued writing to Harry:

7:30 p.m.—still Monday! The personnel here are very perceptive. No pulling wool over their eyes. Alena had already picked up on my inability to get in touch with my feelings; that I must find Donna. From now on, I'm not to refer to you or "the problem" or AA or anything to do with alcoholism (she said I probably know as much about the disease as she does), but that I must concentrate upon myself. I drew the triangle I picture—of Us/Marriage, You, Me—so she understands the interconnection but emphasized, repeatedly, I must concentrate on me.

I described the Feelings Diary and continued:

I'm also to take note of when I'm witty; many times I don't intend to be funny, but people laugh anyway, and how that and my ability to intellectualize can impair communication. I am to accept responsibility for myself and to get in touch with my feelings, and one goal, just for me, is so I—my jumbled head—can be un-jumbled and I'll be able to do creative writing (as opposed to articles and reporting).

I saw the psychiatrist today for a cursory physical exam and oral history taking. We all, individually, liked him. Poolside exercise enjoyable—half hour, then swim, sauna, steam and whirlpool. That was after lunch. Then we saw the Johnson Institute produced film, I'll Quit Tomorrow. At our first group session re communication, one husband's humor reminded me of yours, only yours is better.

Fifi often lapses into an imitation of Lily Tomlin, her bad-good little girl, really funny. Polly went to bed at 8:30 last night but was too uptight to fall asleep before 3 which is when Madeline woke up wide awake and stayed up. My roommate,

Penelope, did not get to sleep until 1:30 and told me this morning I have a very ladylike snore.

I walked a half mile after breakfast. I'm eating lots of salads and fresh fruits; had one bite of someone's cake at noon. I have a cache of yogurt, banana, pear and V-8 on windowsill, window always cracked for refrigeration.

So now that I have a better understanding of how I'm perceived, I can accept the advice this morning and expanded in tonight's counseling re concentrating on me. But, I'm still going to call you. And with the vitamin nonsense resolved, I feel good; feel I can settle in to my program here.

The intensity is ferocious!

Off to another lecture—8 p.m.

Again as in the morning, the final hour-long lecture of the day was presented to the entire patient population. Inwardly I groaned when the subject was announced, "Step One—We admitted we were powerless over alcohol, that our lives had become unmanageable." I considered that Step applied more to an alcoholic than to me and besides, I thought that I as a co-alcoholic had already accepted it. I soon learned otherwise.

The lecturer was a staff therapist, a young, thin woman with long dark blonde straight hair. She was squeaky clean, wore no makeup, and was dressed in faded jeans and cotton shirt. We learned she was recovering from cross addiction—alcohol and other drugs. She began by saying, "Without in-depth understanding of Step One, recovery is almost impossible."

I had admitted my powerlessness over the alcohol Harry drank when, in fact, I was powerless over the effects of alcohol within anyone, including myself. Once I or anyone swallowed alcohol, neither I nor anyone could cancel its metabolic effects. I had admitted I was unable to manage both my outward behavior and my thinking, how I inter-reacted to situations. Yes, I had admitted these things in my head; I had acknowledged Step One intellectually. However, to accept the reality of Step One meant to surrender to it, to integrate its meaning at an emotional level. Perhaps false pride was preventing me from surrendering, that I feared facing a loss of control, when all I had to do was reflect upon my chaotic thinking and know I had become a leaf on the tide. I knew alcoholism was a chronic and progressive illness even when the alcoholic was not drinking but I was still six months away from realizing my co-alcoholism, if untreated, was equally progressive. I knew the disease for the active alcoholic was primary, all-encompassing. I wondered: could that be true for co-alcoholism also? (By the early 1980s, more and more alcoholism professionals considered co-alcoholism as primary an illness as alcoholism.) If Harry continued to drink, the disease would kill him but perhaps not until after he had become insane. Was not co-alcoholism slowly killing the essence of me? Had not Alena only a couple hours earlier told me I must find Donna?

I stopped listening to the lecture as if it applied solely to the recovering alcoholic patients. I heard that it was essential for me to make a commitment to a recovery plan as outlined by the Twelve Steps, that I must follow through with it, despite hassles, even in the absence of pain, because failure to actively pursue my recovery could result in a relapse. I had to realize I had the power to change certain things within myself——resentments, low self-esteem, desire to control, self-centeredness, lack of insight, immaturity and self-pity. I heard I must deal with life realistically. I was comforted to hear that we all—— alcoholics, co-alcoholics, indeed, all people——share a common desire to love and be loved. And I was warned it would be impossible to really work all the Steps until and unless I understood and surrendered to Step One because it was the key to my recovery. The lecture ended with me wondering how I could change my acceptance of Step One into an act of surrender. How was I going to keep my head from getting in the way?

Before I could feel comfortable joining my group back in our rooms, I searched for a pay phone not in use and eventually was able to call Harry. My heart sank when he asked, "Have you met anyone you like better than me?" I was hardly on a shopping trip for a lover or a new husband! I came away from the phone feeling burdened, as if Harry were hanging around my neck. The one word feeling I wrote in my new diary for that hour was "heavy." I unwound by talking with Fifi and Madeline in their room and with others in our group who wandered in and out. Although Alena had cautioned us against playing therapist with one another, listening was interrupted frequently by such questions as "How do you feel about that?" every time the subject rolled into husbands and alcoholism, I kept silent and felt left out while I adhered to Alena's instructions, "...not even euphemistically." When I got the chance, I rambled on about various jobs I had and told raunchy jokes. I felt out of place. At 11:30, I added more to my letter to Harry:

Am in bed. Took a warm bath. In the morning I shower and shampoo. Such full days, nervous tension, that morning and evening "watering" feels good. Chatted a little with Madeline and Fifi about celebrities, plays, movies——a welcome respite from everything else.

I was so relieved to finally get a call through to you. I got good exercise going from pay phone to pay phone. Your voice sounded good, strong. I'm not worried about you, but you are part of me and I like to reassure myself that you're eating (vitamins?) and being good to yourself.

I love you very much.

I'm not about to meet anyone here that I like better than you. Or anywhere. I put all my eggs in one basket. You.

I'm so tired, yet want to savor these moments of doing nothing.

At 7:45 the next morning, Tuesday, I completed the letter:

Here we go again! Just went for vitamins and was told I was to have received them at 6:30 a.m. so can't get any until noon. I'll get it straightened around, and I need my helpers—about three hours sleep total. I could not turn off my head, as if buried thoughts/feelings jousting for position to come out. I only know I slept because I dreamed a little. However, I got up eager and expectant for what this day will bring.

I love you.

Chapter 36

The only poor lecture of the week was given Tuesday morning by a stylishly dressed member of the nursing staff. Her subject, "The Disease Concept of Addiction" was a rehash of what I had read but nevertheless I listened intently.

To qualify as a disease, there has to be a change in the structure or function of the human body. Alcoholism qualifies with three components: Primary (needs treatment); Progressive (gets worse); Chronic (does not go away). In 1955 the American Medical Association recognized alcoholism as a disease. This diagnosis is accepted by many, including AA. However, there are others who eschew the disease definition and instead prefer to call alcoholism a neuropsychiatric disorder. Regardless of its label, out of control drinkers cause problems for themselves (physical, mental, emotional, spiritual) and for those close to them (family, friends, associates). Or, a rose by any other name is still a rose

On that Tuesday in October 1981, the lecturer's statistical data included that one in ten of the general population of the United States is alcoholic; a conservative estimate was there are nine million alcoholics in the USA; only five percent of the alcoholic population ever makes it to a treatment facility. (Based upon a 2002 national survey on drug use and health, an estimated 22 million Americans were classified with abuse or dependence on alcohol, illicit drugs or both. Each one of them was adversely affecting family, friends, work associates.)

Midway into her lecture, in response to the question, "Is there a cure for alcoholism?" she replied, "There are some who return to social drinking, but historically most who try cannot." I couldn't believe my ears. A 1974 experiment in behavioral modification conducted by Linda and Mark Sobel with 20 active alcoholics had received glowing reports but follow up investigation revealed that within one year of discharge, 14 were hospitalized because of active alcoholism. Further investigation negated the Sobels' claims for a cure: eight years after the experiment, four had died from alcoholism, eight were still drinking, seven were dry (and some of the seven were in AA and/or had received specialized treatment) and one could not be found. Recognizing a psychological catalyst as the cause of alcoholic drinking, as touted by the Rand Report, had proven to be deadly wrong: many in the field conjectured how many alcoholics died trying to prove to themselves they could become non-compulsive drinkers. (This was the study that Harvey Dowd, the therapist Harry and I consulted, subscribed to.) Because alcoholism is recognized as being a progressive disease, it is contradictory to suppose it can be controlled while continuing to drink. That is like saying it is possible for someone to be a little bit pregnant.

In the row ahead of me, two women in the 28-day program looked at each other with shocked disbelief. I heard one whisper, "She's planted the seed." Patients peppered the lecturer with questions for absolute medical statements, looking for loopholes, that somehow they would be able to forego abstinence and drink normally. The lecture disintegrated into shambles.

At our Group Session, several of us told Alena what the lecturer said and pointed out the obvious: some CD patients would think they could be among the precious few who could switch from compulsive to social drinking. To the best of my knowledge, anyone who resumes drinking as a social drinker was originally misdiagnosed as an alcoholic. I knew a woman who drank like a fish after her husband ran off with a close friend but eventually she resumed social drinking.

Alena introduced us to another therapist, Julie, who would lead our Group on Alena's days off. Julie appeared to be in her late 30s, attractive, feminine, with softly waved blond hair that just cleared her shoulders and whose eyes reflected her seriousness of purpose but which could also twinkle with merriment. Her quiet demeanor belied an incisiveness that was as penetrating as Alena's.

Alena noted I was less active and interpreted that as a positive sign. She was pleased I did not try to rescue anyone by giving them sympathy, and that

I checked myself when I slipped by referring to Harry. I was less active because I was going through withdrawal from my husband—cold turkey. By trying to follow Alena's orders, I found it difficult to impossible to think of anything else to say. After all, Harry and the disease had become my twin obsessions. The times I wanted to comment on something another member said in reference to her husband, I could not think of how to form a sentence without violating Alena's dictum. Consequently I felt alienated from the group, that I was singled out to be different, and if I could not share with them, how could I still be considered an integral part of the group? I was at Spofford for treatment of my co-alcoholism. Beginning late Sunday and growing throughout Monday, I felt the eight of us were creating a family through the give and take of shared feelings, lighthearted bantering, horseplay, and underneath it all, mutual acceptance. These seven women were becoming my sisters, aunts, children, depending upon which facets of their personalities were evident during any given moment. I was also getting a taste of what it might have been like had I not married Brad and instead gone away to college and lived in a dorm, right down to having a roommate. The comparison with school was strong. We rushed from one "classroom" to another, our blue spiral notebooks in hand, to take notes in lectures or to participate in seminar-like settings. The therapists were our teachers. The administration had strict rules and regulations and did not hesitate to enforce them with disciplinary warnings, even expulsion. Intertwined with my labors to get better, I experienced two long-held fantasies—a caring family unit that excelled in open communication and the stimulation of being an adult student. Here was my opportunity to be a full-fledged participant in each precious fantasy—and I had instructions to be, in effect, not what I had become—an extension of Harry. Without an identity, I felt I was an outsider. I had faith in Spofford, in Alena, but I felt cheated. This new pain—the poor little kid with her nose pressed against the candy store window—intensified with every hour of that memorable Tuesday.

Alena noted that after many of us complained about the morning lecturer, I expressed some positive opinions about her and raised the possibility there might be extenuating reasons behind her alarming statement. I related this to times I felt unfairly judged when people were harsh on me without having the whole picture. On-going issues were examples—the staff's misunderstanding about the role supplemental vitamins play in fostering optimum health and my sense of fairness to Harry, to live up to our agreement to telephone him every evening. No one knew why I had abruptly become less active and more introspective.

Alena knew how agitated I was about counseling with Pennington. I hoped when she talked with him that my feeling I was being discriminated against in favor of my husband's recovery would be validated. Instead, I was disheartened to learn she and Pennington were in agreement about their perception of my controlling and manipulative behavior. I knew I was focused on my husband. But I could not see how I was trying to control Harry's behavior. The consensus was I could benefit from the "one day at a time" philosophy. I knew I could not do that until I stopped letting the past influence the present. That, plus knowing Alena supported Pennington, made me feel I had run up against still another brick wall. I felt more misunderstood than ever. My day was not going well at all.

That afternoon we watched a film about enabling behavior, how people without meaning to actually aid and abet the alcoholic's drinking. Worse yet, once an alcoholic goes into treatment, such as AA and/or professional therapy and the other family members do not get treatment for themselves, they can continue to enable alcoholic thinking and so unconsciously sabotage the alcoholic's recovery. In effect, the untreated family members remain frozen in time with the survival attitudes that worked during the active drinking but now are no longer appropriate; indeed, they are warped. In my notebook I headed a page, "How I Enable":

I conceal many of my true feelings, especially from my "euphemism." (It will come as no big surprise that I find it difficult to switch my focus from alcoholism as it has become a preoccupation.)

I try to make people feel comfortable, not only immediate family but sometimes strangers. I label it as courtesy.

I back away from confrontation with my children, especially my son.

I'm letting my "euphemism" get away with denying the magnitude of recovery— accepting on the surface his statement re his sincerity re doing the Steps.

Following the film, Julie led us in a group discussion. I mixed my thoughts in with her statements as I took notes, but set off her statements in quotes:

"*Enabling is not minding your own business. It's sick love. Enabling is a desire to not let people hurt.*"

I've been using my head to beat feelings off with a stick.

"*Just because you understand something doesn't mean you have to feel differently about it.*"

I've got to get my own act together.

"*What you do means more than what you say.*"

What do I like? What do I want? We've been communicating from defense to defense, not from feeling to feeling. What do I do that's against myself, at my expense? It's wrong of me to expect someone else to meet my needs.

"When you know alcoholics, you are either enabling or intervening. To protect an alcoholic from pain is to deny him good health."

I had not enabled Harry by hassling him about his drinking. I had not poured booze down the sink; I couldn't because I was a product of The Great Depression. But I had marked bottles. I had told people he had the flu when he had a hangover. I had nursed him through at-home detoxification, even handfed him soup. And since he stopped drinking, I had hounded him about his apparent inability to tell the complete truth about his alcoholic escapades. If I did not pull my act together, I could be instrumental in giving him an excuse to resume drinking. I had better stop concerning myself so much with Harry's honesty and start communicating honestly with myself.

That evening I sat at the dinner table with Irene, Penelope and Polly. Penelope seldom referred to her husband; they had been divorced many years. Polly had yet to recognize her husband's alcoholic lifestyle, locked as she was into denial, and she mentioned him often. Irene wove references to her husband into conversation—he had several years in AA—and also spoke of her grown children who were into their own battles with alcoholism and other drugs. For 24 hours I had forced myself to heed Alena's directive: "You are not to mention Harry at all. You are not to refer to him, not even euphemistically." I had been artificially quiet—for me—all day. Suddenly I became aware that I was talking a blue streak. Words tumbled out of my mouth as fast as they did from Polly's, and Polly had the all-time champion machine gun mouth. I stopped and said, "Listen to me! Listen to how I'm talking! I'm going faster than Polly!" and my eyes filled with tears. No one said anything. No one was going to rescue me with kind, sympathetic words. "This is awful," I said as I swallowed and swallowed to get rid of the lump in my throat. What was happening to me? I who tried never to display in public anything other than acceptable emotions was seated in the middle of a crowded dining room, of all places, trying desperately not to blubber. It took every ounce of control to keep my arms and legs from thrashing; my limbs felt like they were charged with electrical current. I wanted to scream and wail. "I feel like I'm cut off from the rest of you. You can talk about your husbands and I can't. I don't feel like I'm part of the group," and the tears spilled over.

"Maybe you ought to talk to someone about it," Irene said quietly. Polly and Penelope agreed.

"Now?" I asked. It was dinnertime. Workdays ended at five o'clock. I silently asked for help, direction, as I was incapable of making any decisions. What right did I have to disturb someone after five o'clock? Still I hesitated. Would it be proper of me to demand attention at such an hour?

Irene said, "Go find Alena and tell her how you are feeling."

"Do you think I should?"

All three said, "Yes."

I left the dining room and walked down a long corridor to the family counselors' offices. No one was around. I did not know what to do next. I felt ashamed for having caused a scene at the table. I turned to go back to the dining room but reversed my direction when I remembered my new friends told me to find Alena. I went to the switchboard. Alena had left for the day. I sank. The receptionist said she would page Julie and for me to go to my room until I was paged. In my room I paced and then sat on the bed. I felt like I was holding myself together with baling wire and chewing gum. I was scared of fears I could not label. I was also afraid Julie was gone for the day, too. But in less than 10 minutes, I heard the intercom, "Will family patient Donna M. please report to Julie Connor's office," and I was on my way before the page was repeated. Most patients were still in the dining room, and the corridors were deserted. I walked into Julie's office, tried to respond to her smile with one of my own and sat down. I described what happened at the dining table and told her that because of Alena's directive, I felt I was not part of the group and that I wanted to feel like I belonged. Julie said the others would be better off if they refrained from talking about their husbands. I began to cry. I told her I resented having to call Harry every evening. She told me I could stop, that I could tell him how I felt. I told her I couldn't do that, not over the phone, not after we had agreed before I left that I would call him every day.

"I don't want to hurt him," I said,

"But what is it doing to you?" Julie asked. I couldn't answer. I blew my nose. "What do you want me to do?"

"I want to be like the others. I want to be able to mention my husband." Just being able to talk about him to Julie relieved some of the internal pressure. She asked, "Why did you come to Spofford?"

"To get rid of the garbage, and that's not happening."

Julie said, "I'm going to overrule Alena," and I thought that at last, on this long, long day I had found someone who understood me, "but only for one hour. I want you to choose someone in your group you trust and go into an empty room and talk all you want about your husband for one hour. You can kick and scream, make as much noise as you want, and get it out. And when the hour is over, Alena's rule goes back into effect."

One hour? Only one hour? How could I get rid of months and years of garbage in only one hour?

Julie said, "Is there someone in your group you feel you can do this with?"

I thought for only a couple seconds and said, "Yes. Irene. She has the most Al-Anon." I remembered it was Irene who broke the ice during our initial group session by opening up and permitting herself to cry in front of all of us. I had marveled at her courage. If she could set appearances aside, maybe I could, too. I thanked Julie and found Irene. She agreed to listen to me, and we decided the best time would be after the evening lecture. During the lecture I wrote in my notebook the subject and one sentence:

The Enabler. If you don't treat the other end, you'll just have problems down the line.

The eight of us sat together like sixteen-legged Siamese twins. The pain I felt was somewhat assuaged by being in physical proximity with my surrogate family. We were all in pain. The wives with husbands in treatment and Irene, whose husband had years of sobriety, did not know if their marriages would survive. My roommate, unbeknownst to me at the time, was in the process of breaking through her denial that she was not only a co-alcoholic but alcoholic as well. Polly was laboring to accept what her children, therapist back home, the family therapists and the bombardment of factual information kept telling her: that her husband was alcoholic. Little Connie wanted to live with her mother but feared she would have to return to her father's house where he was actively alcoholic. Everyone in that lecture hall, with the possible exception of the speaker, was experiencing emotional and/or physical pain. The alcohol and/or chemically addicted 28-day patients were at various stages of physical recovery. Some had distended abdomens, a visual indication of liver damage. Some still had bloodshot eyes and the shakes. Everyone was dealing with a sense of failure and varying levels of guilt and remorse. We were a collection of more than 100 walking wounded. I was aware of the pain of others, but I could not respond to it because the severity of my own pain was overwhelming. I was trying to hang on, not to splinter into a pile of sawdust. By the time the hour ended, I was more afraid than ever, and more determined, to expel the poison that kept me a cripple. No one in the group asked any questions when Irene and I indicated we would catch up with them later. We went into an empty room, a mirror image of mine across the hall, and sat at opposite sides of a small round table. Irene said she would not say anything, for me to go ahead. I lit up a cigarette. Finally I was going to bitch——

even carp—about that lousy, two-timing Harry. But to my great surprise, words about Harry did not come forth. Instead I heard myself speaking of Steve and what a bastard he had been. I spoke of the night he choked the puppies, the excrement I cleaned off the walls because the poor little things had been scared shitless, how frightened I had been, how I could not stand up to him, the abuse of Liz and David, the bulldozer, the tractor, the brute that comprised Steve Black. While I rambled on about Steve, another level of my brain wondered why and when would I get to the purpose of this precious hour and get on about Harry. Venom poured out of my mouth about Steve, and then it hit me: Steve was not only a psychotic but probably also an alcoholic, a troubled man burdened with symptoms of both mental aberrations and addiction.

And then I realized I was talking about Harry. I spewed forth about the personal ads in the sleazy magazines, Harry's ad about "orgasm guaranteed,' and the ad I placed. When I said over 500 replied I heard Irene laugh softly. I talked about Harry reading my diaries, throwing up old boyfriends to me, how I finally wrapped the diaries with chain and padlock, but even that did not stop him from making jealous cracks about men I knew before I met him. I spoke of how I thought I could put an end to Harry's jealous remarks by destroying the diaries, how I tore at the pages, ripping out days and years before throwing them into a dumpster.

I began to sob. The broken trust had killed part of me. Destroying the journals killed another part. I had tried to buy peace in the relationship at a terrible cost to me. I cried, "I feel like I murdered part of myself. I feel like two parts of me are dead and I'm carrying them around inside me—dead." My anger at Harry for breaking trust with me melded with my loss of the destroyed journals, and I blamed Harry for forcing me to destroy my writings. I felt sorry for myself and enraged with Harry. My firsts clenched. "That bastard!" I hissed. Irene moved to the end of the bed and faced me, her knees almost touching mine. She placed a bed pillow on my knees and told me to hit it. I thought, "What a silly idea." I remembered reading about "pillow therapy" and thinking it was silly. How when you wanted to smash someone in the face could an inert pillow be a viable substitute? But I hit the pillow anyway.

"Hit it again," Irene said. "Let it out."

I hesitated before striking at it again with one fist, then waited a moment and hit it again. And then suddenly I could not stop pounding it. I pounded with both fists. I pummeled, clawed and twisted the pillow. Somehow the pillow did become Harry. I cursed. "You bastard! You son-of-a-bitch! I hate you for what you've done! You lying, two-timing prick! I hate you, I hate you, I hate you! You killed part of me and made me murder more of myself! God dammit, Harry, why?" I cried, sobbed, my nose ran.

My arms went limp. I was quiet, the toxin was spent. Irene took my hands in hers. "It's all right," she said. I continued to weep and sniff. When I finally raised my head and looked at Irene, I was touched to see her face was wet with tears. She said, "You did well. But you may have to do this again sometime. That doesn't mean you didn't do it right, but don't be surprised if you have to do this again." We talked quietly for a few more minutes. I blew my nose several times. Irene said, "I won't remember any of this. If someone should ask me about it tomorrow, I won't be able to remember it. It's funny, but that's what happens."

I emptied the ashtray, washed it out, and dried it with tissues. We joked about the pillow still being in one piece. It was wet with tears, and we left it lying atop the bedspread for the maids to find. Ten minutes beyond an hour had elapsed since we entered the room. I went to my own bathroom, washed my face and dabbed on fresh makeup. I found a scrap of paper on which Penelope had written a dear note, letting me know she hoped I was feeling better, that she was outside walking if I wanted to join her. Her note told me more, that her caring, although low key, was strong. I felt a lot of love from that scrap of paper. Then I phoned Harry. He said I sounded strange. I could not tell him about what had just happened, not yet. So I told him what I could—that I was tired, exhausted. I was relieved when the conversation ended. I joined the others in Fifi and Madeline's room. I was asked, "Are you feeling any better?" and I could truthfully answer that although worn out, I felt a lot better. Best of all, I felt I belonged to the group. I was part of it and it was part of me. They could mention their husbands all they wanted; I did not feel like talking about Harry at all.

Of course not wanting to talk about Harry did not last, but the way I thought about him had changed. That one hour released poisonous resentments and gave me insight and perspective. Steve's craziness was undoubtedly exacerbated by his alcoholism. I got crazy from it. The kids got crazy from it. Even Mother got crazy from it. Steve could not help much of what he had done any more than Harry could. What Stan, the alcoholism outpatient counselor, had told me was true: an alcoholic could act rationally one minute and irrationally the next; he could lie and tell the truth almost at the same time. The insanity of alcoholism hit me. Harry had behaved as a horny, unfaithful husband because the insanity of alcoholic thinking gave him license to fool around. He practiced double standards because his mind operated on double tracks. He was powerless over alcohol and his life was unmanageable. My anger towards Harry had evaporated in the room across the hall. I had surrendered to Step One.

Just before midnight, I wrote to Harry:

Dearest love,

So much of what happens here defies accurate description. Video tapes and a certified mind reader are required.

The dynamics of defenses vs. inner feelings—the tearing down of carefully constructed walls designed to shield against pain in order that pain can be experienced so that growth in a particular area may begin.

Our group is evidently as special as I think—FEEL!—it is because the counselors are freely commenting to that effect. They say, "You are all working so hard," which sounds like we are working harder than most groups do. Our strong mutual support is commented upon, too.

We are learning emotionally (we came in here knowing it intellectually) that we are as addicted as the drug dependent patients: we are addicted to the alcoholics in our lives. I know this is true—the obsession. This is why all of us are encouraged to do as is done in Al-Anon: speak of ourselves and our feelings without speaking of our alcoholics or alcoholism. Such is difficult, but none of us can begin to get better until we can do this.

The importance of a sponsor is emphasized. Just as your recovery is dependent upon working your program so is mine.

I've put in two very heavy days, so far. I eagerly anticipate more; they are my keys to getting well.

I've written nothing in my log book since Sunday. Much as I'd like a blow-by-blow "memos of record," there isn't time to make them, and the myriad of feelings being stirred up are too jumbled and intertwined to decipher accurately—yet. By fits and starts, there are flashes of insight, but just as quickly, they're gone and more times than not, I can't remember them. I'm assured they'll return and eventually will be recognized and understood.

Now I understand why Nanette seemed so vague about what happens here. Only an alcoholic can fully understand what goes on within another alcoholic, especially the feelings connected with compulsion. I'll try to fill you in after I come home but I'm afraid I'll be unable to transmit the guts of this program.

This has to be the single best thing I have ever done for myself. I am grateful to be here, to know I have your support. I'm working the hardest I ever have in my life. The pain feels almost unbearable at times; it's scarier than hell to take the risks of exposing myself. But there's no other way if I want to get well. I've joked to the others, "I've become a full-fledged masochist."

Now to bed. I feel quieter inside tonight; a rough evening brought the calm.

I want our marriage to work, really work. I can do my part by getting well. Tiny areas of healing have begun. The process is long. And I haven't told you a thing you didn't already know. It's all in The Big Book.

I love you and your notes and your voice.

s/Your Donna

That night, by breaking through my obsession with Harry, tearing into it and exposing it to the air and to myself, I was confident my recovery process could really begin. The gratitude I had towards Alena for challenging my obsession, for bringing my addiction to Harry to a head, was boundless. I was especially grateful to Julie for sensing how vital it was for me to get rid of the garbage that was choking me, suggesting I take an hour to do so. To Irene I was grateful for accepting my invitation to hear me out, for knowing enough to place a pillow on my lap at the proper time. Irene knew that from belonging to a women's group in which pillow therapy was often used. Once again, I was in the right place, at the right time, with the right people. And to God or Infinite Intelligence or Higher Power, I gave the most thanks of all.

Chapter 37

I awakened the next morning, Wednesday, feeling like a new person; well, maybe not new but certainly freed and able to benefit from what Spofford had to offer. I did not want the week to end; I thought it should be extended because I felt as though I had wasted two days. I loved the women in my group and felt I was an integral and welcome part of a special family unit. I loved Alena and Julie and Carol. I loved Harry. I loved my children, my mother. I felt no anger towards anyone, not even some of the nurses who persisted in letting me know they disapproved of the vitamins I took.

Alena gave the morning lecture on "Alcoholism, A Family Disease" and subtitled it, "Famalcoholism." I sat in the front rows with my new sisters and marveled at how differently I felt than when I sat in those chairs 12 hours earlier. I took notes as fast as I could and wished I had a tape recorder because I found Alena's subject matter most valuable and her presentation outstanding. And when she bobbed her head, I thought the mannerism endearing.

Comparisons were made between families that were healthy and unhealthy due to chemical distortion. In the former, emotion is present; in the latter it is repressed or medicated. Healthy families are physically well; others suffer medical complications. Healthy families are sociable whereas unhealthy families find socializing painful because it hurts to be close to anyone. In a healthy family, the members think clearly, but their opposites experience distorted thinking or they think too much, or both: they need their minds to defend their feelings. Spirituality and hope are present in healthy families, but the unhealthy families cannot trust; they need to be in control; they are saddled with false egos. Members of healthy families have the option of choice-making; they can choose to change things. But members of an unhealthy family feel powerless to make changes; they feel desperate, hopeless.

Alena said, "Unless you set out to become an alcoholic, there is no need to feel guilty or ashamed because you are alcoholic."

In chemically distorted families, each member has key feelings. For the Dependent Person, the one who abuses drugs, it's shame; for the Enabler, anger and guilt; for the Lost Child, loneliness; for the Scapegoat, hurt and anger; for the Mascot, fear and confusion; and for the Hero, guilt and inadequacy. Alena pointed out, "These feelings are not chosen any more than an alcoholic chooses a second drink."

In a healthy family, everyone makes positive contributions, but the members of the unhealthy family contribute negatively. Even the Chief Enabler who takes over the Dependent Person's responsibilities and gives the family care is, in the process, diminishing the addicted person even more. The Hero, or Super Achiever, gives the family something to feel good about. The Scapegoat provides the family with focus and a reason for being because when the Scapegoat acts up and/or gets into trouble, the problem may provide the family with the only time it comes together. The Lost Child provides relief because he makes no waves, the only member who is not a potential "hot spot." And the Mascot with his silly, amusing antics gives the family isolated moments of joy.

Dysfunctional families can get better if they know how to change. First, the unhealthiness has to be recognized. Then it has to be talked about. Feelings have to be communicated. And members can refuse to play their stereotyped roles.

Alena said, "One way you can help someone else is to get your own shit together. And one of the best ways to help someone else is if they want what you have. Communicate and express your feelings so you won't go nuts!"

I hoped that eventually I would understand and believe I was responsible for my own feelings, that I was not responsible for another's feelings. I had to throw out years of conditioning. No longer could I blame another and say, "You make me so mad!" Instead I would have to realize I had chosen to feel angry. And if someone said to me, "I'm disappointed in you," I would know I could not be expected to live up to another's expectations. I would not have to feel guilty.

DONNA BAILEY-THOMPSON

Wednesday was the day Madeline almost went home. Her husband, Max, whose room was just around the corner from hers, waited for opportunities to confront her with real or imagined issues. He badgered her. I had ambivalent feelings about Max: I found him charming but I was intimidated by his physical power. After the lecture that morning, Max stalked like a jungle cat to zero in on Madeline in the corridor outside her room. I started to say something but stopped and retreated because I feared Max would turn on me. I watched helplessly for a few seconds while Max, using the intensity of his words, made her his prisoner. Other sisters appeared and stopped further back. Carol came along, sized up the situation, and walked purposefully to Madeline and Max. Carol was shorter than I, with a soft, gentle demeanor, but she bore the authority of Spofford Hall. She quickly broke up the encounter and told the rest of us to get along to our Group Therapy session. We explained to Alena and Julie why Madeline was not there. I could still see the trapped look on Madeline's face. While I described the fearful feelings I experienced, I understood what happened within me: when Max began browbeating Madeline, I was transported back to the helplessness I felt when Steve was unnecessarily harsh with Liz and David. Even within the protected environment of Spofford Hall, I was a coward. My old guilty feelings were reinforced. My shame was compounded.

I set those unresolved emotions aside and participated in the morning's Group Therapy. Once when I spoke and it was natural for me to refer to Harry in passing, I hesitated, remembering Alena's dictum, and skipped saying "Harry" or "my husband" and substituted, "Euphie." Alena started to chastise me but her sense of humor triumphed. We shared laughter, and then she wagged a finger at me. But I knew something she had yet to know: the night before I had broken the back of my obsession with Harry and now thoughts and references to him could go in and out of my mind without becoming stuck. Throughout the week I continued to refer to him as Euphie which helped me, at one level, to give Harry another identity. Euphie had a light sound and to me connoted an impish quality. The nickname helped me to visualize my husband not as big, bad Harry but as a mischievous elf. The image of Euphie placing suggestive personal ads and visiting a massage parlor became ludicrous—a middle-aged drunk fancying himself as an irresistible lover. I removed the sting from those episodes by recognizing his elfin qualities which had responded to the insanity of alcoholism. I may not have replaced a negative with a positive, but the replacement was definitely more palatable. Soon everyone in our group referred to him as Euphie.

280

During that same session I expressed my displeasure and frustration—feelings bordering on anger—because Joann and Connie ate up so much time saying nothing while the rest of us waited and listened to the hands of the wall clock clicking to the next minute mark. I was aware that the week was speeding along and their reluctance to share robbed them as well as me and the others of gaining new insight into ourselves. Their silence prevented me from getting my needs met. I resented others as sick as I exercising a form of control over my therapy. I wanted to shake them. Actually I was feeling a lot of anger towards them, but my old tapes got in the way: how could I feel angry towards Joann and Connie who were hurting so much they were afraid to talk?

Before it was time to break for lunch, Madeline joined us. Carol, with the help of other staff members, defined limits for socializing between Madeline and Max and evidently convinced Madeline she needed to finish out the week for her own benefit.

Julie observed that I seemed relaxed that morning. Indeed, I was, thanks to puking pain the night before. She also noted that I talked about my defense of intellectualizing. I was able to see so much about myself that I felt like I had taken a handful of smart pills.

I had become a silent mother hen, always counting noses when all of us were supposed to be anywhere. When Irene did not appear for the poolside exercises, I received permission to look for her and found her lying down in her room. Not to report for any scheduled activity was against the rules. Naps were especially frowned upon. Irene did not look well. I learned she was diabetic and had high blood pressure. I knew she, like all of us, was running more on nerves than anything else; sleep was a precious commodity of which we got little. I sat with her for a few minutes, placed a cold wet cloth on her forehead, alerted a nurse and returned to the pool area. After she gave of herself to me the night before, I felt indebted to Irene.

I received mail from Harry and Mother. Harry wrote:

Monday a.m.

Hi, my love,

Sun's out. Flurries later? Cats are fed (they miss you). On my way to work. Called your mother after talking to you last night. Guess all is well.

I slept 10 hours. Kept reaching for my Honya Buncha. God, how I miss you. I love you! Have a good week and then get home.

s/Your H.

He also sent an oversized greeting card that gave me a good laugh:

Just to let you know. . . things are about the same!

And on the inside was a black and white photo of a corner stair landing littered with debris, as if the place had been neglected and abandoned for years. Mother wrote Monday evening, including news about what others were doing. She also wrote:

Harry phoned last night to tell me you had arrived safely. He phoned just now to see how I am doing. Hope you are keeping up with your schedule and are feeling better.

I love you.

s/Mother

That afternoon Julie talked about denial, how it is used to protect the self from something threatening, to block knowledge, to act as a buffer against reality. Often alcoholism is called, "the Disease of Denial." A little joke that I'm guessing got its start in AA and Al-Anon and then jumped into the mainstream is, "I discovered that denial is not a river in Egypt." By the time Harry stopped drinking, I had spent a minimum of 15 years denying I was exposed to behavior related to alcoholism—Steve's, then the children's para-alcoholism, and now Harry's. Denial comes in many gradations, and I used a slew of them. There was the simple denial of not facing facts as they are. There was the minimizing denial when I admitted to some degree there were problems and thus succeeded in conning myself into believing the situation was less significant than it actually was. By blaming denial, I implied that responsibility belonged to someone other than me. I tried the fix-it denial by making adjustments, telling myself, "This won't happen again if I . . ." I made excuses, which is a form of rationalizing denial. I employed diversion denial by changing the subject to avoid discussion about the problem. I exhibited hostile denial which was an attempt to cover up my fears. The type of denial I excelled in was intellectualizing.

My reasons for denial were simple to understand. Alcoholic behavior embarrassed me; it threatened my self-esteem. I used denial to avoid pain. Much of my denial stemmed from ignorance about the illness but when I pleaded ignorant to the handwriting on the wall, I succeeded in compounding my confusion and that of others. I trembled with denial and failed to confront Steve about drinking and related behavior. (As Julie pointed out, "Normal people don't yell and scream at their kids.") I carried my denial to a debilitating degree: I repressed my feelings by blocking out emotional anxieties. Like Scarlet O'Hara, I told myself that I would think about something painful tomorrow, and when tomorrow came, I put it off again and again. I knew it was not uncommon for the alcoholic to have blackouts when nothing registered in the memory or gray-outs when events could be remembered only after prompting. I, as a co-alcoholic, as part of my defense-denial system experienced block-outs. I agreed with Julie when she said, "Sometimes the family is more out of touch with reality than the alcoholic." My growing inability to cope had brought me first into Al-Anon and then to Spofford.

Julie pointed out that denial can be overcome by an objective presentation of facts—being firm, giving specific, factual feedback. I used that technique the previous July that ended by giving Harry the choice of attending AA and counseling or facing divorce. Now, although Harry was making his way into sobriety, I learned I would continue to encounter examples of an alcoholic personality. Therefore, explicit knowledge about denial was coming late but not too late for me to benefit.

The evening lecture was given by still another member of the counseling staff. Therapists seemed to materialize from out of nowhere. Again, I silently groaned when the subject was announced: "Step Two—Came to believe that a power greater than ourselves could restore us to sanity." Grouped with my sisters, I listened and advanced my recovery. The lecturer was a recovering alcoholic, a young man who obviously believed every word he said. His dedication to his own recovery as well as to helping others with theirs underscored his delivery. Although his words were directed primarily to the alcoholic patients, they applied equally to me as a co-alcoholic. With active drinking—Harry's, Steve's—my reality became distorted; I was unable to honestly perceive what was going on. Not only was my trust in Harry destroyed, I couldn't keep promises to myself. I heard the therapist say, "The whole foundation of recovery is trust." Those words scared me half to death.

I was reminded—again—of Harry's and my intellectualizing and our inflated egos. Each of us considered ourselves and our problems unique. We believed we were so different from others that what worked for them, i.e., AA and Al-Anon, could not possibly work for us. Such was part of our collective insanity, the grandiose section department.

I heard the lecturer exhort us to keep an open mind, to resign from the debating society as to whether or not a power greater than ourselves exists. I heard I was not to get caught up in labels as to whether or not I was an atheist or an agnostic. Never mind that I had faith and lost it or that I had considered myself to be intellectually self-sufficient. We were back to trust again, and I needed to become a person of full faith. Only then would I be able to say, "I came to believe." And I heard warnings, too. "Trust what Step Two is all about. Don't be unrealistic. Don't expect a miracle. Don't criticize other people and their way of doing things." Before he said the words, I knew there would be no such thing as doing the Twelve Steps only once, that I would have to—must—do all of them more than once. Recovery was not something I would be handed along with my discharge papers three days hence.

More and more, I wished Harry could be experiencing the dynamics of Spofford Hall too. I was acquiring new perspective. How would we find common ground when I returned? During my nightly phone calls to Harry, I expressed positive feelings, never my fears. I wished we had not agreed to talk every day because hearing Harry's seductive voice interrupted the flow of my mental homework. Finding an available pay phone consumed precious time I preferred to spend in interactions with my new sisters.

On two previous nights following the lecture, Fifi, Madeline and Connie sat with other patients in the whirlpool singing songs while the usual volleyball game among CD patients went on in the adjacent pool. On Wednesday evening those who were not members of Al-Anon were driven to a meeting in nearby Keene. Joann fought going; she was sure she would hate it. She, Penelope, and Madeline went to Al-Anon. Irene was upset because she couldn't go; Wednesday was the night back home of her favorite Al-Anon meeting. She spent much of the evening in the small kitchen down the hall chatting with the CD patients. Connie ("The Kid"), Fifi, Polly and I went to the pool. Later in Fifi's room, we welcomed the others back from Al-Anon. All had positive comments, but Joann was ecstatic. She glowed. She chattered like a magpie. She had a marvelous time. Madeline said she wished I could have heard one member mention she had been married to three alcoholics. "I thought of you at once," Madeline laughed. Later in my room, I began another letter to Harry:

Hi love!

There's a lot to be said for having an in-house pool, sauna, steam room, and massage shower (many nozzles, various heights and angles)—Polly and I shared it; she said she felt like she was in a carwash. Felt good especially at the end of another structured day. As I recall, I got teary only once today, maybe twice, and that's both positive and negative—the tears signal that a hot button has been pushed.

God! What a terrific place this is!

Chapter 38

In the morning at 7:45, I completed the letter:

Our wake-up person got so involved doing some of the girls' hair this morning that she forgot to wake us up. Penelope and I provided another dimension to a Chinese fire drill. We were apparitions, hustling our pointed hair heads to the nurses' station for her medication and my vitamins.

Lake shrouded in fog earlier—so peaceful, serene.

Off! for a half-mile walk. Then our first meeting in 15 minutes. Then I think I'll nap for 45 minutes.

I love you.

s/Your Donna

I had proof I was getting better: I permitted myself to appear outside my room only seconds after waking up—no makeup, hair not combed. Earlier in the week I would not have exposed myself, even to get my vitamins, because my vanity superseded my health concerns. The foray also signified I felt at home at Spofford.

Thursday morning, instead of attending the morning lecture, we reported to Carol in the enormous living room for Art Therapy. Our assignment was to take a box and transform it into something that depicted on the outside how we thought we are seen by others, and on the inside how we perceive ourselves. For supplies there were boxes of various sizes and shapes, old magazines, scraps of cloth, some magic markers, colored tissue paper, glue, scotch tape, and scissors. We pawed through the supplies and set to our task.

Putting that box together stands out as the single most happy event of the week. At times I felt like a little girl surrounded by my dearest playmates spending a rainy morning on a carpeted floor. Flashbacks of kindergarten came and went as we shared the use of tape and scissors. Rummaging through the scraps of material reminded me of playing dress-up. Carol sat in a chair observing us, "Like a mommy," I thought. When we were done, we sat in a conversational circle, some on the couches, some in chairs. One by one we first placed our box in the center of the group where everyone could look at it, pick it up, touch it and explore its contents. Then one by one, we told what we saw and felt. After that, the maker of the box deciphered its intricacies, disclosing what her thoughts and feelings were behind her choice of decorations and contents.

Madeline volunteered to be first. Her box was beautiful, shaped like a house, about the size of an extra tall and thick loaf of homemade bread. She upholstered the outside with lovely cloth. The peaked roof could be lifted up and folded back for viewing the interior. Of the eight boxes, I remember Madeline's and a little about the delicacy of Connie's, and of course my own. Like Madeline, her box was exquisite, worthy of admiration for its beauty. And like Madeline, inside were treasures of her spirit and feelings worthy of exploration and appreciation. I thought that in comparison, my box looked like it had been slapped together. It did not reflect my usual attention to artistic detail. Because mine looked like such a ragamuffin when compared to the haute couture of Madeline's, I volunteered to go next: I wanted to get the contrast over with. Creating the box was fun but as I began to share it, I felt scared I might have revealed too much of myself. I saw it as a self-portrait, from the skin in and from the viscera out.

I used an ordinary cardboard carton with the top flaps pushed flush against the interior walls. According to the inked printing on its side, it had held "third cut, letter size, 11 pt. heavy manila file folders." On the outside of one panel I taped an illustration for vitamins. On anther I drew the eyes, nose and mouth of two female faces—one smiling, the other with a tear falling down the cheek. Beneath these faces was a magazine's cutaway drawing of a house. The faces and the house represented my gladness and sadness surrounding home and family. On another side I taped a packet of sugar to signify I could come across as being sweet-natured, and a magazine photograph of a wintry mountainside, sentinels of pine trees poked up through falling snow, to represent both my appreciation for beauty and particularly the outdoors but more especially that sometimes people perceive me as being cold and distant.

The fourth panel had three magazine clippings to represent my priorities at Spofford. One illustration of eight multi-colored fountain pens represented each of us eight family patients. A grid illustration of various fruits represented the fruits I kept on the windowsill of my room. The other was a photograph also clipped from a magazine of a man in the passenger seat of an automobile, except the top of the photo was replaced by a line drawing of the head and shoulders, the focus placed on the man's head—which was where most of my focus was when I arrived—on Harry's head and what went on inside it.

Taped to the interior side walls were self-explanatory illustrations of stacked pancakes and volumes offered by a book club. A photo of laser fusion bombarding the deuterium with beams from all sides symbolized the bombardment of confrontational episodes beamed at me by family therapists and sister patients alike. Loose in the box was a small section of an egg carton: I was not walking on as many eggs as I had been. Little squares of sponge represented the many different ideas and sensations I was absorbing. A tongue depressor signified I was forced to open up. Rolled up and tied with a string was the sheet music, *I'd Like to Teach the World to Sing*, which covered two areas—my enjoyment of music and my desire to live in harmony with my husband and family. Rolling around was a black film container with an attached long tail of a string to represent how I sometimes felt about Harry, that he was a ball and chain.

Also inside was a separate shoe box which I covered inside and out with pieces of colored tissue paper. The lid was covered with colorful muted plaid cotton cloth. Inside that box were more personal components of my personality. There was a color photo of a heroic oil painting of a naval battle during the era of sail to represent the battles still being waged within me. There were two black and white photo illustrations—one of a smiling middle-aged couple to represent the hope I felt about my continuing marriage with Harry; and the other of a little girl, one hand on a short wave radio she was listening to and the other on a world globe to encompass my desire for wider knowledge and foreign travel. Within the shoe box were two more boxes, but without their lids. The smaller box had plastic wrap stretched across the top and contained a small ball of crushed red tissue paper and pistachio shells which symbolized I could see I still had a small amount of anger to get rid of and that I was still a little nuts. That box set within another that was lined with pink paper on which I had printed "Love" with an arrow through the O, meaning that love was at the core of my being. Taped to the bottom of the shoe box was a black and white photo of Salvation Army women with raised tambourines—eight women smiling in celebration. They represented the eight of us. And taped to the bottom of the large box was a color photo of a person silhouetted against the light at the end of a round tunnel: I felt I could see hope. I choked up a couple times while sharing the box—my box, my self—especially when I spoke of my hopes for a good marriage with Harry and when I said I thought of the eight of us as being sisters. The feeling of comfortableness I had with them was almost more than I could bear.

Carol commented on the openness of the main box, "inviting us to look inside," and of the "honesty" throughout. Later when I had a chance to speak with her alone, I said I appreciated the fact she recognized the honesty. When we were told we could keep our boxes and take them home, I had a stab of panic. How could I ever share all of what the box meant with Harry, in particular the "ball and chain"?

That day's mail brought a Snoopy greeting card from Harry:

"I'm a health nut. I take vitamins A, B, C, D, E, F, G and K . . .

But I can't get enough of U!"

Hi, my love,

Have just spent 2 ½ friggin' hours cutting through roots to the septic tank cover—a shitty pastime. Must rid myself of the anxiety of toilet flushing vs. back-up. Most all wood delivered needs splitting.

Business stinks. All is well, however, and I miss you more and more. Liz was at your Mother's last night wrapping Christmas gifts. AA meeting tonight.

I love you!

s/H.

During Group, Julie spoke about the need to have our needs met, of being good to ourselves, which led into a discussion about sex and sexuality. Some of the wives had not made love with their husbands for months, even years. Such abstinence was due to a number of reasons. Inasmuch as alcohol is comprised of two parts water to one part ether, and ether is a central nervous system depressant, alcohol could be called the original oral contraceptive. I was reminded of Harry's vivid analogy, "Like trying to put a raw oyster in a parking meter." Sharing one's body with a drunk who reeks of liquor, slobbers and employs the finesse of a baboon ranges from being unpleasant to reprehensible. There was also the possibility the co-alcoholic used sex in a manipulative manner—as a reward, punishment, or as a means of barter. Controlling behavior could be contributing to a power play—the male-dominated culture versus a woman's power in bed. When Julie mentioned masturbation, Fifi said, "Oh, I couldn't do that!" Her shock and embarrassment were eclipsed when Julie mentioned a vibrator. I thought Fifi would fall on the floor. Julie's message was clear: a release of sexual tension through orgasm is normal and healthy, and that masturbation is not perverted, not sick.

I couldn't resist teasing Fifi. "If you don't use it, you lose it."

"Then I'll lose it," she said, but at least she was laughing. We all were.

Plain talk was common at Spofford. Not that patients and therapists were purposefully vulgar, but when one is continually exhorted to express oneself in terms of feelings, often so-called unladylike four-letter words did the job effectively. Thus to hear or say, "I feel shitty," or "You're full of crap," seemed natural, never forced. When that all-expressive Anglo Saxon word "fuck" was used as a noun, verb, adjective, expletive, directive, or what have you, it too seemed to fall naturally into idiomatic English. Fifi had a lot of trouble with the F word. Several days in a row she said, "I could never say that." But on Thursday during Group, she did. It just slipped out, as natural as could be, so that she had already spoken several more words before what she said registered with the rest of us. We whooped and hollered and clapped.

Thursday afternoon the reality that our week was winding down hit home when we met with a representative from the Aftercare staff. It was comforting to know that for two years following discharge, we could benefit from Spofford's expertise. We could arrive at Spofford any Saturday morning for an in-house Aftercare session with other current and former family patients, a time for sharing and feedback. We could also telephone Aftercare counselors for support during times of crisis. We were not about to be sent out cold into the dark night.

Thursday evening's lecture was delivered by still another staff therapist, a slip of a girl. This time I did not groan when the subject was announced: "Step Three——Made a decision to turn our will and our lives over to the care of God as we understood him." Step Three is a tall order, and I felt defeated without having begun. Then the lecturer said, "It is humanly impossible to follow Step Three all the time. Self-will can run riot." To any agnostics or atheists in the audience, the lecturer suggested that God be equated with having trust in something greater than oneself and to believe in it. For some a God substitute is the collective power of an Al-Anon or AA group itself. It is difficult for confused, hurting people to realize that when Al-Anon and AA talk about a Higher Power, which some people choose to call God, they are talking about a spiritual concept and not the dogma of organized religions. People of any belief can be comfortable within AA and Al-Anon because the spiritual philosophy does not interfere with other tenets. I could accept that as a fact. I was ready to also put into practice the prerequisites for working Step Three—willingness (keeping an open mind) and faith (becoming dependent upon a higher power and thereby achieving independence which, if explored, is not a contradiction). I had discovered that worrying was an exaggeration of my own importance, as if my worrying had a corrective power. I knew I could achieve patience and tolerance by coping with situations requiring either or both.

The lecturer admonished us not to change or turn the Steps around to fit ourselves, and to remember that the Al-Anon and AA programs are built on action; that one can't work one Step alone but must work them all. We also heard what we knew only too well: that getting better requires experiencing pain, feeling our feelings. Twelve Step programs share a credo: growth towards perfection, but perfection is understood to be unattainable because we are fallible human beings. However, those who have climbed the ladder know that Step One must be learned to perfection, in other words, surrendered to. That I had finally done. According to my notes, the final remarks included: "Living is painful. Pain really starts with Step Four and gets more uncomfortable with Step Five . . . The disease of alcoholism creates an irresponsible personality; it screws up people's lives . . . It requires change to live healthfully."

At 11 o'clock, I began writing to Harry:

My love,

I am sorry you are feeling lonely. I want to fix it so you won't feel this way. I can't do anything about it, at least not before I return home. And then I won't be able to undo any loneliness you have felt. I had mixed feelings about coming here. I was concerned my absence might be too early in your recovery. By coming here, I put my needs ahead of your needs of me. I knew I was affected, am still, from the disease of alcoholism. I felt I had to reach out to this lifeline—literally to begin to get well.

We have Communication Group in the afternoon that includes the eight of us family people (as we are called) and the husbands of three of the women as well as the mother of the teenager. This is the only time we are all together. Yesterday and today we did role playing. The counselor, Carol, described this situation: a recovering alcoholic and his wife have both become so involved in their own programs that they're spending almost no time together, so they make plans to attend a movie together. The husband comes home from work and announces he feels he must attend an AA meeting that night instead. The wife is very disappointed. I volunteered to play the wife, and one of the girl's husbands volunteered for the other role. All of us have built up a big thing about this man—it's a long story; he has harassed his wife here and violated her privacy (staff was summoned and took charge at once). I have had many resentments towards him. We did the scene. The purpose was to communicate how he felt about the AA meeting and how I felt about missing out on a long-awaited social evening together. I stated my feelings of disappointment and agreed that his need to go to AA was more important than a movie.

Later, one of the women (not his wife) told me she was amazed I could play the scene with such compassion and understanding opposite "that bastard." I said I was responding to the real needs of any recovering alcoholic for AA support. I was not seeing the personality of this very troubled man. Also, my reason for volunteering was so I could role play the situation in case you and I ever have a similar situation. And so, the person I was role playing with became, in my mind, you.

Everything I'm doing here is basically for me. But the less troubled (more better?!) I become, the better I feel about myself, the better we will be. Without me getting better, your recovery or our marriage—or both—could go down the tubes. And me, too.

I am convinced a million times over that alcoholism creates a family illness. Our group exemplifies this. One woman is the child of alcoholic parents and has a husband and child in AA as well as another child who is cross-addicted. Another has a father and husband who are alcoholic and children who have been trying to get her to recognize her husband is an alcoholic. (She's a living, breathing example, almost a basket case, of denial.) The teenager in our group lives with her brother and another sibling, and her father is an active alcoholic, but he got custody of the kids when his ex-wife's addiction got out of control before his did. The mother is cross-addicted and is being discharged tomorrow. And the examples of the pervasive insidiousness of this illness go on and on.

Chapter 39

At 6:30 in the morning, I completed the letter:

I almost tore up much of what I wrote about the others for fear I might be violating confidentiality.

I slept fast and I have gila monster eyelids. This is the most tired in the morning I've been. Again today I'll try to catch a nap between 8:30 and 9:15 a.m.

It's so mild today. And today we get into Aftercare and returning home. This program is beautifully integrated: we get what we need at appropriate times. The staff has excellent intra-communication. It's like safety nets are everywhere. It's "support on demand." Fantastic.

We have all expressed fears about leaving and returning home. I think this may be because we realize how affected we are by the alcoholism and know how far we still have to go – and, how different am I now?

I'm much better, I know that. And the light at the end of the tunnel has never looked brighter or held more promise.

I'm coming home, my love, to you – with my warts and all.

And my body!

I love you.

s/Your Donna

P.S. Your notes and cards have made me feel good, wanted, loved. Yes, I'm sorry you've been lonely, but I'm glad I've been missed. Off to breakfast!

Friday morning's all-patient lecture about the advantages of physical activity almost put me to sleep. Two of the Activities staff members shared the presentation, and they did well, but I already had physical activity in my life on a regular basis. The message, however, was important for newly-abstaining alcoholics to hear. An active alcoholic's life revolves around drinking. When he isn't drinking, he's either thinking about it, planning it, buying the booze, or nursing a hangover and thinking about the next "first" drink. Alcohol becomes his God. In fact, it comes before God, country, wife, parents, children, home, job—and any physical activity. A recovering alcoholic can make excuses for not doing something physical on a regular basis, such as, "I can't afford it." How much money was spent on booze? Or, "I don't have enough time." Oh, really? How much time was spent with booze? To meet the demands of his addiction, the active alcoholic found both money and time.

Alcoholism, whether one is addicted or exposed to the illness, causes stress. Recovery is stressful, as I found out. Physical activity helps alleviate stress. The physically fit instructors recommended choosing activities that are fun, to socialize at AA and Al-Anon meetings for the fun of it, and to be flexible, creative, avoiding any ruts, including ruts in Al-Anon and AA activities. We were also exhorted to try new activities, to be adventurous, that the act of taking a risk indicates achievement because it contributes to a growing sense of self-satisfaction, a sensation that far outstrips power and money.

During the morning Group session, we were asked how the Family Program could be improved. Most of us were well satisfied but offered comments. Polly, who had finally broken through her denial and could see she was married to an alcoholic, felt her contact with her Case Worker was shortchanged. Penelope said she did not appreciate the way she was talked to on the telephone prior to admittance and she was especially upset that upon arriving her car keys were taken away "just like I was an inmate in an institution."

Alena smiled. I detected a Cheshire cat quality in her smile. I leaned forward and asked, "Are you saying that Spofford is a mental institution?" She cocked her head and still smiling, looked directly at me as if to say, "What do you think?" Damn, she could be difficult.

I laughed, "Well what do you know? I finally made it!"

Years before, while running the campground, I thought I had coined an original expression: "If I could find a spare 15 minutes, I'd have a nervous breakdown." Evidently I reached my goal or at least came perilously close because my in-patient status at Spofford signified I had emotional and thinking problems; and no matter how I sliced it, those added up to mental problems. Throughout the day I mulled over the reality of being in a licensed special hospital as a family patient with mental disorders.

That afternoon Alena talked with us about the "Do's, Don'ts, and Effects of Sobriety." The single most important statement I heard was, "Whatever the alcoholic needs to do to get sober, you need to do to get sane." To help me achieve sanity, I was instructed not to enable the recovering alcoholic, not to do anything that violated my own values. I was not to try to continue getting well alone but to have a support system. My seven sisters were an important part of my support system. Al-Anon would supply more. I was to take care of myself, to keep my focus on myself. The healthier I became, the fewer demands I would put on another, i.e., Harry. Each person's recovery belongs to him or her, and this meant I was to avoid "recovery program jealousy;" many wives resent the time their husbands spend in AA meetings. I was to continue identifying my own feelings—likes and dislikes; in other words, get to know myself again. I was to figure out what makes me happy and to do it. The easiest advice to follow was to keep a journal and if needed, a "shit book," as I had already done both and would continue. I was to protect myself physically, emotionally, and financially because we were reminded there are no guarantees and especially none when married to an alcoholic. I was advised not to expect a newly-sober person to meet all my needs. And I was to realize that whatever I do is fine provided it does not contribute to sick thinking. When we arrived home we were cautioned not to try to relate everything that happened at Spofford all at once but to delay sharing some aspects until we could do so accurately, with perspective. I thought of my box and knew I would not be able to share it with Harry for some time.

That evening we did not attend the regular lecture but instead held our own Al-Anon meeting in the front lobby. Penelope chaired and chose as the topic, "Attitudes." Half our group had given individual comments when it became my turn to speak. I said that all day I thought about Spofford being a type of psychiatric facility, a special hospital. I spoke of my comment at the time, "What do you know, I finally made it," and pointed out I had used my defense mechanism of injecting humor while simultaneously accepting the fact I was a patient because of my own mental problems. "And after mulling this over all day, I've surrendered to the fact that I am a patient in a MEN-tal in-stih-TOO-shun." Connie was the first to smile and giggle but eventually all laughed. I punctuated my follow up comments with the same sing-song "MEN-tal in-stih-TOO-shun" which while generating more laughter helped take the sting out of the term. I had corrected my attitude of viewing myself as a part-time dilettante of involvement in a recovery program, perhaps to the point of feeling I was superior to others, and at gut level owned up to the fact I was a patient in a MEN-tal in-stih-TOO-shun because that was where I belonged. I accepted the reality I was affected by the alcoholic's alcoholism—mentally, emotionally, physically, spiritually. Somewhere during that day, I surrendered to the deadly seriousness of this family affliction: whatever the alcoholic—Harry—needed to do to get sober, I needed to do to regain my sanity. My recovery was in its infancy.

Chapter 40

In the morning, Saturday, Alena counseled us in Transition Group. We were on the final countdown prior to discharge. I did not want to leave. I was full of fears about returning home. Was I emotionally strong enough? How would Harry react when I told him I had come to think of the seven others as my sisters? Would he be jealous because I was sharing my affection with others?

Alena gave us some tools. If I were asked a question I could not answer comfortably, I could say, "I choose not to answer that question." Sure sounded simple, but would I be able to do it? She cautioned us to be aware of other addictions and means of temporary escape, i.e., food: "If you find yourself focusing on or about food, you're not getting your real needs met." She said that we would arrive home on a high and should be prepared not only for a crash but for a cold. As for the cold prophecy, I felt smug because of the vitamins I took. (I did not get sick after I returned.)

We were peppered with Alena's bon mots: "Part of our perfection is our imperfection. Realize you don't need people around who only love you when you're perfect." She said that if anyone tried to put us on a guilt trip, particularly the alcoholic, we did not have to accept the invitation. We needed to realize that none of us could make up for "all the shit" that had happened to others, "No more than I can make up for all the shit that's happened to you." She also reminded us, "If you feel like you were beaten up with words, then the feelings are the reality." One of her statements seemed to be directed especially to me: "Stop thinking your feelings to death."

Alena asked each of us to select one person, living or dead, other than a relative, we would like to talk to and tell why. Among those mentioned were Golda Meir and Ella Grasso, the first woman elected governor (Connecticut) in her own right. Fifi seemed the most surprised when I mentioned my choice was Jesus, perhaps because I did not talk much about spiritual concerns. He was my choice because I wanted to know how he spent his time through his teens and into his thirties when he began his ministry and specifically, had he indeed studied with the Essenes and developed his amazing abilities under their tutelage? We were also asked to choose one animal we would like to be and tell why. Someone chose an eagle; another a giraffe. Fifi and I chose cats, I because I admire their independence, their ability to live in the "Now."

That gathering was the first time I mentioned an idea I'd been kicking around for a few days; that I would like to write an article about Spofford Hall. I knew which publication I wanted to submit it to—a soon-to-be revised Sunday magazine of *The Hartford Courant*. Just to voice the desire took courage. Alena assured me I would have Spofford's cooperation.

Every Saturday morning at Spofford there were Aftercare groups held for all former patients—one for the recovering CD patients and the other for family members. Together with my beloved sisters, I took a seat in a large circle. With each passing day, Spofford had become mine; together with my group, I owned it. All week I was suspended in time; I spoke of the few former family patients I knew as if they were divorced from Spofford; references to next week's patients were made without a sense they would really exist. But one by one, other chairs in the large circle became occupied by living, breathing human beings who, whether I wanted to admit it or not, had also been family patients at Spofford. My proprietary interest in Spofford was a figment of my own wishful imagination. My first experience in sharing "with the outside world" would begin "at home." I overcame feelings we were being intruded upon and listened intently to how these "old-timers" had made their transitions from the cloistered atmosphere of Spofford back into their homes. Some of my fears were allayed. I also received a happy surprise: I realized that by being a Spofford patient, I was automatically a member of a much larger family.

One returning patient compared herself to a piece of wood, saying that she had developed a core of confidence. Another told of how she was able to deal with some gripes directed her way by saying, "I feel that is not my problem." Some mentioned they had encountered hostility from members of Al-Anon and AA because they had been in an alcoholism treatment center. Alena mentioned that family treatment was where detoxification care had been 15 years earlier—something new and suspicious. Someone suggested that perhaps some members of Al-Anon and AA felt that professional care was in competition with their recovery programs. Those attending the circle who already had years of Al-Anon membership to their credit, said that one complemented the other. I knew that with almost six days of Spofford behind me, I was more receptive than ever to Al-Anon's philosophy.

Alena pointed out, "Whatever has given you the most trouble may take the longest to go away." She cautioned us not to make any major decision for at least six months. Otherwise, we did have options about our behavior: we could keep on doing what we'd been doing; we could change; or we could do nothing at all. What I had already changed, I would keep on with; what I needed to change, I would as soon as I could. To do nothing held no appeal.

An Aftercare plan was drawn up. In my notebook I noted the goals that would demand my attention and effort:

(1) Focus on myself. (2) Get more in touch with my feelings and less with my head. (3) Get Al-Anon sponsor. (4) Take advantage of Spofford Aftercare. (5) Begin own one-on-one therapy. (6) Recognize my needs and find ways to have them met. (7) Explore at-home editing and other freelance assignments towards developing an income. (8) Explore grants available for mid-life educational courses. (9) Reaffirm "new family" ties by keeping in active touch.

I also wrote I would make specific behavior changes on a daily basis in my personal life in order to implement my goals:

(1) Focus on myself, implementing my own recovery program. (2) Acknowledge my feelings—listen to whatever they are trying to tell me. (3) In addition to regular daily spiritual readings (Daily Word, One Day at A Time), also read all the Twelve Steps. (4) Avoid dwelling upon alcoholism and my husband's recovery program by concentrating on my own recovery program. (5) Pray more often, forming the thoughts, asking for God's guidance—in all matters. (6) Have faith in God and myself.

The recommendations from the Treatment Team were that I attend Al-Anon and Aftercare; participate in psychotherapy and eventually marriage counseling. Alena noted I was to feel feelings, to write it down, even if it was "I don't know." And I was reminded to be good to myself. The completed form was signed by Alena, me, and a member of the Aftercare staff.

That afternoon we were back in the front lobby to share the family photographs we had been told to bring. I had photos ranging from my babyhood to the present. The sharing served a dual purpose: we added to our knowledge of one another and more specifically, saw how the postures assumed in candid shots signaled how the people felt about each other. A photo I carried in my wallet taken on the spur of the moment when Liz was pregnant and she, Mother and I were shopping, took on new meaning for me: although we were positioned by the photographer, Liz put her hand on my shoulder. I look at the picture and feel loved.

I also brought a snapshot taken of me when I was 16 and in love and knew I was loved in return because Dane had told me so that afternoon. I kept it and other random photos under the glass on my desk during the years following the divorce from Steve. One night while studying the photo, remembering how happy I was then, I burst into sobs for the lost innocence and the not so happy-ever-after that came later. But at Spofford that afternoon, looking at who I had been or remembering how I felt on that long ago summer afternoon no longer hurt. Was I moving myself out of being tied to the past as well as giving up feeling sorry for myself?

I had brought a Polaroid, and we shot a role of film. Now my new family existed in still another dimension.

Alena gave us two written assignments. Each of us was to write a letter to each member of our group. They would be exchanged the next day, our last day, but were not to be read until after we were discharged. The other assignment was to make a list of things we were going to do after we returned home, things that would give us pleasure. We compared our individual lists which varied widely, and then consolidated them while lingering at the dining table after the evening meal. My contributions are starred:

WE ARE GOING TO:
Learn to say, "No."
Explore mountain climbing.
Play tennis.
Learn calligraphy (use kit I have).
*Paint
*Play piano again.
Join the "Y."
Look at the ocean more often.
Start Yoga.
Water ski.
Resume Yoga.

Take long walks.
Bird watch.
Take "getaway" days.
Play more board games.
Write a letter each week.
Re-decorate my house.
Wallpaper hallway and living room.
Learn how to use makeup.
Become a mailbox watcher.
Go back to school.
Explore area where I live.
Make whole wheat breads.
Read to nephew more often.
*Have a "good read."
Spend more time with granddaughter.
Re-read the classics.
Take computer literacy course.
*Have a massage.
Cut my hair and wear it more casually.
Attend more plays.
Have half-ton truck and 1930 coupe.
Clean my closets.
Take all photographs and make albums.
Have electrolysis.
Become less intense in my job.
*Dance more often.
Resume more active exercising.
Knit.
Go to bed at night when I'm tired.
Have my own bedroom.
Work only 9 hours per day, 5 day week.
Read while I'm eating.
*Attend local theater productions.
Use the library.
*Enjoy candlelight bath, with champagne.
Take positive attitude wherever I go.
Find time for hugging my grandson more often.
*Share feelings with others.

Treat myself to day in NYC.

Go shopping once a week by myself

...and call Madeline.

Throughout the week we were often delighted when a cluster of CD patients in the dining room sang a song to a member of their group being discharged that day. Because we had all arrived and would leave together, we decided to write our own farewell song. I was positive I would have much to contribute and looked forward to the composing session. I missed out however, because during the time I wrote some of my goodbye letters, many of the others were putting the song together. I felt somewhat nonplused when I walked into Polly and Irene's room and was greeted by Fifi and Madeline who said, "Listen to this," and with much clearing of throats and some giggles, a pitch was agreed upon and six or seven of them sang our farewell song. I expected I would find fault with it. Hardly. I loved it. More than that, I loved realizing I did not feel I had been deliberately omitted from the composing process, that I could enjoy the song and singing it even though I had nothing to do with it. My ego was not bruised. I did suggest we pronounce the "k" in "lake" and "take" to add more humor and that we all wear something to tie us together visually as a group. I thought of a scarf and hit upon tying the dining room's red linen napkins around our necks. My sense of theater was still with me. And so, I ended up making a contribution after all.

Saturday afternoon seemed like a Class Day in miniature. We had shared photographs, compiled a list of projected activities, and with the writing of personal letters, I was reminded of the last few days in high school when we seniors dashed from one person to another to have them write something next to their picture in the class yearbook. We had only two scheduled activities left—the evening lecture and a wrap-up session after Sunday breakfast. Fifi wrote out the words to our song on slips of paper so each of us could memorize it. The comparison to graduation was so strong that I would not have been surprised to hear a squeaky student orchestra rehearsing *Pomp and Circumstance.*

In the evening we congregated in the lecture hall a few minutes before eight, only this time we did not sit together near the front of the room as a group needing the physical reinforcement of our togetherness. Instead we felt confident about our bonding to sit in twos and threes, to sprinkle ourselves among the 28-day patients. We passed up the first few rows in favor of chairs beyond the middle. Symbolically, we chose our seats as befitted "upper classmen." However, I counted to make sure we were all present.

Just before the hands clicked into the eight o'clock slot, in walked a rumpled man who could have passed for another patient. This was the lecturer, Dan, still another staff counselor. I overheard a CD patient remark to a buddy, "Be prepared to stand up if he says the word." Relaxed talk rippled among the CD patients and many were quick to laugh. I sensed we were in for a different experience but not in my wildest imagination did I guess how profound and moving the next hour would be.

Dan introduced himself by name as a recovering alcoholic and added, "I'm a plain old garden variety type of drunk." He then said some words about the rule against smoking in the lecture hall. I heard the CD patient whisper, "Here it comes." Another CD patient spoke out, "We can smoke in the living room," which Dan had him repeat. Dan said that was true and asked if anyone wanted to move on. My first impression was that Dan was responding to the wishes of the frustrated smokers in the room. Suddenly there was the confusion of more than a hundred people getting to their feet and heading for the living room. In the corridor, another CD patient said to me, "You realize this is a scam." I wasn't sure I had heard him correctly. "Dan is the one who wants to smoke!" Indeed, a change in venue had been a foregone conclusion. Dan had his props already in place in the living room. On the grand piano were a pitcher of water and a goblet. The couches and overstuffed chairs accommodated many; the carpeted floor the rest. A pot pourri of humanity draped, leaned, and sprawled in anticipation of more surprises.

Dan stood behind the keyboard and played the opening bars of *Saturday Night is the Loneliness Night of the Week* which brought forth a few chuckles. He walked away from the piano and gruffly announced, "And you're right, I am going to play the piano." Then in a voice that boomed with fake exasperation, he continued, "BUT I'VE GOT TO TALK ABOUT DEPRESSION!" The lecture was underway. He lit a cigarette. He skillfully interwove his own story with the known progression of the disease. He cited a few statistics. "Eight million people warrant medical treatment for depression. One quarter million are hospitalized... A frequent outcome is suicide . . . Three quarters are in grim depression." He told us he was a member of AA but that earlier he had been a piano bar player. He said his lecture assignment was, "Make them feel anxious." He asked, "Is anybody depressed?" and laughter was his answer. "I'm a failure," he said, which was underscored by a return of heartier laughter. He told how, because of alcoholism, he lost a job, lost a wife and two children, how he had not had gas for his car, how he "never had shit."

302

Abruptly he wheeled and demanded, "And you think I need someone to make me feel anxious?"

With a cunning and craftiness as subtle as the progression of alcoholism itself, Dan led us down a musical garden path of depression made worse by alcohol abuse. He ran the gamut on the reasons people become depressed. First, there was the lost love. He played and sang, "*Set 'em up, Joe, I've got a little story. . . And make it one for my baby and one more for the road.*". He cited depression brought on by holidays and slid into, "*I'll have a blue, blue Christmas without you...*" He spoke of how depressing other holidays can be, such as "Arbor Day or some of the lesser holidays, like St. Swithin's Day." He spoke of the weekend blues and "any excuse to get blown away." He sang about the appeal of "*Come to me my melancholy baby, cuddle up and don't feel blue...*" Next he played and sang a segment from an old Rogers and Hart tune, "*More than glad to be happy, it's a pleasure to be sad...*" and he jumped up from the piano to shout, "That's sick! I mean, that's SICK!" We howled with laughter. He spoke of all the songs written especially to accommodate people with depression, especially the blues, and musically expanded by playing, "*So cry me a river, cry me a river, I cried a river over you.*" "And rainy days can be very depressing," he said, which tipped us off to the opening bars of *Here's That Rainy Day.*

He told about an evening after he had not drunk for nine months and was called to fill in at a piano bar. A woman asked him to play, *Raindrops Keep Falling on My Head.* She became progressively drunker. Every fifteen minutes, while he struggled not to drink, she repeated her request. He said he allowed her to get to him, and he had two drinks. He stopped responding in any manner to her incessant requests he play, *Raindrops Keep Falling on My Head.* Finally, quite drunk, she said, "Don't you know you're being paid to be nice to me?"

His retort? "For chrissakes lady, they couldn't pay me enough to be nice to you!" Over the roar of our laughter, Dan stated, "I haven't played it since and I'm not going to play it now."

He said that people can go to great lengths to find out why they are depressed, and he played a few bars of, *Why Was I Born?* and then said, "Someone came up with the answer," and he sang, *Born To Lose.* Over the fading applause, he said, "As the disease of alcoholism progresses, what once did the trick no longer does, and there are songs for that, too." He eased into "*I get no kick from champagne. Mere alcohol doesn't thrill me at all ...*" and then he played the opening bars of *The Thrill Is Gone.* By that point, he told us, someone is *Moanin' Low* and they get steeped in various shades of blue, and the syncopation of *Mood Indigo* filled the room until one by one, hundreds of fingers snapped in rhythm. As the applause died away, someone yelled out, "Play *Raindrops Keep Falling on My Head*" but Dan responded with a Jack Benny look. He spoke of how people begin wondering if they are depressed. "And there's a song for that, too," and we heard *Am I Blue?* He demanded, "What's this obsession with being unhappy?" He spoke of one time, while drunk, falling off a piano bench in front of 800 people, an event that he rationalized "happens to everybody." Continuing with the color theme, he plunged into *Rhapsody in Blue* hitting a few sour notes (which I discovered later were due to some faulty keys). The fact he was playing at all was a miracle. The fact he was alive was a miracle. Before the final resounding chords finished bouncing off the walls, the room exploded into applause and whistles. Then quietly, carefully, making sure each of us heard every word, he said, "I have managed to stay sober because I learned a very important thing," and he broke into a rendition of *People*. Every phrase took on new meaning:

People, people who need people
Are the luckiest people in the world.
We're children, needing other children
And yet letting our grownup pride
Hide all the need inside
Acting more like children than children.
Lovers are very special people
They're the luckiest people in the world.
With one person, one very special person
A feeling deep in your soul
Says you are half, now you're whole
No more hunger and thirst
But first be a person who needs people
People who need people
Are the luckiest people in the world.

The fellowship shared by recovering drunks and co-drunks in that forty foot square living room was overwhelming—the sweetness of it all. Strength emanated from the gentleness of caring. Before we could recover, Dan said, "I have one more thing to say," and he began playing and singing "*I wish you bluebirds in the spring...*" Those of us in our group who sat near one another on the floor reached out to hold hands—and Max too. When Dan sang, "*I wish you love...*" I was not the only one with unabashed tears. I did not want to let go of the feeling of community; I did not want the moment to end. I wanted to freeze all of us and the feelings of loving compassion and mutual understanding. The sweet sentimentality felt like a healing balm. The lecture on Depression was over.

No one bolted for the door. Many lingered to thank Dan for all he shared and to compliment him on his unique presentation. Efforts to persuade him to return to the piano were fruitless. A dozen or so who hankered for more music and singing hung around, each of us wanting to prolong the spell. But who could sit down at the piano and follow Dan? Little Connie was persuaded to play but she soon quit. I said I would try, but it had been years since I really played the piano and decades since I had played for others to sing. I was better than nothing, and the longer I played, the more confidence I gained. Fifi exclaimed about my ability to transpose from one key to another. Even I was amazed. Again I experienced the present in conjunction with the past, way back when I was in high school and invariably found myself at a piano to play for those who wanted to sing and dance. Madeline and Max danced. Fifi's joy at singing was infectious. I remained at the piano for an hour and then begged off because I felt the pull to write the letters to my sisters.

I re-read the note I received that day from Harry. Instead of including his name in the return address, he wrote, "The Lone Ranger." Straddling the sealed flap, he printed, "48 Hours And Counting." The note read:

Dear Donna,

Things have changed. I don't know how to tell you this. Guess I should be "up front" and lay it on the line. It takes a lot of courage to spit it out. You are now married to the world's horniest recovering alcoholic. Get your ass home! God, how I love you.

s/H

[When writing the first draft of this book, I asked each member of our family group if she would allow me to share a copy of my letter to her for inclusion here. Two members were willing and are included below.]

I found time late afternoon to write to Connie:

Dear Golden Girl,

Connie, your life stretches out in front of you——so much to learn and see and do and feel! Enjoy all that is your right to enjoy during this time when you are leaving your girlhood for young womanhood.

Your life is yours.

During those times that get yucky, how about closing your eyes again and remembering the fun you had playing water polo in the pool?

And sometimes, remember the scared Connie who was suddenly the only kid among a bunch of nutty women and who grew this week and learned her shyness didn't have to stay in her doughnut.

Connie, I'm glad you are one of us. You helped me to better understand what my children had to go through at your age; you've helped me to get in touch with some of the feelings they have yet to talk about with me.

(You are a lovely pussycat.)

I like to feel that in this wonderful new family of mine that I am your aunt. Can you accept that?

I'm wrapping this note with hugs, and freeing one hand long enough to just stroke your beautiful hair—before you can tell me again that you hate it.

Best of all, you are beautiful on the inside where it really counts.

Much love, Connie-girl,

s/Aunt Donna

There were six more letters to write.

Dear, dear—oh dear!—Polly,

And dear you are. (Oh dear! too.)

From the moment we began talking in the front lobby—actually before that when our luggage was becoming acquainted in the receptionist's office—I've liked you. Before the day was over, I loved you.

But back to that Sunday afternoon. I hoped that maybe we had been assigned as roommates. My smoking blew that. I feared it would be highly unlikely that any of the others coming could be as nice and as friendly and candid as you. I also figured it was also unlikely any of them would talk as fast!

Polly, you made it easier for me to accept my looniness.

Well, none of the rest of our family does talk as fast—except that Tuesday night when I got into my crisis. And everyone was wonderful.

But Polly, you are special—really special.

How you have grown this week! And what joy your breakthroughs have given me! Your ANGER NEEDS WANTS ET CETERA finally expressed and out in the open.

And your struggles with denial are a lesson for me I needed. I was quieter about my denials, but they've been there—not big ones like yours, but because yours were so big and you could come to grips with them, I knew I could.

You know, I could describe any of the other six with no problem. But as I sit here, thinking about you, wondering what words I could use, I get stuck because my whole being is such a big smile from the total joy of you.

Polly is Polly is Polly

And Polly is no longer lost! Polly is alive and getting better. Polly is flapping her *wings, getting ready to fly over the cuckoo's nest.*

With every ounce of honest feeling, I can't think of anyone I would have rather done time with in a MEN-tal in-stih-TOO-shun.

Polly, you're a bundle of bubbling love—depressions and all.

I am convinced you can more than cope with anything—even Mascots.

God bless you and keep you—and our lovely family, too.

I love you, Polly, and I'll never forget the miracle—actually a series of miracles—that brought you to us all. I give thanks for you—YOU, Polly!

s/Donna

Chapter 41

Because the clocks were turned back to Standard Time, we had an extra two hours to sleep; Sunday breakfasts were served an hour later anyway. We rehearsed our farewell song a couple times, and I distributed the red linen napkins borrowed the night before from the cafeteria. Joann and Connie did not want to tie napkins around their necks, but eventually they did. Joann said she would not stand up with us to sing, and I don't remember if she did or not. There was much giggling among us as we walked to the dining room. We made a beeline for a long table on the upper level from where we could be seen and heard by all the other patients. Mid-way through breakfast, some in our group tapped spoons against glasses and cups. Conversation ceased and heads turned our way. With red napkins tied around our necks, most of us stood and with happy gusto sang our song to the tune of *East Side, West Side*.

Good Old Spofford Hall
We've just spent one week at Spofford La-ke
We've taken all the information anyone can ta-ke
We are going home now to practice on our own
The skills we've learned and hoping that
We'll have a home sweet home.

You've made us feel so welcome
We want to thank you all

For making our stay so pleasant
Here at Good Old Spofford Hall.
Rah! Rah!

We received warm applause, and several CD patients complimented us, not only on the song, but on the friendliness of our group. Some even said they would miss us. For recovering alcoholics in a rehab facility to tell enablers they'll miss them is bonafide proof drunks and spouses can get better. (Can you see my smile?)

We returned to our rooms to complete packing and to strip our beds and place the linen outside the door. As instructed, we put our luggage in the hallway, too. Our week was almost over. To return home filled me with apprehension. I had to leave a place where for the first time since childhood I felt protected and secure. The whole learning process was presented lovingly but forcefully by professionals who exuded confidence and who performed their duties with consummate skill. The full seven days were gently orchestrated, guiding people made ill by another's chronic alcoholism into an awareness of their own assets and liabilities. In seven days I received the equivalent of two years of therapy, and my guess is that I learned more about myself than I might have from a decade in Al-Anon. Wisely, Spofford strongly advised ongoing participation in Al-Anon because we needed to learn more than what makes us tick and how we are affected by the family illness: we needed to learn a new philosophy for living.

Our last scheduled activity called "Group Feedback Session" was held in the living room. No mistake about it, we were on the final countdown prior to discharge. When Carol walked in, we serenaded her with our song. She gave us our assignment: one by one, each member of our group would be singled out to receive verbal hugs from everyone. Much of the time I was aware I was quoting what I had already written in the individual letters. I told Penelope she held the distinction of being the only roommate I had not married. I know lovely things were said to me but I can recall only some of Madeline's words. She thanked me for being there, for trying to run interference between her and her husband, and it meant a lot to me to know she realized I had tried to protect her. She mentioned how much my voice had changed during the week, that at first it sounded harsh, strident, but that it had lowered and softened. That was news to me. Many tears were shed during the formal farewells, and boxes of tissues crisscrossed the lopsided circle. Some of us held hands. When the emotionally-charged hour was up, we hugged and hugged.

We exchanged our letters, and Carol reminded us to delay reading them until after we had left the grounds. I had placed the letters I wrote in Spofford Hall envelopes, and above the return address in the left hand corner had printed, "The Mental Institution." I was not about to forget where I had been.

I was ready to leave, in fact, the sooner I could be on my way, the better. I did not want to have goodbyes prolonged because they were too painful. After the gut-wrenching moments of pain that came and went throughout the week, the goodbyes felt like happy pain; I suppose that's why the word bittersweet was invented. Each of us had a list of our names, addresses and phone numbers. We had decided to keep in touch with a Round Robin, and I said I would get it started. Irene suggested she and I follow each other down the highway and stop at a restaurant she liked. She missed the turn, and we ended up at a place serving a brunch in an enormous room where a grand piano sat all by itself. We exclaimed over how perfect the place was for our transition from Spofford back into the outside world. As at Spofford, we served ourselves, the room was vast like Spofford's living room, and the memories of the musical "Depression" lecture were sharpened because of the presence of the grand piano. But how strange it felt to be only two, not eight. We agreed we felt incomplete. It seemed to me that Irene and I were the most vocal about our joy in being part of a new family. We gave each other long hugs in the parking lots, promised to keep in touch, and got into our cars with our own thoughts.

I was eager to get the suspense of homecoming over with. I continued on home by rote. My thoughts leaped between Spofford and Harry. I discovered I felt as I had the Sunday before—could it have been only seven days ago?—only this time I felt some pangs of guilt because when it came time to physically leave Spofford, I thought I didn't feel as sad about leaving as did some of the others.

No doubt about it, I was excited about returning home to my husband.

As soon as I pulled into the driveway, Harry walked out to greet me. We kissed and continued to stand beside the car for many minutes, our arms tight around each other. Our eyes filled with tears. A few times we leaned back to look at reach other, smile, and then re-tighten our embrace. Never mind the trees were bare and the air was raw. I was home. A tall pitcher filled with fresh daisies caught my eye as soon as I walked into our great room. Harry's thoughtfulness brought new tears to my eyes, and we hugged again. I was exhausted and running on nerves. I had averaged less than five hours sleep all week, yet I felt brimming with energy—a typical post-Spofford high—because

I had rid myself of so much pain and confusion and replaced it with seeds of growing self-esteem. I wished more than ever that Harry would take advantage of Spofford but I reminded myself that I could exercise control over only one person in my life—me. I warned Harry that my emotions were at the surface, not to be surprised if I swung between sudden laughter and sudden tears, and to realize the tears came from both joy and fatigue. He wondered about the strange looking cardboard box I set behind the couch; I told him I would get around to telling him about it before long. He seemed to have no trouble accepting that. The couch served as a divider between the living and dining areas, and the box sat behind the couch for weeks.

In spite of Alena's caution that we not try to share our week as soon as we got home and certainly not everything all at once, there was no way I could dam the torrent of words that came out of my mouth. I described our typical days, being constantly on the go, becoming more and more tired and therefore more vulnerable and receptive. I felt like the top of my head had been lifted off and stuff poured into it. I told him a little about each member of my group and became teary in the process. I could feel myself holding back, not daring to tell him they had become my sisters, not wanting him to think I loved him less because I now loved others. The longer I hesitated, the more I was nagged by what I had learned at Spofford: to push down unexpressed feelings was to bury them alive, and I was not responsible for another's feelings. So I took the risk I knew I had to take and told Harry how the eight of us had created our own family, that we were sisters and loved each other. My fears were groundless. Harry expressed genuine pleasure I had become so close to the others and said, "Now I have seven sisters-in-law." That gave me the courage to tell him about "Euphie," and not to be surprised if when he eventually talked with them, they called him by his new nickname. That didn't bother him, either.

I marveled that for the first time—ever!—we were actually communicating. The more I talked from a feeling level, the higher I felt. Much of the time Harry responded in kind. I thought, "How much he has grown!" It was I who had changed. My attitudes were different. I saw our situation differently thanks to surrendering to Step One and to ridding myself of poisonous resentments. Later I heard Harry remark he had never seen someone change as much as I did in one week—"180 degrees."

Before the day ended, I read the letters from my sisters.

Dear, dear Donna,

You've certainly won the gold star for "Roommate of the Year." Compatible,

311

caring, concerned, entertaining, knowledgeable—wise, wonderful—the words could easily fill the page. Our group is by far the best Ho Ho Hall ever had and we've had the added advantages of Alena, Carol and Julie.

You have helped me in so many ways to understand and absorb all the information we've been given. I shall think of you daily and pray for all the best for you.

God bless you.

s/Penelope

Dear Donna,

Sure is good to know you are as close as you are. I have really dreaded the separation of this new family. I love each one of you in a special way. You added a very new personality to my life, one that I'd have run from previously. I have gained so much from each of you. You have given me the confidence I need to say I need this new family. You have the most delightful smile and warmth.

Please keep in touch.

Love ya,

s/Irene

Dear Donna,

Thanks for being!

I love you.

s/Joann

At the top of her letter, Fifi drew a cross.

Dear Donna,

There is so much I want to say to you that it's difficult even to begin.

When this week started, I admired your many obvious qualities and talents. As the week went on, I have learned to love the true essence of just "who" Donna is. I have come to know that you are sometimes very vulnerable, unsure, sad, angry, afraid, but most of all, truly loving.

Your deep sharing of self has left its mark on me forever. Through your sharing, I have grown and have been able to really zero in on my own feelings. I will always be grateful for your gift. Thank you. Your very name means gift. It is a most appropriate one.

It is nice to have a sister named Donna. I've never had that before.

Know that I love you,

God Bless,

s/Fifi

Dear Donna,

During this past week, my feelings for you grew and grew and grew! I learned that you are a soft, gentle, competent, caring, fun and deep woman who has much to give to all with whom you come into contact.

It is my hope that we shall not lose touch but will continue a friendship that began at Spofford Hall.

I have no reservations about your desire to "change" those things you can. What we have taken away from our experience together cannot be forgotten.——Nor will you be. Your hugs, kisses, hugs and words of encouragement were special. Please keep in mind our "family" support system. I will always be there in good times and in bad.

Fondly,

s/Madeline

P.S. I'd like to thank you for standing by me.

Donna,

Thank you for helping me make it through this week. You're a very warm, loving and nice person. I'm glad I got to know ya. I hope everything turns out okay for ya!

Love,

s/Connie

X O X O X O X O X O X

Typically, Polly noted she began writing her letter at 5:30 am Sunday.

Dear Donna,

What can I say? You mean so much to me.

Aren't I lucky I got here early last Sunday and got to have you all to myself for a little while. I really needed you, esp. then. Your specialness and warmth showed right from the start. You sent me the right "vibes" all week to transform the jellyfish into the lion I feel inside today!

The last few days I kept thinking: how can one woman have so much "pizzazz" and talent, and you keep amazing me so I know your talents are never-ending.

My fantasy at this moment is to be around you and have some of your natural charm and un-inhibitions rub onto me by osmosis. I sure have fun just being around you. I get such acceptance from your beautiful face. You may even be turning me into a hugger!

I identify with your feelings and hopes for the future. I know you're aware that "Donna is in God's loving care" each day and boy, that's dynamite!

313

You have been a strong role model for me this week as I have attempted to again join the human race and get interested in life. You're one "hell" of a lady.
I love you and will be thinking of you.
Love,
s/Polly

I was home with my husband who loved me and I him. My new sisters were in their homes and in my heart. My children, Mother and I loved one another, maybe not perfectly or ideally, but still we loved. Silently I thanked God for all the days, months, and years gone by and for the combined efforts of many people—not the least of whom was me—which made it possible for me to look forward to the morning. In the warmth of my husband's arms—and from the electric blanket that covered our king bed—I drifted off to sleep feeling rich beyond measure. In a deeply personal sense, I felt re-born.

Part Three

Recovery

Chapter 42

With Alena's words ringing in my head, "Everything the alcoholic has to do to get better, you have to do to get sane," I plunged into recovery. Never again did I want to feel crazy. I attended the Monday night Al-Anon meeting and gave hugs all around. The following night I attended Al-Anon in an adjoining town and soon joined that group, too. I began each day—in the bathroom—reading first that day's page from *The Daily Word* a monthly booklet published by Unity, a spiritual fellowship, and then a page for the day in Al-Anon's *One Day At a Time* affectionately abbreviated to *ODAT*. Next I kept the promise to myself to read all the Twelve Steps. At various times during the day, I re-read other Al-Anon literature, sometimes pages in AA's *Big Book* and a little volume many AA members read daily, *The 24-Hour Book*. I re-read sections of books about alcoholism I no longer needed to borrow from libraries because I had bought my own copies. Columns and articles in various periodicals seemed to jump out at me, together with television specials and talk shows about drug abuse which often left me frustrated because they were sometimes inaccurate or dangerously misleading, especially when cures were hinted at, and because most times, neither AA nor Al-Anon was mentioned as sources of help. I gave more thought to writing an article about my own experiences.

During my first week home from Spofford Hall, I often looked at my watch and thought, "Now the Family Patients are leaving the morning lecture for Group," or "Now they're at lunch," or "They're in Group Communication

317

now." Each clock-activity connection reinforced my moments spent there. I parlayed my week many times over. And I talked about the week with anyone who would listen. Harry listened the most intently; I rejoiced in being able to share with him. Mother was an attentive listener and asked good questions. Liz tolerated me. I took pains not to talk about Spofford during actual Al-Anon meetings, first because it is against Al-Anon's Traditions Six and Ten to discuss the merits of other sources of help. But outside the meetings, I championed the treatment program and stressed the importance of seeking counseling only from therapists with in-depth knowledge about the disease.

About two weeks after I returned, I was surprised and pleased to have a call from Joann. She needed to talk to someone from our Spofford group because she was having difficulty hanging on to what we had learned. She asked, "Do you feel like you're losing it?" and I was alarmed because I could identify with her question. I wrote in my journal:

1 a.m. Friday

I've not been able to get back to sleep for an hour so obviously something(s) bugging me and perhaps if I write in here, whatever it is will come out. "Write it down; keep a journal," are among my Aftercare instructions. This is the first night since I returned home that I've experienced any sleeping problem. From about suppertime on, I could feel myself becoming agitated.

I lay in bed just now thinking about all the blank pages in this journal, wondering if the privacy of these pages will be violated as were my now destroyed journals. I came to this conclusion: so be it. So, "God, grant me the serenity to accept the things I cannot change . . ." I will not hide this journal.

I do feel like I'm "losing it," like I've regressed the past few days, like I'm slowly oozing back into the old lousy rut and I don't know what to do about it. I returned feeling so much better about myself, feeling a return of self-confidence, of self-esteem, and I don't know what's happening—like I'm getting caught in a whirlpool of molasses.

My homecoming was so sweet and tender. I was genuinely happy to see Harry, to be home again. I babbled on about the seven days, wanting to share, wanting him to share himself with me. Now it feels like we are gradually returning to surface communication, and that's a feeling I deplore. So I tell myself that he's at a different stage of his recovery. He tells me the AA discussion meetings he attends are group therapy, but I don't see how they can possibly be as incisive as what I experienced at Spofford Hall (SH). For one thing, there's no trained professional to pick people up on what they let slip. At SH in the Group Communication sessions that included some of the husbands, the counselors did not pull any punches with the newly-sober alcoholics.

I am actively seeking help. I willingly and eagerly subjected myself to the week at Spofford and wished it were longer. It didn't bother me my car keys were locked up. They could have bolted the doors for all I cared. I was there to learn as much as I possibly could about what's festering inside me, keeping me operating at a sublevel of achievement. What am I afraid of? Surely there are fears of varying kinds and intensities that are incapacitating me. Fears of rejection. Lack of acceptance. Others' censorship. Loss of being loved. I came away determined to concentrate upon my own recovery and I'm beginning to feel I'm not doing right by myself.

Last week I felt I could actually see and feel Harry growing. Maybe that was part of my projected euphoria. Maybe it was real, and the growth has been present this week, too, only I got bogged down in myself too much to notice it.

I took Mother to visit relatives yesterday, more out of duty on my part than anything else. It was an act of unselfishness that I knew wasn't sincere. So I felt doubly bugged. What saved the day for me was finding Irene's house and surprising her. What a classic expression of disbelief on her face when she looked up from the kitchen table and saw me. And what heartfelt hugs we gave one another. Back at the car after I introduced her to Mother, suddenly Irene threw her arms around me and we hugged and hugged. Mother said, "Cut it out, you two. People will think you're lesbians." Irene said, "That's their problem." The more I think about it, the more profound that exchange seems. There were the old messages: "What will other people think?" and "Pay attention to me." If Irene hadn't said, "That's their problem," I think I would have felt the full sting of the reprimand. As it was, Irene's words helped me to hang on to the moment which was one of pure joy at being with someone I love and who loves me, two individuals who have accepted each other as we are.

I extended myself a couple of times this past week as a kindness to others. Why is it that when I do something for my own satisfaction/pleasure I feel guilty? And when I'm consciously putting myself out, I feel guilty because I know I'm not being genuine.

This writing seems to be making me feel even more agitated. Therefore, I must be getting close to some truth about myself that my subconscious does not want to relinquish.

I returned home so full of optimism, especially about our marriage. I'm still optimistic but now I'm coming to grips with the fact we face a long road before our initial stages of recovery are accomplished. How I wish Harry had also been exposed to the same intensive therapy! That he, too, had been forced to acknowledge some *of his feelings as I did mine, to get his feelings out, to experience the tremendous relief after the pain, so that he would share an eagerness I feel for getting everything out. If he were seeing an aggressive counselor, then I feel he and I could make faster headway. Yes, I'm impatient for progress. We don't have a lot of time, not like people 10 or 20 years younger.*

In a book I was reading aloud tonight, Why Am I Afraid to Tell You Who I Am? *by John Power, S.J., it says, "that repressed emotions are the most common cause of fatigue and actual sickness." We've been sleeping too much! I want Harry and me to enjoy full gut-level communication. I want us to both grow up, to be mature and therefore free to really love and appreciate one another. In a nutshell, I want us well (no pun intended).*

My week at Spofford was not only the hardest working week of my life but the most enjoyable. Truly, it was the best thing I've done for myself. There are very few moments or hours from the past I would enjoy reliving just as they happened. My week—a full seven days—at Spofford is one of them. It was both the most painful and happiest week of my life. I was so fortunate to be able to go, that we have the medical insurance to cover the cost, thanks to Harry's foresight. I went there following the most painfully harrowing period of my life. I thank God for being able to go. Now I don't want to lose the momentum of what was begun there.

I suppose it's insanity to still be writing at 2:45 a.m.!

A woebegone Connie phoned that second week and with Harry's blessing, she was our house guest for the weekend. On Saturday morning Connie and I rendezvoused with Irene and then continued on to Spofford for Aftercare, talking non-stop. We verbalized our worst fears about Madeline; seconds after we pulled into the parking lot, Madeline and Max arrived. She said their situation was "lousy, terrible," and although beautifully groomed, she showed the strain. Hugging Max was like hugging stone. I said he was full of anger; Irene said, "Hate." Also at Aftercare was the loving Joann. Five of us eight made it. Fifi, Polly and Penelope were attending a regional Aftercare convenient to their homes. Seeing my sisters helped to recharge my batteries. I got strength just from seeing them, and I sensed the support of those who were missing.

My first appointment post-Spofford for one-on-one therapy with Stan, the same Stan with the alcoholism out-patient clinic I consulted during the summer, was cancelled without notice and postponed a week. By then I had much to talk about; journal writing helped bring old issues to the surface. I needed to talk about the time Mother slapped me across the face. I was 13, we disagreed about something—I can't recall what it was—but I remember feeling Mother was unreasonable and unjust. I pursued my point of view; our voices became slightly raised. We stood in the bedroom facing each other. It was the first time I was "speaking up" to Mother, challenging her. Suddenly this woman who never spanked me slapped me across my face and told me never to speak to her like that again. I was shocked, stunned, totally thwarted. I felt anger and disbelief at the humiliation of being slapped across my face— by my mother! I could not comprehend what I said that provoked such anger but I knew I did not want to provoke more. I stuffed my feelings. Mother's authority prevailed. I was 41 before I crossed her again When we lived at High View, I had divorced Steve, no longer had a car, and had to use Mother's. Through remarks she let drop, I knew she resented having mileage put on her car. I was fed up with feeling uncomfortable every time I used her car. Without consulting her, I bought a used station wagon. She was hurt I didn't consult her, upset I spent the money, saddling myself with the added expense of a car. A discussion begun in the kitchen moved out onto the lawn, a screaming match, like fishwives, and I used the f word effectively which I knew would displease her. I let it all hang out. What a self-satisfying feeling I experienced! In a way I felt like I was cutting the cord, a symbolic gesture of course, but having my own car gave me a feeling of independence. Many of Mother's controlling attitudes were valid and usually stemmed from financial concerns. She had worked hard and long to assure herself of a retirement nest egg and understandably wanted to neither deplete it through frivolous expenditures nor have her daughter go through financial struggles. Intellectually I appreciated Mother's position but I had my own emotional needs. Buying that station wagon signaled the beginning of my postponed teenage rebelliousness.

Spofford may have poured much into my head but my scalp had not been stitched back together: old buried feelings connected with supposedly forgotten incidents kept coming to the surface and wafted out, demanding attention. An entry in my journal reads:

So last week's bummer moments—being placed in a position to think of someone else ahead of myself, being forced into playing Good Samaritan—probably felt like an echo from growing up years: doing what was "nice" and "good," etc. Having the counseling appointment cancelled on short notice with no explanation felt like a slap.

I was on the right track but I had yet to stop thinking of myself as a victim. Writing "being placed" demonstrated I had yet to understand I had allowed myself to be placed in an uncomfortable position, had permitted myself to accept a guilt trip by taking on a Good Samaritan role.

I plugged away with Al-Anon. The Monday group was only a few months old; sometimes only two or three of us were there. Others who wandered in, even if they had previous Al-Anon exposure, were also neophytes at grasping the subtle Al-Anon philosophy. Week after week I returned home on Monday nights agitated about the prevailing negativity in that meeting. To counteract those feelings, on Tuesday night I attended a different meeting, seeking a toehold on elusive serenity. There I heard many references to spirituality expressed by members with as many as eight years of continuous Al-Anon participation. They were wonderfully tolerant of me, the hotshot with alcoholism knowledge and family treatment experience. One evening I inwardly groaned when the topic was announced—methods of relieving tension. Hell, I knew all the methods: meditation, Yoga, reading the *ODAT*, using the phone to talk with other members, getting to meetings. Several spoke of prayer, and they seemed to be the ones who had the most serenity. Before the meeting ended, I said I was disappointed when the topic was announced but I felt I had gained much, especially an awareness of the value of relaxing into spirituality. In my journal I described what happened the following morning:

For the first time since I was a little girl and perhaps the first time ever of my own accord—and without premeditation—I got down from the kitchen stool and knelt and prayed. For only a split second I felt self-conscious. Aloud, I gave thanks to God for bringing me—and Harry—so far into recovery and prayed that His will be done. After I got back onto the stool, I could still feel the pressure of the floor against my knees, and that felt like the prayer was still going on.

When I mentioned this to Stan during our first post-Spofford counseling session, he leaned across his desk, beaming. "You realize what you were doing?" He seemed excited enough to come right across the top of his desk. "You were surrendering!" At Spofford I surrendered to Step One, and thanks to their lectures which were reinforced at the Tuesday Al-Anon group, I surrendered to Steps Two and Three in the privacy of my own kitchen.

With Stan I was as candid as I could be regarding my eagerness and willingness to work hard, to ferret out my hidden feelings. I wanted to get over my need to try to shape peaceful coexistence among others, especially my immediate family, as my anxious efforts were counter-productive: they served to annoy others and to exhaust and frustrate me. With Harry actively working his AA program, my need to protect his feelings lessened. Still, I voiced concern to Stan about being unable to maintain the same level of communication we enjoyed right after I returned from Spofford. Most of the time I felt Harry and I had reverted to communicating from defense to defense, and I wanted open communication. Stan said what I experienced at Spofford was the ideal, that communication there happened in a structured, protected, compassionate and supportive environment. "That wasn't reality," he said.

"Yes, it was reality," I countered. "It was real and it happened."

Stan's point was that in the day-to-day world, I would have to accept a comfortable meeting ground that falls short of the ideal. He asked if I could take whatever I found out. I expected pain but that I knew relief follows pain. He asked, "What if you don't like what you find out?" I didn't think or feel I'd find out anything that was really so awful about me. He pushed more. "Can you survive?" I still did not understand what he was driving at.

"Do you mean can I survive if the marriage ends?"

"Yes," he answered.

"Yes, I could survive, but I really feel the marriage will survive, too." My response gave me verbal reassurance. I came away from that session with a chant in my head: "My wellness is dependent upon only one person—me."

I kept in close touch with my new sisters. Every week I began a Round Robin letter and mailed it to the next person on the list. I wrote individuals and made phone calls. I was concerned about each sister and believed nurturing our group's closeness gave all of us strength. Even if contacts were not reciprocated, I felt my action reinforced my support system, and theirs, too. When I discovered the Round Robin letters were disappearing mid-cycle, I mailed each new letter to a different person; nevertheless, the Round Robins never got beyond a certain point.

Through long distance phone conversations with Fifi, I discovered she had the ability to challenge me, thanks to a combination of her basic personality, more than a year in Al-Anon, and one-on-one counseling with her therapist, Audrey, who challenged her successfully. I welcomed Fifi's confrontations. If I tried to soft pedal anger by saying, "I'm frustrated," she overrode my equivocations until I admitted, "Yes, I'm angry." If I said I was disappointed about something, she reminded me that others did not have to live up to my expectations. For many months I called upon Fifi as my friend, sister, and unofficial Al-Anon sponsor. To keep phone bills down, Harry and I subscribed to a calling plan that also helped lower the cost of his business calls.

Following the intensity of Spofford's treatment, Al-Anon seemed too slow. I was in such a hurry to get well that I equated Al-Anon's gentleness with lack of substance. I thought by not putting demands upon me, my clever subconscious would continue protecting itself. I wanted to be jolted, to lift out repressed feelings no matter how painful because if I did not verbalize them, I knew they oozed poison into my system. I wanted and needed to be challenged skillfully, compassionately, and non-judgmentally. Because I had proven to myself that I could not manage my own life healthfully and because I believed the pros at Spofford knew what they were talking about, my commitment to attend Al-Anon meetings remained steadfast. I wasn't about to give up on them. Thank God Al-Anon didn't give up on me. Around those tables sat my peers. Some still fought the reality of alcoholism as an all-powerful addiction; others, although living with active drinking, seemed to have found peace of mind. Some clung to self-defeating behavior patterns; others took risks by learning new ways to conduct themselves. Some were filled with fear and shame; others had freed themselves from such fetters. Some continued to do what I tried before going to Spofford: select certain aspects of the Al-Anon program to practice what they found easy, relatively painless. Deep down inside, some did not want the alcoholic to stop drinking because they enjoyed their martyr status. Some contending with new soberness found the alcoholic's behavior so frustrating when booze could not be pinpointed as the direct cause that they said they wished the alcoholic were still drinking. Such remarks I could not let go by. Repeatedly, I reminded distraught members that alcoholism is not a simple illness with a beginning, middle and end like measles, but a progressive, fatal disorder. By reminding them, I shook up any feelings of complacency I might have about Harry's recovery. To the best of my knowledge, the longest he had ever gone without drinking was six months. If he drank again, I believed the alcohol could take him to his grave.

Chapter 43

In keeping with my recovery process—following the suggested Twelve Steps—I asked my son to come by after work and have supper with me. Harry left early for his AA meeting to give us privacy. I wanted to take the Ninth Step ("Made direct amends to such people wherever possible, except when to do so would injure them or others") and thereby open up lines of effective communication between David and me, and ultimately pave the way for positive interactions among my children and me. I was nervous about our meeting and took solace from John Powell's words, "No one's feelings are caused by others. Our feelings are caused by our own emotional responses, our own choices and reactions." I knew that David, like Liz, held deep resentments towards me.

David arrived with his girl; I decided I would not let Laura's presence intimidate me. I told him about how I was affected by another's alcoholism and of my week of treatment. I told him all the pieces of the puzzle indicated Steve, among other problems, was alcoholic. I let him know I was concerned about his own drinking habits. David had been in a number of scrapes with the police and all the incidents appeared to be alcohol related. David said he was limiting his drinking to weekends only, and I said that attempting to control one's drinking was a sign the disease was progressing. That night he had a beer "because this is a special occasion." Alcoholics are infamous for finding "legitimate" excuses to drink. David said I placed too much emphasis upon alcoholism just as I had on nutrition and earlier on my spiritual beliefs. He thought his mother was going through sequential phases and did not understand that one nugget of knowledge built upon another. However, our time together was congenial, and I loved hugging and being hugged by my 21-year-old handsome son. I shared my feelings with him and told him I was sorry for causing him pain and anguish. I also planted a seed about his own growing problem with mind-altering substances. In my journal I compared his denial to a wall of steel reinforced with titanium. I felt I had done all I could for now.

Chapter 44

Living with a recovering alcoholic is far preferable to living with active alcoholism, but there were times I wondered if Harry had been drinking. He talked as if he had, not that he slurred his words, but sometimes what he said did not make sense. Other times he was quick to turn on me verbally, lashing out with sarcastic remarks that shocked and hurt. The alcohol may have been out of his system but not the emotional "isms" which continue long after the body is detoxified. I think it's unfortunate the illness/disease/disorder was named after its most obvious symptom——the addiction to alcohol——because if it were called Wilson's Disease, after Bill Wilson, a co-founder of AA, or after E. M. Jellinek, M.D., a scientist-scholar who helped refine and spread the knowledge of alcoholism as a disease, a different name might have helped remove the social stigma, just as what the new name Down's Syndrome did for Mongolism. It is important to dispel the myth that addictive drinking is the only symptom requiring treatment. While I was writing the first draft of this book, Harry slipped me a note: "Being newly sober is like trying to untangle a bunch of wire coat hangers." We were intent upon conducting our lives differently. We no longer lived in the moment-to-moment turmoil of active alcoholism. Now we had time to reflect, the same as anyone does when convalescing from an operation. No longer could we blame the drinking for our problems. We had to take responsibility for ourselves, for the choices we make.

When Harry manifested mood swings I could not understand, I chalked up his behavior to what is called a dry drunk——thinking drunk without the benefit of alcohol in the system. As a further help not to react, I visualized across his forehead the letters, "S - I - C - K". For me to expect logical communication during a dry drunk was senseless. I used one of Al-Anon's slogans more than any of the others: "How important is it?" When Harry slung a barb my way, my first reaction was to set him straight. But by asking myself, "How important is it?" I bought time to decide "whatever" was not important enough to start World War III. There were times I slipped, I retorted, and I was furious with myself. Then I fell back on my belief that everything happens for a reason, and the reason, I told myself, was so I could learn from my slip and not do it again. This does not mean I gave Harry license to walk over me. Sometimes I responded to a cutting remark by saying, "I feel hurt because of what you just said." More often than not, stating my feelings in such a simple, straightforward manner helped Harry switch to a less combative track. On the few occasions he countered with, "That's your problem," I was pissed. He was right, dammit: my feelings were my problem.

One evening Harry said he thought my co-alcoholism was due more to Steve's behavior than to his. "I feel I'm being saddled with more guilt than I deserve." To be sure, my illness got a strong toehold during the years with Steve, but I believe the straw that broke my back—and almost my mind—was Harry's persistent lying about his unfaithful behavior. And since he continued to deny he had done anything wrong, we were at an impasse in our communication. Crazy or not, I had to take responsibility that I had not protected my children from Steve's abuse; being distraught was a mitigating factor, at best an excuse, but such did not absolve me of my failure to intercede. Harry insisted that because he was drunk when he visited the massage parlor and because money was exchanged for the services of a prostitute and because "nothing happened" beyond having his genitals fondled, he, therefore, had not committed an act of unfaithfulness. I asked if I would be considered unfaithful if I allowed a man to fondle me. Harry said, "I'll have to think about that" which ticked me off because that meant the subject was dead unless I brought it up again. I fell back on the wisdom of the Serenity Prayer, "God, give me the wisdom to accept the things I cannot change." That Harry visited a massage parlor no longer mattered to me but not being honest with himself, not owning up to his motives for going there, not putting a realistic label on what he considered a non-event mattered a hell of a lot to me.

When I talked with Harry about the guilt I felt about my kids, he asked if he had contributed to it. I answered, "Yes," and he was surprised and displeased. I said I felt uncomfortable about inviting them to visit us because my impression was he did not like having them around. He began reciting a laundry list of Liz and David's faults. I interrupted. "I'm uncomfortable listening to this because there's nothing I can do about their shortcomings. I want to talk about my guilt feelings, not get bogged down in side issues."

Harry said, "I feel like I've been shot down. I don't want to talk about it any more."

I felt shut out, just like I had when he was drinking and would get in the last word before walking out of the room. I wanted to push for further discussion but I reminded myself, "Donna, if you want your feelings accepted and respected, then accept and respect his." At three in the morning, I was awake and writing in my journal:

I joined Harry in bed and could sense his withdrawal but I was too tired to investigate. So we went to sleep, but the ritual did not feel loving. Aha! Perhaps this is it: I felt rejected because I had stated some feelings which somehow displeased Harry. We have a long road to travel before we are well. My optimism and almost a smugness re how well we are getting along could be due to the fact we have not talked through issues which are really uncomfortable. As I write this, I can feel tears wanting to come forth.

I am very weary from focusing so much on alcoholism, particularly other people's problems due to the disease. I think I would like a break from the incessant reminders of alcoholism. I'm wondering if I'm getting out of balance, if I'm doing too much 12-Stepping. I can't lead everyone to water and expect they'll drink.

Perhaps later today when Harry and I are not so tired we can get to the bottom of whatever nerve button I hit and, in turn, what he pushed of mine.

This evening ended with both of us stuffing our feelings, and that's no way to run a railroad.

I think a pure escape movie would be a real treat and perhaps therapeutic.

During the next counseling session with Stan, I spoke of my guilt feelings. I told him about the time I slapped David across the face when he was a baby. David became my son when he was three months old, directly from a foster home where he was doted upon by a retired couple. Every room featured two to three pieces of baby paraphernalia; he received continuous attention while awake. He was uprooted from such idyllic conditions and transplanted into a home where he had to share his time with an energetic, into everything two-year-old sister Liz, and there was mounting tension between Brad and me. Brad switched his loving focus from Liz to David. Liz assumed a mini-mother attitude towards her new baby brother. And David divided his time between sleeping and screaming. I ran the vacuum so the kids would not hear me crying. I depended upon the children's afternoon naps as a time for me to nap, too, but day after day David fought going to sleep. I ran down the checklist—open diaper pin, soiled diaper, bubble. Walking the floor with him did not help. When he was six months old, after three months of the naptime routine, I lost my temper and slapped him on his left cheek. He stopped crying at once. I was filled with remorse and picked him up and held him while I tearfully apologized. When I laid him back into his crib, he went right to sleep without any further fuss. Liz napped. I napped. When they awakened, I changed Liz and then David and gasped: I could see the outline of part of my palm and fingers on David's cheek. He cooed and smiled. He was in the best mood since coming into our home. When Brad walked in from the office, I told him what happened. The mark on David's cheek had yet to fade away. Brad took David into his arms and told me he would never trust me with the children again. Now neither of us trusted the other.

I also told Stan about not stepping in between Steve and the kids, how terribly David and Liz fought during their teens and continued to spat in their early twenties. Stan spoke of the resiliency of kids, particularly babies, and established I had done no physical harm to David by slapping him on the face (David never screamed again about taking a nap). Stan reminded me of the crazy effects alcoholism has on families and of normal sibling rivalry heightened by continuous tension within the home. He told me guilt feelings would hold me back. While tears streamed down my face, Stan leaned across the desk and said, "Donna, I am absolving you of guilt."

"I don't feel absolved."

Stan's words kept running through my head as I drove home, prepared dinner, and went to the Tuesday night Al-Anon meeting. I noted in my journal the meeting was "a real upper." For days I re-heard Stan's words, "I am absolving you of guilt," until I began to permit myself to be absolved. I wrote in my journal:

When I think back now to those insane years after I divorced Steve, how both Liz and David reminded me of Steve because they acted so much like him, and now I know they were experimenting with pot and booze and pills, so no wonder the atmosphere was charged with insanity. They messed with their heads and mine.

It was Thanksgiving week, and I concluded that entry by writing:

I've done nothing re preparing The Feast. For the first time in years, I really look forward to Thanksgiving. I have much, much to be thankful for—my marriage, Harry himself, our home and home life; Mother, Liz, David, my two grandchildren;

my new sisters; Spofford, Al-Anon and AA. A lot!

Twelve hours later, at noon on the day before Thanksgiving, I suffered my first post-Spofford setback.

I'm getting those lousy feelings again re Harry's social behavior. If I ever find out that he's been unfaithful again to our marriage vows in any way, with or without physical/sexual contact (body or mind), I'll have the s.o.b. castrated—my way.

I've not been focusing upon him at all nor his program. But thoughts are creeping in. I think he's got Step One. He did Step Four, but not in depth. I felt it was more intellectual than emotional. Step Five—he admitted enough to perhaps create a smokescreen. He does not read his "Twenty-Four Hour Book" daily, and it's so easy to do if one is truly committed to the program. I've missed reading ODAT only twice, and then I caught up with myself before midnight.

I feel I should stop being so complacent about his recovery. I've projected my feelings and dedication to my efforts re myself to him. Such is totally unrealistic. I must not let myself fall into the trap—again—of believing what I want to believe about any other person, and especially including my husband.

Oh shit! I can feel the old resentments boiling up. I DON'T WANT THEM!

I want an HONEST marriage. I don't want to be lied to again. I really don't think I could take it, nor is there any reason I should.

I MUST FOCUS ON ME, MY RECOVERY, GET MYSELF TOGETHER, SO THAT SHOULD THIS RELATIONSHIP END, I CAN SURVIVE.

I've been stupid to think he could change—poof!—overnight. Maybe he just can't ever be faithful.

I feel like a pile of shit, and the day began so beautifully. Well, I'll reach down to my toes, and I'll try to apply Al-Anon, and start the day over again.

The next entry was made the following Sunday:

Of course Harry could tell as soon as he came home Wednesday afternoon that something was bothering me, although I thought I had gotten on top of it after kneeling in prayer and almost pleading—no, not almost: I pleaded with God to remove the thoughts from my head. But as soon as Harry returned, I could feel my old fears coming out, and so rather than deceive, I told him—told him about going in his briefcase and finding the folded envelope within an envelope, both with his Post Office Box return stickers in return position. I felt so embarrassed about looking in his briefcase again after all this time. I could feel my sickness coming over me again, like it was going to control me again. I felt I had to tell him the truth because not to do so would be violating The Steps, and if I'm going to live them, then I must LIVE them. He disclaimed any knowledge of the envelopes, said they proved nothing, and asked when I had last looked in his briefcase, "Last summer?" I couldn't remember when exactly and so I said, "Last August or September" and he said that the envelopes were "left over from last summer."

But that isn't true! Because they were not there in August or September. He wrote Steps 4 & 5 to me the end of September, and they weren't there right after that nor before I went to Spofford in mid-October. The last time I looked in his briefcase was JUST BEFORE I WENT AWAY, AND THEY WEREN'T THERE THEN.

I've done everything I can think of to put this out of my mind—but it's in my brain—and I'm scared about telling Harry of remembering now when there wasn't anything there because I can't bear to have him tell me another lie. And if I mention this, it'll cause—oh God! What will it cause? I DON'T KNOW.

I remember Stan telling me last July that I probably wouldn't be able to believe all Harry says for a year. But I put that out of my head when he wrote Steps 4 & 5 and when, after returning from S.H., I felt I had cleansed myself of the poisons and so had freed myself from being obsessed by his behavior. Also, I felt he was genuinely working his program to the best of his ability—at his pace—and so I felt a sense of emotional security, especially—and basically—regarding trust.

My saying anything to him has caused a rift. I've tried to minimize my feelings (and action of going into the briefcase) as a "slip" on my part. But what do I do, how do I apply all I've learned and am learning, when my feelings are a result of logic? I guess my answer is to get on with healing myself.

Tonight, at my suggestion (and I felt as if I were insisting), we attended an open speaker discussion meeting where AA and Al-Anon are all but merged into one meeting. It was a wrong move at this time for me. It put me too much into his program. I'm not strong enough yet to do that. It took my focus off myself and I realize now, several hours later, reinforced my growing obsession regarding his demeanor as it applies to our marriage vows.

He tried to assure me Wednesday that there's no one else, that he's not interested in anyone else, the personal ad stuff is history and that I was being "foolish." But! I heard those same words when he was actively advertising and responding to ads!

God, I wish I hadn't gone into his briefcase! I want to believe all is OK, that we are both genuinely working our programs.

Tears ran down my face on the way home from the meeting. I spoke of everything I could think of that might be causing them, but I had so successfully blocked out the envelopes and what they imply that I never connected anything until I started writing in here.

I can't say this has been the best of weeks. This was the first Thanksgiving I've not spent with David, not even an appearance. I phoned him that morning. A lot of old memories tied to Thanksgiving came rushing in, too. It's now been 10 years since I last saw Steve, that awful Thanksgiving that ended in such rage and tears. I thought of others since then—what a catalog of crap. So I really looked forward to this Thanksgiving—positively—as I'd not been able to do for more than 10 years—perhaps with the exception of the Thanksgiving just before I married Steve, it's been 30+ years.

And then I had to play Pandora.

The only person I can change is myself. And, I want to change. I want to feel good about myself, inside and out. I love Harry. I want us both to get well. I shall continue praying for guidance and for the fortitude to take charge of myself.

Chapter 45

Physical recovery for the alcoholic begins the moment he puts the cork in the bottle. Family life usually improves 50 percent then, too. The next percentage points are hard to come by, but Harry and I had it a lot easier than many. He did not lose his job or his health; we did not lose our home. We did not lose each other. We continued to share a collective neurosis that required not only concentrated attention but a commitment towards achieving a singular and collective wellness. Even without the distractions of young children in the house, rebuilding our lives was slow and often painful. During one of the painful periods, Mary, a wise lady in Al-Anon said, "The growth stops when the pain stops." The reality is that character defects take a long time to work out. The process of Harry changing his alcoholism induced thinking and behavior patterns and my changing my sober but emotionally charged reactions to such residuals was laborious and cruelly frustrating.

When Harry was newly sober, he suffered the pain of withdrawal, both physical and psychological. No longer could he escape into the bottle. I, as the co-alcoholic, no longer knew what to expect. During active drinking, I depended upon certain patterns: he drank too much, became verbally abusive; I reacted and so kept tension at fever pitch. Eventually he shuffled off to bed, and I nursed my invisible emotional bruises. During the first months of not drinking, Harry fell into bed early night after night, except on the nights he went to AA, exhausted from seemingly having done nothing to warrant such fatigue—a typical physical reaction. His mood swings were unpredictable and presented a threat to my recovery. Through Al-Anon I learned I must detach which means not to reject the cantankerous person but to be genuinely courteous and refuse to allow myself to be sucked into "stinkin' thinkin'." The "isms" of the illness for both the alcoholic and co-alcoholic remain until the individuals face themselves with an honesty so intense and total that only their finest selves are in control. Harry and I knew that by owning up to our respective thoughts, feelings and actions, and by accepting responsibility for all we thought, felt, said and did, we would have the ability to free ourselves from a previously debilitating life style. We knew we could never achieve perfection but could strive for it. Our intellectual understanding was fine. But when it came to dealing with our feelings, I was further along than Harry. Inevitably, my frustration corrupted my recovery.

The bottom line for Harry's recovery was not to drink. For me it was to keep the focus on myself, to get out of my husband's head and stay in my own. By not breaking my addiction to the recovering alcoholic, the misery of the "isms" can contribute to a new series of misfortunes. All easier said than done; I had to work at it continuously because if I resumed my obsession with Harry, my addiction to him would take up where it left off, only worse: my obsession had the power not only to destroy me but adversely affect Harry's recovery. I listened to AA people who, after months to years of sobriety, explored the idea they were not alcoholic and picked up a drink to find out. For an alcoholic, one drink is too many and a million aren't enough. Those who tried to become non-addictive social drinkers related tales of suffering more acute than they knew before joining AA. I heard these returnees to AA state they will never permit themselves to forget the horrible progressive pain of a slip that rendered them useless for days to years because they want it to serve as a reminder: they have a progressive, fatal disease, and they cannot, must not drink.

Three months after I returned from Spofford, I labeled my denial of an event as a colossal attitude slip. In the first draft of this book (which Harry read with my permission), I was in such deep denial that I omitted any and all details and shrunk the transgression (another euphemism) into an "alleged" event. Here's what I omitted writing about:

In January, three months after we left Spofford, my sisters and I spent a weekend at Irene's house, reconnecting, reaffirming, sharing, listening, learning, shedding tears and also finding many reasons to laugh. I returned home tired but on a high second to how I felt the day I left Spofford. Harry greeted me warmly; a loving nap was anticipated. But Liz phoned after we laid down. In a clipped voice she said she and Faith wanted to visit. I told Harry that Liz and Faith would be arriving in an hour or so. He rolled away from me. I napped.

Faith, age 16, was Liz's sister-in-law and had lived with Liz and Mike (Faith's brother) ever since they were awarded custody of her. Faith was included in all our family activities; she was shy, sweet natured, and scarred by living with abusive alcoholic parents. Earlier in January during prolonged sub-zero weather, a water pipe in my office had burst. Harry said the ideal time to clean up the mess was while I was away with "the Spofford girls." He said he'd ask Faith to help, that he'd pay her. I suggested that he include Liz. Harry said he wouldn't get anything accomplished if Liz were there because they'd laugh too much. Also, he said that Liz would be too interested in the material being sorted on my desk and he didn't think I would want her to see some of my private papers but that Faith would not pay any attention to them. (Liz was not a snoop.) When I could not talk him out of having just Faith there, something about his attitude made me feel uncomfortable enough to say, "Don't make a pass at Faith because it would only get back to Liz." Harry expressed shock at such an idea.

When Liz and Faith arrived, the confrontation was a nightmare. Liz accused Harry of trying to seduce Faith. He denied it. Faith said it was true. Liz told me to get rid of Harry, to throw him out. I did not know what to do so I did nothing. In part my decision not to decide stemmed from a car-buying incident during my first marriage when Brad and I succumbed to sale pressure and drove a used car home. Within days we knew we had been duped but the dealer would not give us back our car. An attorney said we had a case but said the only way we could win it was if our last name were Rockefeller. To throw Harry out of the house immediately required making an instantaneous major decision based upon emotions. I could not unravel my emotions. I could not sort through accusations and denials. I was immobilized.

At the time of this incident, Faith was 16, Harry was 53. The following day I typed this:

Memo of record from notes made 31 Jan 82 re alleged incident the day before. Faith has accused Harry of making sexual advances. Harry denies any intention of seducing Faith.

1. Two weeks ago while visiting here, Faith says Harry stuck his hand down the front of her blouse and touched her on the chest.

Harry says he chucked her, like under the chin, but near base of throat.

2. After Harry asked Faith to help him clean office, Liz says that Faith

pleaded with her to get out of going or to have Liz come along, too. Faith made it clear to Liz that she did not want to go. Liz insisted that she go and help out after all that Harry and Donna had done to make her feel welcome in the family.

3. Cathy (a friend of Faith's who had spent the night) told Liz that when Harry stopped at house to pick up Faith that he grabbed her ass (Cathy in nightgown).

Harry says he patted Cathy on the fanny.

4. Faith says that on ride to Southwick, Harry said he was glad Liz was not coming along because he and Faith would then be able to fuck. Faith insists he did not say "Fuck around" but "Fuck."

Harry said he said "screw around" and then amended that to saying he said "fuck around" but insisted he never said "fuck" only.

5. Faith said Harry asked her if she's a virgin.

Harry agreed he asked her that.

6. Faith said Harry asked her, "Do you fool around?"

Harry pointed out he has often said this to her in kidding.

7. After finishing the cleanup in the office, Faith says Harry spoke of having a shower, how he really needed one, and asked her if she wanted to take one.

Harry said he offered the shower idea as he thought she might like to take one after dealing with the mess in the office.

8. Faith says Harry rubbed her back while she sat on bar stool.

Harry agrees he did.

9. Faith says Harry asked her if she'd like to take a nap.

Harry says Faith was yawning, acting as if she really didn't care about leaving, and he asked her if she'd like to take a nap.

10. Faith says there was a magazine on the counter when they arrived which Harry quickly removed to coffee table saying it wasn't anything she wanted to see. Then later he told her he'd met a man on an airplane returning from Cleveland and got to talking, the man in publishing business, porno stuff, and that he gave the man his name and address and the man sent him the magazine.

Harry reiterated story about man on airplane and said that magazine arrived three days earlier, that he had looked at it the night before, and didn't know why he kept it, and didn't know how to get rid of it. He said he threw away the man's business card.

Donna insisted upon seeing the magazine right then and there (during confrontation by Faith and Liz) and followed Harry into his office. Magazine was between pads of paper in side desk drawer. Donna said he could have burned it if he wanted to get rid of it. Harry said, "I'll have to think about that."

11. Faith said Harry told her that anything that went on here was none of Liz and Mike's business that Faith would not have to say anything to anyone.

Harry denies having said that.

12. Faith insists all she said is true, that she felt if she had said the word, Harry would have made love with her.

Harry denies any sexual interest in Faith and pointed out she's a child, how he's old enough to be her father, almost her grandfather.

That I originally labeled this event as an "alleged incident" floods me with shame and embarrassment. Based upon what I learned about Harry's other seductions and what constitutes sexually deviant behavior, I believe Harry's sexual addiction was not one of his alcoholism "isms" but a separate illness. I don't like to get ahead of the story but three years later, while we were separated, Harry acknowledged that everything Liz and Faith accused him of was true and two years after that, he denied his confession.

At the time, I had no reason to doubt Faith's story and every reason to doubt Harry's. He was a clever liar, admitting to some of what Faith said but stopping short of confessing he tried to seduce her. He looked guilty. He seemed to shrink. What would happen if I threw him out? What kind of work could I get after being out of the job market (at his request) for almost four years? He was my third husband. I had no career to fall back on. I'd have to move. Again. What I would face overwhelmed me. I did not have the emotional strength I needed to throw him out. Therefore, although I sensed in my gut he was guilty, I could not allow myself to believe Faith.

The more I talked with others, the more I talked myself into believing my rationalizing was logical. No one I talked with thought the Harry/Faith incident, even if true, was worth getting excited about and certainly not worth throwing the baby out with the bath water. The professionals I consulted, all of them recovering alcoholics, raised this question: What had Faith done to signal Harry she would welcome his advances? Al-Anon women threw in the fact Harry was only six months into sobriety. Older women I talked with, including my mother who was fond of Faith, shrugged it off to men being men. The prevailing attitude was that a well-developed 16-year-old girl could wield so much power over men that they were powerless to control their carnal urges. A significant component of the prevailing attitude was sympathy and compassion for the poor, newly sober alcoholic in early recovery. No one I talked with, not even women, expressed compassion for Faith. There was only one exception: Liz.

Back in 1982 I believed the "alleged incident" could have been resolved had hysteria not set in; but that through the re-telling, it escalated into a crisis and family members took sides. I tried to get inside everyone's head, especially the heads of my husband and my daughter who were the principal protagonists. Liz told me she was disgusted with me because I was not divorcing Harry; therefore, she announced, she was divorcing me. I could visit my grandsons by myself but she would no longer allow them to be with Harry because she did not trust him. I was on a mission to ferret out truth in its absolute form, only to discover an age-old truism: there's no such thing as absolutes and especially no absolute truth when those involved view something from a different perspective. As far as I knew, the only person in favor of throwing Harry out was Liz. I regressed—terribly. I was heartsick about Liz divorcing me. Making appointments to see my grandsons, knocking at their door, taking them to fast food places or to visit my mother raised my empathy for divorced fathers. I embraced the Al-Anon tools—extra meetings, extra reading, greater involvement in meetings, phoned trusted Al-Anon friends, increased physical exercise, called Aftercare counselors at Spofford, poured out an agony of words onto the pages of my journal. I became more obsessed with Harry than before going to Spofford.

In effect, Faith's accusation that Harry made a sexual pass at her, an underage girl, was dismissed. That would not happen now, 25 years later. Due in large part to the pedophilia scandals, the public's consciousness has been raised. But in 1982, the prevailing attitude was "Boys will be boys." And in 1982, my integrity was in the toilet. I wrote:

It's three weeks later, and I'm not only not further ahead but further behind. Harry chose to sleep on the daybed last night as he said he'd be hypocritical to sleep with me, that he did not particularly even like me at the time, and said he'll sleep there until I learn to trust him again. By the time we said a clenched-teeth goodnight, I didn't know how I felt; I still don't. I know my name and that I'm so tired of allowing myself to be jerked around, of being so sick and tired of my obsession with Harry. I can spout the Al-Anon party line. How much are financial worries behind my feelings, whatever my feelings are, because I don't know what they are. My head feels like it's the inside of a cement mixer. As long as I act passive, don't make waves, our home life will be quiet. Bullshit!

I turned to Aftercare and to Tom with Spofford's Aftercare Unit. During one conversation, although I was not in tears, Tom urged me to call Stan for an immediate appointment, that very day, to let Stan know I was in crisis. I assured Tom I was not going to do anything foolish: translation, harm myself. He told me to focus on myself, to talk about myself and not about my husband and family members. "Do something frivolous," he said, "anything, as long as it is enjoyable for you." I couldn't think of anything frivolous. I called Fifi. She thought I was being subjected to control, being manipulated by Harry and Liz, and that I was stupid to react to red herrings. She said it sounded like Harry and I had gotten into each other's heads. She reprimanded me for responding to Harry's statements or questions as if they were part of a normal conversation and said the reason I couldn't make any sense out of our exchanges was because, "There isn't any." I wrote:

I think I got sucked into another of Harry's dry drunks because my feelings of frustration and helplessness—of feeling defeated—are the same as I felt during his active drinking. God, this obsessiveness is debilitating.

I fell back on Steps Two and Three: turn my will over to a power greater than myself and have my sanity restored. I did what I'd heard Al-Anon members describe: I wrote a prayer asking God to help everyone involved in this family tragedy to gain insight into themselves and with it perspective and understanding. Then I placed the prayer in a "God Box" which in this case was a silver coffee pot. I had exhausted my efforts to reverse a Mexican standoff so I put into practice the Al-Anon slogan, "Let Go and Let God." I wrote in my journal:

Tom reiterated fact it takes a while for old patterns to disappear. Stuff on the negative side of the ledger has to be changed to permit room for growth—have to change feelings, change reactions—as so much has become part of unconscious patterns. He said it is not only critical but crucial that Harry and I learn communication skills. He advised me to do good things for myself, to get out more, do more, get active—take courses, volunteer work, anything.

After two nights of sleeping alone, that feels comfortable. I'm not ready to make any changes in that area nor do I want to foster more games. Everything happens for a good reason, and being given some privacy by Harry feels good.

The following day I felt better although I was unable to keep the focus solely on myself. The clinic canceled my appointment with Stan and rescheduled it for the following day. I treated myself to a hot box lunch from a deli and enjoyed eating it at home with a glass of sparkling wine. That was about as frivolous as I could get. The next day when I arrived to keep my appointment with Stan, I learned he had to leave due to a family emergency. Although Stan's emergency was beyond his control, I felt abandoned. I felt sorry for myself and wanted to give up, right there beside the secretary's desk. "I'm sorry," I said to her, "but I am going to cry."

"Would you like to talk with someone else?"

"Yes." I would have welcomed talking to a deaf mute.

"I'll see if Harriet can see you." In a few minutes she directed me to the office of Harriet, a recovering alcoholic. Later I wrote in my journal:

God answered some of my prayers. Today's appointment with Stan was cancelled, but I talked with Harriet instead—for two hours.

I handed Harriet a single spaced five-page synopsis of what I referred to as "shitty junk" and asked her to share it with Stan and Luke Pennington who Harry was still seeing every other week. I inundated Harriet with my feelings and concerns about Harry which demonstrated my obsession. I came away with the knowledge my feelings had been understood, validated, and consequently I felt tremendous relief. I wrote:

I felt much better and far more positive towards Harry, deeper understanding of his disease and recovery process—until he started voicing his feelings. He could not omit the sarcasm, barbs. I kept my cool and mentally said, "Tilt!" while imagining "RECOVERING" tattooed across his forehead.

He's back in our bed. He missed the bed, not me.

I felt he was disappointed I did not go to an Al-Anon meeting tonight as I had said I might, and disappointed I'm not going to Spofford in the morning for Aftercare. I felt I was being not so subtly pressured to go.

Anyway, Harriet helped save my sanity.

But the next morning I sank lower than I had been before talking with Harriet. I sank after Harry left to get his post office box mail. I cried. I screamed, the cats scattered. I could not break the association between Harry's post office box mail and his fooling around. I called an Al-Anon friend, Jennie, who asked me, "How are you doing?"

"Yucky."

"You need a meeting. I'll go with you to one tonight."

Jennie had been in Al-Anon six months longer than I; her husband was in early AA recovery. She recognized hurt-in-action: it takes one to know one. She was a little pepper pot. Gung-ho for Al-Anon, she saw to it that I got where I belonged—to a meeting where I felt a sense of peace. But talking with Jennie in the car on the trip over to the meeting and back was what helped me the most. I could curse and make jokes; Jennie didn't care. She kept injecting bits and pieces of Al-Anon, the basics, and that's what I needed to hear. I wrote:

I'm so tired! And the weariness continues. It'll be Al-Anon that gets me through—that and counseling.

On another evening before an Al-Anon meeting I unloaded on Mary some of Harry's hurtful words. She looked directly into my eyes and asked, "Why are you taking it so personally?"

"Because he's saying these things to me." What was she, dumb?

"Why are you taking it so personally?" she repeated twice more.

Of course! Harry was speaking to himself through me. In my emotional turmoil, I had forgotten about transference.

Our friend Cara invited us to her house for Sunday brunch. Initially Harry was pleased to accept the invitation but throughout the week he switched from saying he would go to he wouldn't, and one time he suggested I go alone. If necessary, I would practice being good to myself by going alone, but at the last minute, Harry and I drove to Cara's together. I put on a happy face. One of Al-Anon's lesser slogans is, "Fake it until you make it." My happy face helped me to feel happy inside. When we first arrived, Harry was brusque, unsociable. I smiled and went about my business and whispered to Cara, "He's being a prick. Don't pay any attention to him." She giggled and overlooked his sullenness and maintained a light, carefree attitude. Harry snapped out of his mood and seemed to enjoy himself. Detachment—with love—had worked again.

Another week went by. Harry went to five meetings and said, "I feel like I'm dying inside."

The rift between us deepened and intensified. At bedtime, Harry became verbally and physically aloof, yet he insisted he was not angry and did not want to punish me. He omitted saying goodnight and went to sleep night after night clinging to the edge of the bed. But during his sleep he gravitated towards me and put his arms around me. Harriet said such was a sign of conscious anger and for me to ignore it. "It's part of the alcoholic's old control game," she said. I didn't understand (still don't) how Harriet figured that Harry, while asleep, was manifesting feelings of anger towards me by putting his arms around me.

An exchange of words with Harry prompted me to confront him about the revised nighttime ritual. That elicited angry responses and he denied feeling anger towards me. I heard anger in his voice and said so. He denied it again. Then he got a headache and napped for over an hour. When he got up he seemed more congenial. In another conversation, Harry said he was searching for answers.

"What are the questions?"

342

"If I knew the questions, I'd know the answers."

He harped on what he called a 180 degree turn I made two weeks earlier, the night he decided to sleep alone. I told him, rather sarcastically, I was so glad he had that one thing to hang on to. I hoped I succeeded in making him see how I did not dwell upon any one of the many 180s he executed. He was furious with members of my family concerning Faith's accusations, and he wondered why others weren't examining and questioning their motives about keeping a pot stirred. He said he had started keeping a cash account again because he expected he'd have to account for money he spends. He also said he never left the house without wondering if someone were tailing him. I seized upon that to feed my obsession: either he was paranoid or guilty or a little of both. He was not pleased when I told him I gave Harriet permission to share with Pennington anything I said that she feels will be germane to improving the health of our marriage. He said he was not interested in me or anyone sexually. So when he tried to kiss me before he went out to do errands, I told him it felt phony. I wrote:

He protests too much about asexuality within AA. One of these days he'll get the AA program. I'd like to still be his wife so I can enjoy knowing and being with him. I'm glad I'm seeing Harriet because I know I'm not crazy—sick with obsession but not crazy.

Maybe I wasn't crazy in a technical, legal sense but there's no doubt my judgment had taken a leave of absence.

I heard professionals who were also recovering alcoholics with long term sobriety say that it takes six to 18 months for an alcoholic to "get the program," provided they were really working it. One said, "If they haven't gotten it by the end of 18 months, they're not really working it but are playing games." Another expressed his opinion: "It takes AA years to accomplish what good counseling can do in months provided the client has set goals and objectives. However, a counselor is only as good as his client. A client needs to present issues and is only playing games if he talks about the weather."

Three days later the apex of the crisis occurred. I wrote:

I forgot for a couple hours today that I am NOT crazy. I forgot that Harry is the alcoholic. I forgot all the good advice, counsel, not to get into anything with him, that symptoms indicate a dry drunk. I forgot—and I felt crazy. On my way to an Al-Anon meeting, I heard myself exclaiming out loud, "This is lunacy!"

Earlier that day Harry's attitude seemed good, at least the tension between us was appreciably less; but when he returned from his appointment with Pennington, he was hostile, belligerent, and loaded for bear. I listened while he told me he was not interested in me, that it wouldn't bother him if I had an affair with someone, that he didn't care what I did or what I thought or even what I felt because he had no feeling for me. He said he didn't care about holding me or touching me or even rubbing each other's backs. He said he dreaded leaving the house and dreaded coming back even more because he didn't know what kind of a mood he'd find me in when he returned. He said he couldn't stand my tears and he didn't think many men could.

"I don't ask you what you do or what you're going to do because I don't care. I'm detaching. Call it tough love." He also said Pennington was going to talk with Harriet which was a switch because over the weekend he said he was not in favor of Harriet sharing with Pennington. He said there could be nothing between us until I learned to trust him.

I interrupted him, "All I can do is try."

He said that not everything in the books about the disease and recovery applied to us. He said he was going to concentrate on himself, not me, and find out what makes him tick and that it might take a year, or two years or longer. His next statement was, "I think you have a serious problem."

I thought, "Look who's calling the kettle black."

I looked at Harry, swallowed hard, and said, "Do you have any idea how rejected I'm feeling?"

"Just last week you told me you were not feeling rejected and that you would not feel rejected again because you realized you could choose your feelings. You stood there and told me you no longer felt rejected."

"I thought I didn't, but I do."

"I'm not rejecting you. I love you."

Gears stripped in my head trying to comprehend all he had said. Biff, bam, wham—and then, "I love you"?

It was almost suppertime, Tuesday.

Of course I was having one hell of a time trying to trust Harry! His friendship with Lois in AA did not help, especially giving her rides to and from meetings. I knew that ideally sexual identities were shelved during meetings and recovery-related phone calls, but I also knew how vulnerable hurting and confused people can be especially when exposed to someone with Harry's warmly sympathetic nature. The Monday night Al-Anon meeting had improved dramatically, and I no longer attended the Tuesday meeting on a regular basis. Lois often telephoned on Tuesday evenings. Naturally I attached significance to that, and because I had already taken an inch with my imagination, I went the full mile and thought Harry made a point of letting her know soon after answering the phone that I was at home.

Harry's declarations felt like a frontal attack and made my head spin. All that aggression followed by, "I'm not rejecting you. I love you." I decided to get my hurting self to the Tuesday Al-Anon meeting. I was paranoid enough to believe his custom was to go out onto the patio to make sure my car disappeared in the direction of the meeting. As I was about to leave, Harry asked me for a kiss. On top of everything he said to me, wanting to kiss me made no sense. When I got to the next town, I stopped at a pay phone and called Harry. There was no answer. The AA meeting he planned to attend was only 10 minutes away and did not begin for another 1-1/2 hours. I was too obsessed with jealous scenarios to continue on to where I belonged and I returned home. I looked out onto the patio and sure enough, I saw his footprints in the fresh snow. He had taken two steps out the door and stopped facing the direction of the road below, and then re-entered the house. I wrote in the snow beside his footprints: "Yes, I left."

Joann, a Spofford sister, phoned and said her husband, also a recovering alcoholic, was acting the same way, saying the same types of things to her. I wondered if the residual "isms" made it more than a coincidence. Before Harry returned from the AA meeting, I wrote:

I get the feeling he's trying to drive me out of his life, out of this marriage. If that isn't it, then he's really off in space someplace. He denies he feels any anger towards me. I didn't want to tell him I felt rejected because I didn't want to give him another power tool. But what the hell difference does it make? Sure is a weird feeling to know he watched me drive off, as if wanting to make sure I'd really gone. He says he's not playing any games, and I'm told he may really believe he isn't, but that he's acting out of alcoholic instinct.

After he returned and was in bed, I wrote:

I knew when I printed, "Yes, I left" in the snow by his patio footprints that if he saw it, he would probably make a big deal out of it. He did.

"What kind of games are you playing?"

"I figured you went outside to make sure I drove off."

"I was looking at the moon."

"The moon was on the opposite side of the house when I left."

"I hope you get some help soon."

I referred to what he said earlier about my having a serious problem, and he said, "I'm not going to say anything to you any more." He did say, "Goodnight," and went to bed.

I'm starting to feel physically sick.

By morning I thought it might be helpful if I put some geographical space between us, and the only place I could think of to go was Fifi's. But first, I called Harriet to tell her my plans and to verify I was going to help me and not to punish Harry. En route, I called the house and left a brief message on the machine: "Hello. I need to get away for a couple days. Goodbye." I let Mother know where I could be reached. At Fifi's I was welcomed with open arms and a wonderful hug. For the next 48 hours we talked, and best of all, we listened. Fifi did not yes me to death but made me examine my real feelings and so paved the way for getting my thinking back to a sane level. I met two of her Al-Anon friends; one day we went out to lunch; one evening we attended a lecture. And both evenings we sat up late talking and drinking wine. One small part of me hoped Harry would figure out where I'd gone and telephone, but most of me hoped he would not call. Hashing things over with Fifi while keeping Al-Anon principals in mind helped me to put the previous weeks into perspective. In some respects, my visit was a mini version of the week at Spofford or a maxi Al-Anon meeting. I expressed my feelings openly, exposed my vulnerability without fear of verbal retaliation. What precipitated the crisis did not change as there is nothing that can change the past, nor did the "eye witness" accounts change. What changed was my perception and my attitude; I had allowed myself to get caught up in a situation that was distorted because everyone involved, whether or not they could admit it, was suffering from the family disease. Dismissed was the strong probability that Faith told the truth and instead the blame was placed on a disease.

What insanity! An outsider to the Faith and Harry episode can see that Harry behaved like a predator. He plotted the attempted seduction. I recognized that truth in my gut and overrode it because of the fears I had about how I would survive financially if I threw him out. The perspective of those I consulted was distorted; they were comfortable about shifting responsibility into a convenient catchall: *the disease of alcoholism*. And because such dysfunctional reasoning gave me permission to stick with the status quo, I accepted the consensus as valid wisdom. There are times, and this is one of them, when hindsight is a real pain in the ass: in no way am I absolved for my betrayal of Faith.

But back in 1982, my decision to put 100 miles between Harry and me worked: I interrupted my obsession with him. He was pleased to find me at home two days later when he returned from work, and we spent a pleasant weekend together. On Monday I followed instructions from Fifi, Tom, Harriet and good Al-Anon friends Mary and Idora. and I did something good for myself: at the florist's I bought daisies by the dozens which I arranged in a centerpiece for the dining table. Harry did not notice them for a couple days.

There was still more to go through. Tuesday evening after the Al-Anon meeting ended, I gave Idora a ride to the nearby AA meeting where she could meet her husband and get a ride home. Harry's car was in the parking lot. Idora asked me to come in with her and catch the last half of the open AA speaker meeting. In the hallway Harry was talking with three women, including Lois. I walked over to him, smiling, but he was not pleased to see me, like I was an intruder. I saw someone I knew and wandered off to chat. Harry ignored me. I was embarrassed and wished I could become invisible. Harry caught up with me. "What are you doing here?"

"Idora asked me to come in with her."

"You shouldn't be here. This is an AA meeting."

"It's an open meeting. I have a right to be here," and I left choking on hurt and tears. At home I yanked off my rings and placed them with a note I wrote to Harry:

When you are ready to honor your wife and to make a full commitment to our marriage, then I will resume wearing these rings.

Harry arrived home shortly thereafter and gave me hell for walking into the AA meeting place. He was visibly upset I had removed my rings. I was furious with him. I told him it looked damn peculiar, him standing out in the hallway with three women. I accused him of being rude to me, of not introducing me, of ignoring my presence. He said one of the women had a problem, and he was dragged into it. His next words stunned me.

"When I'm at an AA meeting, I'm not married."

I hesitated for a second and said, "Oh, really?"

He quickly backtracked. "I don't mean that," and he explained that at AA meetings, he was not a husband or father or anybody except Harry and further, that he didn't look upon other AA members as male or female but as people.

The next afternoon Harry told me Lois called him while I was out, about some problem she was having, that he wanted me to know so I wouldn't feel uneasy. He left earlier than usual that night for his meeting. At six, Lois phoned. When Harry returned, I had left another note on the counter:

When Lois phoned at 6, during the course of the conversation, I learned that earlier today Lois did not call you but that you called her—and I am feeling betrayed.

Harry said he knew he should have told me the truth earlier, that somehow

I'd find out because I was so much more sophisticated than Lois I would be able to trap her. I said I did not mind if he talked with AA women before, during and after meetings, but if there were ever any hanky panky, I would put ground glass in his food.

The good news that night was Harry announced he had asked someone to be his sponsor. The term "sponsor" as used by Al-Anon and AA means someone of the same sex in whom you can confide, unburden your heart and know what is shared between you will not be repeated. A good sponsor does not feed into the sickness of the person he's sponsoring, but reminds him of AA or Al-Anon principles, and by operating within those boundaries extends moral support and understanding. The best sponsors, like the best therapists, confront the sponsoree with his or her own behavior. They offer guidance but do not try to feed their own egos by controlling. They present suggestions and never give advice except in life-threatening situations. The best sponsors do what they can to help the sponsoree find his or her own solutions to problems as well as physical sobriety for the AA and emotional sobriety for the Al-Anoner and serenity for both.

Harry said his sponsor had been in AA more than a year. "He has good AA. And he's funnier than hell, very witty." I didn't care if the guy had spots and stripes. Of importance was Harry getting a sponsor, a significant step in recovery, and I set aside catty speculations about Lois.

I had been shopping for a sponsor for myself but could not make up my mind whether to ask Mary or Idora. They were each other's sponsor. Mary did not talk much in meetings but whatever she said was pure gold. She exuded comfort with the whole spectrum of Al-Anon, AA, and spirituality. Idora tended to be more pragmatic and did not hesitate to call a spade a spade. She had divorced an alcoholic and married another one who now, like Mary's husband, was in AA. Both women had more than six years of active Al-Anon membership and were strong keepers of the Traditions. The next day I phoned both of them and asked if they would share in sponsoring me. I hoped I was prepared to be turned down because I knew many other Al-Anon members looked to them for counseling. Each accepted. It was almost five months to the day since I left Spofford with a signed contract promising that I would get a sponsor. I hoped by getting two I helped make up for my procrastination.

Members of Al-Anon and AA are supposed to keep their focus on themselves and to take their own inventories on a continuous basis. I gave Mary and Idora permission to take my inventory any time they wanted to; to feel free to discuss between them any troubling issues I might have. I benefited from their collective wisdom. My recovery process was strengthened. By asking them to be my sponsors, I surrendered to the fact I needed additional help in convalescence. Asking them was an act of humility and something else I can only describe as metaphysical. Each time I called on either of them with a question or problem, I acknowledged I did not have all the answers, that my recovery process was contingent upon the shared experience, strength and hope of others. This is what transpires within Al-Anon and AA: people who were made ill by the effects of a disease and who want to get healthy help one another—"sickies" helping other "sickies"—and it's amazing how well it works.

Chapter 46

The easiest place to practice the Al-Anon program is in an Al-Anon meeting. Like AA, Al-Anon offers a philosophy for living in the day-to-day world, not one that is observed for only a couple hours at a time in church basements (which is where most meetings are held). Within the fellowship are shared nuggets of profound wisdom, and it is not unusual for the most inspirational words to come from those who have the least formal education. To extract that wisdom and then integrate it into one's behavioral patterns takes concerted concentration—and lots of practice.

Ten days after the night I pulled off my rings in a moment of pique—who am I trying to kid? It was more than pique: it was raw anger—Harry said he had a headache and went to bed early. He said he loved me but he didn't believe our marriage stood much of a chance. I wrote in my journal:

I don't know what set him off again. He cited my lack of trust in him, "You'll never trust me." He's said that many times in recent weeks. In turn I say, "I can try," and tonight I also said, "The longer nothing happens to impair the trust, the stronger it can become."

I am feeling so much better than I was ten days ago. God has helped me through other people—Fifi, Harriet, Idora and Mary, the Al-Anon program and Aftercare counselors. I believe that the health of my marriage, Mother's health, the quality of my relationship with my daughter, son, are all in God's care.

Idora pointed out that "Grant me the serenity to accept what I cannot change" can be applied to this day only, that it doesn't mean one has to accept something forever. That interpretation was of great help.

I got in touch again with the reality of the "isms"—the fact that the "isms" of the disease continue unchanged after drinking stops until—if and when— the recovering alcoholic becomes honest with himself and works at changing "stinkin' thinkin' " I wrote:

I believe Harry's sponsor can be good for him, a wonderful opportunity for him to develop a close friendship with another man.

I don't know what set Harry off during the hours I visited Mother. I would have welcomed a loving return, but I'm not letting myself get down because of his mood. I must rebuild my mental sobriety.

That was the night Liz rushed Mother to the hospital with heart attack symptoms and I caught up with them in the ER. While we sweated out Mother's condition who, by then, had regained her color, a patient in the next bay died on the table from a heart attack. We were privy to the medical team's dedicated efforts to revive and save the patient. Mother was admitted to the Coronary Care Unit and released two days later. However, when I returned home, although I knew Mother's vital signs were stable, I was still under a great deal of emotional strain and could not understand why Harry had chosen that particular time to tell me, "I don't believe our marriage stands much of a chance." This was not the first time Harry laid an anxiety trip on me when I returned from being someplace without him nor would it be the last. Eventually I learned not to react, not to ask questions, not to try to determine what his thinking was based upon. I chalked it up to the unwinding of alcoholic thinking, perhaps a carry-over of wanting to be at the center of my attention. The incident was typical of recovery—three steps forward, two back, five forward, three back, but if a curve were plotted, I thought we were gaining better health.

Chapter 47

A day arrived when I was surprised and honored a young woman with several years in Al-Anon asked me to be her sponsor. She had been observing and listening to me for a few months and admired my spirituality. I expressed my amazement to Idora who quietly said, "You have a lot to offer." I knew I had a wider knowledge about alcoholism than some but wondered how I could be a truly effective sponsor after only seven continuous months in Al-Anon. How could I, with my crises track record, in need of my own support system, be a key support person for someone else? I recalled Harriet remarking, "There are no coincidences." I believe that asking to be a sponsor on the heels of climbing out of my latest despair was not coincidental. I discovered I did have much to share. Primarily, I was a good listener. Mostly I reminded the Al-Anon member at the other end of the phone to use tried and true Al-Anon tools and I pointed out time and time again that we have choices, especially how we choose to think and feel. It had taken me months before I understood that the way I perceive something determines how I feel about it. I subscribe to the belief that bestowing carte blanche sympathy on a hurting person can contribute to a crippling attitude, a victim mentality. A few soft words of acknowledgment that validate the person's feelings are helpful, and I found tough questions helped me gain perspective; and so what worked for me, I customized to help others. I had no difficulty empathizing because the odds favored that I had experienced similar situations and had similar reactions.

To anyone dealing with another's alcohol abuse, I echo Al-Anon's suggestion that we learn all we can about the disease and not to expect this can be accomplished only by attending meetings and reading conference-approved literature, but to supplement knowledge by frequenting libraries, bookstores, and now the Internet. To anyone seeking professional counseling, I caution them to seek help from someone with in-depth alcoholism awareness preferably based on first-hand experience; and specifically someone who is a family member and not an identified recovering alcoholic. Why? Because unless the recovering alcoholic experienced, when sober, what it's like to live in the off-the-wall dynamics of an alcoholic home, they cannot really connect with the befuddled emotions of a sober family member. Recovering alcoholics know what it's like to be drunk, craving for more, the demoralizing of hangovers; but they cannot know the ways such behavior impacts the non-alcoholic. Most reputable therapists urge clients to attend Al-Anon.

I believe it can be a mistake for someone to rely solely on their sponsor for one-on-one input outside of meetings because sometimes the same thoughts expressed by another person, even in a different context, will be the words that connect. Having a savvy sponsor means he or she knows you well and is aware of your strengths and weaknesses. When I needed to hash over concerns with Idora, I did not have to give her a lot of history to set the scene: she already knew the background. If Idora were so inclined, she could have written much of this book. Idora was the perfect sponsor for me. She challenged me but she never told me what I could or could not do. Beware of any sponsor who is a controller!

Within another half year, I was privileged to be the sponsor of another five women whose ages ranged from their early twenties to early sixties. I benefited from each call because as I shared, I listened to what I was saying. From long-winded complainers, I learned what constitutes patience and tolerance. During my fledgling months as a sponsor, I did not realize I was not helping some callers by permitting the repetition of the same complaints voiced many times before. I thought they needed to ventilate. I learned singular ventilation is one thing and to have stuff pour out through a sieve is another. Some did not like hearing, "You have choices." Some could not see that because they craved negative excitement, they intentionally created crises. A few presented distorted versions as a bid for sympathy. I was reminded of what my Great Aunt Lizzie used to say: "There are always two sides to anything, but usually one side is a little bit 'side-ier' than the other." Those who chose to play at using the Al-Anon program rather than working it and who developed a dislike for my candid approach stopped calling. I hope they latched onto another sponsor who could find the right key to unlock their bullheadedness. Those who used the Al-Anon tools, and in some cases combined them with professional help, are the ones who got better. One day when Idora and I were talking, she remarked, "I don't know who is sponsoring who."

I said, "Does it make a difference?"

I think developing a viable potential sponsor is the mark of an effective sponsor. Idora was a terrific sponsor. Anyone she sponsored was blessed.

Although I benefited from sponsoring others, I was too early into my own recovery to be giving so much of myself on a daily basis. Tom cautioned me often, "Don't let your cup get too low." I knew what he meant but I thought I was getting back more than I gave. But towards the end of that first year, I recognized I was approaching overload. In meetings while commenting, I'd wonder what in hell I was talking about. I thought I was speaking gibberish. And no wonder. At the rate I was going, I could have drowned in the disease. I was working on my own recovery, exploring feelings and memories and their feelings as they came into my consciousness. I continued to study the disease, attend seminars, talk at length with AA members who dropped by the house and consumed cup after cup of coffee. I swapped my obsession with Harry for a dual obsession—my recovery and wider knowledge about the "family disease." I sought and used all available sources that offered positive, informed help. One day I realized I was holding myself back from developing into a balanced person. I stopped being as quick to share my telephone number; I gave it when asked but seldom volunteered it. When I was asked to be someone's sponsor, I said I would be glad to fill in as a temporary sponsor until they could find someone else. I said I preferred to be called before 9 am and after 4 p.m. as I was trying to observe regular office hours working in my home. That prompted the question, "Oh, what do you do?" and my answer, "I write," was taken seriously by very few. When I answered the phone, I heard, "I know you're writing, but . . ." If the caller were in crisis, I did not mind the interruption.

I had gone ahead with the idea I expressed at Spofford and had written an article for *Northeast Magazine*. They liked it but wanted a narrative. I had started the re-write when I had my "colossal attitude slip"—Harry's thwarted seduction of Faith—which knocked me out of commission and put writing on the back burner. By late spring 1982, I submitted 10,000 words; by late fall, I was notified it would be published after they edited it down to 6000 words to fit their format. I worked on short stories and essays but time and again, I preferred to write about alcoholism. To reach hurting people with facts that could help them help themselves was more important to me than trying my hand at say, a romance novel (which I don't like to read) that would provide escape through preposterous fantasy and so, I thought, make reality seem even worse. A representative of Spofford Hall's Alumni Association asked me to write a few words about my feelings for an alumni newsletter.

After a week as a Family Patient in which my life was turned around, I rejoined my newly sober husband and thought, "How much he has changed!" He said he had never seen anyone change as much as I had in one week—"180 degrees." Prior to Spofford, I spent never mind how many years trying to do things my way and a few months trying to "get Al-Anon" through a selective process. Obviously my way had not worked for my good and I decided to trust the pros. To the best of my ability, I have upheld my Aftercare contract and have proven to myself that both the pros and Al-Anon know what is best for me. I've come through attitude slips thanks in large part to the support network of winners I had in place before the bottom fell out. I devoted a full year towards concentrating on my recovery, learning still more about the disease and how riddled I was by it. Many civilians found me boring. Tough! I used a characteristic of the disease—obsessing—to my advantage: I obsessed about getting better. Three significant components of my on-going recovery process are: (1) feeling comfortable about communicating with my Higher Power; (2) shelving my ego in favor of asking two Al-Anon members to be my sponsors; (3) being asked by others to be their sponsors. In fact, I believe the give and take of sponsorship has helped my growth so much that I almost jest when I say I feel it could make sense to actively recruit sponsorees! Other milestones: learning I have the right to be wrong and that the four letter-word "Time" is my friend.

Chapter 48

The first of October, two months after celebrating his first year of sobriety, Harry learned he would be out of a job the first of the year. Did we panic? Not exactly, but we did put our house on the market because the deepening economic slump made us doubt he would find a job in New England. His first interview netted an interesting offer which meant moving, but we were comforted because the corporation would underwrite relocation hassles and expenses. Six weeks later, the company rescinded the offer because of worsening economic conditions. We were back to square one with six weeks between us and no income. Two other interviews had possibilities. On the night before Thanksgiving, the position Harry preferred was offered and accepted. Best of all, we would not have to move. Harry was hired to run the United States' sales office of a Swiss manufacturing company. I was designated as the treasurer/secretary of the USA division.

I would like to say I was an absolute brick during those eight weeks but I was not. My old fears connected with loss often got the better of me. I was scared about having no income, no nest egg to fall back upon, the possibility of not being able to sell the house and eventually losing it. I also feared the house would sell, and we wouldn't know where to go. The news was full of stories about companies laying off workers, families suddenly without medical insurance, banks foreclosing, long established businesses going into Chapter 11, unemployment figures on the increase, soup kitchens—and I identified with every new bit of bad news. There were days when I moved like a sleepwalker and watched old movies on television. My creative writing attempts were futile. I dreaded going back to work for someone else after being out of the market for five years. I applied for a job and was relieved not to get it. I felt impotent because I could do nothing towards speeding up the job search. The truth is Harry worked his recovery program better than I did. Our marriage felt secure. Most important, Harry did not feel the need to escape through alcohol.

With our stay in the area assured, I joined an exercise program, had my hair cut, and wrapped Christmas presents. My dear friend Martha asked me to join her in New York as her guest for two days and nights of gabbing, shopping and theater. Off I went with Harry's blessing and instructions to have fun, not to worry about anything. Unlike the NYC visit 1-1/2 years earlier, I did not have to play-act about our life being good. This time I felt secure emotionally and optimistic about the future. The complete change of scene and pace heightened by the comfortable camaraderie with Martha helped me realize I was spending too much time wrapped up in alcoholism problems, that I was ready to re-introduce balance into my life. I stepped off the return train exhausted, but renewed and into a one-arm hug from Harry: his other arm cradled daisies.

In the first draft of this book, I omitted references to Thanksgiving and Christmas celebrations. Because of the schism with Liz, I got through the days by rote. On Thanksgiving we visited Harry's Aunt Bibi, and afterwards while driving home, shared an apple. I have no memory of Christmas itself. But two days later, we flew into summer—the Florida Keys. We stayed on the Gulf of Mexico where we enjoyed Camelot weather: it rained only after sundown. We ate breakfasts in our housekeeping unit, then sauntered 75 feet to bathe in the sun, to read, talk, not read, not talk, just be. We went in and out of the water according to our whims. Along about 11, Harry got thirsty for a soft drink and cracked a bottle of champagne for me. Around noon we nibbled on deviled eggs or shrimp or fresh vegetables and dip. Visiting with other guests lasted from minutes to hours. After three, we showered, dressed in casual clothes, poked about in shops, watched fishing boats come in, and headed for any of several fine restaurants where early arrivals didn't have to wait for a table. After dinner we continued our break-neck pace by stopping at a market for whatever caught our fancy, returned to our place to change into even more comfortable clothes and sit under a kiki hut, with or without other guests until nine or so when we strolled back to our room and went to bed.

I began our vacation by almost falling into an old thinking trap: "One day almost gone, seven to go." I reminded myself: "Enjoy the 'Now,' this moment, because this is the only moment that is real." I had to remind myself several times the first day, less the second, and then not at all. On our return flight, I talked about this with Harry. He said time was when he would have boarded the flight to Florida wondering if we would have decent flying weather for the return trip. He would have worried about luggage being lost or damaged, our reservations being lost by the car rental agency, and worst of all, would have continued working in his head. He, too, applied his program for living and stayed in the Now. We agreed that our eight days seemed more like three times as many. It was our finest vacation together.

There were several messages on our answering machine for me to call *Northeast Magazine*. Finally, a year after I first queried the editors if they would be interested in a piece about co-alcoholism, it was slated for publishing in mid-January. I used initials for myself and my two husbands, but the magazine preferred I come up with names, perhaps "George" and "Clyde;" these names sounded so humorous in tandem, like a pair of work horses, that I said, "Those will be fine." (I have renamed them for this book—Harry and Steve.) Choosing a pseudonym for myself was easy: Rebecca Bass was a maternal great-great-grandmother and probably a teetotaler. Two days before the issue of the magazine containing my article appeared on newsstands, I received several advance copies and gasped: it was the cover story for the Sunday magazine. A thick-bottomed overturned glass spilled its lethal contents onto a snapshot of a smiling bride and groom, and that photo was flanked by two melting ice cubes. Beneath the title were the words, "A terrifying personal account of living with an alcoholic." Within the table of contents, the editors wrote, "By now, most people are familiar with the ravages that alcohol can inflict on those who abuse it: the destroyed lives, shattered careers, physical and spiritual damage. But less understood is the torment that the disease of alcoholism wreaks on those innocent individuals whose misfortune it is to live with an alcoholic. One such woman reveals the torture of her experience—and how she fought her way back."

The article began at the center section of the magazine, and this former crazy lady who placed personal entrapment ads chuckled about finally "making" a centerfold. *Northeast* was responsible for the title; they lifted the phrase, "stark, raving sober" from the text. The title in large, bold, black letters dominated the left page and beneath it was this quote: "If anyone had told me that I was as sick as my alcoholic husband, and perhaps sicker, I would have defended myself with every rational fiber of my being. And I would have been wrong." I read every word as if seeing it for the first time. I was sorry that space dictated eliminating most of the words concerning recovery through Al-Anon. But overall, I was tremendously pleased because I had persevered with an idea born while I was at Spofford and excited the piece was given such dramatic treatment. Surely, I hoped, one reader would identify long enough to reach out for help.

I met Harry at the door with the magazine held in front of me. He did a double take. "Cover story!" he exclaimed.

I laughed and said, "How about that? I just read this and I don't know if I should let you in the house. You were such a prick!" And we both laughed.

Feedback about the article began a few weeks later. Al-Anon World Headquarters phoned their enthusiasm and appreciation. Alena phoned to tell me inquiries about Spofford Hall precipitated by the article were keeping her very busy. Irene wrote:

Better late than never, they say, and here I am. I had hoped to be able to see your face when I commented on your piece in the Northeast Magazine. Your letter gave a glowing report, so I could picture your glow as I read it. Congratulations! I have to be honest and tell you that I preferred the original work but I'm no editor, and from the comments and results around here, he knew what he was doing. The first few weeks after the article appeared, at every Al-Anon meeting I attended, there were several newcomers, and they spoke of being there because of the article . . .

The article had surpassed my greatest hope. Not just one reader but many read it and reached out. I wondered: if an article could accomplish that, how many might a book reach? Unless someone writes to me, I'll never know. What is important is that somewhere, someone will know: "I am not alone."

As for the first draft of this book-length manuscript, Harry read it and told me he hoped it would sell; an agent presented it to half a dozen publishers. Several expressed interest but were concerned the book would not sell well because neither I nor the alcoholics in my life were celebrities.

The ending of that draft reads like it was written by Pollyanna. It said:

I could so easily have sat back and nursed my anger, resentments and self-pity while Harry drank himself to death. I had the choice of continuing my own self-destructive behavior while Harry worked at getting better through the help of AA. He would have quickly outgrown me, had my warped attitudes not sabotaged his recovery, and I would have been left with a fail-safe tool for my own misery: bitterness.

Instead I opened my eyes to the gravity of another's alcoholism and my own powerlessness over the disease and my inability to cope effectively. I chose to reach out for help—and health. My goal is to maintain my emotional sobriety, something I cannot have unless I keep my focus on myself. I have learned there is profound wisdom in the adage: Mind your own business.

It's too bad I don't practice it all the time. Just the other day as I walked by the open bathroom door, I noticed Harry peering into the mirror and picking at his face. I said, "Oh do you have a zit?"

A somewhat testy Harry said, "I sure don't get much privacy around here."

I continued walking toward the kitchen, forcing myself to pose the self-question, "How important is it?" and seething with each step. I told myself, "Rebecca, work your program," and I did—for almost 30 seconds. Then standing at the sink, I said in a voice loud enough for Harry to hear, "You can have all the goddamned privacy you want."

There was no response and I hoped that meant he hadn't heard me. I was in the yard when Harry came out and walked to his car. "I'm going to get my mail," he said.

"Okay," I said, but I knew all was not okay. Harry would have had more to say had he not heard my non-Al-Anon remark. About an hour later he returned and gave laconic responses to my attempts to promote a conversation. I did not want a beautiful day to be wrecked over a misunderstanding compounded by my angry reaction. So as Harry stood at the refrigerator door filling a glass of soda. I came and stood next to him. He looked at me as if he were puzzled and perhaps perturbed at my standing so close.

I said, "I'd like a hug."

Harry continued to look blankly at me for another two seconds and then broke into a smile. "You can have all the goddamned hugs you want."

And that's how I ended the first draft. We rationalized that our recovery was on solid ground so we expanded our interests and cut back on meetings. I was getting to only about two meetings every three weeks, and Harry about three meetings every four weeks. We had put ourselves on a slippery slope.

Chapter 49

I found that each Al-Anon group has its own collective personality which is subject to change as membership shifts. I urge prospective members not to judge all Al-Anon meetings by just one or two but to shop around for groups where they feel comfortable. Some are healthier than others, especially the groups that begin meetings by reading the Twelve Steps and Traditions. Al-Anon encourages newcomers to attend six consecutive weeks and then, as the saying goes, "If you decide you don't like us, we'll cheerfully refund your misery." I've seen miracles: faces rife with sadness and anguish that rival the face of the crucified Jesus as painted by the great masters come to Al-Anon and sometimes, in less than a month, can smile. Those who moved like robots soon discover they are capable of moving under the strength of their own free will. Others who were mute from years of conditioning find their voices. Bewildered newcomers without a shred of hope who sat in meetings for weeks half listening and fully crying blossom into active participants who can laugh. As bits and pieces of recovery baby steps are shared, which might strike "civilians" as insignificant trivia, the tumbling of a particularly stubborn block to insight may elicit spontaneous applause and cheers. Recovery is built with smidgens of minutiae. Integrating the Al-Anon philosophy into my life required me to first love and respect myself. Others may have taken a dim view of me, but in Al-Anon I was accepted because everyone there knew what I had experienced—maybe not all the details, but the effects of living in a toxic environment.

But what to call us? By the late 1970s, an awareness developed that so-called significant others shared common symptoms of distress entitling us to treatment geared to our particular needs. Co-Alcoholic (usually reserved for spouse) and Para-Alcoholic (for children growing up in an alcoholic home) drove many long-time Al-Anon members absolutely wild. An old-timer informed me, "It is not our place to diagnose."

I offered this argument: "We refer to our loved ones as alcoholics. What makes co-alcoholic a diagnosis and alcoholic not a diagnosis?" I did not make a friend.

As more data was shared among addictions counselors, it became apparent that co-alcoholic symptoms were common among significant others who had experienced protracted exposure to stressful situations, with or without the presence of alcoholism—a sense of a depleted self, dependent needs heightened, and eagerness to please a driving force. And so the generic term, co-dependency was born. By the mid-1980s, it was increasingly commonplace among the general public. Articles and books that made best seller lists did so through readers' word-of-mouth. Finally, attention was being paid to those, like me, who endured life with alcohol-induced insanity. Best of all, our feelings—and our numbness—were validated. Unfortunately, through erroneous use by those who don't understand the term, the word "co-dependent" evolved into a stigma approaching that of "alcoholic." Often it is used as a catchall, usually a pejorative by those who don't know better, even as a buzz word applied promiscuously and incorrectly to healthy demonstrations of courtesy and concern.

I am not alone in believing that it is not abnormal to react normally to abnormal behavior. An amusing sidelight is that for a time, if all the co-dependency figures proffered by some professionals were to be believed, then in the good ole U.S. of A., there were more co-dependents than there were people.

I became a bonafide codependent. When I wrote "The End" to the book's first draft, I was still codependent.

Chapter 50

In February 1984 when I was in the seventh year of my relationship with Harry, the fourth year of my third marriage, the second marriage to an alcoholic and becoming more codependent by the minute, I had the good fortune to be invited as a representative Al-Anon member to participate in the three-day, two-night Family Recovery Program designed by Parkside Lodge of Connecticut, Canaan, CT. The program was held offsite at a monastery in Litchfield, CT. The program did not have the intensity of Spofford Hall's: the information was factual and generously laced with not only standard alcoholism jargon but also non-alcoholism common sense; the counseling was confrontational but not combative, and it was suffused with gentleness, even love. As a war-weary survivor vacillating between disgust of alcoholic behavior and compassion for whatever drove the poor lost soul to throw away his life instead of really living, I responded with head and heart to the clarity of Parkside's treatment plan. I didn't walk away cured, but even though my codependency had deepened, paradoxically there was also growing within me an awareness of the truths behind the denials I had constructed in order to cope with the diabolical craziness generated by Harry. The truths I buried about Harry's attempted seduction of Faith because otherwise they were too painful to handle, were validated for me by a senior therapist, who said, "Donna, you know what happened." No one questioned what had Faith done to tempt Harry. The onus was placed squarely on Harry. During the two years since that "alleged incident," I had doubted his faithfulness. Anytime I raised the question to Harry, I got wide-eyed denial and a plaintive or argumentative, "When are you going to trust me?" The more I read and watched Phil Donahue, Sally Jesse Raphael and ultimately Oprah, I believed I had the right to believe the doubts generated by my gut.

I had to experience more pain and heartbreak until I decided enough was enough.

For instance: There was a classic Gaslight incident. Harry and I drove to Cape Cod to spend a long weekend, a much desired getaway for me, and he said it was for him. Harry knew what I looked forward to more than anything else was falling asleep on the beach. Anyone who lives with an alcoholic knows how exhausting coping can be, the interrupted sleep, the zingers that come out of nowhere, always braced for the next attack. I was living with an ostensibly dry alcoholic who, according to my common sense observations, was not doing anything constructive towards changing his basic attitudes. But I stuffed my perception because to voice it in front of AA and Al-Anon members was to invite their chastisement and that shaming phrase, "We're not supposed to take another's inventory."

The longer we were on the highway, the surlier Harry became. When we crossed the Bourne Bridge onto Cape Cod, I was thankful he insisted that I open a bottle of champagne for me to drink while he drove. I can hear a chorus of criticism because I drank champagne in the presence of an abstaining alcoholic. Harry never asked me not to drink; in fact, he encouraged me to, even when he was practicing abstinence. "It doesn't bother me," he said. But on that drive to the Cape, I think it bothered the hell out of him. In Wellfleet, he pulled into a roadside snack place and directed me to place the order. "You might as well get it; you have all the money," he said, and that was essentially true: before we left the house, Harry suggested I carry most of the cash, a few hundred dollars, which was not his usual practice. In North Truro, he sat in the car while, again at his suggestion, I went into the market to pick up a bottle of champagne. We checked into the motel and walked into the same king bed efficiency we had stayed in many times before, including while on our honeymoon—directly on the beach of Cape Cod Bay, second floor, with a covered porch running the full length of the long building. The champagne, the summer warmth, the long drive and being overtired at the start made me eager to change into my swimsuit, flop on the beach, and sink into sleep. But first I unpacked.

Harry emptied out his pockets onto the little dining table, changed into swim trunks, and was on the beach several minutes before I was ready to join him. As I walked towards Harry, the sand massaging my feet, I anticipated the comforting blend of sun and salted air easing me into a deep, restorative sleep. Harry was stretched out on an old king size bed throw we used on the beach. When I lay down beside him, he was civil but not particularly friendly. I was asleep within minutes. The next thing I remember, Harry was telling me he was going back to the room to lie down. I was probably back to sleep before he had gone ten feet.

And then, all hell broke loose. Harry was back, telling me to wake up. "Where is your wallet?" he demanded.

I willed myself to come out of a heavy sleep. "It's in the room."

"What did you do with it?"

"It's in my pocketbook." I wished he would go away and let me drift back to sleep. Why was he making such a fuss?

"No, it isn't. I looked. Where did you put it? All our money is in it! All your credit cards! Come on! Get up! We've got to find it!"

I took a few steps towards the motel but looked back to see why Harry wasn't with me. He was folding the throw. Evidently he had determined our afternoon on the beach was not to continue. When I turned back to help, he insisted I get to the room. "Find your wallet!" he ordered. How could he not have seen my wallet in my pocketbook? Of course my wallet was in the room! Why couldn't he have let me sleep? I kept my thoughts to myself. I'd produce the wallet and return to the beach.

The room was about 15 feet by 15 feet. From the beach, one entered through a West door; the king bed was directly ahead, running N-S, the head against the North wall, flanked by small tables and near the foot by a freestanding television. Opposite the bed was the door to the bathroom, and to its right, a closet area consisting of built-in drawers and an open space behind a sliding door for hang-ups. Continuing along that South wall to the West (towards the Bay) was a mini-kitchen unit: a small work surface, a stove and a sink; above were cupboards for dishes and glasses; below left was a cupboard for pots and pans, and to its right a wee refrigerator. The West wall was dominated by sliding glass doors that opened out onto the long porch. Between the bed and the sliders, close to the "kitchen" area, was a small round table and a couple chairs; just beyond towards the bed were two easy chairs.

Harry followed me into the room. "Where did you put your wallet? It's not in your pocketbook! Did you hide it somewhere?" He shot questions at me, not waiting for answers. My brain kicked over into a scrambled mode. Harry's agitation intensified. I reached into the bottom of the closet and pulled out my pocketbook. "It's not in there!" he said. He seemed to be on the verge of hysteria. "You were so drunk you don't remember where you put it! All your credit cards are in your wallet! If we can't find it, we're going to have to go home and phone all the credit card companies, report the cards as missing." I looked inside my purse. No wallet. I got down on my hands and knees to check the closet. I looked in all the drawers where I had so carefully placed our folded clothing. I checked the top shelf. I looked in the bathroom, under the bed, in the drawers of the bedside tables. While I looked in the same places for a second time, Harry described his movements. He said he left the beach because I was snoring so loudly he couldn't sleep. He said he stretched out on the bed but he was thirsty. He said he needed change for the soda machine. And that was why he looked for my wallet.

"Why did you need change from my wallet? Why didn't you use the change on the table?" There was about a dollar's worth of change he had emptied out of his pocket in plain view on the table.

"I forgot about that. I didn't see it." I felt under such pressure that it did not occur to me to challenge his statement. How could he not have seen the table in a 15 by 15 room? What he said didn't make sense, but then, the whole episode wasn't making sense to me.

I looked inside the empty suitcases. I triple-checked everywhere I had already looked. I felt under the edges of the mattress. Throughout, Harry kept up a harangue. He asked me when I last remembered having the wallet. I told him at the store where we stopped. He said we had to drive back there so I could check. I was positive I left the store with the wallet in my pocketbook because I would have noticed had it been light. I was sure checking the store was a waste of time but Harry insisted. We drove the few miles in silence. Harry stayed in the car while I asked the clerks if anyone had turned in a wallet. Of course no one had, but they graciously made a cursory look. I returned to the car. Harry said, "We have to return home. We can't stay. I suppose we'll be charged for the room! All those credit cards! What a mess!"

I felt stupid, angry, resentful, hateful. I wished Harry would shut up. My head swam. "Am I crazy?" Over and over, silently, I reconstructed our arrival at the motel, checking in, unpacking. What had I done with my wallet? While I repacked, my head churned. Harry said maybe someone out on the balcony had looked in and seen the change on the table, forced their way in, found my purse, and stole my wallet. That seemed somewhat plausible but not very likely. (In this scenario, the change on the table was visible to "someone out on the balcony.")

"I don't care about the money," Harry said. "It's the credit cards. You have to call about the credit cards right away. All the numbers are at home in my desk. I don't want to end up having to pay for what someone else has charged! I'll let the desk know we're checking out."

I gathered up our toiletries from the bathroom, even looked inside the toilet tank. Where the hell was the damn wallet? The motel owner came to the room, concerned, sympathetic, and questioned why it was necessary for us to leave. He wondered why we couldn't take care of the calls from there. Harry said he had all the emergency numbers and copies of the credit card numbers in his desk and that we had to go home. The owner tried again to persuade Harry that reporting could be done from there, that there was no reason for us to forfeit our weekend. Harry was intractable. I was embarrassed. I didn't know where my wallet was. I felt I was being punished.

Harry walked over to the kitchen unit. "Did you put it in these cupboards?" and he opened the upper cabinets, "or did you put it in this drawer?" and he pulled out the shallow drawer half filled with assorted cutlery. He bent over and opened the little refrigerator. "Did you put it in here?" He was becoming ridiculous. Then he knelt down, opened the cupboard to the left of the refrigerator that held pots and pans, and turned his face up to mine and asked, "Did you put it in here?" I can see Harry's eyes, fixed upon mine, as clearly as if this happened yesterday and not decades ago.

"No, of course not!" I asserted.

He continued kneeling and staring at me. "Are you sure?"

"I'm sure," I said.

The drive home was a verbal hell on wheels. Again Harry accused me of being so drunk that I couldn't remember what I had done with my wallet. "You were in a blackout. You were drunk. Maybe you ought to think about going to AA."

Could I have been that affected by the champagne? Was the fact I was sure I hadn't been in a blackout a sign I might be denying I had been in a blackout? But if I'd been in a blackout, why could I remember everything except deliberately hiding the wallet?

Harry's verbal assault continued. "You ruined our weekend. I just hope no one has already started to use those credit cards!" As we drove back across the Bourne Bridge, lights twinkled in the early darkness where just hours earlier sunlight sparkled on the canal. I sank into numbness. I stopped thinking about what the weekend could have been like, that we could have been having dinner now in one of our favorite restaurants, all that fresh, tasty seafood. I stopped responding to Harry. He was accusing me of having been drunk but he was acting like he was drunk. Crazy. Crazy. CRAZY!

Then he said something interesting. "I predict one of two things will happen. Either you'll get a call within a few days that your wallet has been found or you'll never hear anything about it."

I had calmed down enough to sort through much of what Harry had been saying. Something inside me made me wonder if Harry had anything to do with the wallet being missing. Why, of course he had seen the change on the table! What was all this about? I had an idea. "Harry, I'm going to contact a hypnotist. That way I'll know exactly what I did with my wallet."

"What are you talking about?"

I explained that whatever occurred was stored in my memory, and through hypnosis, it could be released. I noted that Harry seemed uneasy about that idea. In the dark, I gloated. I couldn't prove he had taken the wallet any more than I could prove he was back to seeing other women if, in fact, he had ever stopped, but his behavior all but screamed, "Liar!" As soon as we arrived home, Harry pulled out a folder containing credit card information. I started making calls to 800 credit card numbers. The first person asked if I had reported the missing wallet to the police. When I mentioned this to Harry, he said, "No! Don't call the police! It hasn't been stolen. It's missing." Gee, what happened to his earlier hypothesis that a thief had come in through the sliders?

I took a stand. "But we don't know if it's missing because it was mislaid or missing because it was stolen." After he left the room, I called the Truro police station and reported the wallet missing. I continued phoning the remaining credit card companies and when asked, I was able to tell them I had reported the missing wallet to the police. When Harry learned I had gone ahead and phoned the police, he said, "There was no need for you to do that. I wish you hadn't done that." He could not give me a reason why.

That was Friday. On Saturday Harry was tense, nervous, but that wasn't out of the ordinary. He phoned his elderly aunt to let her know we were back from the Cape and why; she was very sympathetic about the loss of my wallet and all the red tape connected with replacing credit cards and driver's license and library cards. "Oh dear, oh dear," she sighed. What bothered me the most was losing a poem I had clipped from a woman's magazine 30 years before, had laminated, and carried in my wallet. The poem, *Marriage of True Minds* by Jan Struther captured what I longed for in a marriage. (I wanted to include the poem here but all efforts to track down who holds the copyright failed.)

Harry left to check his post office mail box. I decided nothing was going to interfere with some of the plans I had for the weekend. I changed into a swimsuit, set up a chaise lounge in the sun, and fell asleep. I might not be on a beach at the Cape, but it was the same sun. Later Harry suggested that since I had not planned any meals that we go out for dinner. Any restaurant I mentioned, he found something wrong with it. We drove around aimlessly. Finally, exasperated, I said, "There's peanut butter for sandwiches at home." He chose the Suffield Inn. Conversation was almost non-existent. He tried to talk me into having a glass of wine.

"Go ahead. I don't mind."

I told him I didn't want to take the chance of being accused I'd been in a blackout.

"Are you going to divorce me?" He seemed afraid that I might. How sad he seemed!

"Do you want me to?" I parried.

"No, of course not!" he shot back.

Sunday's atmosphere duplicated Saturday's, except Harry could not use checking his mail as an excuse to leave the house. Again, I sunned and dozed off. We went out to dinner. Tentative conversation resumed, two or three sentences lumped together followed by protracted silence, a typical pattern when Harry was not drinking. With just a few drinks, he could be an engaging conversationalist, but with none, he remained almost mute, and usually glum.

Monday afternoon I received a phone call from the owner of the motel. My wallet was found by the people who rented our room. He passed the phone to the woman. She told me she found my wallet "way at the back of the cupboard, behind all the pots and pans." I could see Harry's face, his eyes boring into mine, as he knelt by that open cupboard. I could hear him asking me, "Are you sure you didn't put it in here?" He had said the wallet would either turn up within a few days or we'd never hear any more about it. How could he have been so sure? Why had he not wanted me to notify the police? Asking myself those questions was a rhetorical exercise. I knew the answers. But I wanted verification, so I spent an hour with a hypnotist. She was impressed by the details I remembered. Nothing bizarre was discovered through hypnosis. I felt as though I had failed. She said as I left her that at some point the recollection I sought would kick in, and that's exactly what happened. Several hours later, while driving, I suddenly felt myself back in the motel room on Friday afternoon, about to walk out to the beach, but first scooping up my purse from the table and swinging it into the closet, onto the floor, around to the left and back of the partition—the first place I had looked for it. I knew I was not the one who stashed my wallet at the back of the cupboard behind the pots and pans.

With the advantage of retrospection, there never was a mystery. Harry had an agenda and found a way to fulfill it. He was in miserable humor before we left for the weekend. I attributed most of his mood swings to jagged nerves, because he wanted to drink or had been drinking. Either condition could have been a factor in any situation. But I think much of the time, more was involved besides booze, and specifically his addiction to sexual conquests. Maybe he was in the early throes of infatuation with someone. I speculated about how thought-out his plan was for aborting the weekend. First there was his sullenness. Next, for the first time, he had me carry most of the cash in my wallet. He left me sleeping on the beach, ostensibly because he wanted to nap in the motel room. He said he did not notice the change on the table. When he opened the upper cupboards, the drawer and the refrigerator, he looked not at me but at what he had opened. But when he knelt by the cupboard that held the pots and pans, he looked up at me. "Did you put it in here?" There was eye contact—sustained eye contact. "Are you sure?" Burrowing eye contact. What would have happened had I fished around in that cupboard and found the wallet? I suppose he would have carried on about my having had so much to drink that I could not remember what I had been doing. Maybe he would have said the episode wrecked the weekend for him and he wanted to go home. We could have notified the credit card companies from the Cape. We could have gotten cash for the weekend by using one of his credit cards for which I did not have a duplicate. Maybe, as more than one recovering alcoholic who heard this story remarked, maybe he was angry because I could drink and was drinking and he couldn't and wasn't and therefore, his warped reasoning dictated I be punished. Maybe his behavior was due to a little bit of everything mentioned. And maybe he planned the whole farce just like he planned to seduce Faith. But the telling point is that his devaluation treatment of me was an indication of how he felt about himself. In which case, I concurred.

Chapter 51

Towards the end of 1984 when I found mushy cards in the car, I blew the whistle and, of course, Harry told me there had been a harmless lunch and she meant nothing to him, and he agreed to counseling. The new psychologist told me exactly what the first therapist told me six years earlier: "He's a loser." I figured this new guy did not understand alcoholism either. Contributing to my denial was that I wanted the marriage—my third—to endure. To initiate another divorce, to rupture those aspects of our home life which were comfortable, to go through moving, to move into the unknown—no, I clearly was not ready.

Desperate for logic to explain why I stayed with him, I extrapolated ordinary, courteous gestures—carrying groceries into the house, taking out the trash, helping me change the bed—into demonstrations of Harry's innate goodness, that he really cared for me. I had become so accustomed to his sarcasm, racial and religious bigotry, nonstop lies and wholesale b.s. that I rejoiced in finding any redeeming characteristic to justify upholding my marital commitment. Even if, in Emerson's words, Harry could not get his "bloated nothingness" out of his own way, I would: I saw his potential and so I loved not what he was but what he could be. Tom, Spofford's Aftercare counselor, described this as the "broken wing" fantasy: a sympathetic enabler ignoring the broken wing and instead imagining a proud, strong eagle. On a daily basis, my ambivalent feelings easily swung between compassion and contempt, affection and loathing.

I misinterpreted some thoughts shared in Al-Anon meetings to mean that the ideal spouse stuck by her alcoholic, no matter what. For years I believed that any behavior exhibited while under the influence was excusable. "Oh, he was drunk," excused the vase smashed against a wall or passes made at other women (Harry never threw a vase). I heard Al-Anon and non-drinking AA members, with shaking heads and shrugging shoulders, speak about AAs who were drinking again, "It's the disease." Yes, I believe alcoholism is a progressive disease with a beginning, middle and an end, and that the disease can be arrested by abstinence otherwise death occurs, usually prematurely, sometimes preceded by alcohol-induced insanity. However, I do not believe the disease label gives an alcoholic license to behave selfishly. I contend that prior to crossing into the final stages when the alcoholic cannot *not* drink, once the alcoholic is confronted with a diagnosis of alcoholism, he or she is handed responsibility for the disease. Between that point and the final stages, alcoholics have choices, beginning with whether to drink or not to drink. Although recovering alcoholics, who include many professional therapists, state that willpower has nothing to do with how an alcoholic stays away from the bottle, I disagree. The decision to stop drinking results from changing one's thinking, and then to stay stopped requires making a commitment to that decision. Whenever temptation occurs, the recovering alcoholic is faced with a choice. By exercising power over his compulsion/addiction, he will not drink. He will have made a conscious choice. He will have exercised the power of his will. I went through identical mental gymnastics when I broke my 30-year addiction to the drug nicotine and eventually, my "addiction" to Harry.

My only consistently frequent contact was with Al-Anon friends—thank God for their patience and loyalty—and Harry ridiculed them. To some he made seductive overtures, by phone and in person. He denied he made passes at other women friends with such outraged vehemence that I thought I had to believe him. His denials included demeaning comments about the women— they were unattractive ("a one-bagger"), not too swift, flaky, too old, or he expressed shock that anyone would dare to suggest he would make a pass at someone younger than his daughters. When he behaved like a predator plotting his seduction of Faith, she was younger than his two older daughters; he was 53, Faith was 16—a 37-year difference. The clincher was telling me I was the only woman he wanted, that he loved me "totally." In time I learned that all the accusations were true. Harry demonstrated equal opportunity seduction—young or old (16 to 70), attractive or downright homely, accomplished or borderline literate, financially upscale or barely scraping by. He charmed them all. In the original *Northeast Magazine* article, I glossed over his womanizing because I thought chasing women was directly related to drinking, and I wanted to believe Harry's expressed wish to become well meant he had stopped drinking which meant he no longer pursued women. Also I thought recounting his adulterous behavior would be counter productive towards achieving sobriety. But the bottom line was I could not bear having others know what I was tolerating. I sensed he was being unfaithful but there was no way I could prove it. And if I couldn't present proof, he called me crazy and denied he was interested in any other woman, and then his standard question was, "When are you going to trust me?" He told me often I was the only woman he loved and wanted as his wife. He referred to me as "my precious girl." "I worship you," he said, often. "I adore you." Such declarations pack great seductive power. Surely, I argued with myself, no one would ever say anything like that unless they meant it. Hah! To protect an addiction—any addiction—to protect his/her image in another's eyes, the abuser lies. I know of no one to whom Harry did not lie. A grandmother who doted on him defended him when he was a little boy: "Oh, Harry doesn't lie. He has a vivid imagination." His Aunt Bibi who loved him dearly, told me, "He's been a liar all his life." He began lying years before he ever tasted alcohol.

In some of the personal ads he placed in *The Advocate* he cited a "handicapped marriage" as the reason this MWM wanted a companion "free to travel." I longed to put a tap on the phone but I thought it would be complicated and expensive. So, for a few weeks I intercepted mail in his post office box. One letter was from a borderline illiterate, whining because she hadn't heard from Harry in a long time. I phoned and told her I was one of his girl friends and asked if she had developed any vaginal problems. When she said she was okay, I told her she was lucky because, I lied, Harry had herpes. I loved her gasp. Paula in a neighboring town, just over the line in Connecticut, told me Harry loved me very much and for me not to be hasty. A secretary from another nearby town who enjoyed the hospitality of my home one Saturday in my absence sent Harry sweet, mushy cards: "My place next time?" Another lover believed that because Harry was raised in a Christian Science home, he was incapable of dishonesty. "God is love," he told her, me, probably others. When bright women can be rendered dumb by even fleeting references to spiritually exalting credos, he would have been a fool not to use such heady weapons in his arsenal of seduction.

I felt no animosity towards any of the women. Had I not been duped? I felt especially sorry for AA women he seduced because they knew Harry was married and by succumbing to his charm, they jeopardized their sobriety. He belittled them. One was a mixed up kid of 19, whom he took to a dinner theater and then to a motel. He referred to her as "The Frog" because she was homely and wore large glasses. Another, Lois, with whom he enjoyed church parking lots and various motels, he nicknamed "Brillo Head" because her predominantly gray, wirey hair was permed in short tight curls. These women represent only a fraction of the women he bedded. To distinguish one conquest from another, he jotted cryptic notes in his personal little black book: "Hangups!" "Small" "Good BJ" "Swinger" "Too serious." His first wife had warned me, "He has women all over Connecticut," and Harry said, "What a cruel thing for her to say." But she was telling the truth.

As I write this, I shake my head, finding it almost impossible to believe I stayed with Harry. I wanted out but I was immobilized by fears. How, after being out of the job market for so many years (at Harry's insistence) could I possibly land an interesting job that would support me? Two of the private detectives I hired offered me jobs because I completed the assignments I gave them before they did but I did not take their offers seriously. My biggest fear was becoming a bag lady. Was Harry a meal ticket and I a prostitute? My respect for myself was almost gone. A victim mentality was entrenched.

By the spring of 1985, I was bombarded by too many clues to pretend there were none. I told him I suspected he was seeing other women and warned him that if I ever got proof, I would not stay quiet, that I would tell his children.

"I don't care," he said.

"Don't you care what your children think?"

"The only person I care about is you."

Early in June, David went into Conifer Park near Albany, NY for a 30-day treatment program for his cross addiction (alcohol, marijuana, pills), part of the same corporation that operated Spofford Hall. His girlfriend and I took advantage of being his significant others and participated in their week-long Family Treatment Program. Before I left the house, I bought the necessary telephone tapping paraphernalia. By following the simple instruction, I set up the voice-activating equipment under Harry's at-home desk. Conifer and Spofford therapists frowned on my action, saying it signified I was becoming even more obsessed with Harry, falling deeper into the family disease—in other words, getting sicker. I felt appropriately demeaned, guilty, but how else was I to determine if I were or were not imagining infidelity? When I returned home to a glum Harry, obviously hung over. I waited until after he left the next morning to play back the tape which covered only the first few days I was away. I had confirmation—at last—of my suspicions. I was infuriated that my husband was not only unfaithful with another "masseuse," he reminisced with "The Frog" about what a good time they had together on a rainy night at a Connecticut hotel. The kicker was that he brought a woman into our home, into our bed, who had advertised in *The Advocate*. The relief I felt, to know I had not been imagining his double life, was greater than my anger. And my anger was huge.

Fresh from seven days in a protected environment, my self-worth bolstered by almost non-stop therapy, I let myself feel my anger. I went a step further: I let my anger work for me. I drove to Harry's office and confronted him in front of his married son, and told him I wanted him out of the house immediately. I never once raised my voice. My control was the stuff of steel. Driving home, I felt buoyant. I reveled in my anger. When he arrived at the house, I unleashed my tongue, unmindful of upsetting "the poor alcoholic." I felt charged with adrenalin—alive, alive, alive!

"Can't we talk?" Harry asked. "Ruby doesn't mean anything to me. She's almost 70!" I envisioned a trim senior citizen thrashing about with paunchy Harry and wondered if he told her, as he had so many of us, "You have the body of a teenager!" Might he also have said, "I'm going to make total love to you"? I never did understand what that meant. He pleaded with me to reconsider. I had no intention of changing my mind. I knew I was doing the right thing for me. I had not felt so vibrant, so self-assured in years. "I love you!" he said. I watched him walk from his closet, through the house and out to his car, clothes on hangers, some draped over his arm. How many times had he played out this scene before we met? His first wife put him out more than once and always took him back. More than ever, my heart went out to her. Like waves, my anger crested and subsided, only to crest again as the significance hit me anew of a Ruby being in my home, in my bed. I felt superficial anger towards her. I knew she was not at fault. I knew only too well the persuasive potency of Harry's manipulative skills. Who could resist his directness, the honeyed compliments, the throwaway quips, the boyish appeal? Certainly no woman, hurting from loneliness, who had fantasized about someone discovering her as the best thing since Marilyn Monroe. Had not I capitulated to his charm which overrode my first impression of him—weasel—the very word that popped into my head the moment I first met him? Had he not lived up to that word, over and over again? No, to Ruby and all the others, I felt sympathy and a form of sisterhood. We'd all been had, in the full sense of the word.

Practical considerations flashed. Now I would have more closet room for myself, the bedroom to myself, the house to myself! Divorce was an option but I had no plans other than to rid myself of a toxic personality, a pollutant who assaulted my sensibilities. I removed my engagement and wedding rings, signifying that at least an emotional divorce was underway.

As Harry was about to get into his car to leave, I threw the sheets and pillow cases at him that he had laundered. Some fell on the driveway. "Take those with you!" I shouted. He looked startled, puzzled. "TAKE THEM!" I yelled.

"They're clean," he said.

"GET THEM OUT OF HERE!" I bellowed.

"You're crazy!" he said as he scooped up the linens and drove away. If I were crazy, it was a most satisfying sensation of temporary insanity.

During the first few days alone, I was in shock punctuated by moments of euphoria and flashes of anger and stabs of pain. I was experiencing withdrawal. Not having Harry around, not being able to observe him, not being privy to even the most superficial aspects of his life, was a tremendous relief. I did not speculate about what he was doing or might do. I knew what he had done, and his history prophesied his history would be repeated.

I knew I was codependent. I knew I had to break my thinking pattern. I knew it would be tough. What I didn't know was how tough.

That summer I seesawed between gaining strength and slipping into weakness. At first I cried—a lot. I think I cried more that summer than all the rest of my life put together. I cried from emotional overload. I cried every time hindsight in conjunction with steadily improving thinking afforded me the ability to recognize what had really been going on. I cried over how callously Harry used me, how selfishly he pursued his pleasures. I've wondered if the times I was literally racked with sobs helped me avoid having a total breakdown. The betrayal I felt was absolute. It penetrated and suffused my whole being. How could I have been such a fool? Almost from the beginning I knew Harry lied. He told me he had four children, not six. Hadn't Lenora mused, "I wonder which two he killed off." I felt so sorry for her, for the 26 years she put up with his drinking and womanizing. Awareness of his multiple deceptions piled up. I repeatedly asked myself, "How could I have been so stupid?" In addition to the five women I could name who had been in our home, there was a mystery guest who had lost a blonde bobby pin in the bathroom. There were others whose presence was disclosed because the window shades were at different levels than I had left them, or the bed pillows were arranged differently. Years later, the next door neighbor murmured, "We wondered what was going on." How could he have violated not only marriage vows but the sanctity of our home? My god, he had Ruby in our bed! I figured out her telephone number by replaying the tape uncounted times, matching tones of the dialing with the numbers. After she recovered from the shock of hearing from me, she said Harry told her he was divorced, that they spent time on the couch before moving into the bedroom. I wanted to heave the couch through one of the square over-sized windows. Everything in the house felt tainted to me. Beyond scrubbing and cleaning, I did what I could afford to change its appearance. I replaced the living room drapes that covered 15 feet of glass. In the bedroom, I installed new carpeting, changed the curtains, bedspread, and pillows. I painted a large rectangular seascape and hung it over the bed. Short of an exorcism, the bedroom became all mine, only mine. And I had both closets all to myself.

Most importantly, I dealt with how I felt about my self-image. I felt split: my head told me that I was okay, that Harry's boozing and wenching had nothing to do with my self, but my emotions triggered doubts about my femininity. Intellectually I had it all together but emotionally I felt bereft. I felt used, even soiled. Sometimes when I thought of Harry's touch, I felt as though my skin were crawling with maggots. Ordering him out of the house was a significant act in the brick-by-brick restoration of my dignity. But so many feelings hurt. I felt wholesale betrayal. I mourned the death of a marriage that had never really existed. I badgered myself with the same questions: How could he value our life together so lightly? How could he speak of dedicated love, tell me repeatedly, "I worship you," and chase other women? How did he have the gall to bring other women into our home, into our bed? Which of all his words of love could I believe? Oh, how could I have been so stupid?

My Al-Anon friends, especially Idora and another close program friend, Lola, gave me their full moral support. My best "civilian" friend, Cara, bolstered my spirits by not talking about Harry. With him out of the house, I was freed from focusing on him. Most of the time, I had no idea what he was doing. But my codependency asserted its obsessive self. A few times I drove by the motel where he was renting by the month (he borrowed the up-front money from his oldest daughter). On his birthday, I baked a cake for him and put it in his car parked outside his office. I believed it was important that his birthday be acknowledged. Go figure. That's how I was thinking. But one day

I stopped myself en route from driving by his motel room. Why? Because I knew I would feel better about myself if I stopped. The obsession was leaving me. I used my time to think about myself and my interaction with members of my family. I could get up and go to bed when I wanted. I did not have to tippytoe in the evenings from as early as 7:15 pm because Harry had gone to bed. I did not have to consider his feelings first. I felt as though I had been paroled from a prison. The tears dried up. My Al-Anon attendance remained high. I used my phone support network so much that a clever plastic surgeon could have made the telephone a permanent part of me.

Late on a September afternoon while I was enjoying a drink before supper, Harry drove into the driveway, unexpectedly and obviously drunk. He sat at one side of the counter, I on the other. He wanted to review some household expenses and bring me up to date about the Swiss business. He said there was something he needed to tell me. "What Faith said was true. I lied." We were in the same spot where that horrible confrontation had taken place. I remembered Faith's tears, Harry's lies, Liz's disgust with me. I remembered having to pick up my grandsons at the door. I remembered Mother's 90th birthday party that Harry would not attend if Liz were present and I felt forced to cleave unto my husband's wishes. I thought of the Christmases and Thanksgivings and other birthday celebrations I could not attend. Most of all I thought of the additional pain heaped upon Faith because I would not let myself believe what she said accurately described the truth. All these thoughts whirred through my head as I walked around the counter to where Harry sat and slapped him so hard across the face that his glasses flew through the air. I wanted to kill him. He retrieved his glasses and left. A year later just before I filed for divorce, he said his confession was a lie.

The first frost arrived and soon afterwards a few days of heavenly Indian Summer. I spent those warm afternoons in the yard trimming hedges, pruning bushes, even some small trees. I got blisters. I sweat. As I walked towards the shed to get another gardening tool, I stopped stock still and exclaimed aloud, "I'm happy!"

Between Christmas and New Year's Day, I went to a few dances. I attended a spiritualist church where a medium told me that in a while I would experience the love, the emotional security I had always wanted. The medium added to make sure my passport was valid because he saw travel "in the spring." When I repeated this to Lola, she said, "Harry?" and I thought, "I hope not." The medium's message was correct: the travel applied to the coming spring; the emotional security to the spring after that.

Chapter 52

On New Year's Day, 1986, Harry phoned to wish me a happy new year. He sounded down in the dumps, but I was used to that. When he phoned the next day, he said, "You've got to help me! I can't get off the booze! Can you get me into a detox?" I called Rob, a mutual friend in AA, Lola's husband, and together we picked up a sodden Harry for the ride to the detoxification unit at Springfield's Municipal Hospital. Rob drove, Harry in the passenger seat, I in the back. Every so often, Harry turned around to smile and to mouth, "I love you very much." His face resembled a melting candle. He seemed to be so saturated with vodka that I wondered why it hadn't killed him. I thought of the first time I drove him to the same detox, seven long years ago. He was in worse shape this time. It took two of us keeping Harry propped up to get him across the snow-rutted parking lot. Once he asked us to stop. He reached into his pocket, produced a container of breath mints, and popped a couple into his mouth. The futility of the gesture hit my funny bone and I burst out laughing. Harry wasn't sure what he had done that was funny but having spent his life seeking approval, he wasn't about to pass up an excuse to laugh. Rob chuckled and said, "That's right, Harry. You take those breath mints and they'll never be able to tell you've been drinking!" Harry's facial expression was heartbreaking. He had done something we found amusing, he had made us laugh, and he drank in the attention he craved. He laughed, swiveling his face from Rob to me, looking like a little boy who has won a great prize. The innate sadness of an alcoholic was never more evident to me. Poor Harry. He spent so much of his life seeking acceptance, and he used humor—sometimes genuinely amusing, too often crass, crude and in poor taste—as an entree. And here he was, two days into a new year, staggering across a frozen parking lot, held upright by an AA friend and the wife he spurned, about to receive detoxification help for still another colossal binge. And we were all laughing.

Less than 48 hours later, against medical advice, he checked himself out of that detox. Five hours later, he was pathetically drunk and ready for another detox. This time Holyoke admitted him. After several days there, he agreed to go into a 28-day treatment program and asked me to drive him to Conifer Park, the same place my son had been six months earlier. At Harry's request, I was there every Sunday for visiting hours. Whenever chemical dependency patients spoke in a meeting or lecture, they were required to identify themselves the AA way. Harry was instructed to say more: "My name is Harry and I'm an alcoholic. Under every skirt, there's a slip." I interpreted this to mean the alcoholism professionals believed that whenever Harry committed adultery, his guilt feelings became so unbearable that he had to drink to blot them out; ergo, if he stopped chasing women, he stood a better chance of not picking up a drink. During this time, Harry's oldest son who had joined his office did not believe any of the directives his father asked me to pass along to him. Harry said he told his son that he, the father, was the liar but that Donna never lies. But who knows what else Harry told his son? I knew how he double talked with my family. I can't fault the son for choosing to believe his father over me. This was hardly the first time someone shot the messenger. The breach between the young man and me was never healed. During his month at Conifer Park, Harry initiated a tentative courtship. I vacillated between believing he was serious about getting better to thinking he wanted me to believe he was. During our seven-month separation, I had not missed the stress of him at all. Still, I was his wife, and according to feedback from the treatment staff and the tone of Harry's communications to me, it appeared that all that was necessary for us to get back together was for me to say the word.

During the last week of his 28-day stay, I became a family patient for the fourth time in five years. Harry and I participated in two to three workshops together every day with the emphasis upon clear communication. I hoped for tougher, more definitive sessions, but I consoled myself, "At least this is a beginning." Could I take him back? He'd have to re-earn my trust but in the meantime I'd try to act as if he already had. My knowledge of the other women had ceased to hurt but I lived with a dull ache. I hoped I'd progressed far enough into my own recovery not to tolerate that kind of emotional abuse again. I'd have to give one of the bedroom closets back to him. I wouldn't be able to read in bed before going to sleep. My socializing with family and friends would be curtailed. There would be post-drinking mood swings. I could choose that we would date prior to resuming a married life but how would I know I was the only one he was seeing? Because he'd been checked out for all kinds of infectious diseases, including AIDS, and was found to be clean, I decided to let him come home.

On the morning he was discharged, Harry asked me, "Did you bring the rings?" meaning our wedding rings which neither of us had worn since the previous summer.

"Yes," and as I fished them out of my pocketbook, I asked, "Are you ready for this? Are you ready to be married? Are you ready to make a full commitment?"

"Yes," he said, as he handed me a wee statuette of a seated teddy bear waving a banner that read, "I'm yours." He added, "I am, you know." We put on our rings and returned to our home in Massachusetts. A honeymoon atmosphere prevailed for a month—the "pink cloud" so familiar to alcoholic families. Suddenly, I had an attentive, romantic husband. There were lunches, walks in parks, flowers, cards, dinners, phone calls. Harry attended weekly Aftercare and AA meetings—one of each per week, nowhere near enough for a newly-dry alcoholic, especially someone with a 20-year history of being in and out of AA and drying-out farms.

One month into our new routine, Harry flew to Switzerland for a sales seminar and then to Italy for a weekend visit with one of his daughters. He spoke at length about meeting a woman on the plane, and I chose to believe his disclaimers about not finding her attractive. He was away only ten days but that was long enough to end his limited attendance routine at AA meetings. His personality remained pleasant but his courtly behavior ceased. Early in May, Swiss business took us to Chicago by way of Niagara Falls, the longest and most enjoyable car trip we ever took together. Two months later we flew to Switzerland on business; we spent long evenings touring, taking advantage of light until almost ten o'clock. For Harry, he was relatively relaxed and a pleasant traveling companion. But by the end of July, on Martha's Vineyard, he was sullen, short-tempered, caustic, laconic, and frankly, a bore. The long descent had begun.

At the beginning of August, our alpha cat Pita, named by Harry, an acronym for pain-in-the-ass—which he wasn't, Pita, I mean—was severely mauled by a dog and not expected to live. Mother, age 93, was hospitalized, and I expected her to live forever. She was diagnosed with congestive heart failure, and a colonoscopy followed by a biopsy disclosed cancer. I spent the days with Mother. When I dragged myself home early one evening, I found Harry sitting on the floor, leaning against a wood cabinet. I knelt. His eyes were open but unseeing. I placed my hands on either side of his face. "Oh Harry, I'm so sorry, so sorry." As I moved away, he toppled forward onto the carpet. I left him there, dead drunk, where he did not twitch a muscle for almost seven hours. I awakened when I heard him vomiting into a wastebasket. Surely I must have known then there was little to no hope the marriage could ever be healthy.

I gave my top priority to Mother. Pita came home, still with drains in his chest, and made a full recovery. I shared that good news with Mother but did not tell her about Harry's drinking. She and I had long conversations; once she said, "You are a good daughter." She became progressively weaker from congestive heart failure and shortly after high noon on September 5th, she passed away in my arms so quietly that I did not know she was gone. She was the only parent I had known (my father died five months before I was born) and suddenly I was an orphan. Harry said all the standard words but I sensed no sincere emotional support. Indeed, I expected none, but how comforting it would have been to have had a husband with inner resources.

During a winter break in Florida, we house-hunted for a post-retirement home. With a small inheritance from Mother, we bought a charming little house in Cape Coral—two bedrooms, two baths, an in-ground pool surrounded by a screened-in lanai, colorful hibiscus, a glorious gardenia bush the size of a small tree, and an assortment of fruit trees bearing sweet juicy gifts. Harry was drunk several times, exhibited wide mood swings, and I speculated he had resumed womanizing. I was expending more emotional energy mourning the loss of Mother than I was thinking about Harry's behavior. By the first anniversary of Mother's death, Harry often smelled of liquor, and frankly, he was a real drag. However during my birthday dinner in mid-September, he declared that he was very happy with me, that he loved me totally, that he felt "good about us." Words. I was emerging from deep grieving and ready to take stock of my life with Harry.

I hooked up the tape recorder. And there it was—Harry lying about going to out-of-town sales meetings that were canceled, adding to the lies when I confronted him. In October he swaggered into the house brandishing a jug of vodka which he set down on the counter with great flourish and announced that if he wanted to drink, he was going to drink, that he'd been drinking for over a year and wasn't in any trouble, and if I didn't like it, too bad. What a grandiose performance! I had never seen Harry look more ludicrous. He also announced he was going to sleep in the other room because he could not stand my snoring. My first thought was, "Hurrah!"

After too long contending with too many emotional demands to do more than think about making an important life-changing decision, I acted. Harry did not know I moved myself out of a victim mentality. The sense of freeing myself was exhilarating. I retained an attorney and quietly gathered facts and figures pursuant to filing for divorce. Through the Red Cross, I was tested for the HIV virus. None, thank goodness. On December 11th, over coffee following dinner at an Italian restaurant, I informed Harry that earlier that day I filed for divorce.

"Why a divorce? Why can't we just go on like we are?" Within a few minutes he said, "You'll be sorry." Later, "You'll regret doing this." Still later, "Where will you live?" I said nothing. "Why don't you go to Florida?" Exactly what I had in mind.

The house sold at a substantial profit——three times what we paid for it. Harry, a whiz with figures——I am not——played number games and presented me with list after revised list until I was thoroughly confused. He worked the numbers the same way he did speculating how much he would inherit from his aunt and ways to pad his business and personal expense accounts. Repaying loans was not on any of his lists. He brought with him into the relationship the couch and daybed. Usually we split the cost of anything we purchased. Everything else came with me; later I bought a new dining table and chairs. He denied my right to be reimbursed for the house down payment I provided. He chiseled me out of money used to buy him a car. And why not? He had a selective conscience. When he whined he would not have any furnishings for the apartment he rented, I loaned him furniture which he later passed along to Liz (when he moved in with his widowed girlfriend whom he eventually married). If I allowed myself to become bogged down in the petty stuff, I would reap added stress, definitely not to my advantage. I reasoned any out-of-pocket losses I absorbed (about $45,000) were worth the price of removing myself from Harry's poisonous persona.

The movers left with the van for Florida. The next day, the end of January 1988, I hugged Harry goodbye. We stood in the driveway, scene of saying goodbye before I went to Spofford, scene of the homecoming from Spofford, scene of throwing the sheets at Harry when I threw him out. Relief I was leaving overwhelmed any sadness I experienced. The car was packed—a roof pouch, luggage in the trunk, the three cats in individual carriers in the back seat. I headed for Springfield to pick up Michael,11, my older grandson, and Liz who shared the driving with me. We stopped overnight in Washington, DC and visited the Smithsonian, The Wall, Lincoln Memorial, and Arlington Cemetery before resuming the trip. A mixed bag of memories were heavy in the vicinity of Goldsboro, NC where I had lived with Steve at the Air Force base; we did not stop, not until we reached South-of-the-Border where tackyness was raised to an art form. My grandson loved the place. The third night, in a heavy rain storm, we stopped near Tampa. Before noon the next day, we rolled into the driveway of my new home. Liz and Michael stayed for five days. We explored the area, visiting Edison's winter home, Larry's Animal Farm, alligator and reptile attractions, the nature refuge on Sanibel Island. When they flew out of Fort Myers, being on my own hit me. Now what do I do?

I had choices. I could either like where I was or not like it. I chose to like it.

Chapter 53

Within two weeks, I had a new Al-Anon sponsor and a new support network and stepped in as a replacement facilitator of a *Women Who Love Too Much* group where I incorporated many Al-Anon approaches and what I learned from my experiences at Spofford, Connifer, and Parkside Lodge. When it came to sharing, I did not lack for germane personal situations. I explored the local Church of Religious Science (based upon the philosophy of Ernest Holmes, really not a religion) and liked it so much that after several months I became a member and soon was appointed to fill the unexpired term of a board member. I enrolled in a philosophy class. I was busy. I loved the house; the serenity it exuded. Every morning I walked through its rooms and aloud said, "Thank you, Mother." Her money had made buying the house possible.

Sounds like I had the world by the tail.

I was healing but there were hours when pain from remembered betrayals sent me reeling—backwards. When I accepted Harry's repeated declarations of love and fidelity, my living in Florida and he in Massachusetts was not what I envisioned. Sometimes I felt as though I'd been sent into exile. And no wonder. I had been shut out of all but a fraction of Harry's life; any work I did for the Swiss company I had to do at home because he never overcame his wimpy posture to arrange a three-way meeting with his angry son. I repeatedly requested the meeting, and he promised to set it up but never did— undoubtedly because he had too much to lose. Before I left New England, I asked Harry about his behavior when we first lived together, and he did not deny he brought women into our apartment. Before we had been living together six months, he was cheating on me—and I was paying half the rent! Searching for insight—and answers—into promiscuity, I read books about compulsive, addictive infidelity. Harry told me that sex with the other women "didn't count for all that much." Rather, it was the chase—the plotting and planning, the sense of danger, the excitement of someone new. By his own description, he was a sexual predator. He started young. His boyhood friend told me about incidents when they were no more than eight years old and Harry straddled girls, rubbing against their bellies, and one particular time while he and the girl were wearing their ice skates. Alcohol played no role in these early seductions.

In one book I read that coping with the feelings that follow betrayal by a "mate" takes more time than dealing with the death of a real mate, that recovery from wholesale, repeated betrayal can take years. If I had been married to a fine, honorable man who died in January, my grieving would have been respected. I would have received compassion because of moving so far away from my loved ones and into a radically different climate and lifestyle. My attempts at keeping full depression at bay would have been commended. I was told that those who have experienced both divorce and widowhood state that recovering from divorce is harder. I was so eager to get through the healing time but being hurt financially on top of everything else did not help. After not working for almost nine years, at Harry's insistence, now he pressured me to find a job. I wasn't sleeping more than two hours at a time; I was waking up unable to swallow or breathe. Most days I had to nap once during the morning and twice during the afternoon. Two years earlier, while watching Phil Donahue's show, I diagnosed myself: sleep apnea. I should have taken care of it then but I procrastinated because I did not want to run the risk of Harry bringing another woman into the house while I spent the night in a sleep clinic. I was afraid that if he did, I might go crazy enough to kill him.

In March I saw neurology specialists for a referral to an overnight stay at Lee Memorial Hospital in Fort Myers. I was wired for sound plus oxygen utilization, temperatures, brain waves, pulmonary and cardiovascular printouts, and whatever else the sleep technicians could think of. According to the literature I had at the time, obstructive sleep apnea is serious if the interrupted sleep episodes last over ten seconds each and occur more than seven times an hour. Test results indicated I had more than 600 impaired breathing episodes and over 100 incidents of considerably more than 10 seconds, averaging out to 20 per hour. Subsequent tests indicated I was fortunate not to have developed two of sleep apnea's side effects—an enlarged heart and high blood pressure. At the beginning of May, I had UPPP surgery—the removal of the uvula—and correction of a deviated septum. When I came to from the operation, I told the surgeon I felt as if my throat had been cut from ear to ear. He laughed, "That's about right." The best part about the operation was Liz flew down to Florida and stayed with me for a week. Within a month I was mostly healed and thrilled that the weight I had worked at losing prior to the surgery was now falling off.

This important note about severe obstructive sleep apnea, which I have: The UPPP surgery helped for about a year before episodes of awakening unable to breathe returned. Eventually a new sleep study indicated my non-breathing (apnea) episodes averaged 50 times out of every hour. I was fitted to a CPAP machine which I wear to bed. I sleep soundly. I no longer snore. Sleep apnea is dangerous; don't ignore its symptoms.

The plot thickened. Harry called to tell me Mr. Baehler, the president of the Swiss company requested us to attend a special board meeting on Monday, July 11. Because I was an officer of the USA subsidiary, Harry said he hoped I'd say yes, that he thought it could be fun. Fun? He said our personal life was none of the Swiss' business; however, he was not requesting separate rooms. If the CEO knew I'd filed for divorce, he would ask questions, and I usually answer direct questions with direct answers. Harry said he thought that for the duration of the trip we could call a moratorium. I'd hoped our first encounter could be delayed until fall, or later, or never. I hurt hearing his voice, the voice that told me so many lies. Before I moved, he left a paper in plain sight on which he was composing a personal ad, something about finding someone "cuddly and nice." I wanted to throw up.

Harry and I met at the Atlanta airport. My first impression was that he was tanned. That was probably a barroom tan. I extended my hand, he took it, and then he gave me a hug. I turned my head so his kiss would land on my cheek. He said, "You've lost weight." He had gained; he said five pounds but looked more like 15 and his belly fell over his belt. He had a good haircut but his shoes were scruffy, his teeth needed cleaning, one lower tooth was broken or missing. The overall impression: he was puffy, pudgy and not well-groomed. He told me I looked very pretty. Our Swissair flight did not leave for three hours. At a snack area he drank beer and I orange juice. I asked that we review the business; he wanted to wait until we got to Switzerland. He had not prepared any reports because "I don't know what Mr. Baehler wants; I can't read his mind."

"Is trying to second guess a standard approach? Sounds like you want to present not what might be good for business but what pleases Mr. Baehler, and in my opinion, whatever is good for business is what pleases Mr. Baehler." I got nowhere.

During the flight, we sat in different sections—Harry in smoking. Mr. Baehler and his wife met us in Geneva and drove us to the inn near the factory. Our room on the top floor rear was the same one we had stayed in on previous visits—twin beds, a big square window that overlooked a large garden, and beyond to a castle. We unpacked, went downstairs for soup and an omelet, then napped, ate supper, and walked around the small picturesque town. Any conversation was sporadic and bland. Adding to the bucolic languor of early evening were the clinking cowbells. We returned to our room, said good night, and laid down in separate beds. Harry fell asleep at once.

I felt okay, relatively strong within myself, secure in feeling emotionally detached from Harry, as if I were seeing him through fresh eyes, not succumbing to his no-fail charm. But with only 10 hours of sleep total in three days, I was not strong enough to foil memories; their emotions surged through me: the same room where we had stayed twice before and made love in the same beds; the last trip together two years ago when some of the good from his Conifer experience still clung to him, making him more often enjoyable company than someone to tolerate; all the crap since then, all the betrayals with all the other women. Suddenly I was focusing on Lenora and her phone call to me so many years ago: "Harry has women all over the state of Connecticut!" and "He's an awful liar! I can't believe a word he says!" and "Oh, he told you he has four children? I wonder which two he killed off." I remembered the pain in her voice when she told me, "I kicked him out. I couldn't take any more." During that phone call, Harry arrived to take me apartment-hunting. More memories rushed in, all to do with Lenora's hurt, how I unwittingly contributed to her pain because I believed Harry's laundered versions of the facts and not her stark truths. After her phone call, I asked my boss who was married and a womanizer whom I should believe. He said, "The wife." My boss may have been a louse but he was right.

I went into the bathroom, closed the door, and cried—bawled—great wracking sobs. I felt so badly about how my being with Harry had hurt Lenora. I was filled with remorse. I lived with Harry for ten years; I could imagine what Lenora probably endured during 27 years, and while raising six children! Harry's sister told me about Lenora coming to her house, pounding the table and crying, "I can't take any more!" I thought how ironic that I was probably the only person who understood what Lenora was subjected to and endured and who, based upon that shared knowledge, had the capacity to offer her not just sympathy but empathy and understanding. I climbed back into bed and lay there, not able to sleep until almost five o'clock in the morning, about 11 pm in Massachusetts.

I began Monday, our first full workday of meetings at the factory, on a total of 13 hours sleep in four days. Over a stretch of seven days, I had approximately 30 hours sleep. That combined with the stress of business meetings, wondering if the USA operation would continue, if Harry's salary would remain the same, and the indescribable stress of being with Harry, pretending to be a congenially married couple seldom separated more than 20 minutes at a time, my emotions were stretched to breaking points, tears staunched. I believed that when I no longer endowed Harry with the power to hurt me, I would not cry. When I had exhausted my anger, I would not cry. That trip could have provided a challenging case study for a psychiatric symposium.

At the factory, the initial meeting started at 10 and was cordial and correct, but I was dismayed at Harry's liberal use of misrepresentation, which is another word for lying. When he asked me how I thought it went, I told him, "It sounded like a lot of bullshit to me." That afternoon while leaving one area to continue the meeting in another room, Harry swatted my fanny. I was livid. How dare he take such a liberty with me! "You have forfeited the right to be so familiar with me." He apologized, a knee-jerk reaction, an effective way to end further dialog. Not until Wednesday morning did I think anything viable was accomplished: Harry was to supply precise information re customers' requirements; and he was to follow through every week with a fax to Switzerland re outstanding issues awaiting answers. In so many words, this was what I suggested to him many times, most recently in a June memo: establish simple office systems. For years he complained about Mr. Baehler not answering questions, of there not being clear communication, and yet Harry did nothing concrete to foster either, no more than he did in his relationship with me or with anyone. During a break in the meeting, while Harry lit up a cigarette, he said, "Don't say anything. I'm on a roll!" He was pleased to have countered strong criticism by verbalizing criticism of his own—tit for tat, a transparent maneuver, childish. The meetings exposed the obvious: Harry had not been expending a full effort. He was led through the basics of efficient selling. Amazing! Harry, the super salesman with egg on his face. I asked him if he realized what a partnership we could have had, what an effective team we could have been had he not given top priority to his secret private life, excluding me from the business while accusing me of my lack of interest when what was there to pique my interest other than a few letters he brought home for me to type? How could I be part of the business when he barred me from the office? As treasurer, I ought to have signed most of the checks, but Harry was such a controller that only occasionally did he bring anything home for my signature. He systematically excluded me from all areas of his life and eventually, in effect, pushed me out of his life.

I wondered if the final push began following my mother's death because he realized I was not inheriting as much as he may have conjectured. He had complained because she gave money to her grandchildren ahead of her daughter. I believe his amorality and hedonism went hand in glove with his monetary greed. He cleverly deflected attention on avarices with small gestures—phone call, a little gift. Throughout my years with him, I listened to him speculate about how much he'd have at retirement thanks to inheriting from Aunt Bibi because other than Social Security, he had no retirement fund.

On Wednesday afternoon after the budget was approved and Harry's salary was left untouched, Harry left the room for a few minutes and immediately Mr. Baehler asked me about Harry's son. "It's as if he's disappeared, evaporated." So there I was, put in the position of defending someone who hated me. I told him he was very much alive, that he'd been working hard, that he was profoundly affected by the death of a newborn, but he'd come out of that, was doing well, very active in the business, that he had a lot of concern about his wife and the new baby on the way, and all was well. Harry thanked me for covering for his son. He said, "The truth is, he's not been working that hard. He's angry because he has not received commissions for his little company."

After all meetings concluded on Wednesday, Mr. Baehler spoke directly to me, telling me he was glad to have me there, not only because of the notes I took and transcribed, but because he thought it was important for me to be informed about what's going on, that I was part of the team. "Next year I would like to present you with a big check," he said referring to a successful, profitable year for the USA division. I was ashamed of my part in the deception—concern about my economic future and the need to protect it by supporting Harry. Back at the hotel, Harry said, "It's easy to get caught up in the enthusiasm. I'm not sure what to do."

"What do you mean?"

"I don't know if I should go back [to the U.S.] and get a lot of inquiries or not."

I was aghast. He had gotten what he wanted—assurance of open communication by doing his part (transmitting precise information and weekly follow-through) as well as willingness of the Swiss to tailor costs to better accommodate customers' budgets, and no cut in salary. He had fudged his way into buying another year (out of a desired two years) of Swiss employment, and he was wondering if he should get to work and produce inquiries? He expressed the same question on Thursday morning. My answer: "I think you should go after the business. You got everything here you hoped to get. Why throw it away?" Why indeed.

Future business plans included a visit in October from the Swiss. Harry said I could fly into Hartford/Springfield, spend five days with Liz. I asked, "What about my coming into the office?"

"You won't have to come in."

"But what about the wrap-up meeting?"

"We'll do that on a Saturday."

Now he had to orchestrate preventing me from bumping into one of his girlfriends as well as his son.

I marveled at how after only 5-1/2 months separation, I could have forgotten so many details about Harry—his sleeping position; his cough, always the cough; the eye contact and vocal sincerity while lying; the avoidance of eye contact; the body English that broadcast, "I'm apart from you," such as his posture at the dinner table Wednesday evening. While Mr. Baehler and his executive assistant hosted an elegant dinner in one of Europe's finest restaurants, Harry sat at the table with arms folded across his chest. Without benefit of booze, his social skills were rudimentary. I knew he had exploited me, and now I was an accomplice in my own exploitation by helping him cover his ass. I knew he was poison and yet I could be drawn to him, anything, I suppose, to try to cancel out ten years of repeated rejection. Simultaneously, I was repelled. He was so obviously an unhappy person, so defensive. I felt sorry for his pain-filled lifestyle. He complained continuously about being overtired. One evening I sat on the edge of his bed and rubbed his head. In the middle of the night when I couldn't sleep, I asked him if he'd rub my back, and he did. The head and back rubbing were platonic.

In a letter from Harry's Aunt Bibi, she wrote, "It must have been an ordeal for you to have to be nice to everyone for those few days…" I wrote back that I had always liked the Swiss people; that I was genuinely fond of Mr. Baehler and his executive assistant, the accountant, and everyone at the plant who had never been anything but friendly. The company chef prepared fantastic meat-free meals for me. The only employee I wondered about was the translator, an American married to a Swiss, as I had the feeling she was capable of devious, two-faced behavior. (My hunch is she and Harry used icy roads as an excuse to stop at a motel for a few hours.) I admired Mr. Baehler and his father who had built a successful, respected business. I thought it was counter productive of Harry and his son to badmouth the Swiss, make "clever" sarcastic remarks about Mr. Baehler, that such attitudes diffused energies which could be used to seek new accounts. A couple months earlier I had sent a memo saying so, and Harry said he agreed with me. But the whining and sarcasm did not stop.

At the Geneva airport, Harry handed me a 50 franc note and told me to buy myself something for our anniversary, a few days away. I was shocked and bewildered because he remembered. There was not enough time to shop so I quickly selected a cologne. I remarked that if I'd had time, I would have liked to get a Swiss Swatch, an inexpensive sporty watch. When we changed planes in Zurich, he said the Swissair catalog featured Swatches, to choose one and charge it to American Express because, "I didn't get you that much for our anniversary." Somewhere over the Atlantic, I selected a Swatch and told the stewardess to see the man in seat 32B as it was a gift from him. I was perplexed Harry chose to remember our anniversary, number eight. Sad, sad, sad. I think the cologne and Swatch were guilt gifts. No matter. I enjoyed them.

Back at the Atlanta airport, he thanked me several times for "all your help and support." He said he enjoyed being with me and that he would miss me. I requested that when talking about the Swiss trip, he express the truth about his appreciation of my contributions and that he not distort what he said to make it sound like what he thought the listener wanted to hear, not to be a people-pleaser. He said he would be honest. We hugged but before I could turn my head, he gave me a quick peck on the lips. All I could think of was the possibility he was a carrier of venereal diseases. His teeth and gums were visibly unhealthy; I suspected minute fissures as well, making him vulnerable to contracting venereal diseases orally. Only recently had the public become aware of rampant VD: gonorrhea resistant to penicillin, syphilis on the increase and AIDS well entrenched among heterosexuals, especially prostitutes and promiscuous swingers. Harry continued to deny that his promiscuity placed him in a high risk category. But such was his pattern: he denied he was an alcoholic, denied how important it was that he stop smoking and start exercising and eating healthfully.

He cracked a few jokes during the five days and I remember one which broke me up. He said, "What's brown and has holes in it?" I gave up. "Swiss shit!" I roared.

I went to the concourse where I was met by Martha who flew in from Oklahoma and from there we flew to Asheville, North Carolina where she continued renovating her cabin in the mountains. The week was bumpy: I was edgy from spending time with Harry, and she was in psychotherapy because she was the daughter of an abusive alcoholic father and now she recognized that her husband Joe was an active alcoholic. Her mood swings were tough to take. While saying goodbye, I suggested she check out Al-Anon. She erupted: "Don't you ever mention Al-Anon to me again!" If a vacation is rated good because of a change of scene, then my week in the Blue Ridge Mountains was good.

I was relieved, grateful and happy to get home.

I discovered summer in Florida is do-able. Every place, except parking lots, was air-conditioned. My alarm clock went off before dawn so I could get my morning walk in before the sun came up; in the evening, I walked at sundown. The "Women Who Love Too Much" support group did not want to stop; I continued in the metaphysical philosophy course and thought often of my lost love, Craig. I was so sure he would enjoy the philosophy that I shot off a letter to him. The post office returned it because the forwarding time had expired. "I'll contact the alumni office at Princeton," I thought, as I dropped the letter into a file folder, but I was distracted and did not follow through. I went dancing once or twice a week, singles dances for seniors, where I was amused by oldsters who hobbled and shuffled when walking in the door but once on the dance floor, watch out! I returned home sweaty and happy, shed my damp clothes, and in the darkness, slipped into the pool for a soothing skinny dip. I joined a Sunday evening singles group for the widowed and divorced and enjoyed potluck suppers in private homes and monthly dances. I attended free lectures and seminars, including one on creative meditation. I knew the only way I could continue feeling better was by keeping my thinking turned around. I did not have either the quantity or quality of support in Florida that I had in Massachusetts which was mostly my fault because I did not throw myself into Al-Anon. Why? I had felt as if I were drowning in the damn alcoholism and sex addiction. I did not want the facts I had lived with to be constantly reinforced by verbalized reminders in Al-Anon discussion groups. I attended Al-Anon once a week and did not make my telephone number readily available. I cut way back on incoming calls, and phoned another Al-Anon member about once a month. The church activities kept me circulating among people who were turned on to thinking, asking questions, eager for knowledge, awareness. I had not become intimate enough with any of them to know their personal problems so that gave me a rest from emotional drama. I arrived in Florida with my cup so low that I did what I could to protect myself from giving away what I really needed for myself. I nurtured myself. Expressed another way, healing was continuing.

I had a few dates with acceptable dancing partners but saw no one with whom I wanted to spend time other than on a dance floor. One of my new friends regaled us with stories about men she dated. My impression was she could not feel okay unless there was a man in her life. I was feeling better and better without a man in mine.

In September, thanks to Mary Jane sending me a check so I could attend her son's wedding, I flew into Bradley International where Harry met my plane. I was pleased to see him and to note, after he pointed it out, that he'd lost some weight, especially around the middle. He told me a silly joke, drove me to the car rental office, and we talked for a half hour or so about the business, the Swiss. From the way he expressed himself, I could tell he did not want me around during the six days when the Swiss were scheduled to arrive in a few weeks. I felt sad when we got into separate cars to go our separate ways but I knew it was okay to feel sad having loved a liar. Once I arrived in Springfield, all sadness left because I was welcomed by family and friends and had a marvelous five days in the bosom of love. At the wedding, Mary Jane was furious that her ex-husband, Barney, showed up with his "new" wife; they'd been together 16 years. I could see how damaging to Mary Jane it was to hang on to the anger she was entitled to have, but nevertheless, the anger was hurting her, not Barny. I knew I had to purge myself of the anger and resentments I had about Harry's mistreatment of me, otherwise it could be the death of me. I left the marriage because to stay would have meant my emotional death, perhaps triggering physical illness; while living with Harry, try as I did, I could not get my thinking to turn around and stay turned. I wanted to be free of painful memories and strong enough to withstand ongoing gestures that demonstrated his rejection of me. After eight months in Florida, and in spite of the trip to Switzerland, I no longer felt sharp anger towards Harry. I was able to laugh (as in snort) when thinking about his behavior which perpetuated his misery, at how foolish he was to sabotage himself in his headlong quest for the secret of personal happiness. I was integrating this indisputable fact: the only person I could change was myself and changing myself was contingent upon my attitude. My emotional dependence on Harry became hard-won history.

I flew back to New England twice more in October. I divided six days between Liz's house and visiting an old girlfriend from high school while I attended my 40th high school reunion, a three-day affair. I don't need notes to remember how much I enjoyed seeing many classmates I had known since kindergarten when we took rests on rag rugs. In my mind they were the first members of my extended family; my heart bulged with tenderness towards them.

After I returned to Florida, unpacked, did a laundry, petted the cats, read the mail, I re-packed, flew back on a Friday, and the next day accompanied Harry to JFK to meet Mr. Baehler and the translator. During that week, I played hostess when we dined out one or two evenings, what Harry called a "dog and pony act." I squeezed in a visit with Aunt Bibi. I have no notes about how that Swiss visit went, so I guess it must not have been a disaster. Not so the meeting that took place the following Spring. At that meeting, Harry was pathetic, unable to answer questions, continuously rifling through papers, like a kid taking an open book exam who had never read the book. I think that meeting marked the beginning of the end of Harry's employment by the Swiss. In the hallway I happened to meet his girlfriend, a secretary in the building, a widow. I introduced myself and sincerely wished her the best of luck. She was nonplused. Poor woman, she had no idea what she was letting herself in for. I gave Mr. Baehler two volumes about Free Masonry because I knew he valued being a Mason, unlike Harry who disparaged Free Masonry and who wore his Masonic pin only when around the Swiss.

I was not surprised when Steve tracked me down and phoned many times, asking me to visit him in Utah, specifically to see the home he built. "After all," he said, "you contributed as much to its design as I did." When he said he was no longer drinking, that he had joined AA, and would send me a roundtrip ticket, I accepted his invitation. He met me at the Albuquerque airport and we sped off in his low slung Lincoln Mark VI, as close to a racing car he could find that also provided comfort for an aging body. He was now 68 but still fit, well-muscled. Beyond Moab he headed northeast alongside the Colorado River through John Wayne/John Ford country where several Westerns were filmed, turning right towards Castle Valley. After more miles through a gritty, stark landscape punctuated by dramatic rock configurations, he took another right down a side road towards a mesa of rust-red and yellow rock and then another right into the entrance to his property. In the paddock beside the drive, two horses trotted towards the fence. Two hundred or so feet ahead, was the large house, the outline of its forward area reminded me of the beautiful barn at the campground we owned. Weathered, nestled among a few tall trees, it was wedded to the earth as if it had been there forever. A medium-size dog of mixed origins, tail wagging, greeted me and his returning master. Steve told me to go inside by myself; he wanted my impression not to be influenced by his physical presence. That was impossible because his imprint was everywhere, from the high, beam-exposed ceiling, the tall windows, massive fireplace, the cook-efficient kitchen that was wide open to the dining corner of the great room. Diagonally opposite was a cozy sitting area where I spotted a rendering of the poem *High Flight* by John McGee I commissioned an artist to create, a long ago birthday gift to Steve. What hung next to it took my breath away: the blue and green silk sash that matched the dress I wore the first time we met. Throughout the house, I recognized architectural features we had sketched and discussed 20 years before. His creative spirit and artistic eye were everywhere. I should have gotten back in the car and left then while proud Good Guy Steve was in control. He did not mistreat me physically, nor did he subject me to insulting harangues. He did not drink. He brooded, deep, dark moods. He said he shouldn't have asked me to visit because seeing me upset him, brought back memories he preferred to keep buried. When he mistreated his dog, I winced but made no comment.

He brought me to a jewelry store in Moab to pick up a necklace of matching gray agate beads he had designed for me, selecting each bead himself. He introduced me to his friends and invited many of them to dinner. When they learned I was Steve's second wife, their interest in me intensified. (Maybe some had been told I died in a fiery car crash?) He showed me photo albums that included pictures taken when he married his third wife. It was before he left on that honeymoon that he called me, asking me to go with him anywhere. When I turned him down, he said he'd call again in two weeks. He did, after he returned from his honeymoon. He wept telling me stories about his third wife, about her alcoholism, her temper, how when driving while drunk and angry, she had an accident and now was a permanent patient, partially paralyzed, and yet somehow he wove the story as if he were at its center, as if he were the injured one. He said that her family was angry with him. Somewhere in the rambling story he mentioned divorcing her. I listened quietly, emotionally detached, fascinated by a performance intended to make me feel sorry for him. Hadn't I heard a similar story before, when he removed himself from taking any blame for Maggie being distraught? He reveled in fabricating self-hurt. No, more than that, he wallowed in assuming a victim role. He spoke about a live-in girlfriend he threw out and her clothes after her. He tried to persuade me to begin my return flight out of Salt Lake City because he wanted me to meet more friends but there was no way I would go over the Rocky Mountains with him again. On our return to the airport in Albuquerque, he drove extremely fast, continually glancing my way to gauge my reaction. I was determined not to react, not to let him see I was terrified. At the airport when he set my luggage outside the car, I surprised him by saying goodbye. "Don't you want me to come in?" I wanted to get away from him. I was impervious to his charm. I could see through his facade to whatever the sickness was within him. Towards the end of January he phoned and afterwards he wrote:

". . . *So many thanks for your card and Xmas letter and your visit. I wish you a very special '89. . .*"

After signing it,

"*Sincerely w/Love,*"

he added,

"*Thanks for listening this morning.*"

and drew a heart.

Chapter 54

Timing is everything, and it's fascinating how issues become resolved.

Although I had sporadic contact with Harry for another year because he did not fulfill his legal financial obligations to me (the State of Florida got his attention by attaching his wages), by mid-November 1988 I had emancipated myself from him as well as Steve. Healing had gone on even when I most despaired. Their effect on me had been linked because of the similarity of their behavior; the years with Harry built upon the years with Steve. Recovering from Harry's mind games and emotional battering was much more difficult than healing from Steve's physical abuse; yet 35 years after the bulldozer incident and the night driving drunk across Arizona abreast of a semi for 15 minutes, any time I am walking or am a passenger in a car and a loud vehicle passes on my right side, I tense. I tell myself to relax. Steve's cruelty and Harry's lying-filled toxicity can no longer damage me and I am able to remember the good moments. I find it easier to remember Steve, perhaps because Steve was a more interesting person than Harry. In effect, the double doors on those chapters closed in November 1988. They had to, otherwise a new door could not have opened.

Early in November, back in my office off the lanai, I came across the letter I wrote to Craig at the beginning of the summer, the letter the post office returned. I thought: "I really ought to call Princeton," and distracted by something else, I started to leave the office when I heard a voice say, "Do it now!" At once I phoned the alumni office and contrary to alumni office protocol, I was given Craig's address—he was living in Ohio. Within an hour, a new letter focusing on Ernest Holmes' philosophy and any personal remarks diplomatically worded so as not to offend a wife, if there were one, was in the mail. When I returned from spending Christmas with Liz, David and our growing family, the pile of mail my neighbor had collected for me included a small package—from Craig. Inside was a tree ornament of a dancing Santa and Mrs. Claus with a note, "I must say they make a wonderful couple!" and also a long letter. That's how the love of my life, after 12 years apart, came back into my life, and the medium's reading I received two years earlier came true—that I would experience the love, the emotional security, I had always wanted.

Spofford Hall

Spofford Hall opened in 1980 and closed its doors within ten years at about the same time as many other highly respected and accredited alcoholism residential treatment centers. It is conjectured the closings were insurance driven; that is, from the insurers' accounting point of view, the expense of covering alcoholism treatment was not cost-effective.

Sandra Cohen-Holmes was hired prior to Spofford Hall opening its doors to create and direct the Family Treatment Program. She hired the personnel, designed each component of the program, and worked to integrate the treatment of family members into the larger population of 100 alcoholics. She trained the staff, many of whom were recovering alcoholics, to understand that family patients were there for themselves, to address their own problems and not there to help their alcoholic. In the Afterword, she describes how she amassed the knowledge and experience to become a key member of Spofford's executive staff.

Afterword by Sandra Cohen-Holmes

I consider my Spofford experience as actually the most exciting and creative professional work I have done. Reading the Spofford Hall section of *Stark Raving Sober* brought it all back. Donna's description of the Family Residential Treatment Program is so accurate that I felt as if I were there.

My interest in alcoholism was piqued by a series of experiences. During the early 1970s while placing under-employed and unemployed clients in job training situations, I noted that those who were in recovery from alcoholism did well, but those who were drinking did not. I wanted to understand the reason for the difference. I attended AA meetings and talked with people at a Portsmouth, New Hampshire recovery club. I brought an open mind to the discussions because I had no personal experience with alcoholism. I had a male friend who was a blackout drinker; I worked part time for him. I learned more about alcoholism driving a taxi than in graduate school where alcoholism was *never* mentioned. At a conference on couples therapy, I had lunch with an alcoholism therapist and a recovering alcoholic. The pieces of the alcoholism puzzle began to fall into place.

My fascination with the effect alcohol has on the mind has lasted my entire career — the way it distorts perception, alters and numbs emotional capacity — especially empathy — and the role of blackouts in making the data of one's behavior unavailable to the drinker, and the crazy-making of those around the drinker. So, too, has the belief that someone with alcoholism is a person first, a unique person with an illness, no two the same, and that alcoholism is never deliberate. It happens and it hurts, and the cost and suffering are immeasurable.

My first work in the field of alcoholism was as an educator for arrested drinking drivers at the Outpatient Alcoholism Clinic (Lawrence, Massachusetts). There I became a therapist counseling alcoholics. I participated in a series of intensive training seminars at the Johnson Institute (now Hazelden) and learned about the impact on families from Sharon Wegsheider Cruse, Vernon Johnson, Claudia Black and others. I implemented more effective treatment for families. In 1979 I left the clinic to have a child. When he was six months old, I read a newspaper ad seeking a Family Treatment Director at Spofford Hall.

I consider myself bilingual: alcoholism is my second language. While I was conducting an intervention, a twelve-year-old boy said, "I didn't know my father had a disease. I thought there was something about me that made him unable to love me." That children and partners take personally the words and actions of those under the influence keeps them stuck, forever analyzing why the drinker drinks and why am I not enough? Like a scene in the movie *The Raiders of the Lost Ark*, when they are searching for the Lost Ark (or the Holy Grail), leading man Harrison Ford yells, "They're digging in the wrong place!" It doesn't matter why a person drinks. What matters is what happens when they drink and how it affects us.

After 30 years of working in the mental health field, I continue to see an assembly line of pain — people affected, damaged and traumatized by drinking and drinkers. I have to wonder why alcohol-related problems continue to riddle our society. The entire criminal justice system (judges, lawyers, police departments, prisons) and to some extent the medical systems are supported by alcoholism. The liquor industry is the largest lobbyist against the legalization of marijuana. I believe the war on drugs is also digging in the wrong place. Alcoholism, like terrorism, is on our streets and highways maiming and killing innocent people and it's in our homes where small children hide powerless under their beds worrying about their parents and learning too well that their own feelings and needs don't count.

I remember a brave young woman in her early twenties who wanted to confront her father with the impact his alcoholism had on her childhood. By then her father had been sober a few years. Before she could speak her piece, she became frightened and disassociative, regressing to about age ten, cowering in the office chair. Her father saw her terror and said, "If the sober me knew the drinking me, I would have killed me."

404

For the past twenty-three years, Sandra Cohen-Holmes has been in private practice in Dover, New Hampshire. In addition to treating adults with a broad spectrum of issues including addiction and co-dependency, for fifteen years she taught a four credit forty-five hour college course she designed entitled "Addiction and the Dysfunctional Family" for the College for Lifelong Learning (now Granite College). She has an M.Ed (with emphasis in counseling) from the University of New Hampshire.

Author's Postscript

Following his marriage to me and two subsequent marriages that ended in divorce, Brad married his fourth wife, Joanna, with whom he will soon celebrate their 25th anniversary. Over the years, Brad and I have talked about events that led up to our marriage and events within the marriage itself. It is my impression that our understanding and appreciation of the persons we were then has benefited from the advantage of perspective gained through both introspection and the gift of time. I value my friendship with Joanna and Brad. The three of us keep in close touch and enjoy celebrating family birthdays, Thanksgiving and Easter together.

Although I divorced Steve in 1972 and Harry in 1988, I was haunted by the unlikely probability our paths might cross, an unpleasant thought if with Harry, alarming if with Steve. There was an outside chance that Steve might contact me. After all, he had done so every year or so for almost 20 years. He tracked me down regardless of where I lived, and the last time, in 1990, he telephoned. He had recently married for the fourth time, and his new bride participated in the conversation. They extended an invitation to visit them. I followed up the phone call with a letter to Steve asking him to write to Liz and David, his former stepchildren, to tell them how sorry he was for mistreating them. They never heard from him. And I never did again.

In August 2005 I learned that Steve had died in 1997 and Harry in 2003. My first reaction was to marvel that I felt nothing. How could that be possible? At one time I had loved them, married them, put my faith and trust in them. For many days, I tried to figure out why I was so unaffected by knowing they were no longer alive. I had no difficulty dismissing Harry because he had played such diabolical games with my head. But why did my thoughts about Steve leap between contrasting flashbacks of positive and negative excitement? The escape from Steve meant freedom from his tyrannical eruptions. With the knowledge of their deaths, I realized that both divorces were truly final. And best of all, neither of them could ever hurt anyone else again. That "nothing" I felt when I first learned of their deaths was actually a feeling I had never associated with either of them. No wonder I couldn't identify it. The feeling is peace.

Permission to Reprint

References to Other Publications
(Fair Use Law)

Getting Them Sober
Toby Rice Drews
ISBN 0961599596

I'll Quit Tomorrow
Vernon E. Johnson
ISBN 0062504339

Marriage on the Rocks
Janet Geringer Woititz
ISBN 0932194176

Off the Sauce
Lewis Meyer
ISBN 0020808208

Why Am I Afraid to Tell You Who I Am?
Insights into Personal Growth
John Powell, SJ
ISBN 08834732332

Printed in the United States
58079LVS00003B/70-264